www.routledgesw.com

Melinda Lewis, The University of Kansas, Series Editor

An authentic breakthrough in social work education . . .

New Directions in Social Work is an innovative, integrated series of texts, website, and interactive case studies for generalist courses in the Social Work curriculum at both undergraduate and graduate levels. Instructors will find everything they need to build a comprehensive course that allows students to meet course outcomes, with these unique features:

- All texts, interactive cases, and test materials are **linked to the 2015 Educational Policy and Accreditation Standards (EPAS) from the Council on Social Work Education (CSWE).**

- **One web portal with easy access** for instructors and students from any computer—no codes, no CDs, no restrictions. Go to www.routledgesw.com and discover.

- **The Series is flexible and can be easily adapted for use in online distance-learning courses as well as hybrid and bricks-and-mortar courses.**

- Each text and the website can be used **individually** or as an **entire Series** to meet the needs of any social work program.

TITLES IN THE SERIES

Social Work and Social Welfare: An Invitation, Fourth Edition by Marla Berg-Weger
Human Behavior in the Social Environment, Fourth Edition by Anissa Taun Rogers
Human Behavior in the Social Environment: Perspectives on Development, the Life Course, and Macro Contexts by Anissa Taun Rogers
Research for Effective Social Work Practice, Third Edition by Judy L. Krysik and Jerry Finn
Social Policy for Effective Practice: A Strengths Approach, Third Edition by Rosemary K. Chapin
The Practice of Generalist Social Work, Fourth Edition by Julie Birkenmaier and Marla Berg-Weger

The Practice of Generalist Social Work

Fourth Edition
by Julie Birkenmaier, Saint Louis University
Marla Berg-Weger, Saint Louis University

In this book and companion custom website, you will find:

- Complete coverage of the range of social work generalist practice within the framework of planned change, encompassing engagement, assessment, intervention, evaluation, and termination—for work with individuals, families, groups, organizations, and communities. This edition features expanded coverage of practice with individuals, families, groups, organizations, and communities.

- Consistent and in-depth use of key theoretical perspectives and case examples to demonstrate essential knowledge, values, and skills for generalist social work practice. But the text does not overwhelm the student reader with a plethora of nuances of intervention and other skills that will occur in a variety of practice settings and roles. *Instead, this book presents clearly the core competencies for general social work practice.*

- Six *unique,* in-depth, interactive, easy-to-access cases, which students can easily reach from *any* computer, provide a "learning by doing" format unavailable with any other text(s). Your students will have an advantage unlike any other they will experience in their social work education. Go to www.routledgesw.com/ cases to see each of these cases on the free website.

- In addition, *four* streaming videos relate to competencies and skills discussed in the book at the three client system levels—individuals and families, groups, and communities. The videos depict social workers demonstrating skills discussed in the chapters and offer instructors numerous possibilities for classroom instruction. In the video for the case, "Brickville," a social worker combines individual and family practice skills with multicultural community engagement as he works with an African American family about to be displaced by redevelopment and facing multiple stressors. Go to http://routledgesw.com//sanchez/engage/video, http://routledgesw.com// riverton/engage/video, and http://routledgesw.com//washburn/engage/ video, and http://routledgesw.com//brickville/engage/video to see *each* of these videos that are included within *each* of the web-based cases.

- At least ten exercises at the end of each chapter provide you with the means to ensure that your students can *demonstrate their mastery* of the theoretical frameworks, skills, and core competencies of generalist social work practice as presented *not just* in the text, but in the free web-based cases as well. Instructors can choose from among the approximately five exercises that relate to relevant practice issues, and five that relate specifically to one of the online cases.

- A wealth of instructor-only resources also available at www.routledgesw. com/practice provide: full-text readings that link to the concepts presented in each of the chapters; a complete bank of objective and essay-type test items, all linked to current CSWE EPAS standards; PowerPoint presentations to help students master key concepts; a sample syllabus; annotated links to a treasure trove of social work assets on the Internet and teaching tips on how to use them in your practice sequence of courses.

- A clear focus on generalist social work practice, informed by the authors' decades of real-world practice experience, at *all* levels of engagement and intervention.

The Practice of Generalist Social Work

Fourth Edition, Chapters 8–13

Julie Birkenmaier
Saint Louis University

Marla Berg-Weger
Saint Louis University

Routledge
Taylor & Francis Group

NEW YORK AND LONDON

Fourth edition published 2017
by Routledge
711 Third Avenue, New York, NY 10017

and by Routledge
2 Park Square, Milton Park, Abingdon, Oxon OX14 4RN

Routledge is an imprint of the Taylor & Francis Group, an informa business

First edition published by Mcgraw-Hill College 2005
Third edition published by Routledge 2014

Library of Congress Cataloging in Publication Data
A catalog record for this book has been requested

ISBN: 978–1–138–05840–8 (hbk)
ISBN: 978–1–138–05651–0 (pbk)
ISBN: 978–1–315–16528–8 (ebk)

Typeset in Stone Serif
by RefineCatch Limited, Bungay, Suffolk

BRIEF CONTENTS

DETAILED CONTENTS

PREFACE

MAJOR CHANGES TO THE FOURTH EDITION

Like the previous editions, this new edition of *The Practice of Generalist Social Work* provides detailed coverage of the knowledge, skills, values, competencies, and behaviors needed for contemporary generalist social work practice. Using a strengths-based perspective, students are given a comprehensive overview of the major areas relevant for social work practice, including: theoretical frameworks, values and ethics, expanded coverage of communication skills for all client systems and examples of their use, and extensive coverage of practice with clients through all phases of the change process. *The Practice of Generalist Social Work* offers a comprehensive discussion of practice with individuals, families, groups, communities, and organizations within the concepts of planned change, encompassing engagement, assessment, intervention, evaluation, and termination and follow-up. Students have the opportunity to learn about generalist practice through in-depth case studies, examples, and exercises integrated throughout the text. This edition provides all the material necessary and relevant for a two- or three-course sequence.

This fourth edition is fully updated to the 2015 EPAS, with connections made between specific competencies and chapter content. This edition also provides additional examples of the application of theory and knowledge through case studies for all client levels, particularly in practice with individuals, families, and groups. For example, many chapters now open with a case and refer back to the case throughout to provide additional connections between content and real-life practice. Additional values and ethics material and cultural competency and humility content provide additional guidance for contemporary practice. Each chapter also now incorporates a link to a Grand Challenge of Social Work, from the American Academy of Social Work and Social Welfare, which facilitates a connection between the profession and the most significant societal challenges of today. The Quick Guides within the text offer students guidance for their field experience and practice after graduation. New Quick Guides in this edition provide students with brief guidelines for community practice.

In sum, this new edition provides expanded resources that contain up-to-date individual, family, group, community, and organizational guidance for the beginning practitioner. New end-of-chapter exercises connect with the wealth of case-based information available at www.routledgesw.com/ and facilitate a dynamic, experiential introduction to social work for your students.

Available with this edition are the following resources:

- Updated companion readings that are linked to key concepts in each chapter, along with questions to encourage further thought and discussion.

- Six interactive fictional cases with accompanying exercises that bring to life the concepts covered in the book, readings, and classroom discussions.

- A bank of exam questions (both objective and open-ended).

- PowerPoint presentations, which can serve as a starting point for class discussions.

- Sample syllabi demonstrating how the text and website, when used together through the course, satisfy the 2015 Educational Policy and Accreditation Standards (EPAS) from the Council on Social Work Education (CSWE).

- Quick Guides from the books offered online for students to print and take into the field for guidance.

- Updated annotated links to websites and other online resources, such as videos and podcasts.

ORGANIZATION OF THE BOOK

The following paragraphs serve to briefly introduce each of the chapters included in this book with emphasis on the updated content. All chapters have updated and specific connections to 2015 CSWE EPAS, and expanded end-of-chapter exercises that use online resources.

Chapter 1

Understanding Social Work Practice provides an overview of social work practice by grounding students in the purpose of social work; social work competencies; types of client grouping; and the practice framework of engagement, assessment, intervention, termination, and evaluation. A discussion of the ethics that guide social work practice, licensure of social work, client populations that social workers work with, and the tensions in social work provides students with real-world information about the profession. Students are also introduced to major theoretical perspectives for social work practice, including the ecosystems, social justice, human rights, strengths, and postmodern perspectives. In this fourth edition, connections made to the Grand Challenges for Social Work are introduced.

Chapter 2

In contrast to a straightforward overview of values and ethics, **Applying Values and Ethics to Practice** provides a brief history of social work ethics and the NASW *Code of Ethics* (2008), then contrasts the *Code of Ethics* with the International Federation of Social Workers' Ethical Statement, and also discusses the limits of ethical codes. A discussion of the intersection of ethics and the law gives students information about the interplay between the two, followed by a discussion of ethical dilemmas and processes for resolving them. Extensive discussion about common practice dilemmas gives students exposure to situations that they may encounter in practice, followed by an emphasis on risk management. Expanded coverage of ethics violations and state sanctions round out the discussion. New content in Chapter 2 includes expanded examples of value conflict, and discussion of the Grand Challenge of Social Work to "Create Social Responses to a Changing Environment."

Chapter 3

Individual Engagement: Relationship Skills for Practice at All Levels provides students with the characteristics of core relationships qualities, as well as a description of the specific skills for dialogue with clients at all system levels, including coverage of common communication pitfalls. As the helping relationship includes the dimension of power, the chapter provides extensive coverage of sources of power within relationships and provides guidance on the use of power through a case study of "Power in Client Lives: Jasmine Johnson." Practical questions guide students toward active listening. Students are also provided with strategies and skills for promoting social justice and human rights within helping relationships. New content in this fourth edition includes discussion of the Grand Challenge of Social Work to "Close the Health Gap."

Chapter 4

Social Work Practice with Individuals: Assessment and Planning includes a focus on the assessment and planning process within the global environment in which practicing social workers live. The chapter begins with a discussion of the history of assessment and moves to an overview of theoretical approaches to social work practice, both classic and contemporary (strengths, narrative, and solution-focused). The application of evidence-based practice approaches is highlighted. The need for practice knowledge and behaviors in the area of diversity within the assessment and planning phases emphasizes the need for cultural humility and competence. The chapter introduces the concepts of compassion satisfaction, intersectionality, and the cultural genogram and includes an exercise to address culture change from the student perspective. The chapter concludes with a discussion of the relevant skills and practice behaviors in the assessment and planning phases of the social work intervention process, including skills needed for strengths-based, narrative, and solution-focused approaches, documentation, and self-care for the social worker. This edition offers content on narrative and solution-focused approaches, documentation, self-care, and suicide risk assessment with vulnerable populations with more examples on applications of knowledge and theory. A discussion of the Grand Challenge of Social Work to "Eradicate Social Isolation" is brought to life with an exercise.

Chapter 5

Social Work Practice with Individuals: Intervention, Termination, and Evaluation introduces students to key areas of social work practice that will impact virtually every dimension of their professional lives. With an emphasis on theoretical perspectives, students learn to apply various intervention, termination, evaluation, and follow-up skills and behaviors. Traditional and contemporary social work roles are highlighted and discussed. Documentation and record-keeping for social work interventions is explained. Interventions with individuals are also framed within an empowerment practice approach. Framed within theoretical perspectives for understanding diversity, students are offered an overview of the skills required to be a culturally competent social work practitioner. New features in Chapter 5 include additional content on connecting the change process to the client's identified goals, therapeutic use of self, managing countertransference, being a social work professional, self-care, and the use of supervision. A Grand Challenge of Social Work, to "Advance Long and Productive Lives," is addressed through discussion, reading, and an exercise.

Chapter 6

Social Work Practice with Families: Engagement, Assessment, and Planning begins with a history of social work practice with families, grounded within a systems framework. Theoretical perspectives, including narrative and solution-focused, are discussed within the context of the engagement, assessment, and planning phases of interventions with families with emphasis on empowerment. Students encounter a broad range of family constellations as they read about contemporary family social work. Practice behaviors and skills are presented for achieving engagement and assessment with families and documentation strategies are included. This newest version of Chapter 6 offers more examples relating to the engagement, assessment, and planning with families. To "Ensure Healthy Development for All Youth" is the Grand Challenge of Social Work that is the focus in this chapter.

Chapter 7

Social Work Practice with Families: Intervention, Termination, and Evaluation conceptualizes generalist social work practice interventions with families. Continuing with the theoretical perspectives discussed in Chapter 6, this chapter develops interventions with families using strengths and empowerment, narrative, and solution-focused approaches. Skills and behaviors for intervening, terminating, evaluating, following up, and documenting family-focused interventions are discussed in detail. New to this edition is more in-depth content on evaluation of family interventions. The Grand Challenge for Social Work, "Ending Gender-Based Violence," is the focus of this chapter with a reading and an exercise.

Chapter 8

Social Work Practice with Groups: Engagement, Assessment, and Planning provides students with up-to-date perspectives on social work practice with groups. The chapter opens with an overview of the role of groups within our communities and profession followed by a historical and contemporary perspective on the use of groups for change. The dimensions of group practice are presented within the framework of theoretical perspectives (i.e., narrative and solution-focused). Planning for group interventions, including the engagement and assessment of group members, is emphasized from a practice perspective along with the importance of cultural competence in the group setting. With this edition, Chapter 8 now includes expanded content and examples on group-level social work skills and behaviors. To "End Homelessness" is the Grand Challenge of Social Work that is highlighted in this chapter.

Chapter 9

Social Work Practice with Groups: Intervention, Termination, and Evaluation emphasizes the development and implementation of interventions with various types of groups. Continuing the framing of skills and techniques within theoretical perspectives, the use of evidence-based interventions with groups is introduced using the strengths, narrative, and solution-focused frameworks. Models for group intervention are described, along with an in-depth examination of the roles, skills, and practice behaviors required for carrying out a group-level intervention. Termination, evaluation, and follow-up of group interventions are also covered. New to Chapter 9 is additional content on group dynamics and leadership. A Grand Challenge of Social Work that emphasizes how to "Harness Technology for Social Good" is discussed.

Chapter 10

Social Work Practice with Communities: Engagement, Assessment, and Planning introduces students to the concept of community. The chapter defines and discusses types and functions of communities. Students learn about various theoretical perspectives, including contemporary perspectives for community practice. Engagement and assessment concepts, including community-based analysis, evidence-based practice, and community needs assessments, are extensively discussed. Examples of types of needs assessments, surveys used in needs assessments, and needs assessment summaries provide additional practice guidance. Community practice skills are thoroughly covered, as are the implications of global interdependence for community practice in the United States. This edition contains new Quick Guides on running focus groups and community forums, as well as content on interprofessional engagement and community planning. Discussion of the Grand Challenge for Social Work, "Building Financial Capability for All" is also new for this edition.

Chapter 11

Social Work Practice with Communities: Intervention, Termination, and Evaluation builds on the engagement and assessment content of Chapter 10 to present strategies and techniques for community practice. Using the insights gained about practice at the individual, family, and group levels, this chapter expands the students' awareness of social work practice with communities through a discussion of today's trends and skills for intervention, including community social and economic development, and community organizing. Included in this discussion is coverage of international community practice. Examples of public and private efforts to promote evidence-based community practice assist students in applying the material. Additional guidance on advocacy efforts and asset-based development are presented. Students also learn the knowledge and skills needed for termination and evaluation of community practice. The fourth edition offers discussion of the Grand Challenge for Social Work to "Reduce Extreme Economic Inequality" and content on follow-up as part of the change process with communities.

Chapter 12

Social Work Practice with Organizations: Engagement, Assessment, and Planning covers a challenging client system for beginning practitioners—the organization. Students learn a wealth of practical and theoretical aspects of organizations, including a discussion about the purpose and structure of organizations, power relations within organizations, and social work within host organizational settings. The chapter provides discussion about the elements of an internal assessment of organizations, including organizational culture and external assessments as well. Material about organizational policy advocacy and nonprofit partnerships help guide practice. Examples of organizational engagement and assessment provide students with contemporary illustrations of key content in Chapter 12. New content in the fourth edition includes discussion of the Grand Challenge for Social Work to "Promote Smart Decarceration" and planning with organizations. A new exhibit displays the organizational hierarchy to help students understand how organizations are often structured.

Chapter 13

Social Work Practice with Organizations: Intervention, Termination, and Evaluation
uses the foundation built in Chapter 12 to discuss approaches, perspectives, and
models for intervening with organizations. This chapter provides extensive coverage
of the relationship between theoretical perspectives and organizational change,
as well as a practical framework for thinking about generating change and the
needed knowledge for a social work generalist in this endeavor. Termination
and evaluation of change efforts within organizations, including a discussion
about the role of the generalist practitioner in this process, help students see their
potential role in a change effort with organizations. Content about the challenges
of implementing organizational change, and persuasion skills to assist in these
efforts, provide direction for the practitioner. In this edition, Chapter 13 has
expanded content that includes discussion of the Grand Challenge for Social Work
to "Achieve Equal Opportunity and Justice" as well as content on follow-up with
organizations.

INTERACTIVE CASES

The website www.routledgesw.com/cases presents six unique, in-depth, interactive,
fictional cases with dynamic characters and real-life situations that students can
easily access from any computer. They provide a "learning by doing" format unavailable with any other text. Your students will have an advantage unlike any other
they will experience in their social work training. Each of the interactive cases uses
text, graphics, and video to help students learn about engagement, assessment,
intervention, evaluation, and termination at multiple levels of social work practice.
The "My Notebook" feature allows students to take and save notes, type in
written responses to tasks, and share their work with classmates and instructors by
email. These interactive cases allow you to integrate the readings and classroom
discussions:

The Sanchez Family: Systems, Strengths, and Stressors   The ten individuals in this
extended Latino family have numerous strengths but are faced with a variety of
challenges. Students will have the opportunity to experience the phases of the social
work intervention, grapple with ethical dilemmas, and identify strategies for
addressing issues of diversity.

Riverton: A Community Conundrum   Riverton is a small Midwest city in which the
social worker lives and works. The social worker identifies an issue that presents her
community with a challenge. Students and instructors can work together to develop
strategies for engaging, assessing, and intervening with the citizens of the social
worker's neighborhood.

Carla Washburn: Loss, Aging, and Social Support Students will get to know Carla Washburn, an older African American woman who finds herself living alone after the loss of her grandson and in considerable pain from a recent accident. In this case, less complex than the Sanchez Family, students will apply their growing knowledge of gerontology and exercise the skills of culturally competent practice.

RAINN: Rape Abuse and Incest National Network The RAINN Online Hotline links callers to local Rape Crisis Centers and hospitals, as well as other services. In addition, rape crisis telephone hotlines have played an important role in extending services to those in communities in which services are not available. Students will learn how and why this national hotline was developed; they will evaluate both qualitative and quantitative data to assess how the program can better achieve its goals.

Hudson City: An Urban Community Affected by Disaster Hudson City has just been devastated by Hurricane Diane, a category 4 hurricane with wind speeds of 140 miles per hour. Students will take up the role of a social worker who also resides in the community, who has been tasked with finding workable solutions to a variety of problems with diverse clients systems. Students will learn about disaster response and how to focus on many clients at once.

Brickville: Families and Communities Consider Transitions Brickville is a low-income community faced with a development proposal that would dramatically change the community. Students will take the role of a social worker who lives in the community and works for a community development corporation. Students will learn about community development and approaches that can be used to empower community members.

This book takes full advantage of the interactive element as a unique learning opportunity by including exercises that require students to go to the Web and use the cases. To maximize the learning experience, you may want to start the course by asking your students to explore each case by activating each button. The more the students are familiar with the presentation of information and the locations of the individual case files, the Case Study Tools, and the questions and tasks contained within each phase of the case, the better they will be able to integrate the text with the online practice component.

IN SUM

When presented as separate issues, all of the aforementioned developmental topics can seem overwhelming to students, particularly when they realize they have to keep at hand all their knowledge when working with clients. However, all of these topics, as well as other topics that are discussed, are set in a framework that will help students to think about the types of problems their clients might be likely to face at different phases in life. Students will also learn that organizing their knowledge about these areas into a theoretical context that "makes sense" to them will help them to manage the seemingly endless stream of information at their disposal. Ultimately, then, students will become more and more proficient at applying concepts to client problems. Meanwhile, students can enjoy the process of learning about them.

Being an effective social worker means being able to understand the complexities of human behavior, the societies and cultures in which we live, and the interplay between them. Being an effective social worker also means having a solid grounding in various disciplines, such as psychology, sociology, and human biology. It means possessing a well-rounded education and an ability to apply this knowledge to the myriad client problems and situations that students will face in the profession. This edition is intended to help students understand this complexity in the field and to help them gain the knowledge and critical thinking skills they will need to practice social work.

ACKNOWLEDGMENTS

We would like to thank the many colleagues who helped to make this book and previous editions possible. To Alice Lieberman, we are grateful for your innovation and vision that has resulted in this series and the web-based supplements that bring the material alive. We appreciate the camaraderie and support of the authors of the other books in this series—Rosemary Chapin, Anissa Rogers, Judy Kryzik, and Jerry Finn. A special thank you to Anissa Rogers, Shannon Cooper-Sadlo, Andrea Seper, and Megan Armentrout whose creativity makes the exercises, test questions, and PowerPoint slides enticing and easy to use. A special thanks to Shannon Cooper-Sadlo for sharing her practice wisdom and exercises. We want to thank the group who participated in the production of the video vignettes: actors John Abram, Patti Rosenthal, Beverly Sporleder, Sabrina Tyuse, Kristi Sobbe, Myrtis Spencer, Phil Minden, Katie Terrell, and Shannon Cooper-Sadlo and videographers, Tom Meuser and Elizabeth Yaeger. A special thanks goes to Megan Armentrout, graduate student assistant, for her extensive assistance with this edition and supplemental materials. Thanks also goes to social work graduate student assistant Dan Stewart for his assistance. We also want to thank:

Joan Allen, Arizona State University
Nancy Barker, Nassau Community College
Robin Bonifas, Arizona State University
Sally Booth, Rivier University
Heidi Brocious, University of Alaska Fairbanks
May Guenin, Mary Baldwin College
Kur Miller, Lancaster Bible College

Paul Sachdev, Memorial University
Mary Thomas, Mary Baldwin College
Gary Whitford, St. Cloud State University
Jeffrey Wylie, Murray State University

for their reviews of the book as it was evolving. Finally, we are most appreciative to the staff of Routledge for their support and encouragement for making this book a reality. It takes a village.

ABOUT THE AUTHORS

Julie Birkenmaier is a Professor in the School of Social Work at Saint Louis University, Missouri. Dr. Birkenmaier's practice experience includes community organizing, community development, and nonprofit administration. Her research and writing focuses on financial capability, financial credit, community development, and asset development. With colleagues, she co-wrote *Financial capability and asset-building in vulnerable households*. She also co-edited *Financial Capability and Asset Development: Research, Education, Policy and Practice*. With Marla Berg-Weger, she co-authored the textbook, *The Practicum Companion for Social Work: Integrating Class and Field Work* (4th edition).

Marla Berg-Weger is a Professor in the School of Social Work at Saint Louis University, Missouri and Executive Director of the Geriatric Education Center. Dr. Berg-Weger holds social work degrees at the bachelor's, master's, and doctoral levels. Her social work practice experience includes public social welfare services, intimate partner violence services, mental health, medical social work, and gerontological social work. Her research and writing focuses on gerontological social work and social work practice. She is the author of *Social Work and Social Welfare: An Invitation* (4th edition). With Julie Birkenmaier, she co-authored the textbook, *The Practicum Companion for Social Work: Integrating Class and Field Work* (4th edition). She is the Past President of the Association of Gerontology in Social Work and currently serves as the Managing Editor of the *Journal of Gerontological Social Work* and is a fellow in the Gerontological Society of America.

CHAPTER 8

Social Work Practice with Groups: Engagement, Assessment, and Planning

© SerrNovik/Thinkstock

Alone we can do so little. Together we can do so much.

Helen Keller (1880–1968)

Key Questions for Chapter 8

1. What competencies do I need to engage with and assess clients in social work group practice? [EPAS 6 and 7]
2. How can I use evidence in research-informed practice and practice-informed research to guide engagement and assessment with groups? [EPAS 4]
3. What potential ethical issues may arise in social work practice with groups, particularly in the early phases of the group's development? [EPAS 1]
4. What knowledge and skills do I need for culturally competent group-level engagement and assessment practice? [EPAS 2]

The residents of the Riverton community (see case at *www.routledgesw.com/cases*) are becoming increasingly concerned about alcohol consumption and its negative impact on the residents and businesses, particularly on the children and youth who live in the neighborhoods. As this chapter will highlight, there are multiple strategies and formats for intervening in this problem at the group level. The Riverton community members have proposed three potential group interventions to address their concerns about alcohol use in their neighborhoods: (1) Riverton Against Youth Drinking (RAYD)—a voluntary group of residents and professionals who receive in-kind support (meeting space, office supplies, etc.) from the Riverton Association of Neighborhoods whose goal is to prevent problems by creating alternative activities and options for the community's youth as an alternative to substance use; (2) Riverton Children's Grief Support Group—a group facilitated by the Community Service Agency for children who have lost a family member to drug- or alcohol-related death; and (3) Riverton Mental Health Center Groups for Persons with Co-occurring Diagnoses—a therapeutic treatment group for persons who are experiencing substance abuse and mental health challenges.

NONE OF US LIVES WITHOUT SOCIAL CONNECTIONS. Many of us spend much of our lives negotiating our closeness to family, neighbors, friends, associates, and colleagues. Regardless of the ways in which we experience connections and whether we perceive them as positive or negative, virtually everyone has relationships to small collectives of other people or groups. In this context, **group** refers to the natural or planned associations that evolve through common interest (e.g., supporting the local Little League Association), state of being (e.g., having a child with a disability), or task (e.g., working together at a place of employment to improve workflow). Connectedness to groups depends not only on an individual's needs for affiliation but also on cultural norms; social arrangements (e.g., marital/relationship status, family status (parent or child), and personal affiliations); and social location (e.g., faith traditions, children's school, or neighborhood of residence). Within social work, **group work** is a "goal-directed activity that brings together people for a common purpose or goal" (Toseland & Horton, 2013, para. 1).

This chapter addresses the nature of groups, briefly reviews the history of group work in social work practice, and explores the dimensions of group work that relate to types and purposes of groups. In this chapter, you will explore the purpose of groups and the relationship of groups to other areas of social work practice along with engagement and assessment skills. Chapter 9 will build on the engagement and assessment of group practice addressed in this chapter by presenting skills and behaviors for approaching the various aspects of the process of group work through intervention, termination, evaluation, and follow-up.

GROUPS: THE SOURCE OF COMMUNITY

The social dimension of social work implies that people need and want to relate to others within the context of a "community." Yet the ways to meet this need are not always clear to social work professionals or to the clients they serve. In contemporary U.S. culture, there is a pervasive emphasis on independence, mobility, and the pursuit of success. Employment opportunities for many that are far away from home; socioeconomic achievements; and/or pressures to advance professionally, socially, and economically influence people and have spurred new definitions of and parameters for community. Such influences are not necessarily negative, but they can take a heavy toll on one's sense of connection and linkages (i.e., community) to stable, consistent groups on which they can depend over time.

A brief online search using the term "support groups" or a review of the advertisement section of any major newspaper provides evidence of our need to connect with others. The number of announcements for therapy groups, support groups, community groups, and educational groups suggests that, as a western culture, people are looking for a way to relate to others that is outside of themselves. In other words, people seek out groups in order to form community. Such groups provide a safe environment in which to share goals, information, give and receive mutual aid, and make connections with others (Steinberg, 2014). By implication, social work practice with groups affords people the opportunity to participate in meaningful experiences that the contexts of their personal and/or professional lives do not provide. Family, friends, and co-workers may be empathetic to and supportive of our challenges and form one type of group that provides community, but it might not be enough. We may find a stronger connection with nonfriends or family who share lived experiences, issues, or perspectives than our natural groups.

Group Orientation as a Cultural Dimension

Culture has an important impact on the amount and type of connections people seek. "People relations" (Diller, 2015, p. 99) is one of the cultural paradigms that distinguish one cultural group from another. For example, European Americans are more inclined to be individual in their social relationships; this contrasts with the collective focus of many other cultures—Latino/a Americans, in particular. The social worker facilitating the group must be culturally astute, aware of group participants' cultural backgrounds, and attuned to the cultural influences that affect group dynamics. Brown (2013) offers the following strategies for culturally competent group facilitation:

- Ask questions of group members to draw out cultural differences and attempt to integrate learning into the group process.

- Do not overwhelm group members with too much information at one time.

- Regularly check in with group members to ensure clarity of understanding by all members of the group regarding goals, purposes, membership, and processes.

- Attend to your communication skills; use open-ended questions and avoid technical words and jargon.

- Ask group members to share their own traditions related to respectful interactions, culturally sensitive issues, and taboos (p. 52).

Exhibit 8.1 provides additional suggestions for developing culturally competent group practice skills.

EXHIBIT 8.1

Cultural Competence in Group Work

Social workers practicing with groups can benefit from incorporating culture-specific strategies, like those listed here, that build on culturally competent practice with individuals and families. These practice guidelines do not apply to all members of these populations, and they should be used in conjunction with, and not in place of person-centered skills that focus on the individual members of a group.

Latino/a Americans: With a commitment to collectivism, family traditions, harmonious interpersonal relationships, and respect, consider the following as you develop a group:

- Attend to issues of language, both written and oral, including ensuring that written materials are available in Spanish, pronouncing names correctly, and asking if group members prefer English or Spanish and, if the latter, clarifying the word/phrase meanings if group members speak different variations of Spanish.
- Assess level of group member acculturation within various contexts, including physical and mental health, school, family, and work and consider potential conflicts if members are newly arrived in the country or if they are longtime residents.
- Make no assumptions about group members, and be open to learning about individual group members' language, origins, and history.
- Be flexible and fluid with the timing and flow of the group meeting.

EXHIBIT 8.1

Continued

- Allow adequate time for engagement and for trust and relationship building. Encourage facilitators to share personal information about themselves and their families.
- Use story circles/storytelling to enhance relationship building, collaborations, and social action.
- Integrate activities that encourage artistic expression (e.g., painting, acting, theater).
- For curriculum-oriented groups, ensure content and materials are culturally specific and appropriate.

Source: López and Vargas, 2011, pp. 144–145; Paniagua, 2014, pp. 104–105.

African Americans: To consider the use of an Afrocentric approach that brings together Western and African cultures:

- Emphasize the interconnections among the individual, family, and community to enable the individual to see her or himself within those contexts.
- Maintain a focus on African American culture and its strengths.
- Present yourself as respectful and genuine.
- Upon gaining the group's acceptance, maintain a consistent and active role in the group process.
- Be aware of and attend to group members' expectations regarding the group experience (e.g., will the group be multi-racial/ethnic and or have a communalistic focus?).

Sources: Greif & Morris-Compton, 2011; Harvey, 2011, p. 268; Paniagua, 2014.

Asian Americans—Understanding Asian American cultures can help you to:

- Recognize that the importance many Asian Americans place on what Westerners might sometimes see as conflicting values (such as family (versus the individual), harmony, independence, privacy, expression of feelings, and respect for authority) can complicate a group intervention.
- Consider your own assumptions, biases, and lack of information with regard to the diverse groups within Asian cultures. Take heed of the implications of each of these for the intervention.
- Understand that potential differences in communication styles (i.e., emphasis on nonverbal communication) can, for example, enable you to be comfortable with silence.
- Acknowledge group members' strengths, particularly in terms of bicultural skills.
- Consider the impact of similarities and differences in terms of: length of time in the U.S., cultural origins, migration and loss issues, acculturation to Western culture, intergenerational and gender roles/conflicts, and experiences in the U.S. (particularly related to discrimination and oppression).

EXHIBIT 8.1

Continued

- Consider normalizing feelings and experiences, psychoeducational activities, noncon-frontational approaches, and self-disclosure.
- Assess member's level of comfort with sharing feelings and avoid invasive questions until trust and communication norms are established.

Source: Paniagua, 2014; Ringel, 2005.

Native Americans: While few group work approaches have been developed with specific emphasis on Native American culture, consider the following strategies:

- Strive to ensure that each member's voice is heard, specifically in terms of sharing individual stories and making decisions for the group.
- Acknowledge and gather information on tribal-specific traditions, ceremonies, spiritual implications, and context.
- Incorporate positive and honest humor.
- Be consistently "present" and genuine with group members.

Source: McWhirter et al., 2011, pp. 79–80; Paniagua, 2014

Undocumented Immigrants: With their diverse array of personal and family histories and potentially high level of anxiety regarding legal status and possible deportation, group work with undocumented immigrants can benefit from the social worker's use of the following specialized skills:

- Acknowledge and celebrate group members' resilience in the face of challenges and the strengths they have developed as a result of their lived experiences.
- Be knowledgeable about the legal issues associated with undocumented status.
- Ensure that agency administration supports the provision of services to this population.
- Consider active outreach to enable this population to feel comfortable joining a group.
- Clarify for yourself what you do and do not need to know—group members may be reluctant to share specific information regarding their living situations.
- Promote relationship building and trust by inviting members to share their stories and later addressing such issues as marginalization, isolation, and discrimination.

Source: Chen, Budianto, & Wong, 2011, pp. 90–93

Implications of Global and Cultural Connections for Social Work Group Practice [EPAS 2]

An increasingly global perspective on social work practice underscores the need for sensitivity to global awareness in social work group practice. In 1996, NASW amended its *Code of Ethics* (2008) to include the following statement: "social workers should promote conditions that encourage respect for cultural and social diversity within the United States and globally" (Standard 6.04). This addition to the *Code of Ethics* called on the social work profession to embrace a more global consciousness, a perspective that has become well integrated into social work practice, in general, and with groups, in particular. Due to the increased globalization of our society, social workers engaged in group work will need heightened awareness of the expectations and needs of group members of diverse cultures.

As a practicing helping professional, you will benefit from exploring the degree to which your own orientation to achievement, independence, and competition as cultural variants might be incompatible with the cooperation and collaboration that clients from other cultures may value more highly. Regardless of your own cultural heritage, be careful to avoid valuing your orientation to the ideals in your culture or privileging your cultural values as normal just because they are familiar. Suppose, for example, that you encounter a child, Jared, in a school setting who appears to lack an eager, competitive spirit; who seldom raises his hand when a teacher asks a question; and who always defers to others, and you attribute these behaviors to a personal deficit. You may find him slow, shy, or lethargic, and you may see him as dependent, or even as depressed or developmentally delayed. Rather than correlating with some deficit, however, Jared's behaviors may simply reflect a cultural orientation to cooperate, to prioritize the communications of others, and to maintain modesty in the company of people who are older and who have authority.

The nature of "groupness" is complex and variable according to social location. While all people need and seek social connections, their cultural expectations related to family and community, customs, propriety, loyalty, authority, individualism, and the way in which these factors fit together can temper and shape this phenomenon. Although Western values of competitiveness and individualism have been responsible for much of the accomplishments and power of U.S. culture, these values have the potential to create disconnection, isolation, and detachment. While individual self-determination is an important hallmark of social work practice, a group social worker must also understand that it could be perceived as oppressive to clients whose cultural orientation is more collective in nature. Group social workers should be able to adjust group work processes and expectations to account for the range of cultural orientations about collective versus individualistic orientations of group members.

Historical and Contemporary Contexts for Group Work

Like other legacies in social work, social work group practice has roots in the settlement houses in England in the 19th century. The political and economic context of this time period disrupted lives and broke down social connections within and among families. Such a sense of isolation led people to come together in groups around common interests and needs. With a sense of mission, volunteers, often through charity organization, of this era brought groups together for socialization, recreation, advocacy, and social action. The time was ripe for the development of group social work, although there were disagreements among professionals regarding the question of whether social or individual change should be the focus of group work (Alissi, 2009; Furman, Bender, & Rowan, 2014 requested; Toseland & Horton, 2013).

Group work developed in the United States in the late 19th and early 20th centuries at a time when many in our society perceived a need for public, religious, or philanthropic organizations to involve themselves in the lives of U.S. citizens. Inspired by the work of religious and philanthropic organizations in the U.S. with individuals and families, the concept of bringing people together in small groups became a popular strategy for helping clients within community-based settings (e.g., YMCA/YWCA, Boy/Girl Scouts, and faith-based community centers). One approach focused on individuals and their need for change. In contrast, another group of helping professionals of the time focused group efforts on social reform with a humanitarian impulse and believed that social change was the critical ingredient in making a positive difference in people's lives. These reformers were more likely to see the group (rather than the individual) as the medium for that form of intervention. The differences between these groups of professionals echo the social control/social change tension discussed in Chapter 1. By the end of the 19th century, the Progressive Era promoted continued growth of group work. In response to the influx of immigrants and needs of the teeming urban environments, group work (particularly groups with a self-help focus) were being offered within settlement houses and community organizations, and self-help groups. These organizations stressed group methods (e.g., language classes, cooking groups, recreation, the arts, and youth services) and aimed to address the social justice issues of inclusion and acculturation. They sought to increase access to society's assets for newly arrived residents in order to maximize their ability to achieve their desired quality of life. Still, group work was not clearly identified with social work during this period.

Throughout the 1930s, many social work professionals tended to assign lesser status to group work than to social casework. This perception was due in part to the fact that recently developed curricula in schools of social work, reflecting Freud's pervasive influence, focused on individual casework. With the pervasive Freudian focus, existing group work was strongly associated with recreational activities (e.g., sponsoring dances or creating arts and crafts with children) as well as inclusion and acculturation. Such activities were not held in as great esteem as more clinically focused casework. That slowly changed, and as the profession began to accept group work as equal status with casework, practitioners declared it a part of social work, but as a discrete unit with distinctive methods.

In the 1950s, group work expanded from the community into hospitals and psychiatric facilities and social workers introduced **therapeutic group work** or **treatment groups**. These therapeutically focused groups were designed to heal or help people change. This shift took a more professional stance than the former community-based model. Through the process, the distinctions between group work and casework began to blur.

Three classic models for group practice—the **social goals model**, the **reciprocal model**, and the **remedial model**—emerged between the late 1950s and the 1970s. Social workers still use these perspectives in contemporary social work practice with groups, and we will discuss them in detail later in this chapter and in Chapter 9. See Exhibit 8.2 for a brief description of the origins and aims of these three classic models.

By the 1970s, the Council on Social Work Education (CSWE), the accrediting body for social work education in the United States, required all schools of social work to adopt a generalist focus throughout undergraduate programs and for the first half of master's programs. With an aim toward integrating all practice methods across levels, the generalist focus requirement served to de-emphasize the distinctive role of group work as a method and, many believe, to lessen its importance. Most school curricula already emphasized casework, and with the CSWE mandate, there was little incentive to develop more group work courses. As a result, many social work students did not complete coursework that focused on social work practice with groups. Nevertheless, a strong core of social workers committed to the

EXHIBIT 8.2 _Classic Models for Social Group Work, 1950s to 1970s_	MODEL TYPE	MAJOR FOCUS	SOCIAL WORKER ROLE	EXAMPLE	ORIGINAL AUTHORS
	Social Goals	Democratic values, social conscience, responsibility, and action; uses strengths of members.	Fosters social consciousness and serves as a model for democratic values.	School groups that promote student affiliation and contributions to student governance.	Pappell and Rothman, 1962
	Reciprocal	Interaction in an attempt to fulfill mutual affiliation goals; mutual aid.	Serves as mediator between each member and the group as a whole; finds common ground.	Adolescent children of incarcerated parents developing coping skills.	Schwartz, 1961
	Remedial	Prevention and rehabilitation aimed at behavior change and reinforcing individual behaviors.	Works both inside and outside the group to ameliorate conditions in environments; acts as motivator.	Discharge group in mental health settings to increase patient capacity to negotiate community.	Vinter, 1974

power of social work with groups remained, and they founded the Association for the Advancement of Social Work with Groups, Inc. (AASWG) in 1979 (later renamed as **International Association for Social Work with Groups (IASWG))**. The IASWG first issued *Standards for Social Work Practice with Groups,* a guide for effective practice with groups that is widely used in contemporary social work practice, in 1999. The second edition of the *Standards,* issued in 2006 and updated in 2015, provides practitioners with guidelines and practice perspectives for gaining the knowledge, tasks, and skills needed in group work. These guidelines include core values and knowledge, phases of the group process (i.e., pregroup planning, beginning, middle, and ending), and ethical considerations. The Standards are derived from practice wisdom, theories of group work practice, and empirical evidence (AASWG, 2013, p. 270).

The climate of social work practice today offers practitioners a unique opportunity to work with groups to help individuals meet their needs for genuine connection and social action. A group-focused orientation is one of the characteristics that distinguish social work group practice from psychology or mental health counseling groups. In group work, the social worker's effort focuses on the development of the group as a whole through which individual well-being is promoted through interactions and group structures.

DIMENSIONS OF SOCIAL WORK PRACTICE WITH GROUPS

For this discussion of the dimensions of type, form, and function and the logistics of social work group practice, we define a social work group intervention as a small, face-to-face gathering of people who come together for a particular purpose which can be focused on the individual or community. The major feature of a group experience is the interdependence among person, group, and social environment for such purposes as individual or community growth and social advocacy/policy change.

Types, Forms, and Functions of Groups [EPAS 4]

At the most basic level, social work groups are either formed (or constructed) groups or unconstituted, **natural groups**. Natural groups occur in the context of socialization and are not organized from the outside. These may be based on spontaneous friendships, common interests, or common social location, such as living in the sophomore wing of a college dormitory. Families are the original natural group. Natural groups usually do not have formal sponsorship or agency affiliation, but social workers may have occasion to work with them (particularly families). Social workers and their agencies can also provide support to these naturally formed groups in a variety of ways (e.g., offer meeting space, access to office equipment, or staff consultation).

© Blaj Gabriel

Social workers are more likely to engage with or facilitate **formed groups**, which are organized by an institution or organization, such as a school or hospital, an agency, or a community center. There are three primary models of formed groups that accomplish different functions: **task groups**, which are designed to accomplish a specific purpose; **social action** or **goals groups**, a type of task group that focuses on advocating for social justice; and **client groups**, which are geared toward personal change. More specifically:

1. Task groups include task forces, committees and commissions, legislative bodies, staff meetings, interprofessional teams, and case conferences and staffing. A task group aims to facilitate a change that is external to the group with a focus on a specified purpose, such as developing policy, completing a product or a plan, or creating a mechanism for collaborative decision-making (Strand et al., 2009, p. 42). The social worker can function as a convener, member, chair/leader, facilitator, or a combination of these roles. The social worker in the leadership role is responsible for initiating and monitoring the meeting and the group's progress toward stated goals and objectives, managing group interactions, and maintaining focus (Furman et al., 2014, p. 18). We explore task groups in more detail in Chapter 10. You may also visit http://routledgesw.com//riverton/engage/video to learn about a task group, the

Alvadora Neighborhood Association that oversees the activities and growth of the community of Riverton. The video provides an example of a social worker-led task group in action as the members use Roberts Rules of Order to discuss purchasing streetlights and issuing a liquor license.

2. Social action or goals groups are a form of a task group that addresses a social issue to empower individuals or a community (Toseland & Horton, 2013). A social action group inevitably incorporates a political focus that may address issues of social justice, equity, and human rights, all of which require the social worker to have knowledge of the political and social challenges faced by those being served (Dudziak & Profitt, 2012). The social action approach has a number of strengths: (1) the collective effort of a group of people can be more powerful than that of an individual; (2) the social worker is not the expert leader, but rather a facilitator or supporter of the group; (3) groups can help harness the individual's capacity to create social change; (4) professionals and group members work in partnership; (5) group members determine the agenda; and (6) groups can create a safe environment for the individual and collective exploration of issues of oppression, discrimination, and disadvantage (Fleming, 2009, pp. 275–276). As with task groups overall, the social worker can function in a variety of roles. For example, as described at the beginning of this chapter, a group of residents of the Riverton community came together with professionals who work in the community to address their growing concerns about alcohol abuse among the youth in their neighborhoods by forming a social action group, Riverton Against Youth Drinking (RAYD). With in-kind support of the Riverton Association of Neighborhoods, RAYD has established the goal of developing organized activities and programs to deter the youth from engaging in drinking behaviors and worse. To reach their goals, the group plans to apply for grants, hold fundraising events in the community, and partner with family service organizations.

3. Client treatment groups may be aimed at support, education, growth, therapy, socialization, empowerment, and remediation. Client groups can be formed for two purposes:

    a. **Reciprocal groups**, also referred to as support, self-help, and mutual sharing groups, form to enable members who share a common experience to provide mutual aid to one another. With an emphasis on self-help and not specifically on therapeutic intervention, reciprocal groups can range from informal to highly structured to **psychoeducational** (blending mutual support and educational focus). Reciprocal groups provide members with an opportunity to experience "shared empathy," which is the experience that brings members together and provides the potential for cohesion and mutual problem solving (Furman et al., 2014, p. 69). Finding others who share similar life experiences can be validating and affirming for group members and can provide them with opportunities to share valuable insights and coping strategies.

This model for group work intervention has wide applicability, particularly among adults who face a new or unanticipated struggle and can benefit from education and group support. Psychoeducational groups focus on educating group members regarding a psychological condition. One approach in particular has been especially helpful to parents of young adult children experiencing mental illness. These individuals frequently develop new symptoms in their early 20s, and their parents may not have been touched by mental illness before. Local community mental health agencies often offer group sessions to these families to help them learn more about mental illnesses, what to expect in terms of their children's behavior and symptoms, how they can best provide support, and how they can cope with their own grief. The **National Alliance for the Mentally Ill (NAMI)** first established these groups, and they have been particularly effective. Psychoeducational groups usually incorporate considerable factual information, but they also rely on the supportive and accepting attitudes of worker/facilitators and other group members. Groups can be structured, with a curriculum and lessons in sequence, or they can be freer in form. In some locations, parents who originally attended these groups have become group facilitators themselves, generally with training and technical support from the local agency.

Social work involvement in reciprocal groups can range from initiator to facilitator to "silent" support person. The social worker role will be related primarily to the origins of the group (i.e., a larger role if social worker-initiated and a lesser role if member-initiated). In the case of a psychoeducationally focused group, the social worker may play a more formal role based on possession of particular knowledge or skill expertise. A grief support group for children living in the Riverton community who have lost a family member to alcohol or drug abuse is one example of a psychoeducational group. As described at the beginning of this chapter, the Riverton Children's Grief Support Group is offered by the Community Service Agency and facilitated by a social worker. The group relies primarily on community professionals from the school, Community Service Agency, and Alvadora Community Mental Health for referrals.

Groups for persons who are in the early stages of dementia are one example of contemporary support groups. Social workers frequently work with persons who either have dementia or live with or love someone who has dementia. The stigma and isolation some of the men and women living with dementia experience can be as devastating as the disease itself. This makes support a critical component of work with these individuals, and the support group can offer a chance to share feelings, combat loneliness, gain information, exchange resources, and normalize the overall experience. Similar issues arise for families and other loved ones of someone with dementia, and social workers may facilitate groups for them as well. Social workers need to understand the effects, symptoms, and issues that people with or effected by dementia's experience. Alzheimer's disease and other dementia can invoke volatile emotions; therefore, it is particularly important for facilitators to acknowledge and understand their own reactions to and biases regarding the disease and those living with it.

b. **Remedial groups** aim to change behaviors, restore functioning, or promote coping strategies of the individual members who either voluntarily or involuntarily join the group (Toseland & Horton, 2013). The social worker's role in these groups is typically that of facilitator or leader because they bring the clinical knowledge and skills needed to direct the group. Returning to the Riverton community as an example, a remedial group may be formed at a mental health center or hospital to provide therapy for persons struggling with **co-occurring illnesses** (i.e., substance abuse/addiction and mental illness). The Alvadora Mental Health Center Groups for Persons with Co-Occurring Diagnoses is co-facilitated by two clinical social workers with training in addictions and mental health treatment.

Groups may also be distinguished by the role the social worker plays. In treatment or therapy groups, the social worker may use methods consistent with counseling and interpretation, while educational groups may focus on teaching and processing. Task groups are likely to direct the social worker's focus on facilitation, as she or he assists the group in taking action to address an undertaking. See Exhibits 8.3–8.5, which depict phases of group interventions, including social worker and member roles. Using the descriptions of the four groups in the Riverton case, these exhibits give examples of the beginning phases of group processes—pregroup planning, engagement, and assessment—that illustrate the social goals/action, reciprocal, and remedial models.

During the group planning process, a decision you must make is to determine if a group experience will meet the needs you have identified. Group interventions can be powerful and have the potential to address a number of individual, community, and societal needs. A group approach is more suited to some situations than it is to others. In addition to bringing together people who have a common life experience, concern, or need, a group effort can promote creativity and problem solving, influence individual thoughts and behaviors, and provide a convenient strategy for delivery of services to a large group of clients with similar issues (Garvin & Galinsky, 2013). While all of these can be valid reasons for launching a group intervention, consider whether the potential gains for the group, both as individuals and as a collective, are optimally efficacious and efficient or if another type of intervention will be better given a particular situation or need. For example, having a number of male and female clients of all ages who share a life experience (e.g., childhood sexual assault) does not ensure that developing a group intervention is the most appropriate intervention as practice wisdom has shown that mixing ages and genders around an issue as sensitive and personal as childhood sexual assault is not

<table>
<tr><td rowspan="2">

EXHIBIT 8.3

Riverton Against Youth Drinking ("RAYD"): An Example of Social Goals/ Action Group

</td><td colspan="2">

PHASE I: BEGINNING

Background: Concerned about the use and abuse of alcohol among their adolescent children, a group of parents, residents, and professionals in the Riverton community approaches a local community service agency to ask for help addressing this problem. Chapter 9 will highlight later phases of the group's work.

Note: While the stages of group interventions are not linear and may, in fact, overlap, the following depicts a possible approach to responding to the identified need.

</td></tr>
<tr><td>

PREGROUP PLANNING AND ENGAGEMENT

</td><td>

ASSESSMENT

</td></tr>
</table>

PREGROUP PLANNING AND ENGAGEMENT	**ASSESSMENT**
Meet with parent groups to gather information	Determine individual and group members' "agendas"
Identify current and potential stakeholders who are/may be invested in the issue	Conduct community assessment, including needs, assets, and resources (see Chapter 10 for further information on community assessment)
Identify interests of group members	
Research evidence on approaches for facilitating social goals groups on this topic	Gather and analyze data from assessment; identify and prioritize options for intervention
Determine general focus/goal of launching an intervention	Re-determine/confirm focus of intervention
Identify roles for agency and social worker	Finalize plan for intervention, including objectives, tasks, activities, persons/ groups responsible, time frame, and plans for evaluation and sustainability
Arrange first meeting and logistics, including time, location, refreshments, etc.	Re-clarify agency and social worker roles and responsibilities
Develop agenda for first meeting	Revisit needs
	Make plans for continued assessment

the most effective approach. Individual and same-gender/age interventions may be more helpful to the clients.

Recognizing that the individual's work is completed within the context of the group's fluid, interactive, and sometimes conflictual dynamic, ask yourself if your desire to establish a group meets the client's needs or your needs to efficiently serve a larger group of clients. Would group work primarily meet your agency's revenue goals, or would it mount an advocacy effort, or some combination of the two?

PHASE I: BEGINNING

Background: A social worker in a local community service agency has become aware of a number of children in Riverton who have lost a parent to alcohol and substance-related deaths. The social worker takes steps toward offering an educational support group in the community. Chapter 9 will highlight later phases of the group's work.

Note: While the stages of group interventions are not linear and may, in fact, overlap, the following depicts a possible approach to responding to the identified need.

PREGROUP PLANNING AND ENGAGEMENT	ENGAGEMENT AND ASSESSMENT
Gather information to support the need for and appropriateness of this group intervention	*Pregroup*
	Prior to first meeting, meet individually with parents/guardians and separately with children to assess interest in and appropriateness (i.e., "fit") for a psychoeducational support group
Analyze data and confirm plans to move forward with forming a group	
Research evidence supporting approaches to facilitating reciprocal groups with children	
	First Session
Determine group components:	Lead introductions
• Composition of group (number, age range, and gender)	Orient members to the group; review purpose, goals, rules, norms, format, time frame, intervention plan, termination, evaluation, and confidentiality
• Recruitment strategies	
• Format (open or closed)	Assess individual member goals, functions, and interactions with other members
• Time frame (time-limited or ongoing)	
Determine and implement appropriate recruitment strategies	Assess group cohesiveness
Conduct screening interviews with potential members (see note in Assessment regarding group membership)	Continue to assess individual and group needs (for support and education), interests, strengths, and "agendas"
	Monitor and assess social worker role
Invite group members (for minors, obtain written permission from legal guardians)	Administer pregroup measurements to be used in the evaluation process
Determine roles of agency, social work facilitator, children, and legal guardians	

EXHIBIT 8.5

Riverton Mental Health Center Group for Persons with Co-Occurring Diagnoses: An Example of a Remedial Group

PHASE I: BEGINNING

Background: A new social worker at the Riverton Mental Health Center has recently assumed co-leadership with another social worker for a clinical intervention group for persons with co-occurring diagnoses (i.e., substance abuse and mental illness) who receive outpatient services at the agency. The group is diverse; members represent a mix of gender orientation, racial/ethnic group, and age and both mandated and voluntary participants. Membership turnover depends on members' "graduation" from the treatment program; therefore, group membership is fluid. Two new members have been referred to the group. This will be the first time new members have been referred since the social worker took over co-responsibility for the group. Chapter 9 will highlight later phases of the group's work.

Note: While the stages of group interventions are not linear and may, in fact, overlap, the following depicts a possible approach to responding to the identified need.

PREGROUP PLANNING AND ENGAGEMENT	ENGAGEMENT AND ASSESSMENT
Obtain information on potential new members from referral sources and agency records, as appropriate	*First Session*
	Facilitate introduction of new members to group and review group expectations, norms, and rules
Research evidence on incorporating new members into an existing group	
Determine structure for admission, including criteria and process	Assess individual member goals, interests, and "fit" with group
Meet with potential new members to screen for potential "fit" with group purpose, goals, and other members	Assess member reactions to new group members
	Assess group cohesion
Invite new members to first session, introduce self, and provide orientation (e.g., composition, goals, expectations, norms, and rules)	Monitor/assess progress of other members

Quick Guide 24 provides a set of questions to consider as you weigh the pros and cons of forming a group.

Group Work Logistics

Social work groups may form and meet in community agencies, schools, community mental health centers, medical practices, public assistance offices, job training centers, residential care settings, church or faith organizations, or any other setting in which participants come together. The physical location may be a setting that

QUICK GUIDE 24   THE PROS AND CONS OF CREATING A GROUP: QUESTIONS TO CONSIDER

As you weigh options for intervening with client, organization, and community systems, first determine if a group intervention is the most effective approach. To clarify your goals, consider the following:

- What are my reasons for choosing a group intervention over an individual or family intervention? Specifically, what needs have I identified within my clients, my agency, or the community?
- What type of group intervention am I considering—social action, task, reciprocal, or remedial? What are my reasons for selecting this format?
- What would the goal(s) of the group be? For the group? For me? For the agency or community?
- Will the group be an open or closed group (i.e., continuous group of members or open to members entering and leaving as needed)?
- Will the needs of members best be met in a time-limited or open-ended group?
- Who and what will determine the eligibility criteria for group membership?
- Do I have the requisite competence to facilitate a group intervention?
- Should I be the sole facilitator, or would having a co-facilitator better serve the group?
- Do I have the support of my supervisor and agency administration? If not, am I aware of the process for gaining approval?
- What resources do I need to offer the group? Possibilities include meeting space, supplies, and funds for recruitment, refreshments, transportation, and child or adult care.
- What options exist for gaining the resources needed for the group?
- If this is a client group, will there be a charge for participation?
- What is the optimal group size?
- Is there an adequate pool of potential group members within those my agency serves or the larger community?
- If I am uncertain about the pool of candidates for the group, how would I recruit members? What marketing strategies would be appropriate?
- What are the appropriate meeting dates, times, frequency, and longevity for the group?
- When will group meetings begin?
- How much time do I need to prepare to lead the group?
- How will group activities be recorded and evaluated?

group members already use (such as a school), or it may be a local community facility that makes itself available to group activities (a community hospital that houses a grief and loss group, for example). Many residential settings that host social work groups, like law enforcement centers or mental health facilities, restrict their use to residents and their significant others.

Social work groups may differ in other ways, such as the number of group meetings or the way in which they are organized. A group may meet for a fixed number of sessions, or it may be ongoing, with changing membership over time. Some groups are structured as **closed groups** in which group membership and the number of sessions are fixed. Many others are **open groups**, which allow new members to join at any time (or occasionally only at fixed times, such as after the third and sixth sessions). Group interventions are often intentionally time-limited because of the nature of the work (e.g., mandated groups or psycho-educationally focused groups), financial or agency resources, or characteristics of the group members (e.g., children or adolescents). In developing plans for a group intervention, consider which of these formats will best meet the needs of the target population. Open groups may offer flexibility for the facilitator and group members and economic advantages for the organization, but this format may lack the cohesiveness and continuity of a closed group format. Consider also the similarities and differences in the skill sets required to facilitate each type of group. For example, to effectively lead an open group, the social worker must be able to quickly develop an empathetic connection to group members, promote cohesion in each meeting, and know when it is appropriate to use more active or less active facilitative skills (Turner, 2011).

Whether group participation is voluntary or mandated is another important distinction. In mandated situations, the social worker may have lower expectations (not always realized) of member investment, and the influence of the mandating institution (such as the court) is likely to be greater than it is in voluntary groups. Many involuntary treatment scenarios employ groups. For example, recall the innovative family group decision-making model in Chapter 7, which used a large group of community and extended family members in a case of a child protection violation. More traditional models also use involuntary groups for work with clients who experience intimate partner violence, parenting issues, and substance abuse/ addictions. Group work focuses particularly on interrelatedness and extension to the "outside" world, thus creating opportunities to engage involuntary clients in a process from which they can benefit long after completing treatment. During the engagement, assessment, and planning phases of group work with members who are mandated to participate, the social worker's role is to take an empathetic stand toward the goal of finding a mutual purpose, including acknowledging to her- or himself and the clients the presence of anger and hostility while creating options for decision-making (Doel & Kelly, 2014). For example, consider your approach if you are facilitating a group for adolescents who have been convicted of nonviolent criminal offenses in which the members are mandated by the court system to participate and are, not surprisingly, unhappy to be there. Rather than attempting to create an illusion of willingness or complacency about their situations, you may opt to address the involuntary aspect at the outset of the group with a statement such as,

I know that you are each required to participate in this group as a condition of your legal situation and that you may prefer not to be here. I also know that you have a choice in how you want to handle your time in this group and I want to let you know that I will respect your right to participate at the level you feel comfortable.

THEORETICAL APPROACHES TO ENGAGEMENT AND ASSESSMENT WITH GROUPS [EPAS 6 AND 7]

As with social work practice with individuals and families, developing competencies for engaging, assessing, and planning in group practice begins with identifying a theoretical stance from which you will work. Just as in social work practice with individuals, families, and communities, social workers are obligated to utilize a theoretically evidence-based intervention that incorporates empirically supported group interventions and process, evidence-supported guidelines, and practice evaluation (Macgowan & Hanbidge, 2015).

Regardless of the theoretical perspective selected for group work, you should maintain a commitment to the strengths-based perspective. The following discussion is grounded in the premise that all members in a social work group have strengths on which the goals and objectives can be built. As Kurland (2007) notes, "the very act of forming a group is a statement of our belief that every member of the group has something to offer the others, something to give to others, not just to get from them" (p. 12).

Since all groups are created and function as a system, most theoretical frameworks for group practice derive from the systemic perspective (Garvin & Galinsky, 2013). You can apply your knowledge of systems theory as it relates to work with individuals and families to your work with groups. You may begin by viewing groups as fluid, dynamic interactions between a set of individuals who become interdependent. Any change in group composition (e.g., a member joins or exits) changes group dynamics and interpersonal interactions. A systemic perspective suggests that, through group members' exchanges and feedback, the work of each phase of the group process "coalesces into a meaningful whole" (Manor, 2009, p. 101). Group work can be highly effective when approached from a strengths-based perspective. When a group focuses on members' strengths and abilities as opposed to their limitations, it can have a powerful impact on those individuals (Ephross, 2011). Building on the conceptualization that systemic and strengths-based frameworks guide social work group practice, the following discussion looks at narrative and solution-focused perspectives within group work.

Narrative Approach in Group Engagement and Assessment

Social workers have integrated narrative theory with other theoretical and practice approaches to group work just as they have in their practice with individuals and families. Incorporating a narrative approach with groups begins with viewing the clients as collaborators with one another and the social worker. With a group, the number of potential collaborations is significantly increased as compared to individual work. Having a group of individuals who share common experiences can further aid in the process of engaging the individual group member to elicit her or his story, then challenging the client's perspective and partnering to reconstruct a new story/reality. Members can benefit, not only from sharing and reconstructing their own narrative, but also from listening to other group members and contributing as they reconstruct their own individual stories.

The narrative framework emphasizes the client's expertise on her or his life (Kelley, 2013). Within the context of assessment in group practice, group members can work with one another and with the social worker to identify members' strengths. The assessment process can also help members externalize or separate themselves from their problems for the purpose of planning for change. Next, we explore using a narrative approach blended with a solution-focused approach.

Solution-Focused Approach in Group Engagement and Assessment

Recall from earlier discussions of social workers using a solution-focused approach with individuals and families that this approach emphasizes brief, targeted interventions. A solution-focused approach "encourages more purposeful interaction among group members" (De Jong & Berg, 2013, p. 286). With its grounding in a strengths-based perspective and its emphasis on solutions, this approach can quickly focus group members on the issues that brought them to the group, aid them in collaborating with one another on the development of a plan for change, and activate the planned change—all with the input and support of other group members and of the social work facilitator.

In engaging potential group members, the social worker can emphasize the time-limited, targeted, future-oriented nature of a solution-focused group. This orientation clearly sets the stage from the engagement phase that the work together will be purposeful, will occur within a specified time period (ideally 6–12 meetings), and will emphasize concrete, achievable outcomes. Such an approach is likely to appeal to potential group members who may be reticent about joining a group. De Jong and Berg (2013) report that the relatively brief, time-limited nature of the solution-focused group intervention can serve as motivating and purposeful for group members. Solution-focused strategies have been shown to be particularly helpful when addressing bullying behaviors with children and youth (Young, 2013), with clients mandated for intervention (e.g., prison inmates and offenders of intimate partner violence) (Uken, Lee, & Sebold, 2013; Walker, 2013), and substance abuse (SAMHSA National Registry of Evidence-based Programs and Practices (NREPP), 2012).

Because of the pragmatic, outcomes-oriented nature of the solution-focused approach, the assessment phase of solution-focused group work can promote a range of helpful techniques. For example, creating individualized therapeutic goals and using scaling questions to gauge members' concerns enables group members to monitor their own progress throughout the intervention. Using a standard series of solution-focused questions to introduce assessment highlights previous successes, strengths, and resources while focusing the individual client (and the group) on viable solutions. For example, as a social worker working with the group of Riverton residents who have lost someone to substance abuse/ addiction, you could begin the assessment phase by asking individual members the "miracle" question: "How would your life be if you were no longer acutely grieving the loss of your loved one?" You could then ask the group member to recall a time when he or she successfully coped with a challenge or crisis. Recognizing that grief is not easily resolved, you can guide group members to consider alternative strategies for coping with their loss. The benefit of such a pragmatic, time-limited nature of the group process is that group members can share ideas and strategies, help identify strengths in themselves and others, and support and nurture one another.

Social workers can effectively integrate solution-focused approaches with other intervention approaches. For example, incorporating strategies from the strengths- and narrative-based schools of thought can enhance the impact of the intervention (Kelley, 2013). All three approaches emphasize engagement, assessments, and planning focused on the resources of each person with the goal to empower and change. Narrative-focused techniques can elicit the stories of the group members and help develop alternative and unique change outcomes for the individual and the group. Specifically, the interactional nature of the group experience can promote the group members' comfort and motivation to articulate their stories as well as enable them to support one another as they explore and strategize potential solutions that will work for them.

Regardless of the orientation(s) to which you subscribe, remember that your client in group work is, in fact, the group itself, and the group experience can be powerful for both you and for group members.

CONTEMPORARY TRENDS AND SKILLS FOR THE BEGINNING PHASES OF GROUP WORK: ENGAGEMENT AND ASSESSMENT [EPAS 6 AND 7]

As with practice with individuals and families, pre-planning, engagement and assessment, and planning are critical to an effective social work intervention with a group. These areas coincide with the phases of the group intervention: (1) engagement including preplanning and planning for the group experience; (2) assessment and planning for the group process planning; (3) intervention focused primarily on the middle phase of group work; and (4) termination, evaluation, and follow-up encompassing the ending phase. Group practice skills build on the skills and knowledge needed in work with individuals and families; here we will discuss new skills for pregroup formation planning (i.e., screening, engaging and assessment, group logistics, and process (Macgowan & Hanbidge, 2015).

Pregroup Planning

A successful social work group intervention requires careful planning prior to the first meeting. As the practitioner, there are nine areas you need to consider before organizing a group (adapted from Kurland & Salmon, 1998, p. 24):

- Client need

- Purpose

- Composition, eligibility, and appropriateness

- Structure

- Content

- Agency context

- Social context

- Pregroup contact

- Contacting prospective group members

You should think about each of these areas within the context of the agency, your supervisor's input or direction, and the larger social environment. These areas are interrelated; decisions in one area may influence decisions in another. The considerations here do not presuppose certain answers. They are simply areas to keep in mind in order to avoid unexpected obstructions later. See Exhibit 8.6 for schematic drawings related to preplanning models and Exhibit. 8.7 for an example of the operationalization of the preplanning process.

Let us return to Jasmine Johnson's situation in which she asks for your help to learn alternative strategies for interacting with her teen son. A component of her contract with you was to participate in a Parents of Teens Support Group. Look at Exhibit 8.7 from the perspective of the social worker who will create and lead that group.

Client Need To determine if a group approach would be most appropriate for clients, you may begin by identifying the major relevant issues that confront the client population. You want to know your clients well and to be aware of their needs as they perceive them. In order to establish a vital, functioning group, you must understand members' lives and struggles and be able to focus on some aspect of their lives that is important to them. In-depth knowledge of your target group can influence your recruitment and retention strategies, meeting location, group agendas and activities, and the impetus for potential members to participate (Finlayson & Cho, 2011, p. 491). For example, in working with the parents of teens group in which Jasmine Johnson is a member, consider the decisions you will make

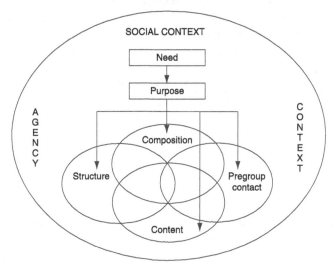

Pregroup Planning Model
(for use when group composition *is not* predetermined)

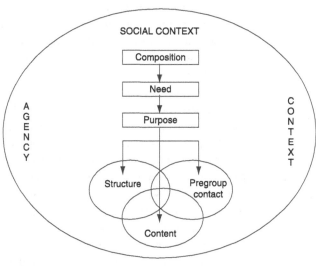

Pregroup Planning Model
(for use when group composition *is not* predetermined)

Source: Kurland & Salmon, 1998, p. 209

EXHIBIT 8.6

*Pregroup
Planning
Models*

Your agency has experienced an increase in the number of parents of teens seeking services out of concern for their relationships with their adolescent children. Together with your supervisor and colleagues you reach a decision to form a support group for this population. You have been asked to lead this effort. Building on Kurland & Salmon's (1998) classic list of preplanning tasks, you consider the following:

Preplanning Issue/Task	Consideration for Parents of Teens Support Group
Need	62% increase in the past six months of parents of teens seeking services out of concern for their relationships with their teenage children.
Purpose	After discussion at a staff meeting, family service staff agree that parents can benefit from a reciprocal, psychoeducationally focused group intervention.
Composition, eligibility, and appropriateness	*Composition:* The group will target parents of adolescents aged 12–19 years and will not have a minimum or maximum number of participants.
	Eligibility: Based on the changing needs of the target population, the group will be open to any interested parents of teens. Participants need not currently receive services from the agency.
	Appropriateness: Due to the psychoeducational/support orientation of the group, any parents who feel they need support will be appropriate for the group. This type of group is consistent with other services your agency offers.
Structure	The group will meet monthly for 90 minutes in the agency's multipurpose room. You will serve as primary facilitator while the social work student completing practicum with you this year will serve as co-facilitator. The agency will provide refreshments and will offer child care for any parents with young children. Service learning students from a nearby university will oversee the childcare area.
Content	As the group intervention focuses on the provision of mutual aid and education, each session will begin with a brief presentation by one of the facilitators or another professional. The parents will collaborate with the co-facilitators to determine topics of interest.
	Following the presentation and discussion, members will be given the opportunity to "check-in" with one another, raise issues, and ask for input from the group regarding their concerns.

Agency context	With support from your supervisor, agency administration, and your co-workers, this group intervention helps promote the agency mission to provide services to families and children.	**EXHIBIT 8.7** *Continued*
Social context	A psychoeducational, reciprocal support group meets a need within the community that no other agency or institution is currently meeting. Should members need additional support, your agency provides individual and family services.	
Pregroup contact	Together with your social work student, you will develop a program flyer to circulate among agency staff and post on the agency's website and bulletin boards. You will also promote the program to other social service agencies that serve this population, school social workers, a community service website, and in the organization section of the local newspaper.	
Contacting prospective group members	Social service professionals may refer prospective group members or prospective members may contact the agency directly. You and your social work practicum student will conduct a brief intake interview with each potential member to determine her or his appropriateness for the group. If you determine that the individual is a good fit, you will invite her or him to the first meeting.	

regarding the scheduling and location of meetings and the parents' schedules, transportation, and child care needs. Keep in mind the challenges these parents face in balancing challenging parenting situations with work, the needs of other family members, and their own well-being and focus on an issue relevant to their lives rather than on something they may deem irrelevant (e.g., retirement planning). On the other hand, self-care strategies (e.g., exercise, social activities, or creative arts) may be very appealing to parents who are feeling stressed and concerned for their teenage children. The point is to know your clients' needs and respond to them in a way that is consistent with your agency's purpose. Community needs assessments, agency service statistics, and interviews with staff and clients can all provide data that can help you make these decisions.

Purpose   Consider both collective and individual objectives: What hopes will the group as a whole have? What expectations will individuals have? Ask yourself, what is the function of the group and what will your role be? The group may focus on, for example, counseling, teaching, or facilitating social action. Consider ways in which member interaction will contribute to the purpose of the group. A structured group intervention should always focus on meeting participants' goals for growth and to gain knowledge that they can apply to their own lives (Ephross, 2011). Returning to the parents of teens group in which Jasmine is a member, the group as a whole may hope to normalize the experience of living with and parenting their children during the often turbulent years of adolescents. Individual goals may be to gain strategies and wisdom for responding to the challenges of parenting an adolescent that can be gained through group member sharing and psychoeducational content.

Composition, Eligibility, and Appropriateness   Group composition refers to the number of group members and their characteristics, such as gender orientation, age, experience, skill, beliefs, and values. The major concern in determining the composition of a group is the degree of homogeneity or heterogeneity that is most conducive to achieving desired outcomes. In general, scholars agree that some common characteristic or situation optimally provides a unifying focus, but there should also be enough difference to sustain members' interest and the potential for growth through exposure to different ideas. Frequently, a particular condition, such as living with cancer or caregiving for a family member with a chronic illness, can bridge many differences on other dimensions, such as age or ethnic background, but these aspects should be evaluated carefully in each situation. In the case of the parents of teens group, Jasmine and the other parents share the experience of finding challenges in trying to help their children through adolescence, which can be a shared similarity, but each will bring a different lived experience, attitudes, and beliefs about their situations which can show diversity of perspectives.

In addition to individual descriptive variables, behavioral characteristics are also important. The group has the potential to be more successful if members have compatible interpersonal styles, levels of verbal development, and understandings of the potential for groups. Different types of groups will vary on the balance of these components—for example, similar ages in children's groups would probably be more important than in most adult groups. In thinking about the parents of teens group, the parents will likely be a range of ages and varying degrees of parenting experience, both of which can be an asset in the group's ability to support and guide one another.

The need and purpose of the group intervention helps determine the eligibility criteria and type of members that are appropriate for the group. As you explore the possibility of forming a group, take into consideration the focus of the group and members' ability to connect to one another. For example, consider these questions. Will caregivers of spouses with Alzheimer's disease have issues that are similar to or different from caregivers of adult children with a developmental disability? Will people in recovery from an addiction be eligible to remain in the group if they are found to have relapsed? Focusing on the goals of the group intervention will help you answer these questions and create a group who will be able to help each other.

Structure   Determine if a group will be open or closed and if there will be any "trade-offs" for your particular group. What is the agency's position on this question? What challenges might you face in an open-ended group? What about challenges in a closed-ended group? What type of group will best address the short- and long-term needs of group members?

Group leadership is another area to address as you begin developing a group intervention. Will the group have a sole facilitator, or will co-facilitators better meet the needs of the group? While a single facilitator may be more economical in terms of time and financial resources, there may be compelling reasons for co-facilitation, including physical safety for members and facilitators, opportunity for a student to gain group experience, and the benefits of facilitators as role models (Ephross, 2011).

Structure also refers to the logistical arrangements of the group—location, frequency of sessions, time of meetings, and duration. Other practical questions include: What type or size of room will work best? Will group members require transportation or child care? Will there be a fee for participation in the group? How will members maintain confidentiality? What level of agency coordination will be required? Using the parents of teens group as an example, taking into consideration the parents' work and family obligations and schedules will be critical to the parents' ability to join the group. Similarly, knowing that the information that each one shares will be maintained inside the group will enable the group to share more openly and without fear of their family issues becoming public knowledge.

Content   You should determine the content the group will cover by analyzing the purpose of the group, its members' needs, and agency and personnel resources. The activities or other means used to accomplish the group's purpose may require special equipment or educational or art materials. Consider the agenda and content of the meetings. Who will be responsible for making arrangements for the group, establishing timelines, creating an agenda, and developing a group purpose? If the group will use discussion, will the content facilitate interaction among members? For the parents of teens group, providing the members with an opportunity to establish their own rules, agendas, and areas to be discussed can serve to more accurately meet the parents' needs and to empower them as individuals and parents.

Agency Context   Consider how the agency will affect the group and how the group will affect the agency. Specifically, do agency administration and personnel endorse group work for the population served, and is group work consistent with the agency's mission and emphasis? Do not assume you have the agency's support without confirming it. Your group is likely to have repercussions for others. For example, a children's group that meets at the agency is often noisy and may be disruptive to other staff and clients. The addition of group work to the agency's repertoire of service may increase the support staff's administrative responsibilities. Individual social workers may feel possessive of their clients and may be reticent to refer current clients to a group experience. It is to your advantage to address these and other concerns as directly as possible prior to creating the group.

Social Context   Consider social and cultural influences that may influence the group's bonding and functioning. Will the group complement other community services? Are there appropriate supports and resources for members after the group to help them maintain changes? Do members' cultural contexts support group participation? For example, if you want to facilitate a group for adolescent girls, consider whether their families will approve of and provide support for the group and their daughters' participation.

Pregroup Contact   Prior to a first meeting, consider the following questions: How will members be recruited or referred to the group? Will you conduct individual pregroup screening interviews to determine whether individuals are appropriate for the group? How will members prepare themselves for the group experience? How will you facilitate members' orientation to the group process so they can experience maximum participation and benefit? While each group and each potential member is unique, developing a plan to address these questions can enable you to assemble a group with whom you are familiar and who are already oriented to the purpose, structure, and format of the group they may be joining. While raising each of these questions is important, in general, meeting with each potential group member is an appropriate strategy for providing relevant group information to the person, for determining if she or he can benefit from a group experience, and for determining if there is a fit between the individual and the other members of the group.

Pregroup contact can also be an opportunity for the social worker and the client to discuss the client's participation in and balance with other services. The client may be receiving individual and/or family services so strategizing about ways to maximize benefits from both types of services can be helpful for the potential group member. The social worker can also let the potential group member know that, during the group experience, it is not unusual for the social worker to suggest individual or family services be initiated. The social worker can help the client who receives multiple services process and make use of the information gleaned from each of these intervention approaches.

Contacting Prospective Group Members   There are many ways to build up the membership of a prospective group and to connect with potential group work clients, including outreach and on-site service referral. **Outreach** is a method for contacting people in their homes and communities to inform them of services and information about which they may not have been aware (Barker, 2014). You may reach out to potential group members through connections with other professionals in the community (e.g., school social workers). Other times, outreach may require a more concerted coordination campaign (e.g., advertising, posting to agency website or social media, and individual contacts), particularly if potential clients fear discrimination or barriers to eligibility. It may be helpful for current group members to recruit prospective group members. Having firsthand knowledge of the group's purpose and focus can be an effective strategy for recruitment of new members.

On-site service referral is often a useful way to connect with potential members. You may, for example, recruit members from your caseload of individual clients, or you might ask your colleagues for referrals after they give you their support. Postings and announcements are helpful, but they must be paired with personal contact, such as another staff member's enthusiastic recommendation, to be effective.

In nearly all scenarios, a pregroup interview is ideal. First, it allows you to get an in-depth sense of the potential member to determine her or his "fit" with the goals and purpose of the group and whether she or he is an appropriate member. A pregroup meeting also provides an opportunity to assess any potential concerns about the person's interaction with other members of the group. It also provides the opportunity for the prospective group member to air any anxieties, to develop a sense of this new experience, to ask questions, and to make a more empowered choice about joining the group. A pregroup meeting is a time to raise questions or concerns regarding fees or costs associated with joining the group. Finally, this contact with group members is a form of engagement, assessment, and planning. As such, it requires the same level of knowledge and skills as individual engagement and assessment and planning.

You can ease a potential or new group member's entry into the group by providing online or printed information regarding the group experience. Such a document may contain information on (Brown, 2013):

- group purpose and goals;

- the format of the group and techniques, activities, and procedures that will be a part of the group experience;

- the individual's right to refuse participation;

- limitations of the group intervention;

- potential risks and benefits;

- the leader's credentials and group experience;

- the leadership of the group if the leader is not available;

- implications of any diagnoses that may have been made and the role of testing, if it occurred;

- documentation, including recordkeeping, reports, and client access to records; and

- payment process, if applicable (pp. 19–20).

Engagement

Overlapping with the important pregroup planning phase, engagement is the beginning phase of the group intervention. The *Standards for Social Work Practice with Groups* (IASWG, 2015, pp. 6–9) provides behavior guidelines for the practitioner working in the engagement or beginning phases of the group work intervention, including such pregroup activities as:

- identifying member aspirations and needs as perceived by the member, agency, and yourself;

- confirming organizational support for offering a group;

- determining the group type, structure, processes, and size that will complement group purpose and goals;

- developing strategy for and recruit potential group members;

- completing organizational requirements for admission to group;

- clarifying member goals and expectations along with the person's feelings about joining the group;

- establishing meeting time and location to ensure comfort, safety, and access;

- developing a group purpose (will be finalized during first group meeting); and

- planning group content, activities, and documentation format and obtaining needed resources.

Following the pregroup phase of work, skills and behaviors needed for continuing the engagement and assessment of group members include:

- developing contracts for explication of individual and group goals, tasks, and activities for the duration of the group and beyond;

- following your own introduction and clarification of your role in the group, inviting members to introduce themselves and to share their reasons for joining and their hopes for the group;

- in collaboration with group members, developing a clear statement of purpose, rules and norms, and roles that incorporates the individual and group member and agency goals, needs, and perceptions;

- developing, as appropriate, content, activities, and resources relevant to the group's purpose;

- highlighting common interests and goals, direct interactions, and potential linkages in order to promote group cohesion among members, and between the members and you;

- in cooperation with group members, establishing the work plan for the group for the rest of the beginning phase and for the remainder of the group's planned time together (or for the individual's time in the group if the group is open-ended and not time-limited); and

- building awareness and overt recognition of the unique characteristics of each group member, including but not limited to cultural and ethnic heritage, age, gender, sexual orientation, presenting concerns, and note that each person brings strengths to the group process.

The first session ideally begins with you and group members sharing your expectations for the group. Be transparent about what you (you alone or with a co-facilitator) hope to accomplish. Likewise, encourage members to talk about their perceptions of their roles. Confidentiality is often one of the first dimensions you will discuss, and, as you can imagine, unless all members feel safe in revealing their struggles and feelings, it is not likely that many will participate fully.

Establishing **norms**, or expected rules of conduct, creates a productive group climate and requires members to actively participate so the social worker is not in the position of dictating group regulations. The actual norms will depend on the type of group. For example, the major expectation for a socialization group for 7-year-old boys in residential treatment may be "no hitting." "No shouting" might be applicable to an anger management group, or "celebrating holidays and accomplishments" to a single-parents' group. Some groups also discourage members from contacting each other outside the group because it may dilute the group process, and others encourage it because it fosters translation of group benefits into the "real world." The primary purpose of norms should be to facilitate group members' involvement through a relatively clear set of behavioral expectations that in turn will increase their comfort in the group and encourage their maximum participation. If, for example, group members have differing cultural heritages, and some members interpret lateness as disrespectful while others view it as culturally appropriate or simply flexible, the social worker may opt to explore timeliness as an area for negotiation. Knowing the membership can help you anticipate particular issues that may affect group process. Like the interview, all of these early negotiations with group members serve as important opportunities for both engagement and ongoing assessment.

The engagement phase can be challenging for both the social worker and for group members. The social worker is trying to engage with each individual member and the group as a whole, to promote cohesion among the members themselves, to establish the group structure and format, *and* to keep the group on task and on target for the previously stated goals. Creating an environment that is safe, comfortable, and supportive is essential to group members' ability to establish rapport and engagement with the process and with you as the facilitator (Furman et al., 2014). When a group is engaged, group members become empowered to begin sharing with and supporting one another, alleviating the need for the social worker to take full responsibility for leading the group. Engaging new members or facilitators who join an established group can be challenging. The social work facilitator is responsible for engaging the new member and for encouraging the group to do the same, or, if the social worker is new to a group, he or she is responsible for reaching out to members. If members do not feel engaged in the first meeting, attrition may occur. Members who join a group voluntarily but who do not feel connected to the group or to the facilitator may feel reticent about returning to the group.

The beginning phases of group work can present challenges for group members as well. Whether the group member is voluntarily or involuntarily participating in the group, she or he may be reticent to engage with the group facilitator, fearing possibly that the facilitator does not understand the member's situation or is judging the member for life choices or circumstances. Regardless of the reasons for the member's hesitancy, the social worker can use "**tuning in**," with each of the individual members. In "tuning in" to the individual members, the social worker conveys empathy, acknowledges the reasons that the member may be reluctant to engage with the social worker or other group members, and invites feedback (Shulman, 2015). Being attentive to individual reactions and responses will ensure that individuals are not "lost" or deterred from investing in the group experience. "Tuning in" to the group members can also help to create a **therapeutic alliance** (i.e., development of a trusting working relationship) with the members of the group as individuals which can then allow the individual members to create alliances with the other members of the group (Shulman, 2015).

Assessment and Planning [EPAS 1]

As with social work practice with individuals and families, the transition from one phase of work to another is rarely linear or clearly defined and must relate both to the group and the individual members. Just as engagement can be an ongoing process, you can revisit assessment and planning throughout the duration of the group experience. Both assessment and planning logically and naturally occur as you recruit and screen potential members and again as the group forms and collaborates on the development of individual and group contracts. You may find that you need to assess and plan at different points throughout the life of the group as individual and group goals change and evolve, as members arrive and depart, and as unanticipated events influence group interactions (e.g., conflict, change of facilitator, or termination). Ongoing assessments must be conducted to establish the individual member's goals and desired outcomes, the group's outcomes, and the group processes (e.g., group cohesion and productivity) (Macgowan & Hanbidge, 2015).

Regardless of the timing and frequency assessment occurs, bringing a biopsychosocial-spiritual lens to the information is essential for the group intervention. Within the context of group practice, the biopsychosocial-spiritual assessment is a strategy both for determining the context of the client's situation, if the issues and characteristics a group member presents are consistent with those of other members, and for monitoring individual and group progress toward goals. Recall the earlier example of the group for Riverton children who had lost a family member to substance abuse or addiction. As the facilitator of this group, you may initiate a group discussion about the biopsychosocial- spiritual aspects of addictions and grief.

You can also conduct assessments to measure group-related issues such as cohesiveness (Macgowan, 2009b). Upon determining what you want to assess, you can opt to use standardized measures, observation, group member self-reports, or feedback from an external source (e.g., in person, through videos, through audio recordings).

As with any area of social work practice, group leaders must be cognizant of the ethical obligations associated with engaging and assessing members of a new group. Social work ethical guidelines dictate the following (Brown, 2013):

- All assessment techniques and instruments must have sufficient and appropriate validity and reliability.

- Group facilitators must have formal training and supervised practice assessing group members.

- Group leaders must always practice within their areas of competence.

- Group members must provide informed consent for participation in the group experience and the group leader must inform them of any information resulting from the assessment that will be shared with others (p. 23).

Planning within the assessment phase of group work often requires vigilant attentiveness and flexibility. While most group facilitators spend considerable time and effort on pregroup planning and developing an agenda or plan for each group session, the experienced group practitioner can attest to the need to be willing and able to quickly and creatively shift plans. Regardless of the type of group you are facilitating, it is likely that at any meeting a member or members will have an issue, crisis, request, or behavior that will take precedence over your plans for that session. While you will want to be responsive to each individual's needs, you must try to balance the needs of the entire group. You may be able to set aside your plans for that session to devote time to one or more specific individuals, but use caution to ensure you do not sacrifice the needs of other members or agenda items in the process.

Shulman (2011) offers the following suggestions for helping group members manage their feelings during these early phases of a group intervention:

- Reach inside the silences by asking the members of the group to share the reasons for their silences.

- Help the group member to put their feelings into words.

- Convey to the group members that you understand their feelings.

- Share your own feelings with the group members (p. 18).

STRAIGHT TALK ABOUT GROUP ENGAGEMENT AND ASSESSMENT

Acting as a facilitator or co-facilitator can help you develop important practice skills as you learn to share the helping role and some control of relationship(s) with group members and to allow the group to forge its own path. For many students and new social workers, however, learning to trust the group process and to maintain a stance of facilitator (not necessarily "leader" and certainly not "runner of") can be challenging. A tolerance for relinquishing control will serve you well. That said, despite your best efforts to refrain from controlling the group and to strive for empowering the group to assume increasing levels of power, it is important to recognize that there may be a hierarchy with you being perceived as having more power than the group members. Addressing these issues to both the group and yourself can directly diffuse any potential conflicts (Doel & Kelly, 2014). Fortunately, early anxieties regarding control and its management usually abate with experience.

When embarking on an experience in which you will serve as a group leader or facilitator, it is particularly important to think about the experience in the context of the members' participation. With that in mind, consider the following assumptions one can make about group members and their roles (Brown, 2013):

- Each group member has a unique personality and history and can make a unique contribution to the group.

- Group members are not always aware of the fantasies and fears that may influence their lives.

- Some group members may be at a crossroads in their lives that prompts fears and anxieties about group participation. Such dilemmas may present in the form of defensiveness within the group.

- Group members use different strategies to make sense of their experiences (p. 59).

Preparation

Surprisingly, many social workers fail to adequately attend to the logistics of group preparation and implementation. While it is important to consider the philosophical dimensions of launching a group intervention, equally important is logistics, such as making sure there are enough chairs, the meeting is not scheduled on a religious holiday, that all members have transportation, and that child/adult care is provided as needed. Ensure, for example, that a group for male perpetrators of violence does not meet at the same time and place as a group for their survivors. Consider competition with other known schedules, so that a parenting group does not conflict with a mothers' and children's group. While it is not possible to avoid all conflicts or awkwardness, giving thought to as many of these aspects as you can is worth the effort.

Engagement

Actively listening to the messages group members convey to you is particularly important to the engagement and assessment phases of group work (Shulman, 2009). This requires you to be aware of your own thoughts, feelings, and reactions and to have empathy for those of group members and others (e.g., family, staff, or referral sources). For example, if you are facilitating a group for Riverton residents concerned about local teens' use of alcohol and drugs, it is crucial that you "tune in" to your own experiences and feelings related to substance use and abuse and to the origins and meanings of what the Riverton residents have to say about the problem in their community. Tuning in can enable you to understand the influence your own attitudes, feelings, and experiences may have on a client situation. For example, if you grew up with a parent who is an alcoholic, you may not be completely objective when a group member in a substance abuse treatment group talks about her or his inadequacies as a parent. Listening is important to your work with any population, as it enables you to determine if you have biases, unresolved personal concerns, or conflicted values that may prevent you from objectively and empathetically serving a client.

In keeping with being in tune with the needs of group members, be mindful to use the following additional facilitative strategies (Ephross, 2011):

- Say less (as opposed to more) to avoid interfering with the group's process. You may need to play a more active role in the beginning, but your role should decrease as the group process unfolds (i.e., eventually group members should be doing approximately 80 percent of the talking).

- Recognize that the power of the intervention comes from the group interaction, not from the social worker.

- Summarize group members' discussions and provide a bridge to the next topic or area of work.

- Set limits. Use clear and transparent expectations and policies, negotiate individual and group contracts for work, and transition the group through the various phases of the group process.

Assessment and Planning

The early phases of a group experience can present unique and possibly unexpected challenges for the social worker, particularly related to the ongoing assessment and planning activities. To your surprise, you may find that group members have conflicting agendas and roles from what emerged during your assessment and not all members will be committed to supporting other members (Zandee-Amas, 2013). You may encounter situations in which your goals for the group differ from those of group members or your role as a provider of individual and family services conflicts with your role as a group facilitator. Or you may find that some members of the group are not able to or interested in productively engaging with other group members. Challenges that can occur within any group experience include: norms and patterns of nonproductivity being established by group members and conflict between group members and one or more members and the social worker (Macgowan & Hanbidge, 2015). Each of these situations relates to group member expectations and dynamics. Group members who struggle to see how the group process benefits them, particularly when compared to an individual helping relationship or in an immediate time frame, may leave the group. Group members often find that their common experiences extend beyond the group; this can lead to alliances within the group session and/or socializing outside the group. While not necessarily a problem, such relationships can be disruptive to the group process.

© Yuri Arcurs

As assessment and planning are activities that continue throughout the entirety of the group social work intervention, it is critical to have skills that will enable you to engage in evaluating the individual members' concerns and issues. Shulman (2011) offers these recommendations for helping the group members manage the issues they are facing: (1) to decrease the possibility of the members having unrealistic expectations of the social worker, regularly clarify your purpose and role in the group; (2) utilize the group members to provide feedback to one another and to you regarding the issues being raised; (3) identify and partialize the concerns being introduced; and (4) when the members bring up sensitive or "taboo" topics, provide support so the issues may be discussed openly (p. 18).

Documentation

Another logistical detail that social workers sometimes fail to adequately address is that of documenting the group experience. While documenting the process of the group experience presents a unique set of challenges, it need not be an overwhelming or complex task. Documenting any group experience serves a range of purposes. It records (1) the group process, including interactions and dynamics; (2) assessments and evaluation of individual and group change and outcomes; (3) group leadership skills; (4) referrals; and (5) accountability for payment and the sponsoring organization (Doel & Kelly, 2014; IASWG, 2015). Typically, the facilitator maintains two separate records of the group experiences. The group's record includes information on attendance, general themes, cohesion, interactions, and plans, while documentation in the individual group members' record includes only information regarding that client and her or his goals, needs, etc. In order to protect individual client confidentiality, the names of other group members should not be included in an individual client's documentation. Typically, these two records are never co-mingled in the same paper or electronic record; the only exception to this would be if the records are subpoenaed by the court. At that point, the social worker would need to clarify for the court record that the information contained in the group document on any members not related to the court action should be redacted to protect their confidentiality.

Documentation should reflect the tenor and flow of the session itself. For example, if you are using a solution-focused approach, your assessment documentation should focus on solutions rather than problems (De Jong & Berg, 2013). Exhibit 8.8 provides samples of documentation that you might include for assessing potential members of a client-oriented group, while Exhibit 8.9 provides a list of questions a social worker can ask an individual client to assess and document whether she or he is appropriate for membership in the group.

AGENCY/ORGANIZATION NAME

GROUP NAME

Demographic Data:

- Name
- Contact information
- Legal status and needs
- Group participation needs (e.g., child or adult care needs, transportation, etc.)
- Presenting concerns as they relate to the group purpose or focus
- Current living situation (level of stability, support, safety)
- Social environment (level of activity, satisfaction, relationships with others)
- Cultural environment (client satisfaction with and views on help-seeking and cultural views of help-seeking, particularly in the group environment)
- Religion/spirituality (statement of beliefs and levels of activity and satisfaction)
- Military experience (branch, time in service, discharge status, coping with experience, view of experience)
- Childhood (supportive of the client, strengths, and significant events—including trauma)
- Family (composition—parents, siblings, spouse/significant other(s), children, and others; level of support; family history of mental illness)
- Sexual history (activity level, orientation, satisfaction, concerns)
- Trauma history (physical, sexual, and/or emotional abuse or neglect and experience with perpetrator(s))
- Financial/employment circumstances (employment status, satisfaction, financial stability, areas of concern or change)
- Educational history (highest level achieved, performance, goals, challenges)
- Substance use/abuse (history of addictive behaviors, alcohol, drugs, gambling, sexual, other)

History of Emotional/Behavioral Functioning:

For each of the following areas, gather information regarding current status (current, previous, or denies history), description of behavior, onset and duration, and frequency.

- Self-mutilation
- Hallucinations
- Delusions or paranoia
- Mood swings
- Recurrent or intrusive recollections of past events
- Lack of interest or pleasure
- Feelings of sadness, hopelessness, isolation, or withdrawal
- Decreased concentration, energy, or motivation
- Anxiety
- Crying spells
- Appetite changes
- Sleep changes

- Inability to function at school or work
- Inability to control thoughts or behaviors (impulses)
- Irritability or agitation
- Reckless behavior, fighting, or fire setting
- Stealing, shoplifting, or lying
- Cruelty to animals
- Aggression

Past and Current Behavioral Health Treatment History (i.e., individual, family, and/or other group experiences):

- Date(s)
- Program or facility
- Provider
- Response to treatment

Mental Status Exam:

- Attention (rate on scale of good, fair, easily distracted, or highly distractible, and describe behavior)
- Affect (rate on scale of appropriate, changeable, expansive, constrictive, or blunted, and describe behavior)
- Mood (rate on scale of normal, depressed, anxious, or euphoric, and describe behavior)
- Appearance (rate on scale of well groomed, disheveled, or inappropriate, and describe behavior)
- Motor activity (rate on scale of calm, hyperactive, agitated, tremors, tics, or muscle spasms, and describe behavior)
- Thought process (rate on scale of intact, circumstantial, tangential, flight of ideas, or loose associations, and describe behavior)
- Thought content (note normal, grandiose, phobic, reality, organization, worthless, obsessive, compulsion, guilt, delusional, paranoid, ideas of reference, and hallucinations, and describe behavior)
- Memory (note normal, recent (good or impaired), past (good or impaired), and describe behavior)
- Intellect (note normal, above, below, or poor abstraction, and describe behavior)
- Orientation (note person, place, situation, and time, and describe behavior)
- Judgment and insight (rate on scale of good, fair, or poor, and describe behavior)
- Current providers (including psychiatrist, primary care physician, therapist, caseworker, etc.)
- Community resources being used (including support groups, religious, spiritual, other)
- Client goal(s) for treatment
- Summary, including social worker's assessment of client "fit" with the group (see Exhibit 8.9 for assessment questions).

Source: Adapted from St. Anthony's Medical Center, 2010; Safe Connections, n.d.

EXHIBIT 8.8

Continued

EXHIBIT 8.9

Screening Questions for Group Assessment

When you determine a client's appropriateness for membership in the group, you ensure the emotional and physical safety of all group members. The following list of general questions can help you evaluate clients for possible group membership.

- How does the client respond to opinions, thoughts, and insights that differ from her or his own?
- When the client becomes angry or upset, what is her or his reaction and thought process?
- Is the client able to express her or his emotions in an appropriate way? Does the client assume responsibility for the emotion?
- What triggers the client's emotional responses?
- What is the client's developmental age? Is the client able to cope with negative emotions and thoughts at a level appropriate to the developmental level of other group members?
- Does the client demonstrate:
  o Impulse control challenges?
  o Appropriate boundaries?
  o Self-awareness?
  o Self-destructive behaviors?
  o Potential to monopolize or disrupt the group?
  o Ability to respond to social cues?
  o Sensitivity toward others?
  o Potential for personal growth?
  o Appropriate group interaction behaviors?
  o Difficulty making decisions?
- Might the client's behavior limit group participation or benefit?
- If the client is currently experiencing a crisis, will the benefits of participating in the group outweigh risks for the client?

Source: Adapted from Safe Connections (n.d.)

While the documentation of the work of nonclient groups—social goals/action and task groups—may include some of the same basic information you would record with a client group (e.g., attendance, themes, and plans), the focus is more typically directed toward recording actions and decisions. Often compiled in the form of minutes or notes, the documentation of group process and outcomes for social action/goals or task groups emphasizes the work being completed as opposed to the interactions among group members. See Quick Guides 25 and 26 for templates you can use to record the work of nonclient groups. Quick Guide 25 provides a template for a matrix-style record, while Quick Guide 26 provides an outline for a narrative-style document.

QUICK GUIDE 25   TASK GROUP NOTES TEMPLATE

AGENCY / ORGANIZATION NAME
GROUP NAME

Date
Present:
Absent:
Minutes submitted by:

ISSUE	DISCUSSION	FOLLOW-UP/ RECOMMENDATIONS	PERSON(S) RESPONSIBLE
Call to Order			
Minutes			
Announcements			
Old Business			
New Business			
Adjournment			
Future Meetings			

QUICK GUIDE 26   TASK GROUP MINUTES TEMPLATE

Agency / Organization Name
Group Name
Date

In attendance:
Absent:

1. Call meeting to order
2. Review meeting agenda
3. Review minutes from previous meeting
4. Announcements
5. Old business
6. New business
7. Adjournment and next steps

Respectfully submitted,
[Note taker's name and title]

Regardless of the challenges you may encounter as a group facilitator or leader, maintaining a transparent, open, and equitable style will best serve you and the group. Remember, the "basic reason for doing group work is the power of the group, *not the worker*" (Ephross, 2011, p. 13). Gaining as much group experience as possible throughout your social work education, particularly as facilitator or leader, can prepare you for being a contributing member and capable leader throughout your social work career. As we continue to explore social work practice with groups in Chapter 9, consider the valuable lessons you can learn from experiencing different roles within a group, including member, facilitator, and observer.

GRAND CHALLENGE

End Homelessness

The American Academy of Social Work and Social Welfare Grand Challenges for Social Work Initiative identifies one of the areas the profession should address is to end homelessness. The authors of Grand Challenge Working Paper No. 9, *The Grand Challenge of Ending Homelessness* (Henwood et al., 2015) emphasize that philosophy regarding homelessness has shifted from management and reduction to elimination:

> To eradicate all forms of homelessness in 10 years, interdisciplinary and cross-sector collaboration will be necessary for accurately assessing the scope of the problem; improving data; establishing innovative and clear solution to family, youth, and other subpopulation homelessness; and disseminating existing effective solutions. Ending homelessness cannot be accomplished simply by focusing on how best to respond to individuals who experience homelessness; it will require ongoing effort to address the structural, macro-level factors of poverty and income inequality (p. 4).

With the profession's expertise in working across all levels of social work practice, social work can and should have a significant role in the effort to end homelessness. However, new strategies are needed to provide housing and access adequate health care and educational opportunities. The authors of the Grand Challenge charge the social work profession to engage in such innovative activities as: gather evidence to accurately measure the number of persons who are homeless, particularly those who are transient or hidden, and evaluate the efficacy of interventions; better utilize community resources and services; promote evidence-based intervention practices; and identify and leverage funding to support interventions (p. 14). These activities could involve the extensive use of task groups among a wide variety of professionals, including social workers, working in an array of settings, such as government agencies, nonprofit social service agencies, and for-profits (e.g., banks and other lenders).

To familiarize yourself with the issues related to ending homelessness, visit the Grand Challenges website and read Working Paper No. 9, *The Grand Challenge of Ending Homelessness* (Henwood et al., 2015) at: http://aaswsw.org/grand-challenges-initiative/12-challenges/end-homelessness/. (See Exercise #a1 for additional exploration of this Grand Challenge within the context of the Riverton community.)

CONCLUSION

This chapter advocates for social work practitioners to address the culturally imposed isolation of many individuals through groups. We have explored some of the exciting adventures into group work using contemporary theoretical perspectives in the pursuit of social justice. Group work can provide opportunities to address issues related to social justice, diversity, and human rights connections that give social work its meaning.

Chapter 9 will turn to the next phases of social work practice with groups. Building on preplanning, engagement, and assessment work, the social worker–facilitated group moves first into the intervention or middle phase of work and then to the termination, evaluation (or ending), and follow-up phases of the group experience.

MAIN POINTS

- All people are members of groups that provide meaning to their lives and interactions and critical human connections. Western culture tends to de-emphasize the gifts and powers of group connection.

- Group work in the social work profession remains a vital part of practice that lends itself especially to social justice, diversity, and human rights perspectives.

- Organizing a group requires careful planning and continuous consideration of the value the work to the group as a whole and its individual members.

- Traditional theoretical models for group work include the task group, social action or goals model, the reciprocal model, and the remedial model.

- Social work group practice employs a variety of theoretical frameworks. This chapter highlighted strengths and empowerment, narrative-focused, and solution-focused perspectives.

- Engaging and assessing group members individually and collectively from a biopsychosocial-spiritual perspective is the first step in group formation.

- While primarily completed during the beginning phases of group work, engagement and assessment can be ongoing aspects of the group experience. The fluid and evolving nature of group work can result in changing membership and leadership, new and unexpected issues, and interpersonal dynamics and conflicts that can influence the course of the group intervention.

EXERCISES

a. Case Exercises

1. To apply your learning of the Grand Challenge to end homelessness that was highlighted in this chapter, visit the Grand Challenges website and read Working Paper No. 9, *The Grand Challenge of Ending Homelessness* (Henwood et al., 2015) at: http://aaswsw.org/grand-challenges-initiative/12-challenges/end-homelessness/. To examine the issue of homelessness in the Riverton community, review the case information at www.routledgesw.com/caseStudies. After reading Working Paper No. 9 and reviewing the information on Riverton, complete the following items:
   a. Using the town map, sociogram and interaction matrix (matching the homeless community icon with each of the other community entities), prepare an analysis of the homelessness situation in Riverton.
   b. Develop a plan for engaging members and organizations in Riverton in group work using task groups and conducting an assessment of homelessness in Riverton, including but not limited to identifying potential partners, strengths, barriers, and resources needed.
2. Go to www.routledgesw.com/cases, review Carla Washburn's video vignette, and complete the following tasks:
   a. Summarize the group's activities as depicted in the vignettes.
   b. Document the group practice behaviors that the social worker, Shannon, uses.
   c. Identify any potential challenges that may occur in a group intervention with the members of this group.
   d. Brainstorm the next steps you would take as a social worker facilitating this group.
2. Review the Carla Washburn video vignette and explore options for facilitating this group using a range of different approaches, including the following:
   a. Psychoeducational group
   b. Reciprocal group
   c. Remedial group
   Now respond to the following questions:
   a. How does the focus of each group differ?
   b. How does the social worker's role differ in each group?
   c. What engagement skills did the social worker use?
   d. Using the case vignette as an example, role-play with classmates the group as one of each of the following:
      1. psychoeducational
      2. reciprocal
      3. remedial
3. Go to www.routledgesw.com/cases and review the case for Brickville, focusing on Virginia Stone and her family. In the Intervention section, review Vignette

#3, which describes the use of a social action group intervention focused on Virginia's efforts to save the park memorializing her family members who were lost in an apartment fire twenty years earlier. Using the information available to you, develop a written plan for:

a. Determining the need for this group

b. Identifying the purpose a task group would serve in this situation

c. Propose appropriate group composition and each member's potential contributions

d. Develop your thoughts regarding group structure (e.g., meeting time and place, documenting group activity, and leadership) and content

e. Reflect on the meaning of forming this group in the context of the agency and the community

f. Describe your plans for initiating pregroup contact, engaging group members, and assessing members' potential commitment and contributions

g. Assess available and needed resources and potential barriers to success

4. Go to www.routledgesw.com/cases and review the case for Hudson City. Recall from Chapters 6 and 7 that the Patel family experienced significant impact from Hurricane Diane. Several weeks after the hurricane, Sheetal (wife of Hemant and mother of Rakesh, Kamal, and Aarti) confides in you that she is concerned that her 12-year-old daughter, Aarti, is not coping well with life following the hurricane and the family's displacement from their home and restaurant. They have been able to return to their home and are working on re-opening the restaurant. Aarti has returned to her school, but she continues to have nightmares about the storm, is uncomfortable being away from her parents, and seems to have less of an appetite. Other parents whose families were affected by the storm are expressing similar concerns, both to you and to your co-workers. Describe in writing your plan for developing a group intervention to address the needs of children who survived the hurricane, including:

- Type of group approach (include format and structure)
- Plans for member eligibility, recruitment, and parent involvement
- Strategies for engaging group members in a culturally competent manner, keeping in mind the diversity of the community and its large immigrant population
- Strategies for assessing group members' appropriateness for the group

5. Go to www.routledgesw.com/cases and review the case for Riverton, then, referring back to the discussion of the Riverton community's concerns about alcohol consumption at the beginning of this chapter and Exhibits 8.3, 8.4, and 8.5 in this chapter, conduct a search of the literature on group-level practice in order to find evidence to support development of the following group interventions:

a. Riverton Against Youth Drinking (RAYD): evidence-based practices for facilitating social goals groups on teen drinking.

b. Riverton Children's Grief Support Group: evidence-based practices for facilitating reciprocal groups with children.

   c. Riverton Mental Health Center Groups for Persons with Co-Occurring Diagnoses: evidence-based practices for facilitating a treatment group for this population and for incorporating new members into an existing group.

b. Other Exercises

6. As a skilled individual and group practice social worker at a local community health center, you have several young clients who have been diagnosed with attention deficit hyperactivity disorder (ADHD). The clients are Hispanic children between 6 and 8 years of age. When they come to pick up their children, you notice that some of their parents appear sad about their children, while others appear anxious, frustrated, or angry. The children themselves seem somewhat isolated and all are experiencing social, academic, and behavioral problems in school.

   Assume that you have the time, interest, and agency support to offer to form and lead a group. Choose one of the following interventions from this list that you think will be the most helpful:

   a. A play/social skills group for the children

   b. A support group for the parents

   c. A psychoeducational group for the parents

   d. An empowerment group for the children

   Be prepared to provide a rationale for your choice to your classmates. How might one choice intersect with another? Compare with peers.

7. You work for a child welfare organization and are facilitating a support group for adolescent females who have recently given birth and are preparing to return to their high schools. In some cases, the babies' grandparents are helping with their care, and some babies have been adopted through the agency. Some of the group members have concerns about returning to school while others are eager to get back into a "normal" social life. Most group members are participating well, although one member, Janine, has said almost nothing in the first three meetings. All members of the group are African American. You are a white, 23-year-old female social work practicum student.

   At the beginning of the fourth meeting, the mood of the entire group seems contentious. After you share in brief preliminary pleasantries and restate the agenda for this session, you realize that Janine is quietly crying in the corner. At the same time, two of the other members start calling your name angrily, competing for your attention. They tell you they are annoyed at the group, at the plan for today, at the agency, and at Janine who is sitting there acting like a "baby."

   Respond to the following:

   a. Identify two skills from the chapter that you would use in this situation and give an example of the way in which you would use these skills.

    b. Provide a rationale for your selection of these particular skills. What results do you expect from the use of these skills?

    c. Which of the models described in this chapter offers the best explanation for these group dynamics?

8. Attend a mutual aid group in the community and write a reflection about your experience.

    a. Describe the group type, purpose, and structure.

    b. Identify group leader and member roles.

    c. Reflect on your previous experiences as a group member. What role do you often play? Why? Do you want to do things differently?

9. In small groups of three or four, create your own social action group.

    a. Identify an issue of mutual interest to group members.

    b. Determine the roles for each member.

    c. Develop a plan of action for the group. Prepare a presentation for the class.

10. Your field instructor at your practicum has invited you to join her in co-facilitating a psychoeducational support group for persons who serve as caregivers for a family member experiencing Parkinson's disease. Most members of the group are wives and adult daughters. In addition to co-leading the group each session, your field instructor has suggested that you assume responsibility for leading one session on a topic of your choice that will be relevant for this group. This is your first group work experience, and you are unfamiliar with this medical condition. To accomplish your task:

    a. Review the literature to learn about Parkinson's disease.

    b. Develop a plan for the session that you will lead, including identifying a relevant topic and strategies for engaging the group members in the discussion.

Social Work Practice with Groups: Intervention, Termination, and Evaluation

I found myself slipping into that self-trashing thing, man, you know, putting myself down, thinking and saying I'm a dumb broad, ugly and worthless, just like J. used to tell me. But they got on me, those awesome women! They told me I was breaking the friggin' rules! Me! Breaking the rules, and then I remembered what they meant. We're not doing that stuff in this group. The end. Not okay. They are really the most awesome! What would I be without them?

Marcy (of the Debbie, Joan, Marcy,
and Kate Group for Survivors of Intimate Partner Violence)

Key Questions for Chapter 9

1. What competencies do I need to intervene, terminate, and evaluate with clients at the group level of social work practice? [EPAS 8 and 9]
2. How can I use evidence to practice research-informed practice and practice-informed research to guide the evaluation of a group I am facilitating? [EPAS 4]
3. What is the appropriate response for a social worker leading a group if one group member violates the confidentiality of another member of the group? [EPAS 1]
4. What is the distinction between the appropriate social worker role in facilitating an intervention with a self-help support group and a therapy group? [EPAS 8]

From the perspective of social work practice with groups, there are multiple opportunities to work with the Stone family of the Brickville neighborhood (www.routledgesw.com/cases), including: (1) Virginia Stone, who is a family caregiver of her mother who may benefit from participation in a support group for caregivers of older adults; (2) Virginia's son, David, a participant in the Brickville Community Development Corporation's Youth Leadership Program (YLP) who is developing his leadership skills by serving as the Chair of the youth-led Committee for Healthy Teens; (3) Virginia's two granddaughters, Tiffany and Suzanna, who are the children of an incarcerated parent and are both having behavior and academic challenges in school that might be addressed in group work; and (4) the trauma of the tragic fire twenty years ago and the family's sense of racial bias by the fire and police departments has been reignited by incidents that have occurred across the U.S. from which groups like Black Lives Matter have emerged.

THE EFFICACY OF SOCIAL WORK PRACTICE INTERVENTIONS, terminations, evaluations, and follow-up with groups stems from effective engagement and assessment. The middle and ending phases of work—the interventions, terminations, and evaluations—are the parts of the group experience in which the "majority of the work of the groups gets accomplished" and is "the time to consolidate the work of the group" (Toseland & Horton, 2013, para. 22, 23). Terminations and evaluations are complex because of the dual focus on both the individual and the group.

To complete our exploration of social work practice with groups, this chapter follows the group experience from the development of the intervention process through the termination, evaluation, and follow-up phases. We will focus on theoretical frameworks for group interventions and models of group intervention and look at the social work behaviors you will need to intervene with groups. The chapter then examines the final phase of the group intervention: termination, evaluation, and follow-up. To set the stage for delving into the middle and ending stages of group work practice, let us first consider social justice, diversity, and human rights.

INTERFACE: SOCIAL JUSTICE, DIVERSITY, AND HUMAN RIGHTS [EPAS 3]

Social work with groups is a natural setting for practitioners who are committed to social justice, diversity, and/or human rights concerns. As discussed elsewhere in this book, much of social injustice is rooted in exclusion—from resources, opportunities, respect, and supports. This kind of exclusion is especially evident in the experiences of those persons and groups who are considered by society as "other" or

© Glynnis Jones

different. Those may be persons with disabilities; persons of color; people living in poverty; people from other racial or ethnic backgrounds; older adults; persons who are gay, lesbian, bisexual, transgender, or questioning—unfortunately the list is long (see Greif & Ephross, 2011). The most appropriate and effective social work response to diversity within the group intervention is a subject of ongoing debate. For example, are group interventions more effective if the group is heterogeneous or homogenous? Most scholars agree that evidence-based practice is critical for group work; therefore, social workers must provide evidence to support the intervention(s) and to inform the decision to offer a heterogeneous or a homogenous group structure (Toseland & Horton, 2013). The need for supporting group work with evidence will be discussed within this chapter. Diverse groups reflect the world in which most people live, but not all individuals may feel comfortable or safe taking personal risks around others who are different from them in some way meaningful to them, or with others whose reasons for joining the group are different from their own. In addition to utilizing research on group diversity to inform and guide interventions, social workers can also benefit by examining their own views (including their own "isms") on the groups (e.g., population, ethnicity, and affiliations) they will be bringing together for a group intervention (Toseland & Horton, 2013). Social workers must also factor in their prior life and professional experience and the preferences of the members of the group.

Group work practice brings people together in meaningful ways that can serve as a forum for increasing understanding, appreciation, and respect for others. In short, group membership can reduce the effects of exclusion and the injustices associated with feelings of marginalization. When working with groups, you can identify, establish, articulate, and mediate the rights and the needs of group members. This can be an important and empowering experience for those who may have rarely (or never) understood their own social contexts in terms that affirmed their rights as human beings (Kurland et al., 2004), and model such behavior for other members of the group. Viewing group intervention as reinforcing human rights can further integrate human rights practice into the profession.

Approaching group work with a focus on social justice requires a commitment to learning about and embracing a number of conceptual foundations. Singh and Salazar (2011) suggest that social justice-oriented group work is based on the following foundations:

- *The centrality of multicultural competence:* Social workers must strive to become culturally competent with many different cultures (multicultural competence) throughout their entire social work career. The diversity of our contemporary society means that, as a social worker, you will routinely interact with and serve a wide range of individuals who are members of various groups; thus, the need for not just cultural competence, but *multi*-cultural competence and cultural humility becomes paramount to your practice.

- *The interplay between content and process:* A commitment to a social justice orientation enables the social worker conducting groups to address the substance and interactions related to social inequities and oppression that may occur in any group setting and among the group members.

- *The influence of privilege and oppression:* Delving into the impact of group leader and members' experiences with privilege and oppression is critical for social justice-oriented group work. Questions to consider may include: "What are group members' needs, perceptions, experiences, and wants with regard to the injustices they face? What are their efforts toward their own empowerment and freedom from self-blame? How are these injustices experienced by others in the community? How do community members, both individually and collectively, define and perceive empowerment?" (p. 218).

- *Effects on power dynamics within and outside groups:* Emphasizing issues of power within the group can and should have the added benefit of empowering group members to engage in advocacy and change in other areas of their lives.

THEORETICAL APPROACHES TO INTERVENING WITH GROUPS [EPAS 4]

Just as there are many theoretical models for social work intervention with individuals and families, there are well-developed theoretical approaches related to group interventions, processes, skills, and ending points. When the social worker subscribes to a specific theoretical perspective, she or he can use the theory to guide the formation of the group, define roles, and impact group dynamics to guide the content of the group experience (Macgowan, 2013).

In this section, we will continue our examination of theory-driven approaches to group practice. Following an overview of theoretical applications to group interventions, we will explore several classic, contemporary, and developmental models. Later, we will look at intervention skills, examples of current groups, and, finally, contemporary innovations in group work.

Strengths and Empowerment Perspectives on Group Intervention

As you recall from Chapter 8, this book is grounded in the premise that social workers should approach practice with groups from a strengths orientation. A strengths approach can affirm and motivate the individual's change process through a focus on "possibilities versus problems." The strengths perspective helps identify and integrate individual members' strengths into strengths for the whole group. For example, within the intervention itself, the social worker can use group members' strengths for a range of purposes, including developing individual and group goals and sharing resources. Individual strengths can serve as models when group members share ideas and resources. For example, the group member who has experienced multiple losses in her life (Virginia Stone from Brickville, for instance) and continues to remain strong can serve as a role model for other group members. Approaching the group intervention from a strengths-based perspective requires the social worker to help create an environment in which all group members accept the following three norms (Benard & Truebridge, 2013):

- *Participation:* Group members recognize one other as equal participants, each with the same rights and opportunities.

- *Communication:* Interactions among group members and the facilitator must be respectful (e.g., everyone should be allowed to speak without interruption or side conversations).

- *Interactions:* In order for all group members to contribute equally, members and the group leader should be committed to arriving on time and staying for the duration of the group (p. 215).

A strengths-based perspective integrates easily with other theoretically-driven intervention approaches, such as the empowerment perspective. Arising from an ecological perspective, empowerment-focused group interventions align with a strengths perspective in their emphasis on addressing social injustices and fostering reciprocal connections with members' environments (Hudson, 2009, p. 48). Within this context, empowerment is a process as well as an outcome that encompasses the personal (individual person), the interpersonal (interactions between persons), and the social (interactions within society) (Cattaneo & Goodman, 2015). In **empowerment groups**, committing to joining a group can itself support the personal and interpersonal dimensions as well as the empowerment felt from helping and receiving help from other members. Critical analysis of the political environment and individuals' participation in change efforts is also important to the empowerment process. This means that group members are empowered from the earliest planning for the group and participate in the identification of needs (Breton, 2006).

In helping to negotiate a change between group members and their environment, the social worker's role is to collaborate with members to mediate between them and the entities or issues within their environment that create oppression or injustice (Hudson, 2009). The social worker is a "co-activist," working with the group to achieve their goals. Such an approach works with many types of group interventions, including social goals/action and reciprocal mutual aid groups.

Recall Georgia's situation from Chapter 1: Georgia experienced intimate partner violence, and after working with a social worker individually, she joined an empowerment group with other women who had been in violent relationships. This group supported Georgia's needs for esteem and dignity; offered her the opportunity to identify her priorities (for example, have a viable safety plan, stable work situation, and protect her children); built new skills so she might competently access needed information, services, and help; and enhanced her self-efficacy through increased confidence, sense of community, and asking for and accepting help (Cattaneo & Goodman, 2015). The quote from Marcy, another survivor of intimate partner violence, that opens this chapter, shows us just how powerful the group process can be.

Narrative Theory and Group Interventions

Building on a strengths- and empowerment-focused engagement and assessment process, a narrative approach to intervening with groups emphasizes, not only the collaboration between the client and the social worker, but also the collaboration among group members. A narrative-oriented group intervention requires the social worker and group members to listen to each member's voice and to aid in the deconstruction and subsequent reconstruction of the individual or group "story" (i.e., their experience through their own perspective). In the case of a mutual aid or therapy group, stories are individual, but in a social goals/action group, the "story" may be the group's story. Reshaping individual or group perceptions can provide a basis for setting a plan in motion for members to achieve the unique outcome the individual group member(s) desire(s). Group members can then work together to brainstorm and process members' motivations, options, and behaviors.

One of the hallmarks of the narrative approach is the use of witness groups and community supports. The social worker calls people together into **witness groups** to "witness" discussions between the social worker and the client and/or among group members. In the case of a group intervention, group members are in place to serve as witnesses to their own discussions. Known as the outside-witness group (because they are outside the individual's personal situation), these group members both contribute to, and listen to, dialogues and provide feedback to the social worker and to individual group members (Morgan, 2000). Such feedback can include questions, observations, and interpretations. The individual receiving feedback may then ask questions and respond. This process can help the client develop an alternative approach to her or his current dilemma or concern.

Using "insider" knowledge (i.e., hearing from others with similar life experiences) is a staple of the narrative approach. Group interventions are good opportunities to use this practice strategy, particularly if group members share similar life experiences and are at different phases of those experiences. For example, Hall (2011) describes how a social worker used a narrative approach with a group of males who had battered their partners. Using narrative strategies, the group leader was able to work with group members to address issues of male power, privilege, and entitlement by externalizing the violence outside of the individual. This helped the males in the group to gain insight into the origins of their belief systems, which freed them to determine if they wished to continue their behavior or to change (Hall, 2011, p. 180). Understanding the beliefs that underpin your behavior promotes assuming responsibility for one's choices. As noted in Chapter 8, narrative approaches are also well suited to many other theoretical frameworks.

Solution-Focused Group Interventions

Solution-focused interventions with groups are similar to family interventions and require the same knowledge and skills. During the beginning phases of group work, you asked clients a series of questions to identify their desired new realities and the strengths and resources available to help achieve the clients' goals for change (De Jong, 2013b). When you develop a solution-focused intervention plan, you can ask clients to reconsider the "miracle," "exceptions," and "scaling" questions to solidify the plan for change. While you pose these questions to individual group members, the entire group can contribute to the development, implementation, and evaluation of individual change plans, and they can continue to be a resource throughout the change process, presenting their own questions, observations, and experiences. Once the plan is developed and underway, you can monitor members' progress by asking group members to describe the changes they are experiencing (i.e., "What's better?").

Solution-focused approaches at all levels can be used in conjunction with other approaches (e.g., solution-focused, empowerment, and narrative therapy approaches) to enhance the effectiveness and accountability of interventions. De Jong and Berg (2013b) suggest that social workers implement a solution-focused intervention with a group after becoming competent with solution-focused work with individuals and families.

The solution-focused group intervention is well suited for a variety of client populations and settings. With its emphasis on positive changes in the client's life and client-developed individualized treatment plans, this intervention has reaped promising outcomes with adults, adolescents, and children and with involuntary clients (Greene & Lee, 2011). When used with adults who are incarcerated, in mental health settings (in- and out-patient), and in substance abuse treatment programs, solution-focused interventions "can often be like doing individual therapy in front of a group" (Greene & Lee, 2011, p. 203) when individual clients are engaged in dialogue about their individual situation in front of the group.

The integration of solution-focused group interventions with adolescents and children is equally promising. Social workers and their adolescent and child clients can build solution-focused group interventions around a specific topic or theme. In addition, their brief time-limited format, flexibility, future-oriented focus, and de-emphasis on problem "talk" makes solution-focused group interventions particularly well-suited to work with adolescents and children (Greene & Lee, 2011).

Developmental Models

One of the classic theoretical perspectives on group work, the **developmental model**, is based on the assumption that group members (individually and collectively) grow and change as the group process unfolds. Developmental models assume that groups change and grow in semipredictable ways. This assumption does not mean groups go through rigid progressions but rather that group relationships ripen. Members are perhaps ambivalent about joining the group at the beginning. Then they jockey for position within the membership, grow closer together through the work of the group, establish differences from one another, and finally separate at the group's ending. This perspective reflects the idea of stages (also referred to as phases) and has been extremely influential in contemporary group work. Developmental models are still the norm in many practice contexts. They are frequently useful in alerting the social worker to possible dynamics, gauging what is happening, and thinking about how to intervene. We now examine two different developmental models—the Boston Model and the relational model.

Boston Model   First developed at Boston University's School of Social Work, the **Boston Model** outlines five stages of group development: preaffiliation, power and control, intimacy, differentiation, and separation (Garland, Jones, & Kolodny, 1965).

- During **preaffiliation**, members may feel some ambivalence or reservations about joining the group as well as excitement and eagerness. For example, someone joining a support group for people diagnosed with an illness may be eager to connect with others who have a similar experience but may at the same time wonder if she or he will find others in the group who share common experiences, fears, and needs.

- In the **power and control stage**, members vie for influence and status within the group. In a support group for individuals who share a diagnosis, members who are further along in their illness, treatment, or recovery may perceive themselves as having more status and influence than those who are recently diagnosed.

- **Intimacy** occurs when group members, having worked through their power issues, become closely connected; they may seem more homogeneous at this stage than at any other time in the group. Having processed the issues of power and control, they can begin to support each other around their common life experiences. Members will often share coping strategies and develop relationships outside of the group sessions to help each other through crises.

- During **differentiation**, members feel they are safe enough to express and value the differences among themselves and the worker; the homogeneity of the former phase matures into a respect for difference. In this phase, members of an illness support group may become comfortable enough to confront one another on differences of opinion, coping behaviors, or lack of compliance. Such confrontations can occur successfully only when members have reached a point of mutual respect for one another.

- In the final stage, **separation**, members begin to withdraw from the group in anticipation of its ending. Members of an illness support group may separate as they finish treatment, recover, or learn that their illness is terminal.

Although the creators of the Boston Model propose a general progression through these stages, they do not assume that progress will occur as a rigidly linear sequence. There are likely to be points in the life of a group at which one or more members seem to loop back to the behavior typical of a previous stage or tend to jump ahead to another one. See Quick Guide 27 for ways these developmental stages can be applied to three different group populations. As you can see in the Quick Guide, some of the groups exhibit these stages in slightly different orders than the Boston Model, or skip some stages. While these phases of group process are not typically associated with task groups, one could argue they are, in fact, relevant for work with tasks groups since task groups form, bond, and progress through similar relationship-building stages.

Other models of group development divide the stages slightly differently, and some include additional substages. The group population also influences the degree

	QUICK GUIDE 27 APPLICATIONS OF THE BOSTON MODEL PROTOTYPE TO THREE POPULATIONS			
	BOSTON PROTOTYPE	**FEMINIST**	**FEMALE ADOLESCENT FOSTER CARE GROUP**	**OLDER INSTITUTIONALIZED PERSONS: FLOOR GROUP**
	Garland, Jones & Kolodny, 1965	*Schiller, 1995, 1997*	*Lee & Berman-Rossi, 1999*	*Berman-Rossi & Kelly, 1997*
Stage 1	Preaffiliation	Preaffiliation	Preaffiliation: • Approach-Avoidance • Power and Control	Approach-Avoidance
Stage 2	Power and Control	Establishment of a Relational Base	Intimacy and Flight	Intimacy
Stage 3	Intimacy	Mutuality and Interpersonal Empathy	Differentiation	Power and Control 1: Challenging the Institution
Stage 4	Differentiation	Challenge and Change	Termination	Power and Control 2: Challenging the Worker
Stage 5	Termination	Termination		Differentiation & Empowerment

Source: Adapted from Berman-Rossi & Kelly, 2003

to which members progress through the phases and the ways in which they progress. For example, in an application with an online group of nurses developing best practices, Kelly, Lowndes, and Tolson (2005) found that separate stages emerged, including preaffiliation, work/intimacy, work/amalgamation, with a return to work/intimacy, and group development was influenced by member characteristics, structure, and group purpose.

With its emphasis on power and control, the Boston Model may be most appropriate for use with group members who are more comfortable with competition, power, and conflict (e.g., younger groups) and groups that can move through stages quickly and with independence from the facilitator (Schiller, 2007).

Relational Model Feminist theorists and practitioners established the relational model in response to developmental theory building that excludes women. Many feminists challenge Erik Erikson's famous male-normed psychosocial sequence of life stages on the grounds that he stereotyped girls as being concerned with "inner space" and boys with "outer space." Some feminists believe the intimacy stage, a clearly relational dimension, actually precedes the identity stage in girls, which reverses Erikson's order. Over two decades ago, Carol Gilligan (1993) suggested that the identity and intimacy stages are intertwined in girls.

The feminist orientation to the importance of the relational aspects of development appears in group work models as well. The **relational model** proposes that women go through different stages than those in the Boston Model. The second and third stages of the relational model emphasize the relationships established before the conflict, or challenge, stage. The model is as follows (Schiller 1995; 1997; 2003):

- *Preaffiliation:* Members experience ambivalence about joining.

- *Establishment of a relational base:* Members build strong, affective connections with others.

- *Mutuality and interpersonal empathy:* The connections deepen into a commitment to mutual aid.

- *Challenge and change:* Members recognize differences, and the connections may change in nature.

- *Termination:* Members conclude their work and separate.

While useful in all groups, this model is particularly helpful in feminist groups or in groups composed mainly of women because it supports one of the more accepted

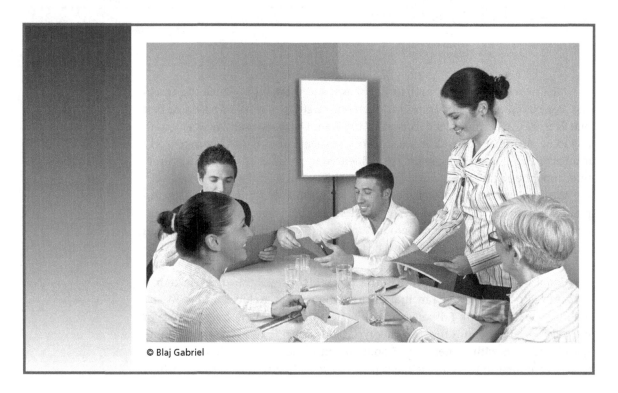

© Blaj Gabriel

gender constructions relating to women's development and theory (Lesser et al., 2004): that is, the importance of established relationship and relational patterns as a precursor to engagement in challenge, such as self-advocacy, or taking risks previously not attempted. Specifically, women benefit in a group environment when they are able to develop relationships with other women who share similar life experiences and/or are similar to one another in other ways. Creating connections can enable participants to feel secure and safe within the group, leading to a comfort in sharing with others (Lesser et al., 2004). A relational approach may also be applicable for other groups who may have experienced oppression or displacement and for whom confrontation is not motivating (e.g., immigrants and refugees) (Schiller, 2007).

Relationships and connections lie at the heart of this model of group intervention. Thus, a key role for the social worker leading a relational group is to help empower group members to feel safe so they may move into the phases of the group process in which they will take risks and address areas of concern (Schiller, 2007).

Many valid theories and perspectives can guide group interventions. Each social worker must determine the theoretical perspective that is most compatible with her or his philosophy and professional and personal value systems, given agency structures, guidelines, and funding sources. Once a practitioner identifies one or more perspectives with which she or he is comfortable, that practitioner must develop competency in the chosen approach(es). Regardless of which theory you choose, it is essential that you demonstrate competent behaviors.

© Design Pics/Don Hammond/Thinkstock

CONTEMPORARY TRENDS AND SKILLS FOR THE MIDDLE PHASE OF GROUP WORK: INTERVENTION [EPAS 8]

In the middle phase of the group experience, the social worker, the client, and the entire group implement the plan to work toward their goals. The social worker and the group move into a pattern of interaction that enhances cohesion, unity, integration, trust, and communication (Macgowan, 2013). The primary function of intervention phase of group work is to carry out goals that were established during the assessment phase of group work. The *Standards for Social Work Practice with Groups* (IASWG, 2015) provides guidelines for organizing this phase of work and identifying needed skills:

1. *Support progress toward individual and group goals:* Having established both individual and group goals in the assessment phase, members can develop and implement a plan to accomplish the goals. The social worker must be attentive to the potential need to re-negotiate goals during this phase of work.
2. *Attend to group dynamics and processes:* The social worker must be vigilant in her or his ongoing observations of group dynamics and processes. As group members become familiar with one another, they may feel more confident confronting one another, which can create conflict within the group. Moreover, the social worker must be mindful of alliances that form within the group and outside the group and of the impact of those relationships on individual and group functioning.
3. *Use evidence-based group practices (see discussion next) and utilize resources inside and outside the group:* As the work phase progresses, the social worker should be aware of and have access to resources that may be helpful to group members.

Examining the literature for evidence-based group interventions can help your group practice. Group work that is informed by both quantitative and qualitative evidence to support the "best available" practices is known as **evidence-based group work** (EBGW) (Macgowan, 2009a, pp. 132–133). Using rigor, impact, and applicability as the criteria for determining the strength of the evidence, EBGW enhances practice and policy accountability, enables social workers to improve practice competencies using empirically validated tools and research outcomes, and ultimately bolsters the efficacy of the group intervention. Exhibit 9.1 outlines the seven considerations of an evidence-based approach to implementing and evaluating a group intervention.

Examples of Different Types of Social Work Group Interventions

As we discussed in Chapter 8, there are four types of groups within which practitioners often work—task groups, social action/goals groups, reciprocal groups (including psychoeducational groups and support groups), and remedial groups.

When reviewing the research on approaches to group interventions, consider each approach with regard to the following:

1. The way in which the approach assesses client needs and strengths
2. How the approach identifies desired outcomes
3. Potential legal and physical risks involved
4. Group member compliance with the intervention plan developed by group members
5. Client responses to intervention
6. Assessment of outcomes
7. Distinction between individual and group outcomes

Source: Comer & Meier, 2011, pp. 464–470

EXHIBIT 9.1

Considerations for Evidence-Based Group Work

These groups often have overlapping outcomes. For example, the support group promotes mutual aid among members, the psychoeducational group supports and educates, the social goals group educates and advocates, and all deal with some aspect of social justice, diversity, or human rights. In each type of group work, the members are experiencing some dimension of exclusion or are concerned about others experiencing exclusion (such as intimate partner violence and groups concerned with those in correctional facilities), which in turn leads to unmet needs and violation of rights (see Goodman, 2004).

Each effort described here represents an attempt to counter the negative effects of a contemporary social issue, and each demonstrates creativity and courage. Note that, as works in progress, these efforts may not be proven effective. Although they are based on recognized social work perspectives and guided by research inquiries, they will no doubt evolve in response to evaluation procedures that gauge their effectiveness and pinpoint needed improvements. In forging new territory, they take risks and reflect group work's potential.

Constructionist Groups for Women Experiencing Intimate Partner Violence A **constructionist group** is a group intervention facilitated from a social constructionist perspective. In this approach, the facilitator recognizes that group members create reality through shared meanings. The constructionist group process offers members the opportunity to develop new understandings of themselves. A constructionist group intervention embodies feminist and narrative theories as well as the postmodern approach of the way in which a person develops a new and preferred **representation of the self** (i.e., view of her or his own worth and identity). In a feminist group for women experiencing intimate partner violence, members accomplish new representations of the self in part by resisting and protesting male violence. The work of the group includes three processes: (1) revealing and undermining society's oppressive discourse relating to women experiencing violence, which has historically been manifested through *political* processes; (2) identifying and detailing the protest that women can and will use in response to violence, the recognition of which reflects *change*; and (3) reconstructing participants' identities based on the protest. These activities work together to encourage members to first seek resistance (i.e., to confront difficult issues) and to then anchor resistance (i.e., identify potential change), culminating in a new story that elaborates a new identity (Roche & Wood, 2005). Group members celebrate this last process in an empowering **"definitional ceremony"** (a concept developed by Myerhoff, 1982, and applied by Wood & Roche, 2001, p. 17), which allows the women to present to an audience of people important to them their new understandings of self. In the definitional ceremony, one group member tells her story, a witness responds with a retelling of the story, and finally the original speaker retells the story, incorporating the new insights the witness provided (Leahy, O'Dwyer, & Ryan, 2012).

In one example, the social worker points out the common themes that arise in the women's conversation relating to their reactions to violence. Some women adopt a socially imposed understanding that incorporates shame and guilt when male partners are violent toward them. They believe that their own shortcomings cause violence against them and that they are responsible for changing their behaviors in exchange for safety. After first expressing support for the women, a social worker can help to counter the woman's feelings of shame and guilt by asking perspectival questions that help to break the logic of self-deprecation (for example, "What would your sister say about the way Mike treats you?" or "What did the court say about this?"). Over time, such questioning encourages a focus on multiple realities by helping women see that others would not think they "deserved" violence, "had it coming," or should "just put up with it."

At this point, the social worker seeks descriptions from the women in the group regarding their actual responses, that is, the ways in which they have resisted and protested. Protest may take the form of simply not accepting the batterer's negative statements, or it may be considerably more confrontational, such as obtaining a restraining order. Some protests may be viewed by the client and the social worker as passive (giving older bread and milk to an abusive partner while saving fresher food for a child). Incidences of protest, however they are expressed, begin to form the basis for a new understanding of the self as a person of agency who can make real and meaningful life changes.

Group members ask where a woman got her ideas for the protest or the courage to carry it out, and they also consider what the protest says about her. These explorations lead to a new view that challenges the woman's identity as helpless and worthless. The social worker and other group members then reinforce, or anchor, this new more positive representation by seeking to enrich the story through the woman's further detailed description. Finally, they celebrate her new identity as she sees it through a collective definitional ceremony. By emphasizing process rather than group stages, the group commits to helping each woman discover the other side of their survivorship and become who they want to be.

Models like this one, based on narrative ideas of story and constructionist ideas of self, are especially useful in political contexts that highlight contemporary views of gender and power relationships. In particular, they are appropriate in any situation in which the goal is to strengthen an individual's self-esteem (e.g., community mental health centers and for groups addressing sexual assault, intimate partner violence, and relationship issues).

Restorative Justice Groups for Combating Crime   Seeing the criminal justice system as mired in practices that neither heal nor rehabilitate, scholars and practitioners have developed what they believe is a more relevant approach that better responds to the issues of offenders as well as survivors, particularly in cases involving gendered violence against women (see van Wormer, 2009). A loosely associated collection of strategies called **restorative justice groups** focuses on crime as an interpersonal conflict with repercussions on the victim, the offender, and the community at large. Well suited to the social work profession's grounding in the value of the biopsychosocial-spiritual perspective, the strategies of restorative justice emphasize healing, growth, and enhanced functioning for all those affected by crime (see, for example, the systematic review of social work involvement in restorative justice in Gumz & Grant, 2009). Communities suffer when their members are engaged in crime, and they benefit when healthy and productive climates are restored within the community; therefore, it is important to focus on securing community involvement when addressing crime.

In one example, a series of three groups of offenders conducted at the Washington State Reformatory focused on balancing (1) offender accountability, (2) the rights of victims, and (3) citizen involvement in the justice process. The three groups accomplished their work through participants' stories of their personal crime experiences. Each week, one victim, one offender, and one community member shared her or his personal accounts of experiencing crime. Such storytelling increases understanding, validates experience, reduces isolation, and increases the vision for change. Group participants then determined how offenders could respond to the needs of individual victims and what offenders and community members could do to repair the harm.

The progress and process variables of these groups were largely consistent with classic models of developmental group work theory (that is, initial anxiety and a stage of conflict, followed by greater connectedness) with individual members also influencing the meetings so that each reflected different stages of development. A number of additional obstacles to the development of group unity occurred, such as the emphasis on crime, the large number of participants, emotional fragility, at times problematic group dynamics, safety concerns, confidentiality issues, and the implications of diversity, among others. This emphasis on an alternative crime response strategy that heals and helps people reconnect with each other holds promise in a society struggling with the alienation of both victims and perpetrators. A recent addition to this concept is the enactment of Neighborhood Activity Boards. In many communities, groups of volunteers come together to meet with first-time, nonviolent offenders and those people victimized by the criminal activity to discuss the impact of the crime. Typically, the offender must complete community service along with participating in the impact panel.

Motivational Interviewing Groups   Chapters 5 and 7 discussed motivational interviewing (MI) in the context of working with individuals and families. MI is also useful in a group setting, where it is known as GMI (group motivational interviewing). GMI builds on the same premise of engagement, focus, evoking, and planning. GMI in particular requires the facilitator to emphasize collaboration, autonomy, support, and empathy through reflective listening and change talk (Hohman, 2012). MI scholars Miller and Rollnick (2013) support the use of MI with a range of group interventions, but they offer two cautionary notes: (1) the group leader should be competent in the facilitation of MI with individuals before attempting to incorporate it into a group experience, and (2) due to the larger number of participants, there will be fewer opportunities for change talk, which may result in less predictable outcomes.

The examples provided here present just a small sampling of the types of group interventions available to social workers. Identifying the intervention approach, format, and structure that best fits your goals for working with groups is the key issue to consider whether you are developing a task, remedial, reciprocal, or social action group.

Social Work Skills for Group Interventions

While social workers must possess certain skills to apply any theoretical model, and while group work interventions may seem different from one-to-one models in social work settings, many of the same generalist practice roles and skills that social workers use in individual and family interventions are both applicable to and vital for group work interventions. As you work to maintain a group-centered focus during an intervention, you will find that listening, supporting, and empathizing all play as important a role in group work as they do in work with individuals. Exhibit 9.2 provides a comprehensive list of general skills that are important for group interventions, and the section that follows discusses specific skill areas in greater depth.

The following additional skills critical to group practice are adapted from the authors' practice experience as well as from Brown (2013), IASWG (2015), and Middleman and Wood (1990, pp. 96–102).

Leadership Skills   Social work practice with groups requires the social worker to demonstrate leadership in initiating and facilitating the group, including:

- To maintain a **"thinking group"** posture, you, as the social worker, consider the group as a whole first and individual members second. This concentration

As a social worker, you will use a diverse array of skills when working with groups of any type, including the following:

1. Understanding your relationship to your agency and the way in which you and your agency fit within the context of the larger community.
2. Understanding the flow of group work from beginnings through endings, including the ongoing assessment of and attention to the group's level of cohesion.
3. Conducting group interactions with multicultural awareness and sensitivity.
4. Advocating for individual clients, the group, and your agency.
5. Practicing within the ethical guidelines of the profession.
6. Helping the group establish adaptive norms.
7. Ensuring that self-disclosure is consistent with agency policy and meets the needs of the group (as opposed to your personal needs). Use of self (incorporating your own experiences) can help reflection and role modeling for the group.
9. Collaborating with group members to identify individual and group short-and long-term goals.
10. Ensuring that the goals the group establishes are consistent with the purpose of the group.
11. Regularly seeking feedback from the group regarding members' feelings about the group and the process.
12. Clarifying members' perceptions of time needed to make change, since we often expect change to occur more quickly than is realistic.
13. Providing group members with information that is relevant to the purpose of the group (e.g., medical/health information or information about legal processes).
14. Admitting when you lack information or knowledge.
15. Incorporating a variety of strategies and techniques into group process (e.g., art or writing projects; role-playing; relaxation exercises; or videos, speakers, or exercises).
16. Promoting expression of feelings within the group.
17. Demonstrating your respect for the group when members share feelings by listening actively, reflecting, and tracking.
18. Normalizing group members' feelings.
19. Engaging members on a cognitive level (i.e., thoughts and feelings).
20. Incorporating past experiences and family history to help group members connect with emotions.
21. Partializing (i.e., separating and prioritizing) the presenting issues to help group members avoid feeling overwhelmed.
22. Confronting individuals and the group as needed regarding issues related to compliance or engagement, for example.
23. Maintaining a focus on the present, such as using current events to emphasize human nature and social justice.
24. Offering strategies for resolving interpersonal conflicts.
25. Modeling empathy and the use of "I" statements and contracts.
26. Promoting member self-esteem and competence.

EXHIBIT 9.2

Knowledge and Skills for Group-Level Interventions

Source: Adapted Greif & Ephross, 2011, pp. 489–493

on the whole can require a paradigm shift. For example, you may avoid a prolonged exchange with a single group member because that focus would hinder the group's communication.

- Exhibiting "**balanced leadership**," you encourage the group to have some control over the process and outcome. This leadership can challenge social workers who believe they must have complete control of the group and its agenda or it will explode or become chaotic. If the social worker allows the group to evolve without close attention to process, it *can* become chaotic, members' feelings may be hurt, or the group may fragment and lose its meaning for group members. The social worker's ability to effectively facilitate depends on many factors including group connection, group functioning, and the presence of internal or **indigenous leadership**, that is, leadership that evolves within the membership.

Generally, the social worker is more directive in the early stages of groups, in groups with lower-functioning members, in groups with little indigenous leadership, in open-ended groups, and in task-oriented groups. As the group progresses, the social worker's role is to gradually retreat and to encourage growth in the group's ownership of the activity. The key here for any social worker is to recognize group needs and to be flexible with the degree of direct leadership. Typically, the overall goal for social workers in groups is to reduce their activity to as little as possible while maintaining self-awareness and a safe environment and encouraging members to take charge of their own group.

- **Scanning**, engaging in ongoing observation and engagement with all members of the group, is a strategy for maintaining visual observation of all members—the group version of the attending skill.

- Maintaining **cohesiveness**, or connectedness, means sustaining a sense of "we" through the use of "we" language, the encouragement of rituals (for example, marking the beginning and end of each meeting in a specific way), and the recording of the group's progress. When groups have too much or too little cohesiveness, the leader can attempt to uncover the causes (e.g., group member anxiety) (Berg, Landreth, & Fall, 2013). The use of these skills can contribute to group members' spirit and can facilitate a sense of belonging to something significant. Development and recording (through a chart on the wall, for example) of the group's agreed-upon norms or customs contributes to a sense of connection as well.

- **Facilitating change**, which can occur by assisting group members in making progress toward goals through support, programmatic activities, addressing obstacles, assessing progress, and making new contracts for goal achievement, as needed.

- **Promoting the development of mutual aid**, which may involve a review of group norms, group values, and conflict resolution.

- **Facilitating and monitoring groups**, which is completed by reviewing and reiterating definitions and rules related to confidentiality, particularly those germane to sharing information about other group members outside of group meetings.

Leadership Communication Skills

- Carefully choose the patterns of communication you will use in your group. If you respond only to the members who speak up, you will likely marginalize or exclude a subset of members. On the other hand, if you always go around the group, member by member, some members may feel pressed to contribute, and all will feel a certain amount of routinization. Instead, endeavor to encourage a respectful balance so that all members have an opportunity to speak without any one member dominating. Alternatively, you may choose to invite all members (especially those members who remain quiet) to participate and ask if others in the group share the speaker's thoughts or feelings. Periodically remind members of the norms they agreed upon and emphasize the group's accomplishments and history when appropriate.

- Responding empathetically is a critical skill in the group intervention that requires the group leader to: focus on the person speaking, restrict questioning to only those areas that need clarification, allow the group member to finish speaking, and resist the temptation to provide answers to client situations.

- **Redirection**, or redirecting questions and concerns away from you back to the group or to individual members, can be challenging. Some members will continue to address you as the source of authority for the group. Given the power dynamic, many group members may have experienced as clients in other services, such behaviors are not unexpected. Some members may complain about other members through a third party (often you). In both of these situations, you can redirect the message. Your goal is to facilitate direct, constructive communication within the group and its supporting environment. Exhibit 9.3 provides an example of a redirection within a group using the two scenarios mentioned here.

- You establish both consensus and difference when you invite agreement and disagreement on issues. A group member who has not been especially vocal will likely find it challenging to register dissent when a group approves something heartily. Early feelings of connectedness and strong group bonds can make that dissent even harder. Later, as the group matures, expressions of difference should be less troublesome, but you should continue to support difference and encourage others' capacities to respond.

EXHIBIT 9.3

When Redirection Is Needed in Group Work

As the group facilitator, you can use the following example to redirect a group session in which one member of the group appears to be leading the group away from its goal.

A member asks if visitors can attend a group meeting. Because the group has not addressed the issue before, you submit the question to the full membership:

"How do others see this question?" or "How do you as a group want to handle this?"

You may invite quieter members to participate and attempt to soften the messages of louder voices.

A second scenario involves one member of the group complaining about another member. In this scenario, you may simply say:

"Why don't you tell Bernice that?" or "I don't think you need my help talking to Kate about that."

- If the facilitator is talking, members cannot, so it is important that you, as a facilitator, work on **exercising silence**. The social worker's well-placed silence encourages the group to engage in the bulk of the interchange, which allows members' communication patterns to develop.

Leadership Problem-Solving Skills

- *Connecting progress to goals* by summarizing progress, identifying options, prioritizing decisions, mediating conflicts, confronting lack of progress and group interactions, and weighing potential outcomes are skills and activities that a social worker employs in problem solving during the intervention phase of group work. On occasion, the social worker may have to negotiate an amended contract with individual members or the entire group. The social worker may also identify the next discussion areas for future group meetings.

- In problem solving with groups, it is important that the social worker participate in *locating resources to benefit group members*. This involves working with members to identify resources, to include natural assets (e.g., friends, family, or neighbors) into the helping network, and to emphasize the connections between the group and the community. Engaging in a joint discussion among members early in the process conveys the expectation that the group has both the ability and the responsibility to deal constructively with its own issues. Identifying resources outside the group expands the potential network for all members and supports the interdependence between members, groups, and the environment. Another potential resource for the members of a group can be to incorporate activities in which the members can engage, including outside speakers, videos, group exercises, or journaling.

- The social worker can *make use of the unique characteristics of the group in the act of problem solving.* A social worker's goal in work with groups is to nego-tiate the tension between individual member and whole group needs, coming to a genuine compromise that encourages creative enrichment that benefits both the individual and the group. The group must establish an acceptable expression and appreciation for difference. Consider the following example from a social worker's notes of the eighth meeting of a socialization group of 12-year-old girls.

The girls were bustling around preparing crepe paper streamers and searching for birthday candles, giggling and joking about how old Lila was really going to be. Some said she was probably going to be 60 or so, judging by how glum she had seemed last week about the party they were planning. Lila was late, and when she finally showed up, she looked more miserable than ever. Finally, she blurted out, "I HATE BIRTHDAYS!!" in a voice very unlike her usual somber tones. The other girls were horrified and silent for a moment—almost unheard of in this group. Lila started to cry. Finally, she choked out the story: Her mother had died the night before her birthday two years ago, and she didn't know how to tell anybody in the group that before. The very word "birthday" was a terrible reminder. She didn't want to celebrate.

The girls seemed to feel sorry, they liked Lila, but they also really wanted to cele-brate birthdays in this group. It was an important ritual for them. I confess that, as their facilitator, I didn't have a clue what to do. After a moment, Betsy, whose grand-mother came from France, cheerfully volunteered, "Well, let's be trés français in this group and say we're celebrating our anniversaries! That's what the French call them, the anniversary of birth!" The others responded loudly, hoping their ritual was rescued from certain demise. Lila was silent. She looked up. Finally she almost smiled and said, "I think that would work." And that was that. The group took on a "French theme" ever after and was the only group of 12-year-olds I ever knew that celebrated their anniversaries!

Management of Group Function and Process   All effective social work interven-tions make use of the social worker's ability to interact competently with clients with strengths-based and biopsychosocial-spiritual perspectives. Within those inter-actions, the social worker and group members may fulfill a broad spectrum of potential roles. While this and the previous chapter have highlighted social worker roles within groups, this chapter will focus on the role of the social worker during the intervention, termination, evaluation, and follow-up phases of group work. The summary of those roles is examined here, followed by an overview of the roles group members play.

Social Worker Roles

While the social worker's primary role is to provide leadership for the group intervention, the type, format, and goals of the group determine what specific role the social worker will play. The social work group practitioner may find her- or himself needing to function in one or more of the following roles (Berg et al., 2013; Furman, Bender, & Rowan, 2014; Collins & Lazzari, 2009, pp. 299–302; Reid, 2002, pp. 435–436):

- As a **facilitator**, the social worker must be a skilled listener who invites sharing and participation, reframes and links issues, and maintains group boundaries and rules to promote appropriate interactions. In a task group, the facilitator may set the agenda, maintain the group's focus on tasks, and document the meeting. Regardless of the group setting, the social worker should foster an ongoing awareness of the "unconscious group process" (i.e., understanding issues that permeate the group's functioning) (Levy, 2011, p. 155).

- As a **synthesizer**, the social worker summarizes group members' discussions, identifies themes and patterns, and connects content from one session to the next to promote continuity and substantive discussion.

- When a social worker models appropriate group behavior and directs feedback, she or he acts as a **setter of norms**. For example, the social worker establishes appropriate group interaction by encouraging the use of direct interactions, "I" statements, appropriate challenges, and concrete examples and by helping set the rules at the beginning of the group. Norm setting includes the challenging issue of self-disclosure. As the leader, you can appropriately share information about yourself and suggest group activities that focus on attitudes, values, and beliefs rather than more threatening exercises that emphasize sensitive content areas.

- Social workers functioning as **educators** or teachers within a group setting provide factual information specific to group goals.

- As group leaders, social workers can empower group members by promoting **self-advocacy** that can be applied both inside and outside of the group setting. The group can serve as a place for members to rehearse their newly learned self-advocacy skills.

- As with social work practice with individuals and families, social workers may **collaborate** with other professionals. Co-leadership is often an effective strategy in group interventions as it can involve equal commitment, motivation, and vision on the part of each of the co-leaders that can build on the strengths that each leader brings to the intervention.

Group Member Roles

Group members bring their unique characteristics and traits to the group experience regardless of the type of group or its purpose, often serving as both learner and teacher (of others in the group). The social worker may experience these qualities as both strengths and challenges. Ideally, group members will be open to new information, growth, and change and will be willing and able to actively participate in the group process to provide the same for others (Furman et al., 2014). These are obvious strengths, but even challenging behaviors can be reframed and used for positive individual and group outcomes. If a group member displays resistant behaviors (e.g., disruption or an unwillingness to engage) and cannot fulfill their roles as learner and teacher, she or he may lack trust or feel insecure (Berg et al., 2013). See Quick Guide 28 for a list of questions that may be helpful in managing resistance. The social worker can encourage appropriate group member interactions by setting expectations from the outset of the group intervention, but individual group member's idiosyncrasies may still lead to challenging interactions within the group process.

Some group member roles commonly emerge. Individual personalities influence and interact with group dynamics (much like the dynamics of a family interaction). The competent group practitioner can begin to anticipate these roles and behaviors and, having previously considered these possibilities, can be prepared with an appropriate response. You must exercise caution, however, to ensure that you do not generalize or stereotype group member behaviors but respond to each person as unique. Six potentially challenging group member roles you can expect and possible social worker responses include the following (adapted from Berg et al., 2013; Furman et al., 2014; Yalom & Leszcz, 2005, pp. 391–405):

- *The "silent" group member:* The "silent" group member is challenging because it is difficult to determine if the individual is not speaking because she or he

QUICK GUIDE 28   QUESTIONS THAT MAY BE HELPFUL IN MANAGING RESISTANCE

If you encounter a group member or members who seem resistant to engaging in the group process, consider the following questions:

1. What is the nature (e.g., behavior and attitudes) of the resistance?
2. Are the member's behaviors disrupting group function and process?
3. How does resistance impact other areas of the individual's life?
4. How do other group members respond to the group member who is displaying resistance?
5. How are you responding to the group member displaying resistance?

After reflecting on these questions, share your observations with the group and collectively brainstorm possible causes and responses.

Source: Berg, Landreth, & Fall, 2013, p. 125

is not engaged or because he or she is uncomfortable or intimidated and thus not able to benefit from the group experience. Silence does not necessarily mean that the person is not engaged. While it is possible to experience vicarious gains without active engagement, the social worker typically strives to turn the reticent group member into an active participant. Inviting the individual to participate, noting nonverbal gestures, and speaking with the member outside of the group about her or his silence are all strategies for promoting participation. Should these strategies fail, the social worker may either allow the individual to continue as a silent member of the group or develop an alternative intervention outside the group for the individual. As you consider the way in which you will address the silence, take into account the responses from the other group members.

- *The "monopolizer":* Equally as challenging for a group leader is the "monopolizer," who is perceived as talking too much. In this role, the group member may attempt to offer her or his opinion on virtually every statement made by others or may spend an inordinate amount of time describing her or his own situation or needs. Monopolizing can present itself in different forms, including the "compulsive talker," the "intellectualizer," the "special interest pleader," or the "manipulator," all of whom may be operating out of fear or a need to control the situation. While understanding the reasons for this person's behavior is important for changing the behavior, the impact on the group process and members can potentially be negative as members may perceive that the person is being singled out, the group is not safe, and/or they may be next to be confronted. As with the "silent" group member, the social worker may personally address a group member's monopolizing behavior or may encourage the group to address the behavior. The social worker might work with the monopolizer outside the group to address the reasons she or he feels compelled to speak so frequently, or the worker may develop an alternative intervention strategy.

Subgroups or cliques within the group can also monopolize the group's time and energy and can isolate some members or create internal divisions or conflicts. Allowing the group to manage any subgroups when they form is ideal; the social worker can ensure that the process is fair and respectful.

- *The "help-rejecting" or complaining group member:* A social worker may view a group member who appears to reject help or ideas as both a challenge and a resource. Avoidant behavior can signal a member's depression or lack of problem-solving skills. The "help-rejecting" or complaining group member is likely to have a negative influence on the group's dynamics and may be unable to experience change or to grow. On the other hand, other group members may use the avoidant member's negative perspective to see alternate possibilities (if only as a reaction to the negativity). The social worker can respond in a way that maintains a focus on concrete feedback and on the group process and that encourages the group to respond to this member as well. The leader may also seek to build trust with the member displaying avoidant behaviors.

- *The "caregiver":* A "caregiver" (also known as the coordinator or rescuer) is a group member who strives to take care of others, including the group facilitator. Not surprisingly, caregivers often use caring for others as a way to avoid addressing their own individual challenges. The social worker can respond to caregivers by acknowledging their history of altruistic caregiving, praising their willingness to now take care of their own needs, and gently confronting them when they attempt to care for others as a way to avoid dealing with their own issues

- *The "attacker":* An "attacker" may verbally assault another member or the facilitator, which may either stimulate or disrupt the group. Acknowledging an attacker's aggressive behavior is a first step toward exploring the underlying reasons for that behavior. Confrontation is required if attacks become personally targeted.

- *The "dependent" group member:* Certain "dependent" behaviors can be challenging in the group setting. For example, the "harmonizer" strives to maintain peace within the group, the "clown" uses humor (often to mask depression or fear), and the "poor me" member seeks constant affirmation.

© vm

QUICK GUIDE 29   SUMMARY OF INTERVENTION SKILLS FOR
SOCIAL WORK GROUP PRACTICE

The social worker engaged in the intervention phase of social work practice with groups should:

• be knowledgeable and skilled in group leadership (e.g., logistics and time management);
• facilitate group communication and group dynamics;
• be competent with individual and group problem solving;
• focus on promoting progress toward group and individual goals; and
• manage group functions.

As a facilitator, you can initiate a discussion focused on the interactional and communication styles the members possess and the functions those styles serve in their lives. As the discussion of the intervention or the middle phase of the group work process comes to a close and the exploration shifts to the termination and evaluation phases of group work, a review of the skills needed to competently intervene with groups may be helpful. See Quick Guide 29 for a recap of these skills presented.

CONTEMPORARY TRENDS AND SKILLS FOR THE ENDING PHASES OF GROUP WORK: TERMINATION AND EVALUATION [EPAS 9]

While the concepts we explored in our discussions of terminating (i.e., ending), evaluating, and following-up with individuals and families can be applied to work with most clients, there are some additional considerations and dynamics to consider in social work practice with groups. As in social work terminations and evaluations with individuals and families, the intensity of the phases of ending a group and evaluating the work will depend on the type of group and its purpose.

Social Work Group Endings

The social worker's role in termination is to "help members examine their accomplishments, review their experience together, and prepare for the future . . . and express and integrate positive and negative emotion" (Garvin & Galinsky, 2013). Social work practice with groups can end in many ways. Terminations may occur when a member opts to leave the group, when the group reaches a predetermined time limit or meets its collective goals, or when the leader leaves the group (Furman et al., 2014). Regardless of the reason for the group's termination, endings may evoke a range of member responses and interactions. Group members may experience positive emotions, including feelings of success and elation, and/or negative emotions such as loss, threat, rejection, abandonment, or anger—all of which may relate both to their individual and group experiences (Furman et al., 2014). At termination, the group leader may notice that group members regress back to previous behaviors, withdraw from the group, panic, or begin to devalue the group experience (Brown, 2013). Response often depends on the group purpose and lengths. For example, members of an educational or task group are likely to experience fewer highly emotional responses than those of a treatment group. A group that has met only six times will probably not be as highly invested as a group that has met for three years.

Negotiating terminations with groups is an often-complex endeavor in which the social worker deals with endings on three different levels:

- The relationship between group members and the social worker

- Relationships among the group members

- The structure of the group itself

The theoretical framework a practitioner uses should guide the termination phase of group work. We will now consider endings from each of the theoretical perspectives discussed earlier in the chapter.

Using the Strengths and Empowerment Approach in Group Work Endings
Integrating strengths and empowerment concepts into the termination phase can enable both individual members and the whole group to review progress toward their goals and to develop strategies for sustaining change. The social worker can invite each member to review and reflect on her or his individual experience in the group, including: the strengths they brought to the group process; their status in the beginning, middle, and endings phases of the work; the changes they experienced; and their plans for using the group's strengths to maintain the change(s). Having individual members engaged in this review and reflection process provides an opportunity for the social worker and other group members to contribute to that individual's own experience of the group process. Group members can take advantage of fellow members' reflections for their own review and sustainability processes.

A strengths-based perspective can further enable the social worker and group members to reflect on how the group's strengths have evolved as the group moved through various phases. For example, a group strength may be the respectful and supportive way in which the members interact with one another. The social worker can provide feedback on the changes she or he has observed in the group's engagement, cohesion, and work, and group members can reflect on taking part in a strengths-focused group experience. Such reflection can empower group members and the social worker to integrate this enhanced sense of confidence and competence into the group process.

In situations in which individual or group goals are not realized, the formal ending of a task or social action group can still be oriented toward a strengths perspective. One strategy is to engage in an exercise in which members review the strengths the group had from the outset, those strengths they gained or mobilized during the group, and those strengths members can carry on after the group is terminated. While group members (and the social worker) may be dismayed at the group's failure to achieve its goals, planning ways in which members can continue to work toward achieving those goals can be empowering.

Narrative-Focused Group Work Endings   Ritual or ceremonial activities and public acknowledgement of growth and change work well in narrative-focused group terminations that emphasize strengths. Group members and the social worker can collaboratively plan a celebration to recognize the formal ending of the group's work together. This "definitional" ceremony can acknowledge the achievement of goals and the next phase of growth as well as help individuals reclaim or redefine themselves (Morgan, 2000, p. 121).

As with individual and family work endings, the group termination process involves public testimonials (Morgan, 2000). Group member feedback on individual testimonials can reinforce members' changes and solidify plans for maintaining change beyond the formal group experience. A social worker can use a process similar to one she or he might use with individuals, with group members serving as outsider-witnesses. The definitional ceremony begins with the social worker and group members listening as an individual group member re-authors her or his work in the group. The witnesses then reflect that re-authored story back to the individual, the individual member responds to the feedback, and the entire group engages in a discussion about the process. This activity can be helpful both as a tool for recognizing individual and group strengths and goal attainment and as a means of evaluating the change process.

Solution-Focused Group Work Endings   Termination of the solution-focused group intervention can be viewed by the social worker and the group members as the achievement of the initial and overall goals for the work of the group even if all of the members' individual goals were not realized. Solution-focused group interventions identify issues and plan and implement a change effort. In group interventions, group members provide opportunities for individual members to process their issues and potential solutions. Recall that solution-focused interventions are grounded in the ongoing use of a series of questions to elicit strengths, thoughts, and feelings regarding change and to develop plans for change. During the termination phase, you can ask members about the progress they've made via scaling progress questions (e.g., "On a scale of 1 to 10, where were you when you joined this group? Where are you now? Where do you need to be in order to maintain this change when you leave the group?" "How will you know when it is time to leave the group?" "What will be different?") (De Jong, 2015). Group members can provide their own observations of an individual member's change process. Shifting the emphasis from the present to the future can help the individual and group members to perceive themselves as separate from the group and from the social worker leading the group, thus enabling them to view themselves as empowered to implement and maintain the desired changes.

Regardless of the theoretical perspective you choose to guide a group intervention, you will need a number of competencies to effectively bring an intervention to an end. As with any social work intervention, groups are made of unique individuals and situations, and the social worker must be attuned to those aspects. In addition, a social worker needs to possess a set of termination-related skills specific to group practice.

Skills for Social Work Group Terminations

Even planned group endings can be complex and intense, and social workers need a skill set that reflects the unique features of the group intervention. During the termination phase, the social worker emphasizes bringing together the different phases of the work, beginning with the engagement, assessment, and intervention, to achieve closure for the individual group member, the group itself, and for her- or himself (IASWG, 2015; Toseland & Horton, 2013). The social worker should recognize and attend to all the feelings of the group members as well as her-/himself and frame the ending as a new beginning (Furman et al., 2014). Individual and group reflection during termination is particularly powerful. Group members and the facilitator can reflect on accomplishments as well as the way in which each person experienced the group process and ending (Furman et al., 2014). Let us take a closer look at each of the multiple skill sets social workers use in group endings.

Ending the Relationship between Group Members and the Social Worker   The end of the relationship between group members and the social worker places particular demands on the social worker. In this final phase of any type of group (i.e., task or client group), you, as the social worker, have several responsibilities with respect to the entire group, including the following (Brown, 2013; IASWG, 2015; Furman et al., 2014; Kurland & Salmon, 1998; Toseland & Horton, 2013):

- Preparing members for ending (from the mid-point of the group intervention)
- Assessing progress toward achievement of group goals
- Helping stabilize member and group gains
- Anticipating and eliciting individual and group responses to ending
- Planning timing and content to maximize remaining sessions/meetings

© Yuri Arcurs

- Helping group members express their ambivalence about the group's ending and addressing individual and group reactions and behaviors to individual or group accomplishments, including affirmations and confidence building regarding achievements

- Sharing observations of progress and confidence in members' abilities to function successfully without the group, or, in the case of a task group, continuing to work toward identified goals (it may be helpful to identify any obstacles to success and needed connections to resources outside the group)

- Supporting members' efforts to begin the process of separating from the group and identifying strategies for implementing change and applying new knowledge

- Developing awareness of ways in which individual and group change will impact systems external to the group

- Helping members connect their experiences in the group to life experiences in the future

- Developing awareness of your own feelings regarding ending and reflecting on and sharing feelings with the group

- Eliciting feedback from group members about the group process

The social worker's task is to help the group end positively and to help members translate their achievements into the "real world" outside the group. The social worker also has to monitor her or his own responses; after all, she or he has invested a great deal of effort in facilitating an effective experience, and groups in which significant personal and group changes have occurred can experience more difficult endings as groups may be reluctant to end as they have developed strong bonds with one another and the social worker. Recalling the overall purpose of the group and focusing on the specifics of the process can help the social worker to balance her or his response between task and emotion.

There are also a number of group behaviors typical to endings that may be directed either at the social worker or at the group as a whole. These include: (1) denial, or simply "forgetting" that the group is ending; (2) **clustering**, moving toward more connection rather than less; (3) **regression**, either claiming verbally or acting out in behavioral terms that the group is not ready to end; (4) withdrawal or passivity related to active participation; (5) rebellion; or (6) flight, leaving the group before it ends (Furman et al., 2014; Reid, 1997).

The responses to ending in groups are similar to those that occur in intervening with individuals and families. The fact that the number of people in the group may multiply those responses can make them feel quite momentous to you as the social worker. For example, when an entire collective of 13-year-old girls makes it clear, through sudden and orchestrated hostility toward you, that they do not want the experience to end, you can certainly feel the power of the group. In this case, just as in individual or family work, you can view the group's reaction as a function of the process (and perhaps of the success of the group), rather than as a focused personal assault.

Social work skills that are particularly useful in ending work with groups include the following (IASWG, 2015):

- *Preparing for termination:* The social worker has the responsibility to ease the transition and promote sustained change by ensuring that the end of the group experience (whether individual or entire group) is anticipated and planned.

- *Discussing impact of the group experience on the individual, the group, and the group facilitator and reflecting on gain:* Reflecting with the individuals and group-as-a-whole on the gains made and not made and strategies for sustaining changes is a useful strategy for ending group work because it allows the group to discuss their achievements and verbalize plans for maintenance.

- *Preserving group information:* This skill involves the facilitator verbally and in writing documenting the group goals, processes, achievements, and referrals/ connections in individual and group records. In the process of ending, the social worker can help the members to focus on maintaining the changes they experience as a result of the group into their world outside of the group.

Ending Relationships among Group Members   In ending relationships with other group members, individuals may exhibit a range of responses, from denial or flight behaviors to gratification to actual celebration. Some members may not attend meetings specifically dedicated to ending activities. Others may attend but refuse to enter group interactivity about endings, or they may simply resign themselves to feeling they have been rejected by the other members or the social worker. Individuals may become increasingly short-tempered and impatient with other members, as if to negate the importance of their relationship and to render the ending insignificant or even a relief. This behavior may occur among those members who have worked the hardest to connect with one other.

In other situations, individual members may question their ability to maintain change without the assistance of the group and the social worker. These members will sometimes lobby for individual sessions with the worker or a reconstituted "mini group" in which only a few members of the original group would attend. Some individuals may initiate more intense relationships with other group members outside the confines of group meetings, as if to negate the need for the group. The most helpful thing you can do is to articulate your observations regarding group dynamics, reflecting on your perceptions of their individual and group starting places, work completed, changes made, and goals achieved with the group members. Such a reflection can help the members examine their own experiences through the lens of another person. Staying focused on the group, rather than on individuals, can be challenging, but it is part of negotiating a successful ending.

Ending the Group Itself   The ending of the group itself is at once philosophical and technical. On the philosophical level, it requires you to reflect on your feelings about ending this unit of work and this group of unique characters. How will the experience contribute to your professional growth? What could you have done differently? How will group members benefit from it? If the group has been difficult, you may struggle with feelings of inadequacy or a sense of work left undone. When there is an overall sense that the group went well, you may feel exhilarated by a sense of accomplishment, of having crossed a particular hurdle, or of entering into the realm of the skilled. What metaphor will you use to describe your experience? Death? Divorce? Disengagement? Completing a required course? Graduation?

On a much more practical side, when the group ends, you will need to close out records of participation, complete the evaluation process (discussed in the next section), and terminate logistical arrangements such as space and place. Finally, you will need to honor follow-up commitments and successfully make any referrals or transfers.

Consider the issues that arise in the following group termination scenario:

A community-based agency that serves new immigrants offers a group for high school-aged students focused on the students' transitions from their country of origin to their newly adopted country. The group also has a secondary purpose: it provides an opportunity for the students to practice their English skills in a safe environment. The group is composed of a mix of genders and ethnicities. The social worker charged with facilitating the group has developed her cultural competency through a commitment to learn as much as she can about the students' heritage and traditions, language, cultural rules and norms for gender interactions, and faith traditions. She personally interviews each student who is referred to the group and her or his parents/ family/guardians so she can be familiar with the individual student's needs and goals for joining the group.

The social worker has become aware of a potential dilemma. The current group of students has developed into a cohesive group, particularly around becoming "Americanized" as they enthusiastically adopt the customs of teens in their new country. The time-limited group is scheduled to come to an end, but a number of parents who are distressed that their children are abandoning their heritages have approached the social worker and have asked her to continue the group for the purpose of reconnecting the teens to their ethnic and cultural roots. While the teens enjoy the group, they have already planned their "graduation" celebration and appear ready to move on with life outside the group. The social worker is conflicted—she empathizes with the parents' concerns but believes the group should terminate as planned.

What options or alternatives might the social worker in this scenario consider in order to meet the needs of both groups?

Endings can and should be a time for reflection and celebration. It is important that all social workers in group practice, particularly those in the early stages of their career, review the group process as it has impacted their personal and professional growth.

Evaluating Social Work Practice with Groups

Evaluating practice with groups serves the same purpose as evaluating practice with individuals and families: to assess the work, the process, the progress, and the social worker's skills (Furman et al., 2014). Unlike family intervention evaluations that focus exclusively on the unit and individual intervention evaluations that focus solely on the individual, the evaluation of a group intervention encompasses both the individual and the group, thus elevating group evaluations to a higher level of complexity.

As noted previously, individuals arrive at the group with distinct goals, personalities, needs, and expectations. Oftentimes, the social worker must consider evaluative strategies within the context of a large, diverse group of individuals who perceive their experiences differently from one another. You must frame an evaluation of any group intervention within the context of the purpose, type, structure, and format of the group. Further complicating group evaluations, the social worker must work within the agency or organizational structure in which the group is conducted. Having to address multiple needs with a group of individuals requires the social work group practitioner to have a clear and thoughtful approach to evaluation of the group intervention *prior* to the first meeting of the group.

Regardless of the method(s) used to evaluate the group intervention, it is important for everyone involved in the intervention to participate in the evaluative process (Garvin & Galinsky, 2013). The many strategies for accomplishing the goals of this phase of the group intervention include the following (Bloom, Fischer, & Orme, 2009; Furman et al., 2014; Garvin & Galinsky, 2013):

- Related to individual and group goals, reviewing individual and group member accomplishments with an emphasis on preparing for the future, sustaining change, and ensuring the inclusion of support systems to reduce risk for failure.

- Gathering group members' impressions of the group experience and the activities/programming. You can collect data publically as part of the group process (orally within the group or in written evaluations which are discussed in the group) or anonymously (in writing), using caution to avoid "satisfaction-only" surveys in which members are asked if they enjoyed the experience, as they typically do not accurately reflect growth and change, but members' feelings about the facilitator, setting, etc.

- Administering pre- and postgroup measures of behaviors, attitudes, and group function. Consider the use of previously validated and standardized measures that have been used with comparable groups. Such measures will provide you with evidence-supported data from which to interpret your findings. While standardized measures of the individual are appropriate for use in group interventions, also consider the use of standardized measurements developed specifically for group interventions (e.g., see Group Engagement

Measure (originally developed by Macgowan, 1997; further psychometric testing and review of research: 2000, 2003 (with Levenson), 2005 (with Newman), and 2006).

- Through direct observation, documenting behaviors and changes in individual group members and in the group. You may gather data quantitatively and/or qualitatively.

- Completing a self-evaluation, including exploration into such areas as: meeting group member needs, developing appropriate structures and interventions, and assessing your own performance as a social work practitioner. As part of reflecting on your role within the group, you may want to conduct a self-evaluation so that you can grow and evolve as a group facilitator. Quick Guide 30 provides a strategy to help you engage in a self-evaluation.

- Soliciting direct observation and feedback from other professionals.

While each group develops its own personality and each group experience is unique, there are aspects of each phase of the group process that are often replicated. Recall from Chapter 8 the examination of the engagement and assessment phases of three group models (social goals/action, reciprocal, and remedial models) used within groups of parents from the Riverton community. Returning to the Riverton example, Exhibits 9.4, 9.5, and 9.6 depict the intervention, termination, and evaluation phases from the perspectives of the three models.

QUICK GUIDE 30   GROUP FACILITATOR SELF-EVALUATION

When reflecting on your experience leading a group, ask yourself the following questions:

1. How did the group experience me?
2. What feelings did I experience in this session? Did I express those feelings? Did I have some feelings with which I did not feel comfortable?
3. What were my reactions to various group members? Did I feel "turned off" by some members, or rejected? Do all members know I care about them? Do they feel that I accept them?
4. What general message did I communicate to each member? Did I say what I really wanted to say? Did I clearly state my message?
5. How much time did I spend focused on the content of the discussion rather than on the interaction taking place or the feelings and needs subtly expressed?
6. What do I wish I had said or done? What would I do differently next time?
7. Did I dominate? How willing was I to let someone else assume the leadership role?

You can complete this reflection following each session as well as when the group comes to a close. Upon finishing this reflection, consider ways in which you may strengthen your group skills.

Source: Berg, Landreth, & Fall, 2013, p. 138

PHASES II AND III: MIDDLE AND ENDING WORK

Background: A group of parents in the Riverton community, concerned about the use and abuse of alcohol among their adolescent children, approaches a local community service agency to ask for its help.

Work thus far: Stakeholders and their interests and goals have been identified. The social worker's role has been agreed upon. A community needs assessment has been conducted, including strengths, resources, needs, and priorities. A plan for intervention, termination, and evaluation has been established; it will focus on developing and mounting a public education campaign to raise awareness about the issue of teen drinking.

Note: While the stages of group interventions are not linear and may, in fact, overlap, the following depicts a possible approach to responding to the identified need.

INTERVENTION	TERMINATION	EVALUATION
Identify community partners who will support and help to disseminate the education campaign	Conclude campaign	Conduct evaluation
		Analyze data gathered from evaluation effort
Confirm the plan, time frame, and resources for intervention, termination, and evaluation continue to be viable		Implement plan for sustainability
		Document findings
Launch the intervention		
Monitor progress, particularly dissemination and relationships with community partners		
Adapt the intervention, as needed		
Revisit plan for evaluation and sustainability		

PHASES II AND III: MIDDLE AND ENDING WORK

EXHIBIT 9.5

Riverton Children's Grief Support Group: An Example of a Reciprocal Group

Background: A social worker in a local community service agency has become aware of a number of Riverton children who have lost a parent to alcohol and substance-related deaths. The social worker takes steps toward offering to the community an educationally-focused support group.

Work thus far: Based on the social worker's assessment of community need and interest, group members were recruited, screened, and invited to join the group. A first session was planned and has been held, at which time the social worker and group members collaborated to determine group rules and norms. Individual group goals and needs were shared. The social worker's role as a facilitator/educator was established.

Note: While the stages of group interventions are not linear and may, in fact, overlap, the following depicts a possible approach to responding to the identified need.

INTERVENTION	TERMINATION	EVALUATION
Social worker begins each session by reviewing group rules and norms and conducting member check-in	Begin termination as planned	*Individual* Determine if goals were met (informal or formal)
Social worker engages in ongoing assessment of individual member needs, group interactions, and group cohesiveness	Check in with each group member regarding feelings about the termination of the group and the process	Administer post-group collection of data *Group* Determine if group goals (informal or formal) were met
Social worker has developed a repertoire of available agency and community resources to suggest as needed	Invite each member to talk about individual gains and continuing needs	Ask members to provide feedback regarding satisfaction with the group process
Revisit group needs and adapt intervention and educational programming plans as appropriate	Discuss plans for sustaining change and any perceived obstacles to maintaining desired changes	
Share information, as agreed upon prior to group initiation, with legal guardians	Provide resources as needed to help members sustain change	
Monitor individual and group progress and adapt as needed	Conduct termination ritual or celebration	

	INTERVENTION	TERMINATION	EVALUATION
EXHIBIT 9.5 *Continued*	Regularly revisit time frame and plans for termination and evaluation Invite suggestions from group members regarding plans for recognizing group termination		Document findings

EXHIBIT 9.6 *Riverton Mental Health Center Group for Persons with Dual Diagnosis: An Example of a Remedial Group*	**PHASES II AND III: MIDDLE AND ENDING WORK** *Background:* A new social worker at the Riverton Mental Health Center recently assumed leadership for a clinical intervention group for persons with dual diagnoses (i.e., substance abuse and mental illness) who receive outpatient services at the agency. Group membership is diverse and includes a mix of genders, ages, and mandated and voluntary members. Membership turnover depends on members' "graduation" from the treatment program; therefore, members are often entering and exiting the group. Two new members have been referred to the group. This will be the first time new members have been referred since the new social worker took over responsibility for the group. *Work thus far:* The social worker has gathered information on eligibility criteria for group membership and integrating new members into an ongoing group. The social worker has met with the two persons who have been referred and determined they would be appropriate for inclusion. The two members have been oriented and attended their first meeting. During this session, the social worker introduced the new members to the group, revisited group rules and norms, and assessed the individual goals and needs and group cohesion. *Note:* While the stages of group interventions are not linear and may, in fact, overlap, the following depicts a possible approach to responding to the identified need.

INTERVENTION	TERMINATION	EVALUATION
At the beginning of each session, social worker reminds members of group rules and norms	Ongoing, as membership is open	Complete formal evaluation as required by agency

Social worker conducts check in by asking members to share with the group events/actions since the last session

Social worker assesses individual member needs and goals and monitors progress towards goals (critical as each person may be at a different point in their progress)

Social worker assesses group cohesion

Members with longer membership serve as guides/mentors for newer members

Determine termination ritual appropriate to an open-ended group

Prepare existing and remaining members for termination

Check in with members regarding their feelings about termination

Obtain information from existing members regarding achievement of goals and experiences with group format and process (e.g., open vs. closed and time-limited format) and social worker leadership

Document findings

EXHIBIT 9.6

Continued

In addition to the type(s) of evaluative strategies for examining group interventions that we have discussed, consider using the data that you gather and analyze to develop evaluation tools that you can use with future groups (Garvin & Galinsky, 2013). For example, you and other group facilitators may find it helpful to have a menu of strategies for monitoring group progress or a manual for conducting a group intervention. Exhibit 9.7 offers a sample of a facilitator evaluation that group members can complete.

STRAIGHT TALK ABOUT GROUP INTERVENTION, TERMINATION, AND EVALUATION

The social worker's overall role and purpose is to encourage and mobilize the group's strengths. The social worker's concern for individual well-being and growth is augmented by the individual relationships within the group, one member to another. Consistent with trusting the group process, the social worker should strive to avoid overinvestment in the centrality or power of her or his role. The goal, after all, is for the group to gain its voice and develop its strength, even as individual members continue to grow. You will not be able to take credit, even in your own mind, for all of the potential successes in your group. In exchange, you will have the

EXHIBIT 9.7

*Group
Counselor
Rating Scale*

Instructions: Rate your group counselor as you see her/him functioning in your group.

Respect: Shows respect for group members by attentiveness, warmth, efforts to understand, and supports freedom of personal expression.

	5.0	4.5	4.0	3.5	3.0		2.5	2.0	1.5	1.0
Very high			high		moderate			low		very low

Empathy: Communicates an accurate understanding of group members' feelings and experiences. Group members know the counselor understands how they feel.

	5.0	4.5	4.0	3.5	3.0		2.5	2.0	1.5	1.0
Very high			high		moderate			low		very low

Genuineness: Realness. Everything she/he does seems to be sincere. That's the way she/he really is. This person doesn't put up a front.

	5.0	4.5	4.0	3.5	3.0		2.5	2.0	1.5	1.0
Very high			high		moderate			low		very low

Concreteness: "Tunes in" and responds to specific feelings of experiences of group members. Avoids responding in generalities.

	5.0	4.5	4.0	3.5	3.0		2.5	2.0	1.5	1.0
Very high			high		moderate			low		very low

Self-Disclosure: Lets group know about relevant immediate personal feelings. Open, rather than guarded.

	5.0	4.5	4.0	3.5	3.0		2.5	2.0	1.5	1.0
Very high			high		moderate			low		very low

Spontaneity: Can respond without consistently having to "stop and think." Words and actions seem to flow easily.

	5.0	4.5	4.0	3.5	3.0		2.5	2.0	1.5	1.0
Very high			high		moderate			low		very low

Flexibility: Adapts to a wide range of conditions without losing her/his composure. Can adapt to meet the needs of the moment.

	5.0	4.5	4.0	3.5	3.0		2.5	2.0	1.5	1.0
Very high			high		moderate			low		very low

Confidence: Trusts her/his abilities. Acts with directness and self-assurance.

	5.0	4.5	4.0	3.5	3.0		2.5	2.0	1.5	1.0
Very high			high		moderate			low		very low

Open-ended questions like the ones below may also yield insightful group perceptions about the facilitator:

1. Of what changes have you become aware in your attitudes, feelings about yourself, and relationships with other people since your group experience began?
2. How did the group experience help these changes to come about?
3. What did the group leader do that was most helpful and least helpful to you?
4. Was the group experience hurtful to you in any way, or did it have any negative effect on you?
5. Briefly identify any group exercises you especially liked or disliked.
6. In what ways do you wish you had been different in the group?
7. How are you most different as a result of the group experience?

Source: Berg, Landreth, & Fall, 2013, p. 143–144.

EXHIBIT 9.7

Continued

privilege of experiencing the power of group connection and the autonomy the group ultimately can exercise as it liberates the power of its members. The emphasis on the group does not mean that your own role is any less important. You are responsible for the structure of the group, for the emotional and physical safety of each member in the group, and for ensuring the group processes its own activity. Accordingly, your role is to evaluate group process and functioning on an ongoing basis, just as you do in other forms of social work practice interventions. This evaluation will vary according to the nature of your group purpose, goals, and format. For example, if you are working in a task group, the intervention and evaluation processes will focus on monitoring progress in completing the group's project. If you facilitate a group for school-aged children, you must make sure to use an appropriate developmental level. Other forms of evaluation that are especially useful come from members: Is the group meeting their social and affiliation needs? Do members continue to feel safe in the group? Is it a helpful forum to address the issues they want to deal with? As always, consider the work of evaluation as an ongoing process.

The American Academy of Social Work and Social Welfare Grand Challenges for Social Work Initiative identifies one of the areas the profession should address is to use technological innovations in social work practice, including group practice. The authors of Grand Challenge Working Paper No. 12, *Practice Innovation through Technology in the Digital Age: A Grand Challenge for Social Work* (Berzin, Singer, & Chan, 2015) charge the social work profession with investing in resources to leverage information and communication technology (ICT) to enable the profession to better prepare students and practitioners and serve consumers:

GRAND CHALLENGE

Harness Technology for Social Good

GRAND
CHALLENGE

Continued

Technology shifts at a rapid pace and social work is poised to be part of these advances. Social workers can begin to play a more active role in guiding the development side with their content knowledge and exploiting technology created for other purpose by ensuring . . . meaningful progress (p. 13).

While the profession must consider the ethical and practical implications of further integrating technological advances into individual, family, and group practice, there are a number of potential benefits, including: increasing accessibility and flexibility in service delivery; using social media to reach more people, using global positioning systems (GPS) and sensor systems to personalize treatment processes and gather evidence for practice innovations; and redefine social work roles and boundaries. The authors of the Grand Challenge advocate for the social work profession to promote evaluation of cutting-edge technologies to support practice interventions, develop training programs to encourage adoption of technologies, and advocate for regulations to support online service delivery (p. 13–14). This Grand Challenge is timely as Technology Standards in Social Work Practice are jointly launched by the National Association of Social Workers, Association of Social Work Boards, Council on Social Work Education, and the Clinical Social Work Association to provide the profession with guidelines related to the use of technology in social work practice (for more information, visit www.socialworkers.org). To familiarize yourself with the issues related to the use of technology, visit the Grand Challenges website and read Working Paper No. 12, *Practice Innovation through Technology in the Digital Age: A Grand Challenge for Social Work* (Berzin et al., 2015) at: http://aaswsw.org/grand-challenges-initiative/12-challenges/harness-technology-for-social-good/. (See Exercise #a1 for additional exploration of this Grand Challenge within the context of the Hudson City community.)

CONCLUSION

This chapter has presented social work practice with groups as functioning to mediate a range of social and emotional issues, including isolation, oppression, and life crises. Group work harnesses the relationship component of humanity toward individual and group goals. Currently, there are many exciting adventures in social work practice with groups that build upon contemporary theoretical perspectives, social justice, and diversity. The scenarios presented in this chapter that emphasize process over stages and story over problem all point to the empowering direction that social group work is taking. Social work practice with groups offers significant potential for the future and is particularly relevant for the social justice, diversity, and human rights connections that give social work its meaning.

MAIN POINTS

- Effective social work practice interventions with groups provide an interface for the promotion of social justice, diversity, and human rights.

- Strengths and empowerment, narrative, and solution-focused approaches are useful middle-phase (intervention) and ending-phase (termination) strategies.

- Developmental models, such as the Boston Model and others based on it, are widely used in group work. Many applications of and departures from these models can be found in the contemporary practice environment.

- Social workers working with groups add to the skills they've honed for intervening with individuals, developing additional skills for group intervention in the areas of group leadership, community, problem solving, and management of group functioning.

- Contemporary examples of innovative, evidence-based group practice models, such as constructionist groups and restorative justice groups, help to provide vision and possibility for responding to current cultural and social issues.

- Termination occurs in three distinct areas of group practice interventions: between group members and the social worker, among group members, and of the group itself.

- While evaluation of group practice shares some commonalities with evaluation of individual and family interventions, evaluating group interventions is more complex, as it requires both examinations of the individual members of the group and of the group itself.

EXERCISES

a. Case Exercises

1. To apply your learning of the Grand Challenge to use technology for social good that was highlighted in this chapter, visit the Grand Challenges website and read Working Paper No. 12, *Practice Innovation through Technology in the Digital Age: A Grand Challenge for Social Work* (Berzin et al., 2015) at: http://aaswsw.org/grand-challenges-initiative/12-challenges/harness-technology-for-social-good/. To examine the potential use of technology in the aftermath of Hurricane in the Hudson City area, review the case information at www.routledgesw.com/caseStudies. After reading Working Paper No. 12 and reviewing the information on Hudson City, complete the following items:
   a. Using the town map, sociogram, and interaction matrix, identify potential

group interventions in each of the four areas of social work group practice discussed in this chapter.

b. For each of the proposed group interventions, research existing technological models and resources that could be utilized to provide or enhance the social worker's ability to develop and conduct the group intervention.

c. Reflect on the potential strengths, weaknesses, and ethical dilemmas associated with each of the proposed technological strategies.

2. Go to www.routledgesw.com/cases, review Carla Washburn's video vignette and consider the roles each member plays in order to complete the following activities and answer the following questions:

a. *Gather into groups*: Start with the group session from the conclusion of the video vignette, and role-play the next session. What happens next? Process the group session with the class.

b. *Round robin:* Each student takes the opportunity to role-play the social worker. Change roles when the "social worker" is not sure how to proceed with the group. Debrief about the experiences and practice behaviors demonstrated for each role-play. What were strengths and areas for growth for each student as a facilitator?

c. Select a member of the group and discuss her or his role in the group process.

d. Identify the social worker's strengths as a group facilitator along with those practice behaviors that she or he may be able to improve.

3. Terminating a group intervention can be challenging. Returning to the grief support group depicted in the Carla Washburn video vignette, role-play the final session. Consider the following:

a. What is the most important role the social worker plays at this stage of the group process?

b. What practice behaviors are critical for the termination phase of a group intervention?

c. Brainstorm strategies for responding to the array of possible member reactions to the ending of the group experience.

4. At the conclusion of a group intervention, the evaluation of the effectiveness of your interventions is critical. Research various evaluation tools and complete the following for the grief support group in which Carla Washburn is a member:

a. Create a satisfaction survey.

b. Create a pre-test/post-test.

c. Create a six-month evaluation tool.

5. Go to www.routledgesw.com/cases and view the Riverton video vignette that depicts a group meeting of the Riverton Neighborhood Association. Upon viewing the video, respond to the following:

a. What model of group intervention is being conducted in this vignette?

b. Identify the practice behaviors and skills covered in this chapter that the group facilitator demonstrates in the meeting.

c. Compare and contrast group facilitation skills needed for a group such as the Riverton Neighborhood Association and for a client-focused group.

6. Go to www.routledgesw.com/cases and view the Riverton video vignette that depicts a group meeting of the Riverton Neighborhood Association or the Carla Washburn video vignette that depicts a grief support group. Using the Group Counselor Rating Scale (Exhibit 9.7), evaluate the group leader. Write a reflection identifying the group leader's strengths and areas for growth and change.

7. Go to www.routledgesw.com/cases and review the case for Brickville, particularly Virginia Stone and her family. In Chapter 8 (Vignette #3), Virginia was involved in the creation of a social action group targeted at saving the park that was built in memory of her family members who were lost in the apartment fire twenty years earlier. The exercise in Chapter 8 focused on determining the need, purpose, composition, structure, and content for such a group. Using the information available to you, develop a written plan that includes the following:

a. Development of the social action plan

b. Strategies for implementing the plan

c. Resources needed to implement the plan, including individuals, groups, organizations, and funding, as appropriate

d. Plan for determining the success or failure of the social action effort

e. Your reflection on the process of implementing a social action plan at the community level.

8. Go to www.routledgesw.com/cases and review the case for Hudson City. Recall from Chapters 6, 7, and 8 that the Patel family experienced significant impact from Hurricane Diane. As a result of her response to the experience, you refer the 12-year-old daughter, Aarti, to a group to help her develop her coping skills. While Aarti was a regular and active participant in the support group, there is mounting concern that she continues to struggle with the challenges that resulted in the referral to the group (e.g., nightmares, discomfort when required to be away from her parents for activities other than school and group, and decreased appetite). Describe in writing your thoughts about the concerns her parents and the leader of the support group express and a plan for addressing the ongoing challenges that Aarti and her family are experiencing, including:

• Continuation in the support group

• Alternative intervention strategies

• Resources needed for a revised intervention plan

9. Go to www.routledgesw.com/cases and review the case for Brickville, then, referring back to the discussion of the Stone family potential participation in group interventions at the beginning of this chapter, conduct a search of the literature on group-level interventions to find social work skills needed to conduct and evaluate the following group interventions:

a. Through a community needs assessment of services for older adults, the Bethany Catholic Church additionally identified a number of community members who are caring for older family members and determined that offering a group for family caregivers would be of service to the caregivers and their older family members.

b. The Brickville Community Development Corporation Youth Leadership Program (YLP) uses evidence-based practices for training and facilitating a task group focused on helping teens to make healthy life choices.

c. The Catholic Charities Community Center offers a group for children experiencing behavioral concerns.

d. A group of residents in the Brickville area have banded together to form a group to bring attention to issues of police and fire department lack of/slow responses to their community.

b. Other Exercises

10. To relate the information covered in this chapter to your own group experience, reflect on a specific experience you have had as a member of a group by responding to the following items:

a. Describe in detail a group to which you belonged (may be a current group). Include the following:
   - Type of group (may use one of the types described in Chapter 8)
   - Purpose of group
   - Structure of group (e.g., open or closed membership, time-limited or open-ended, number of members, eligibility for membership)
   - Your role within the group

b. Consider the quality of your involvement by reflecting on:
   - How did you feel about being a member of the group? How did you feel about your role? Your contributions?
   - Did the group fulfill stated expectations? Your expectations? If not, explain the reasons.
   - What were the strengths of the group?
   - What are areas for the group's growth or change?
   - Was group leadership formally determined or did it evolve naturally? What was the style of the leader(s)?

c. Based on your experience and your new knowledge of the group process, reflect on the following:
   - Would you engage with the group differently? If yes, how would your involvement change? Explain your reasons.
   - Was the group formally or informally evaluated? What were the outcomes?

11. Develop a plan for the way in which you, as a group leader, will respond to each of the following behaviors that may emerge during the course of your experience in group work:

a. "Silent" group member

b. "Monopolizer"

c. "Help-rejecter/avoider"

d. "Caregiver/coordinator"

e. "Attacker"

f. "Harmonizer"

g. "Clown"

h. "Poor me" group member

   After developing your response plan for each behavior, reflect in writing on the challenges you anticipate facing and strategies for learning and growing as a group facilitator.

12. Recall from Chapter 8 that you, as a practicum student, were invited to serve as a co-facilitator for a psychoeducational support group for family caregivers of persons experiencing Parkinson's disease. In the previous exercise, you focused on familiarizing yourself with Parkinson's disease and developed a plan for the session that you would lead. In preparing for the intervention, terminations, and evaluation phases of group work, respond to the following items:

   a. Identify potential needs for ongoing psychoeducational support that caregivers of persons with Parkinson's disease will likely experience.

   b. Develop a plan for evaluating the support group with a specific emphasis on strategies you will use to gather feedback from group members.

CHAPTER 10

Social Work Practice with Communities: Engagement, Assessment, and Planning

Change will not come if we wait for some other person or some other time. We are the ones we've been waiting for. We are the change that we seek.

Barack Obama, Feb. 5, 2008

Key Questions for Chapter 10

1. What competencies do I need to engage and assess communities? [EPAS 6 and 7]
2. What are the social work practice behaviors that enable me to effectively engage and assess communities? [EPAS 6 and 7]
3. How can I utilize evidence in research-informed practice and practice-informed research to guide engagement and assessment with communities? [EPAS 4]
4. How can I apply social work values and ethics to community engagement and assessment? [EPAS 1]

Many issues that arise in individual, family, and group practice can also be addressed through community practice. Community practice includes social planning, which means planning human services for a geographic community based on resident needs. It also includes community organizing and development work. The Sanchez family members (see www.routledgesw.com//sanchez/engage/casefiles) have a range of challenges that could be the focus of community practice. For example, Celia struggles with low English proficiency, and the family has financial struggles and does not access health care often due to barriers. These struggles may be shared by other families in their community and may be addressed by community practice. Beyond

*just being referred to existing services for their challenges, the family may also ulti-
mately benefit from a community engagement and needs assessment process
(discussed in this chapter) to uncover how common these issues are in the community, and whether there are other issues that need to be addressed community-wide.*

IT IS IN COMMUNITIES THAT PEOPLE FIND identity and meaning for their
lives in their various roles as individuals, parents, children, partners, friends, and
professionals. **Community** is the structure, both tangible and metaphoric, that
supports interaction and connectedness among people over time. The characteristics of the community in which people grow, live, and develop can have important
implications for the resources and opportunities available to them. For example,
growing up in some communities that offer a safe environment and strong schools
helps children grow into secure and well-educated adults with strong prospects for
the future. Communities are the central context of social work practice with all
types of clients: therefore, community practice is an important aspect of generalist
social work.

This chapter examines the concept of community and your relationship to it as
a social work practitioner. It will explore the types of community and the functions
that give community meaning. We will consider methods of inquiry into the study
of community, including community analysis; community needs assessment; and
community asset mapping. Finally, the chapter will consider the need for and
avenues by which to have a global perspective on community practice.

FAMILIAR PERSPECTIVES AND SOME ALTERNATIVES ON COMMUNITY

Encouraging individuals, families, and groups to work to improve their communities is part of social work practice. Sectors such as education, housing, health, recreational opportunities, local businesses, religious/faith communities, and
employment opportunities are important to the quality of life for the residents of a
community. Local relationships, experiences, resources, and opportunities continue
to play an important role in our daily lives, and local residents invest time, energy,
and resources into creating community resources and opportunities that will positively impact their quality of life. For example, local residents and business owners
work hard to maintain and increase property values and to decrease crime in their
neighborhoods. Similarly, residents strive to keep materials that are hazardous to
the environment (e.g., some chemicals and landfills) out of their neighborhoods
and to garner resources to increase the quality of public education in their communities. Challenges and issues compel residents to take action on behalf of their
communities. **Interdependence**—the idea that individuals depend upon on one

another—resonates in practice models with individuals, families, and groups that emphasize health and recovery based on both professional and peer support.

Forces Working against Connections within Communities

Much of contemporary research and literature about community focuses on how the increasingly impersonal and complex nature of U.S. society works against some types of community work (Brueggemann, 2013a). As an example, the forces working against connections within local geographic communities include technology that allows people to share interests and build bonds with people outside of their immediate community and all over the globe and the individualistic character of U.S. culture, which provides less social reinforcement for community involvement than other cultures. Globalization provides another example; it may also work against the development of strong place-based community connections, as corporations and financial capital shift quickly from place to place to find the most profitable locations for business, and workers move to find optimal employment opportunities. Third, the human service system also reinforces society's focus on individualism in its emphasis on the individual and family and the perpetual pursuit of self-fulfillment. Many human service agencies focus on individual and family counseling. Encouraging individuals, families, and groups to work to improve their communities is part of social work practice.

Community Practice and Generalist Practice

Promoting community involvement is important for social workers working with clients at every level. Communities are critical because it is within communities that individuals live their lives, and communities are the formal conduits through which resources; formal and informal systems; and political, social, and economic forces shape individuals, families, and neighborhoods. Communities therefore influence our experiences and the ability of social workers to affect outcomes for their clients. Even when social workers never go outside of the traditional one-to-one social work relationship, the success of their efforts depends, in large part, on the nature and responsiveness of the clients' communities. For example, a community's overall capacity to provide decent, affordable housing for single persons who receive public assistance will impact a young, low-income client with two children who is seeking shelter. If this client asks for your help finding housing, you need to know about the resources for shelter, transitional housing, and low-income housing available in her community, as well as resources to combat discrimination if she suspects that she is denied housing illegally (if, for example, she is denied rental housing because the landlord will not rent to single mothers who receive public assistance). Other factors to consider surrounding her housing choices may include employment, schools, child care, the quality and quantity of afterschool programs, and the existence of a community center. She may be interested in information about the overall safety of the community, including the rate of crime, the proximity of a former partner who may pose safety concerns, and the presence of specific gangs in the area. To practice competently, social workers need knowledge of community resources and skills to address challenges related to those resources; the entities that make decisions about resources; and ways to secure resources for clients. A social worker also needs to know about the various dimensions of a community in order to be an effective catalyst for change in that community. Skills honed working with individuals, groups, families, and organizations are vital to community practice, and skills honed working with communities are important to every other type of client.

Working with communities requires mastery of many social work competencies and behaviors (CSWE, 2015). For example, social workers must be able to respond to the contexts that shape practice [EPAS 7] by being proactive and engaging in community work that will seek to prevent problems and unnecessary challenges from occurring. As in work with other types of clients (individuals, families, and groups), social workers in community practice must also employ ethical principles [EPAS 1] and cultural competence [EPAS 2]. Community practice uses research-informed and evidence-based practice [EPAS 4] to advance human rights and economic justice [EPAS 3]. Lastly, like practice with all other types of clients, community practice utilizes the change process (i.e., engagement, assessment, intervention, termination, and evaluation) [EPAS 7, 8, 9, and 10]. This chapter will explore many of these competencies and will discuss the practice behaviors associated with them. We will also consider the different types of communities, the nature of community functions, and ways to understand a community.

DEFINITIONS AND TYPES OF COMMUNITY

Several types of community are discussed in the social work literature. This section describes three of the most common—spatial, social, and political—as well as personal communities (Chaskin, 2013).

Spatial Community

One type of community is a geographic entity, such as a town, city, small neighborhood, or college dormitory. These **spatial communities** are structures of connectedness based on a physical location. In some cases, these communities have clear, physical boundaries, such as a river, mountain, gate, wall, or a legally defined boundary. In other cases, **stakeholders**—those who have an interest in community affairs, such as county or city officials, or neighborhood leaders—agree upon their boundaries. People also construct cognitive maps of their communities that inform their relationship to their physical space, movement within their spatial community, and their social interaction. These boundaries may provide safety and security for community members, but they may also be a means of excluding others. The degree to which community residents perceive themselves as community members depends on many dimensions, but access to the community's benefits is among the most influential. Those residents of a community who do not have access to community benefits such as community centers, public libraries, and other resources may not feel personally affiliated with the communities in which they live. In large spatial communities, such as New York City, there are likely to be many smaller communities within the larger community. Spatial communities of all sizes can be diverse. For example, Jackson Heights, New York, a community within the borough of Queens with 175,000 residents, is one of the most diverse communities in the U.S. and the world, with 167 spoken languages (New York Times, 2015).

Social Communities

Groups that share common interests, concerns, norms, identity, or interactions and share a similar sense of belonging are **social communities**. One type of social community, a community of identity, relates more to affiliations than to a location. Student communities, Asian communities, lesbian communities, veterans' communities, and skateboard communities are all examples of communities of identity. As in spatial communities, members attach different meanings to their communities and affiliate with those communities to varying extents over time. For example, the Jewish community may play a significant lifelong role for some but have less significance for others, or a community of skateboarders may play a very important role in members' lives for several years but fade in importance as they reach adulthood. Some social workers focus their careers on specific communities of identity, such as women who experience intimate partner violence or those who have lost a partner to Alzheimer's disease or related dementia. Social workers may develop interest in a particular community of identity based on their personal experiences or early professional experiences. While social communities have the potential to function as exclusionary associations, they can also offer members a powerful sense of connection and commitment.

People are often part of more than one type of community. For example, a person may be affiliated with a spatial community in which they live, a worship community, an online community of gamers, a community of yoga teachers, her/his dorm, and a community of undergraduate students. A social community consists of a collection of both spatial and social communities, where people can build a sense of belonging. They often serve to provide meaning to one's identity. These unique arrangements of place and nonplace communities are networks within which one interacts, and they serve to integrate one's personal and professional lives. Social workers may be interested in clients' social communities because social communities provide socialization and resources, such as helping networks (formal and informal), that may be helpful for clients facing a crisis or challenges. Social communities can also provide cross-cultural dimensions that aid in a wider world view.

© vm

Political Communities

Political communities serve as venues through which people participate in democratic governance and promote social change through community organizing and political mobilization. The spatial community, as a formal political unit, and the social community, through which people interact, are both incorporated in a political community since they can both serve political functions. Efforts to promote democracy using political communities focus on increasing the capacities of both geographic and social communities to practice self-determination and be involved in governing. Social workers may utilize the political community of clients to encourage civic engagement through attending neighborhood meetings, supporting candidates for office, meeting with elected officials to share ideas about local needs, voting, and being involved in grassroots community organizing efforts.

COMMUNITY FUNCTIONS

A traditional view of community holds that communities perform certain necessary functions for their residents or members, including the following (Streeter, 2013):

- *The production, distribution, and consumption of goods and services:* This may include basic needs like food, clothing, shelter, health care, and employment. Communities provide adequate wages so people can access goods and services.

- *The transmission of knowledge, social values, customs, and behavior patterns:* This socialization process guides how residents view themselves, others, and their rights and responsibilities. Both formal institutions, such as schools and faith communities, and informal institutions, such as friends and peer groups, can be involved in this function.

- *The maintenance of conformity to community norms through social control:* Formal governmental entities, such as law enforcement and court systems, enforce laws, rules and regulations. Informal systems of enforcement, such as schools, families, peers, and organized neighborhood watches, reinforce community standards. Patterns of service provisions that regulate access to resources (e.g., eligibility guidelines for local food pantries) also serve as mechanisms of social control.

- *Social participation through formal and informal groups:* Interaction with others through groups, associations, and organizations provides social outlets and helps build natural helping and support networks. People engage in social participation when they join sports leagues, volunteer, vote, attend Parent Teacher Association (PTA) meetings, and attend local music festivals.

- *The provision of mutual support:* Families, friends, neighbors, and volunteers provide aid, support one another, and assist individuals and families to solve problems independent of professional help. Due to the complexities of modern society, the work of human service professionals, such as social workers, often supplements this function.

UNDERSTANDING A COMMUNITY

Given their complex nature, understanding the many ways that communities can be conceptualized is imperative before moving into the change process of engagement, assessment, intervention, and termination and evaluation. We will examine communities as social systems; as ecological systems; as centers for power and conflict; and from two contemporary perspectives: the strengths, empowerment, and resiliency perspectives and the postmodern perspective.

Community as a Social System

General systems theory offers a helpful framework with which to analyze and understand communities. General systems theory posits that a system, such as a community, is composed of multiple intersecting components that relate to one other and that are also part of larger systems, such as a larger community. Some communities are part of subsystems that perform specialized functions for the larger system—the community as a whole (for example, a community of business owners within a larger geographic community). Through community assessments (in the "Assessing Communities" section), social workers can critically assess the extent to which subsystems, such as the function of mutual support or the business subsystem within a community, meet the community's needs. If necessary, they can then advocate for higher functioning to improve the subsystem (Netting, Kettner, McMurtry, & Thomas, 2017; Streeter, 2013).

Community as an Ecological System

The ecosystems perspective focuses on the interdependence of people and their environment in our understanding of communities. It emphasizes the spatial organization of community resources, the relationship of these resources to one another and to groups of people, and the corresponding social and economic consequences. For example, a major road or highway bisecting a community can have implications for the social organization and economics of the community. It may bring in more customers for some businesses and shut down others. The social organization implications of the road include the possibilities that individuals and groups may interact more or less with one other. The ecosystems perspective is also concerned with competition for resources: one or more communities may compete with each other, or groups within a community may compete. For example, competition for land is common in many communities, as some groups want to develop land for residences and businesses, while others would like to keep land available for parks, community centers, and hiking trails, and still others may advocate to keep land devoted to family-based agriculture. The political or economic dominance of communities over one another or of one group over another group within a community often results in decreased access to resources for some groups that have less power and has consequences for the social interactions within a community. A group's dominance can ensure its access to better schools, employment, health care facilities, and public services such as police and fire protection. The ecological systems perspective can therefore help in understanding a hierarchical, uneven power structure in a community. Other related concepts including segregation (i.e., the isolation of groups within a community); centralization (i.e., concentration of resources in one part of a community); and succession (i.e., the movement of groups of people into and out of areas of a community) are also useful in analyzing communities (Netting et al., 2017; Streeter, 2013). These concepts help explain the ways in which populations move and settle in various areas of communities and why resources differ among particular areas of communities.

Communities as Centers of Power and Conflict

Political and social dynamics and conflicts are powerful forces in communities. Power significantly influences opportunities and constraints for community members. Often, the interests of one segment of a community clash with the interests of another segment, and a struggle can emerge. Applying conflict and power theories can create conditions that promote change (Weil & Ohmer, 2013). The following theories assist in our understanding of the community as a setting for power and conflict (Hardina, 2002). Individually or together, the theories can help explain power and conflict within communities.

Power dependency theory focuses on the dynamics associated with a community's dependent relationships with the external entities that supply needed resources. The effects of these dynamics can be dramatic. For example, a community's dependence on a funding source with close ties to a large retail chain may influence its decisions about promoting small, locally owned businesses. Therefore, the small businesses may go out of business due to the community's dependence on the interests of a funding source.

Conflict theory views the community as divided into influential ("haves") and noninfluential ("have-nots") groups that compete for limited resources. This theory further assumes that the influential group has power over the noninfluential group and that dimensions of diversity play a central role in oppression. For example, people with greater income and political connections may have more influence over decisions that affect the community than those who are of lower income and fewer connections. Therefore, community decisions may favor those with more income and political connections over those with less of both.

Resource mobilization theory focuses on the conditions needed to promote change through community practice. Large-scale community change occurs more easily when groups that feel excluded from a decision-making process come together and protest their exclusion as a group. These groups can use an appealing message and an inclusive structure to attract more members. For example, delegates to the 2016 Republican National Convention from all over the U.S. who did not endorse Donald Trump as the Republican Party candidate for President came together at the Convention around the message of "Never Trump" and staged a protest.

Taken together, the theories just discussed inform the social work profession's thinking about the community as a setting in which power and control play crucial roles. Groups within a community vie for power and control to implement change that will benefit their interests, even if the change may oppress others within the community. Communities can bring about change through rational planning and collaborative efforts, or through confrontation, efforts to build power, and negotiation. Dimensions of diversity, such as race, socioeconomic status, and ethnicity, as well as special interests, such as area of the community, can be driving factors in community conflicts, and underscore the need for cultural competence in community practice. Viewing the community as a center for power and conflict can help social workers assess the community power structure and understand the process of community decision-making, the reasons behind it and their roles in community processes. Social workers may also use this lens to learn more about ways in which marginalized groups are oppressed in communities and how powerful forces in communities maintain their power (Netting et al., 2017; Streeter, 2013).

Contemporary Perspectives for Community Practice

Now that we have a general understanding of communities, we turn to a discussion of the strengths, empowerment, and resiliency perspectives and the postmodern perspective. These perspectives move us toward a deeper understanding of community and toward assessing communities.

Strengths, Empowerment, and Resiliency Perspectives   As previously mentioned, the strengths perspective, originally presented by Saleebey (2013), focuses on identifying possibilities and assets of individuals, groups, and communities, rather than on their deficits and problems. It may be challenging to apply the strengths perspective in communities that have few resources. As in all communities, identifying strengths in these communities can help them empower themselves. Assisting them to recognize the resources they possess helps them develop the power to effect change. The recognition of resources can lead to resiliency and can increase the potential for successful problem solving. For example, the strengths perspective can encourage leaders in communities with large plots of vacant land and boarded-up homes to think about the land and homes as valuable assets, rather than as problems. Perhaps the vacant land could be used for community gardens or for greenhouses for small businesses. A community's strengths also include the skills and talents of its residents. Later in this chapter, we will discuss community asset mapping as a means to implement the strengths, empowerment, and resiliency perspectives (Kingsley, Coulton & Pettit, 2014; Netting et al., 2017; Hillier & Culhane, 2013).

Community in a Postmodern Perspective   The postmodern perspective assumes that knowledge is socially constructed and that multiple "truths" exist, depending on a person's perspective. Postmodern approaches, including social construction and critical social construction, invite the examination of the cultural assumptions that underlie many arrangements of power and politics. These approaches tend to be critical of assumptions or theories that claim absolute or authoritative truth. Social workers using postmodern approaches are interested in assumptions, explanations, and causes of perceived problems in the community and in examining situations from multiple perspectives. For example, social workers using the postmodern perspective would seek out different perspectives and assumptions surrounding the presence of undocumented immigrants in a community to learn about various community members' views and assume that there could be multiple "truths" about how welcome they have been and how they are viewed by other community members. They would also be interested in the cultural symbols and norms a community uses, such as the ways in which the social structures of specific populations are organized, and the cultural symbols used to signify those structures (Weil & Ohmer, 2013).

ENGAGING COMMUNITIES [EPAS 6]

This section will discuss traditional and contemporary perspectives on community work and the ways in which these perspectives can inform engagement and assessment with communities. Traditional and contemporary perspectives on community allow us to use different lenses to understand the dynamics and decision-making processes in communities. The perspectives also help explain the sources of and barriers to change in ways that inform the change process (i.e., engagement, assessment, intervention, and termination and evaluation with communities).

Engagement of Communities

In their work in communities, social workers can approach engagement, the first step in the change process, in many different ways. Engagement with communities involves working with clients and institutions on behalf of entire communities. Many of the engagement and assessment skills we discussed in previous chapters are helpful in work with communities. Active listening skills, for example, are as useful in working in community practice as they are in work with individuals, families, and groups and organizations.

Social work with communities begins with a focus on challenges and opportunities. For example, a social worker working for a community-based education program attached to a local public school may discover that community residents lack adequate employment opportunities. Alternatively, social workers employed by a local or state correctional system may learn about an opportunity to apply for funding to prevent juvenile crime and engage community members to plan and write a grant to benefit the local community. Social workers may also engage in community practice through their work with a particular population. A social worker in a health care setting may learn about a lack of respite services available for the family caregivers of older adults. The social worker may help the caregivers organize themselves to approach a potential funder—such as local, state, or federal legislators or a local foundation—to advocate for funding for respite care. Social workers also engage with communities based primarily on setting. For example, a social worker employed by an elementary school may learn that a local factory is dumping hazardous waste materials in a nearby neighborhood, endangering the health of the children of the community. The social worker may work to engage local community leaders to conduct community-wide meetings and/or communicate with appropriate decision-makers and work toward a resolution to protect the health of the children. Social workers become engaged with communities in many ways, either through formal employment or volunteering at the community level or through involvement with a challenge/opportunity, population, or setting they learned about through their primary professional roles with individual, family, group, or organizations (Netting et al., 2017).

Engagement with community members can take place in a wide variety of ways. Often different types of groups are used to learn more about community issues. For example, using the Sanchez family, a school-based group of parents may be formed to try to engage parents and families about improvements needed in the school for children with disabilities. As part of the group process, many issues may emerge, including the difficulty in accessing primary health care in the community. With skilled facilitation that encourages members to share their stories and build group solidarity, groupwork can also facilitate engagement in wider community issues (Hardina, 2013).

Interprofessional Engagement Community engagement often includes interacting with institutions and professionals that provide resources or potential resources, make decisions for, or have influence in a community. Engaging institutions and professionals that specialize in health, public health, mental health, counseling, psychology, urban planning, theology, education, business, and/or law is common in community practice. Professionals with these backgrounds work in a variety of roles, such as business leader, politician, community planner, program manager, faith leader, and others. Interprofessional collaboration skills, including such interpersonal skills as active listening and building trust, are needed to effectively engage these professionals and their institutions. Social workers also need a strong understanding of social work values and ethics to guide them in collaboration. Other professions often have different values and ethics, or codes of ethics; therefore, interprofessional collaboration requires a curiosity about the differences between and among the knowledge, skills, and values of various professions, as well as a strong social work identity. In the engagement process, the goal is to build relationships useful for working together on a shared vision within a climate that is trusting and capable of resolving conflicts productively and professionally (Hardina, 2013).

For example, a social worker who is facilitating the school-based group of parents that includes the Sanchez family may work with other professionals, such as those with legal and educational degrees, along with the parents, to pressure the school district to provide more resources for children with disabilities. Throughout the process, the social worker should be mindful of the National Association of Social Workers' (NASW) *Code of Ethics* (NASW, 2008) to guide her in the advocacy work and should be aware that those with legal and educational background may be guided by different professional values and ethics.

ASSESSING COMMUNITIES [EPAS 7]

The assessment process in community work often occurs in tandem with the engagement process, and it can involve several different techniques. The following discussion will explore two prominent techniques: comprehensive community-based analysis and a community needs assessment. Community asset mapping will also be discussed as a strengths-based community assessment technique.

Comprehensive Community-Based Analysis

Social workers in different settings and jobs need an understanding of the overall community in which they serve clients, as well as an understanding of the specific population they serve and the primary challenges that population faces. Understanding communities involves learning about their structures and how they function. Developing an accurate knowledge base about a community can lead to more effective assessments and interventions with individuals, families, groups, organizations, and communities.

When you learn about key aspects of a particular community, you discover its unique characteristics, including its strengths, challenges, and history and the concerns of its residents. You can use the answers to the questions suggested next to create a formal document for an organization or community or in an informal fashion.

One useful tool for understanding the connections among aspects of a community is the **sociogram**. A sociogram (similar to an ecomap) is a visual tool for assessing community connections and dynamics. It is important to note which subsystems interact and the nature of the interaction. It is also important to note which subsystems do not yet have any interactions so that you can consider potential linkages. The use of a sociogram can lead to understanding both isolated and well-connected aspects and the nature of those connections. The focal system is considered the "client," that is, the system that is the focus of intervention, as displayed in Exhibit 10.1.

To achieve an overall understanding of a community, the following major community domains must be explored during a community assessment (Netting et al., 2017) using assessment techniques discussed later in this chapter. The following provides a guide for domains for a spatial community:

- *Physical setting:* The physical setting of a community includes the geography (e.g., presence of water or flat or hilly land), main geographical boundaries and natural barriers, and the degree to which communities are integrated into or isolated from surrounding neighborhoods. For example, is the community near a downtown area, a vital entertainment or shopping district, or a medical complex? Do the streets dead-end or go through to other communities?

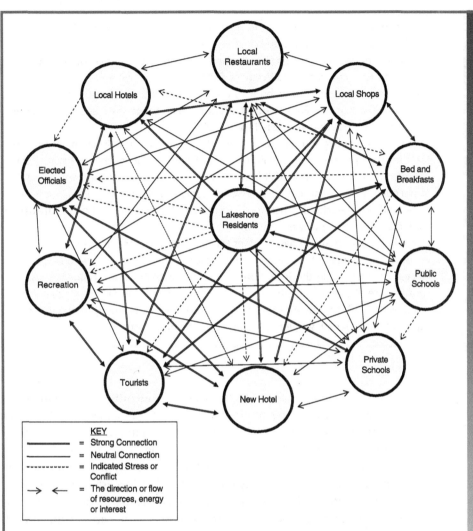

EXHIBIT 10.1

Lakeshore Sociogram

Lakeshore is a town in the northern part of the United States. It is a popular tourist destination in the warmer months because of the beautiful lake and beaches that surround it. Its many restaurants and shopping districts prosper in those warm months. As evident from the sociogram, the relationships among the various entities in the town vary. A few are described in the following list:

1. The restaurant owners have a strong positive relationship with the local shops because the shops recommend the restaurants to tourists. The residents also are supportive of local shops, and they enjoy a strong positive relationship.

2. There are many thriving small bed and breakfasts and locally owned hotels, but this year a large, high-rise hotel is scheduled to be built in the town. This will be the first hotel of this kind in Lakeshore, and there are mixed feelings about what this hotel

EXHIBIT 10.1

Continued

will bring the town. Therefore, the relationship between the hotel, the bed and breakfasts, and smaller local hotels is stressed/conflicted.

3. Due to the tourism industry at the lake, there are many recreational opportunities in the town such as miniature golf courses and lake/water activities, but residents get upset in the tourist months when they are very crowded and increase their prices. Therefore, the relationship between the residents and the tourists, and between the residents and recreation, is stressed/conflicted.

4. There are both public and private schools in Lakeshore. The public school leadership feels that the private schools drain resources from the public schools, because the parents of the private school children are not as supportive of campaigns for additional public funds for schools, and fewer students in the public schools means fewer state funds for the schools. Therefore, the relationship between the two is stressed/conflicted, with a one-way energy flow.

5. Elected officials voted and passed plans for the addition of the new, high-rise hotel in town. The owners of the new hotel therefore have a positive relationship with elected officials, while the local hotels, bed and breakfasts, and residents have a conflicted relationship with the elected officials. While some residents believe the hotel will benefit the town's small businesses and overall economy, most prefer to support locally owned, smaller hotels and bed and breakfasts.

- *History:* The history of a community includes the identity of the population(s) that originally settled the community, when it was settled, and the major historical events that shaped the community. Additionally, you might also consider the ways in which the architecture and layout of the community reflect early inhabitants and whether the community history impacts the current dynamics of community functioning. Consider asking the following: What is the history of different populations settling in the community? Have transitions occurred? If so, have these transitions been marked with conflict?

- *Demographics of the population:* Knowledge of the current population of the community, as well as the well-defined and informal subpopulations with their own distinct cultures within the community, is very important. Questions to consider include: What are the largest population groups in the community? Can the community be characterized as homogeneous or heterogeneous, considering different variables?

- *Economic system:* The economic system includes employment for community residents; types, number, and industry of large businesses; the presence of small, locally owned businesses; the presence of stores that residents can utilize for their basic needs, such as grocery stores and co-ops, farmers' markets, clothing stores, and hardware stores; the rate of employment in the community; and the type of transportation available to community residents. You may ask: Who are the major employers? Where are the jobs located? Are the jobs conveniently located to the unemployed or underemployed? What is the employers' relationships to the community? What are the needs of the employers?

- *Political system:* An awareness of a community's political system provides helpful information about who makes key decisions affecting the community. To understand the community, it's important to learn about all types of elected officials who have the authority to make decisions for the community. It's also important to seek information about the level of political activity in the community (for example, by looking for bumper stickers and yard signs). Information about the degree to which the business community is organized into a business association and involved in politics is also helpful. You might inquire about the degree to which human service systems are involved in the local political system, the degree to which the political system is organized and connected to community residents, and the level of activity of local politicians.

- *Social characteristics:* Social characteristics include the demographics of the residents in terms of social class, race, ethnicity, age, and other dimensions of diversity, as well as places where people gather. Questions to consider regarding the social characteristics of a community include: Do new residents and visitors consider the community friendly or unfriendly? Are there many places of worship? What size are the congregations and which denominations are present? Are there formal or informal meeting places besides places of worship (i.e., coffee shops, meeting halls, clubs, associations, etc.?) What is the condition of the parks or recreational areas? What are housing conditions in terms of upkeep, quality, and the proportion of rental versus family owned? Does it vary by neighborhood? Is housing for sale? Is the for-sale housing dispersed or clustered? Is there evidence of construction and home repair? Are there strong institutions in the community related to social needs?

- *Human service system:* The human service system includes education, health, and social services of all types. Questions to consider include the following: What kinds of public and private schools are located in the community? Investigate their educational quality, physical condition, and funding sources. What kinds of voluntary agencies are located in the community? How available are services to residents? How well organized are the organizations within the community? Are professional networks in the community strong or weak?

- *Values, beliefs, and traditions:* While observing and building relationships to learn about values, beliefs, and traditions, consider what community residents value. Are differences based on race, ethnicity, and sections of the community, or on another dimension of diversity? Do members of the community celebrate specific traditions that may be unique to that community or to a sub-population of the community?

- *Evidence of oppression and discrimination:* A social justice perspective requires social workers to look for oppression and discrimination within the community, and/or from other communities. Questions to consider include: Is there a history of oppression and discrimination in the community (such as separate recreational facilities, housing patterns that suggest discrimination, and/or school enrollment and quality patterns that suggest discrimination)? Are there current patterns of discrimination and oppression?

Community Needs Assessment

A community **needs assessment** is a formal process for identifying unmet community needs, placing needs in order of priorities, and planning to target resources to solve problems. A needs assessment can be conducted to focus on the overall functioning of a community. Alternatively, many social workers begin to learn about a community through the focus of the predominant population they are serving, or because of a specific community challenge such as poor quality housing, gangs, or truancy. A focus on a particular community of identity or population and to assess the degree to which the social services system meets their particular needs is another way to do a needs assessment. The process concentrates on the gap between needs and resources. The findings inform the planning process for specific social work community interventions and are often more practical than comprehensive studies. Ideally, community analyses and needs assessments are integrated processes rather than an either/or choice.

The overall process of a community needs assessment can be compared to a research project. As with a research project, the goals of the sponsor of the study may shape the purpose of the assessment. For example, a social service organization may want more information about the needs of the older adult population in a community, but may not be as interested as you are, as a researcher, in examining the growing LGBTQ older adult population. This difference of interest may require a negotiation about the needs assessment process, tools, data sources, and reporting. Regardless of the sponsor, the social worker should use the following six recommended steps to conduct the needs assessment (Mulroy, 2013);

1. Reviewing the evidence
2. Assessing local knowledge
3. Selecting study methods
4. Conducting the study
5. Processing and studying the data
6. Reporting the findings

The principles of evidence-based practice, as discussed in the next section, should guide the research process.

Using Evidence-Based Practice in Community Practice [EPAS 4]   Following the steps of evidence-based practice, social workers begin community practice with a review of relevant research literature about similar communities and theories of change to guide the design of the needs assessment. The next step is to clarify the unit of analysis for the study, whether that is a specific population, a geographic area, a particular challenge—such as homelessness or a combination of units. Consultation with community members, the sponsor, and other interested parties about the current evidence; local knowledge; research design; study methods; analysis; and the structure of the report can help achieve the highest-quality needs assessment (Mulroy, 2013).

Social workers can use the same research methods they used for comprehensive community analyses when they perform comprehensive needs assessments or needs assessments focused on particular populations or challenges. An understanding of each approach can help determine the most appropriate evidence-based method(s) to use in a particular situation. In the following discussion, we consider several sources of data gathering, including observation, census and administrative data, interviews with key informants, focus groups, community forums, and survey data (Royse, Staton-Tindall, Badger, & Webster, 2009; Ohmer, Sobek, Teixeira, Wallace, & Shapiro, 2013). We go on to discuss the use of maps to visually display data and community asset mapping.

Community Needs Assessment Process   Social workers are involved in community needs assessments for many reasons, including seeking new resources and support for a program, targeting a program to best meet community needs, or simply getting to know the community in order to better serve individuals, families, and groups. Funders considering a request to back a program will often ask the agency or institution making the request to justify the proposed program or services by demonstrating community need. Policymakers can use the findings of a community assessment to modify policy. For example, if, due to increased demand, a food pantry must consider changing its eligibility policy, the program can use data from a community assessment to determine which population has the highest unmet need. Organizations that wish to improve services for a particular group of clients may undertake a needs assessment to learn about, for example, the unmet needs of single men in the community. Finally, social workers may become involved in a needs assessment to establish or strengthen partnerships. For instance, a homeless shelter may increasingly encounter children who are medically fragile. The staff of the organization may conduct a community needs assessment to collect data about the health needs of homeless and near-homeless children so that they can present that information when they approach local health providers to develop a service partnership.

Sources of Data for Community Needs Assessments

There are many potential sources of data, including primary and secondary sources of both quantitative and qualitative data, for a community needs assessment. Some of the most common and useful forms include observation, service statistics and previous studies, census data, administrative data, interviews, focus groups, community forums, and survey data. Several of these types, as well as guidelines for making decisions about methods, are discussed next (Mulroy, 2013; Netting et al., 2017; Iowa State University Extension and Outreach, 2016; Ohmer et al., 2013).

Observation   The purpose of observation is to collect information about community processes and events as they occur. Observers can attend popular community events such as free concerts, plays, and/or political rallies to notice aspects of community life including ethnic composition, geographical divisions, and apparent patterns. For example, an observer may detect the presence or absence of late-night street activity, the number of older adults visible in a community, the number of children playing outside during school hours, and the number of young adults hanging out on the streets during the day. Other aspects to notice include interpersonal relationships, patterns and styles of how residents relate to one another, and residents' relationships to the community space. An observer may simply witness events, or she or he may actually participate in the community activities being observed.

As a nonparticipant, an observer may walk around and/or attend events within the community in places like the city hall, coffee shops, community centers, busy parks, commercial strips, fairs and markets, and schools. Using this method, the observer can gather notes about observations, items in local newspapers, pamphlets that describe community resources, local maps, local directories, and historical markers.

Participant observation occurs when an observer joins in community events and interacts with local residents. For example, a participant observer could learn about a community by eating at local establishments and interacting with patrons and staff. During the interaction, a participant observer asks questions from the perspective of a respectful learner and avoids taking the stance of an expert or a change agent.

Service Statistics and Previous Studies   Data from local human service organizations may be helpful for the needs assessment. Such data can include rate of utilization of services, types of services provided, waiting list information, and caseload data. Data from other types of organizations, such as businesses, faith communities, neighborhood groups, and youth organizations, can also be helpful. This information may be available through a variety of sources including annual reports, public data available on the Internet, a contact person at an organization, or an elected or appointed community official. Similarly, previous studies about the origins of community problems, such as studies from the public health department or community organizations, may be helpful.

Use of Census Data   The U.S. Census Bureau conducts a national census every ten years, gathering extensive demographic information about people living in the United States. The Census Bureau also conducts the American Community Survey each year, collecting some data from a sample of residents. A variety of databases and websites, some of which are very user friendly, provide access to census data. These resources allow you to access data at small geographic levels within broader communities.

Administrative Data   School districts, public assistance offices, child welfare offices, public health agencies, and police departments make administrative data available to the public. Administrative data can help illuminate a wide variety of community issues including local academic performance, truancy, child abuse, rate and prevalence of sexually transmitted disease, teen pregnancy, crime, and other issues. These data are typically available at the zip code level. The data may provide information about the topic you are interested in directly or indirectly. For example, the drop-out rate and teen pregnancy rate together may serve as a proxy for the number of young people who drop out of high school because of the demands of parenting, which may be data not directly collected by any institution or organization. See Exhibit 10.2 for ideas for sources of census and administrative data.

Other Data   Many state, local, and human service organizations provide data about the clients they serve and/or community-level data on populations or issues. These data may be publically available, or organizations may be willing to make them available at the social worker's request. These organizations may collect data to ensure that their services are meeting the community needs that are the highest priority, or they may be required to collect data in order to retain funding. The data may be collected across the community, or it may be only a sample.

Mapped Data   Mapping can help to establish relationships among different sets of data. **Geographic information systems (GIS)** are enhancing the usefulness of data that is attached to a specific geographic location. GIS utilize the geocoding of spatially mapped data to allow researchers to identify spatial patterns among challenges and resources (Hillier & Culhane, 2013). Using GIS, census and other types of data may be visually combined onto one map. For example, as Exhibit 10.3 demonstrates, plotting both minority populations and home purchase loans on the same map can add to the depth and complexity of a needs analysis and provide even more useful data. This map can illustrate the possible relationship between subprime minority populations and home purchase loans in the St. Louis, Missouri region, informing a local task force's efforts to encourage minority homeownership. GIS also offer the possibility of adding more layers of data, such as income, to this map, so that

EXHIBIT 10.2 *Sample of Sources for Census and Administrative Data*	National Center for Health Statistics	This Center for Disease Control and Prevention site provides access to information regarding recent health surveys and data collections on vital statistics.
	Bureau of Labor Statistics	The Bureau of Labor Statistics site, updated by the Department of Labor, provides FTP links to download raw data on Local Area Unemployment Statistics and Geographical Profiles.
	County and City Data Books	County and City Books, from the U.S. Census Bureau, provide information about individual cities and counties in the United States by year.
	FedStats	This site includes a listing of approximately 100 federal agencies (e.g., National Center for Health Statistics) with links to information on statistics and other resources.
	U.S. Census Bureau	This site provides the most up-to-date information from the U.S. Census Bureau. The "QuickFacts" feature allows you to search statistical information about a particular state.
	Bureau of Justice Statistics	This site contains information on crime, criminal offenders, victims of crime, and the operation of justice systems at all levels of U.S. government.
	Statistical Abstract	This U.S. Census site provides a summary of statistics on the social, political, and economic organization of the United States.
	National Neighborhood Indicators Partnership	This network of the Urban Institute and 36 cities supports the development and use of neighborhood indicators across many domains. Each partner city maintains neighborhood-level indicators across topic areas.
	DataPlace	DataPlace is a free resource for housing, economic, and demographic data. It includes guides and analysis to help users understand data sources and interpret indicators.
	The Census Bureau's Data Ferret	The Data Ferret allows users to map census data for specific geographic locations.
	The Centers for Disease Control and Prevention	The Centers for Disease Control and Prevention site provides available health-related data, such as mortality, births, and sexually transmitted morbidity, for specific locations.
	Annie E. Casey Foundation Data Center: Kids Count	The Kids Count website provides access to hundreds of measures of child well-being on a national and state level.

Sources: St. Louis University Pius XII Library (n.d.); Ohmer et al., 2013

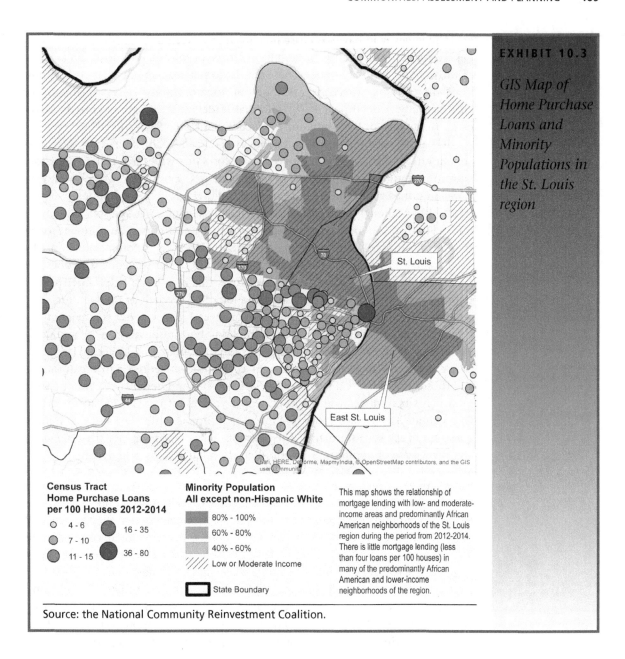

EXHIBIT 10.3

GIS Map of Home Purchase Loans and Minority Populations in the St. Louis region

Census Tract Home Purchase Loans per 100 Houses 2012-2014

○ 4 - 6   ● 16 - 35
○ 7 - 10   ● 36 - 80
● 11 - 15

Minority Population All except non-Hispanic White

■ 80% - 100%
■ 60% - 80%
■ 40% - 60%
▨ Low or Moderate Income
▭ State Boundary

This map shows the relationship of mortgage lending with low- and moderate-income areas and predominantly African American neighborhoods of the St. Louis region during the period from 2012-2014. There is little mortgage lending (less than four loans per 100 houses) in many of the predominantly African American and lower-income neighborhoods of the region.

Source: the National Community Reinvestment Coalition.

the task force might study possible relationships among race, home purchase loans, and income.

Interviews with Key Informants   Although any person with some level of knowledge can be an informant, relationships with key informants who can act as guides to the inner workings of community life can be particularly useful. **Key informants**

are individuals who have expertise in a given area, such as the history of the business sector of a community, or who have formal or informal influence on an issue or with a population of interest. These may be formal leaders (e.g., mayors, business association chairs, executive directors of organizations, clergy members, or alderman/city council people), or informal leaders (e.g., longtime citizens' advocates, volunteers for the community association, or gang leaders).

If you are seeking information about systemic and political barriers to solving community problems, carefully select key informants who have extensive history with the community, population, or issue studied. Choosing a key informant who is well informed about the institutions involved in shaping the community, population and/or challenge, both past and present, is also helpful. This person can provide information about both the day-to-day dynamics and the past and present forces that impact those dynamics. If you are just seeking a key informant to learn the lived reality of community life, you may want to consider someone who does not necessarily have the qualities mentioned here, but who has a helpful perspective to provide to the data collection, such as a longtime resident or the matriarch of a family who has been in the community for several generations. This type of key informant may be able to provide information about residents' lived community experience, values and beliefs, oppression, and discrimination. To locate key informants, begin by approaching leaders of community meetings and organizations and those quoted in local news sources like websites and newspapers. Your first key informants may direct you to other people you might contact for an interview. Quick Guide 31 provides a structure for a key informant interview and examples of questions to ask key informants. The questions relate to informants' personal views and their sense of significant community facts, relationships, and dynamics.

Focus Groups   A moderated discussion among a group of people who share a common characteristic, or a **focus group**, is another method of collecting data about a community. The common characteristic among participants might be that they are enrolled in the same program, living in the same community, or caring for an older adult. In focus groups, you can ask questions about the issues that are most important to participants, the reasons they find something challenging, and how a challenge exists in a community. You can ask participants about their attitudes, beliefs, and opinions. Focus groups are an inexpensive, flexible, and efficient way to collect data. The open discussion allows participants to build their thoughts and ideas off of comments from others. Quick Guide 32 provides more detailed guidance for focus groups.

Community Forums   When people meet in a public space to exchange and debate information and to consider and critique strategies, they are engaging in a **community forum**. In these forums, community residents can learn about an issue, state their preferences, and/or present their demands. Forums can be organized to introduce an idea for solving a problem or debating an issue. Forums may be open to all community residents or to a select number of persons chosen based on specific criteria. Quick Guide 33 provides in-depth discussion of community forums.

QUICK GUIDE 31   GUIDE TO KEY INFORMANT INTERVIEWS

General Guidelines

Based on your previous research about the community, prepare a few general questions prior to conducting the interview.

The format should be flexible enough to allow for more depth on some questions, depending on the informant's answers.

Prepare for a 30–40 minute interview, with the option for a longer interview if the key informant is amenable.

Educate yourself ahead of time with available census and administrative data, prior needs assessments, observation, and/or other available data.

Interview Format

Practice the interview skills discussed in Chapter 3, such as empathy, genuineness, and warmth.

At the beginning of the interview, develop rapport by engaging the key informant, define the purpose of the interview and agree on the time allotted for the interview. Provide the key informant with the interview format (such as the topics and number of questions, the issue of confidentiality, etc.) and information about what you will do with the data you collect. If you want to tape the interview, obtain the informant's consent to do so.

At the end of the interview, consider asking the key informant to share any other pertinent information that may not have come up.

Questions

Consider funneling the questions (i.e., moving from general questions to specific).

Avoid using jargon. Avoid double-barreled, leading, long, and negative questions.

Ask about the strengths of and challenges to the community.

Ask about the internal structure of the community (i.e., organizations and decision-makers within the community) as well as the external structure (i.e., organizations and decision-makers outside of the community).

Sample Questions for Key Informants

- Tell me a little bit about your history with the community. Why have you chosen this community in which to live/work/volunteer?
- What are the advantages to living/working/volunteering in this community? What are the main challenges?
  What are the organized groups in this community? How do these groups relate to one another?
- Who is significantly involved in community affairs in this community? To which groups, if any, do they belong? Are they elected or appointed to any official positions? Who are key decision-makers in this community? Who influences them?
- Who has been involved in efforts to make changes to or advocate for the community?
- What were those efforts? What were the results of those efforts?
- What groups or types of individuals is the community not serving? In what ways?
- What groups or individuals are not involved in community affairs? What might explain their lack of engagement?

Key Informant Interview

© CREATISTA

Survey Data   Surveys are a common method of collecting data for community practice. Survey data can help researchers gauge attitudes, beliefs, and opinions about an
issue or a proposal. Researchers should disseminate surveys widely, and surveys
should be clear and easy to complete. In order to quickly survey a large number of
people door-to-door, via web, telephone, or other technology, or face-to-face in
public spaces, researchers should focus on closed-ended survey questions. Surveys
can deliver information about specific needs within a community or population that
even census data and administrative data cannot provide. Surveys can provide information about the availability and accessibility of services, and they can identify
unmet needs or gaps in services. Depending on the amount of resources available,
you can create a survey or purchased one that has been tested in the past. Targeted
surveys involve collecting data from a small group within a larger group or community without trying to generalize the finding to the larger population. Small surveys
may be given to certain types or groups of residents, business owners, organizations,
and service providers. For example, you might collect data on the impacts of the use
of methamphetamine in a community by surveying treatment providers, physicians,
social workers, clergy, health providers, lawyers and judges, and others directly
involved. Quick Guide 34 provides sample needs assessment survey questions.

QUICK GUIDE 32   GUIDE TO FOCUS GROUPS

General Guidelines

Focus groups can get closer to what people are really thinking and feeling about problems or ideas and can assist to obtain public opinion in an interactive method. They have a specific, focused discussion topic, such as the improvements needed within a particular school or the features of a new planned playground. Like with Key Informant Interviews, preparation is needed to facilitate effective focus groups. Use prior research (census and administrative data, prior needs assessments, observation, and/or other available data) about the community to prepare a list of questions prior to conducting the group. However, focus groups are seeking more depth, nuance, and variety of responses than can be typically obtained with many other data collection methods. Facilitators encourage members to express their opinions and to comment on each others' thoughts and ideas. Nonverbal behavior and group interactions can also be observed.

Logistics

Focus groups' discussions should be recorded—either audio recorded (using, for example, a smartphone app or a digital recorder) or through note-taking. Either way, group permission should be given for recording the discussion. Generally, focus groups run for approximately 45–60 minutes, and consist of 8–10 people.

Group Composition

Group members should be a representative sample of those whose opinions you want. For example, if you are collecting information about the needs of older adults in a spatial community, you want to consider inviting older adults from various areas of the spatial community, as well as those with varying demographics, such as age, race, ethnicity, marital status, gender, ability status, and others. You might run several focus groups to ensure that you hear from a variety of the population of interest. To get people to the meeting, you might consider offering transportation, food, a small monetary incentive, child/elder care, public recognition, or other things that prospective members might need or want. Participants can be recruited through personal invitation to specific people, or publicity for willing volunteers.

Sample Questions

- What are some of your thoughts about what is going on now?
- Are you satisfied with the current situation? Why?
- What needs to be changed about the current situation?
- Some people have suggested [XXX] is needed. What do you think about this? Do you agree?

Facilitation

Facilitators should feel free to follow up participant answers by asking

- Can you say more about that?
- Can you say why you think that?
- Can you give us an example?

Facilitators should also work toward a balance of discussion by asking the quieter participants directly for their thoughts. If some members are dominating, the facilitator can ask people who have spoken already to wait until others have spoken before speaking again. It is helpful to occasionally summarize the group discussion to check for accuracy.

Source: University of Kansas Work Group for Community Health and Development, 2016.

QUICK GUIDE 33   GUIDE TO COMMUNITY FORUMS

General Guidelines
Like focus groups, community forums also collect public opinion but in a more public and open format than focus groups, and with potentially a wider group of people (such as a broad cross-section of the whole community). Additionally, forums can provide a link to people interested enough in the topic that they might later be involved in a community intervention.

Logistics
If possible, hold several forums in various locations comfortable to various populations and at various times to facilitate attendance by a broad cross-section of people. Publicity is key to getting people to attend, so all avenues should be utilized (print, media, word-of-mouth etc.). It is helpful to personally invite people as well and ask them to recruit others to attend. Providing food/drink, transportation, childcare, and other incentives can be helpful. Like with focus groups, community discussions should be recorded (audio and/or note-taking).

The Program
The format usually consists of a short formal presentation, and a general or breakout sessions to facilitate a higher level of interaction. There should be some sort of interactive portion, such as discussion, prioritizing issues or ideas, and/or voting. Next steps should be announced at the end.

Sample Discussion Questions
- Did the presentation include the most important challenges/ideas? What was missed?
- What are the barriers to solving these challenges? How can they be overcome?
- Are the challenges widespread? Who is most affected?

What resources are needed to address these challenges?

Facilitation
The facilitator should be someone who is neutral on the topic, and can keep the program and discussion moving. Careful facilitation is needed to ensure that everyone feels welcome to participate and that a small minority of participants do not dominate the discussion.

Source: University of Kansas Work Group for Community Health and Development, 2016

Determining Your Assessment Approach

There are several important considerations to take into account when designing a community needs assessment. Key principles include the following (Mulroy, 2013; Ohmer et al., 2013):

1. *Value participation from diverse constituencies:* Seek multiple perspectives on the community and experiences in the community, particularly those of disadvantaged and oppressed populations that may have been overlooked and undervalued in the past. While it may be difficult to gather data from diverse constituencies, carefully consider the way in which you can fairly report on dissenting opinions in your final report.

QUICK GUIDE 34   SAMPLE NEEDS ASSESSMENT SURVEY QUESTIONS

Circle any of the following that are needs for you or your family.

Medical Health Care	Job Transportation	Childcare
Dental Health Care	Medical Transportation	Elder Care
Vision Health Care	Housing	Legal Services
Prescriptions	Disability Assistance	Utilities
Mental Health Care	Housing Loans	Counseling
Hospice	Housing Repairs	Domestic Violence Services
Clothing	Employment	Income Tax Preparation
Food	Education	Senior Services

What are your barriers to childcare services, if any? (Circle all that apply)

None needed	Location of childcare providers	Not enough childcare providers
No barriers		
Cost	No transportation	Quality of childcare providers
Hours not sufficient	Children have special needs	

How many household members do NOT currently have health insurance? (Including insurance from Medicare, Medicaid, CHIP, Private Insurance) _____

Of those with NO health insurance, how many are: Under 18: _____ Over 65: _____

What are your barriers to health care? (Circle all that apply)

No barriers	No doctor in my area	No childcare during
Cost	No doctor will take my	appointment
No insurance	insurance	No transportation to doctor
Fear		

What are your barriers to employment? (Circle all that apply)

No barriers	Pay too low to support	Lack of training or
No jobs for my field	family	experience
No transportation	No childcare during work	Mental disability
	Physical disability	

What are your barriers to reliable transportation? (Circle all that apply)

No barriers	Price of gas	No routes near work
No car/Can't afford car	No private transportation	No public transportation
No routes near home		

What are your major housing concerns? (Circle all that apply)

Rent too high	Utility costs too high	Can't find house in price range
House needs major repairs	Can't afford house payments	No concerns

Circle if you HAVE a:

Phone	Computer	Internet access

QUICK GUIDE 34   CONTINUED

What do you feel is the primary cause of unemployment in this community? (Check only one)

☐ Lack of child care

☐ Not enough jobs

☐ Wages are too low

☐ Lack of encouragement to work

☐ Lack of education

☐ Not enough on-the-job training

☐ Lack of transportation

☐ Not enough help available to find a good paying job

☐ Other

_____

What do you feel is the primary cause of transportation barriers in this community (Check only one)

☐ Suspended driver's license

☐ Lack of reliable/ affordable vehicle

☐ Insurance prices

☐ Gasoline prices

☐ Bus service not available/ reliable

☐ Other

_____

What do you feel are the biggest problems facing youth (ages 5 to 17) **in the community? (Check up to three)**

☐ Not much to do away from school

☐ Lack of adult role models

☐ Adults not in touch with needs of youth

☐ Stress

☐ Depression

☐ Alcohol/drug abuse by youth

☐ Alcohol/drug abuse in family

☐ Other _____

☐ Lack of opportunities to develop skills needed as an adult

☐ Violence

What do you feel are the biggest problems facing adults in the community? (Check up to three)

☐ Inability to pay all bills and on time

☐ Stress

☐ Bad credit

☐ Lack of education

☐ Lack of assets

☐ High rent/mortgage costs

☐ Alcohol/drug abuse

☐ Low wages

☐ Nowhere to turn for help in crises

☐ Unemployment

☐ Other

_____

Do you have and use a bank account (checking or savings)? Yes No

Do you presently use a prepaid card, check cashing, or cash advance services instead of banking services? Yes No

Source: University of Kansas Work Group for Community Health and Development, 2016

2. *Use multiple methods:* Both quantitative and qualitative methods offer unique types of data for the project. Quantitative data, such as service statistics, census and administrative data, mapping, and survey data, offer reliability, repeatability, and transferability. Qualitative data, including participant and nonparticipant observations, interviews, focus groups, and community forums, offer a richer, holistic picture of communities and their inhabitants. The most informative community needs assessments use both types of data.

3. *Encourage civic participation in technical elements:* Encourage key stakeholders and/or community members to participate in the design and selection of technical elements. Seek their input when formulating research questions, and when selecting data collection methods, survey questions, focus group participants, and key stakeholders. Involve them in the collection and analysis of data and in formulating recommendations, if appropriate. Their full participation helps build capacity in the community while ensuring that the data gathered is relevant and that it may be useful for efforts to improve the community.

4. *Keep the assessment realistic:* Community stakeholders and agency staff want usable evidence for local community and agency decision-making and community improvement. Lengthy assessments and overly long documents may not be helpful.

5. *Value strengths and asset building:* Along with needs, note the strengths and assets of the community. Institutional resources, such as churches, locally owned businesses, nonprofit organizations, schools, financial institutions, networks of organizations, and individuals can all be considered strengths. Asset-building programs, such as those that encourage savings, employment, small businesses, local investment of resources, and other types of assets, are intended to increase the individual and collective assets of a community. Local control of resources empowers residents and strengthens the community.

When selecting your methods, the purpose, desired impact, and potential uses of the assessment and resources must be major considerations (University of Kansas Work Group for Community Health and Development, 2016; Ohmer et al., 2013). Questions to consider include:

- What do you/your sponsor hope to learn?

- How will you use the information?

- Can existing data provide the needed information?

- Can you combine existing data with newly gathered data?

- What resources do you have for the project?

- What might be some of the other potential benefits of choosing particular methods?

The purpose of the assessment will help to shape the specific data you collect. For example, if you are conducting a needs assessment about financial services for low-income residents in a community, you might ask a key stakeholder, "When you think about the residents using financial institutions in this community, what services do they need that currently do not exist locally?" or "What type of institutions, if any, would be more beneficial to local residents?"

If the public or decision-makers view your project as controversial, or if you anticipate a skeptical or even a hostile response to the findings, plan the most rigorous data collection your budget allows. Political issues surface in a needs assessment, because the data may be used to convince decision-makers to approve and/or fund a program or service, to modify or end a program or service, or to acknowledge a previously unrecognized challenge in the community. Assessments can challenge the status quo in communities, and therefore, they may be contentious. Including specific influential individuals and organizations in the assessment may lend credibility to the findings. Using data supplied by less credible individuals and organizations may cast doubt on your findings.

It's also important to consider the financial resources and time available for an assessment. For example, social workers interested in creating a new financial education program for local youth may have few resources to conduct a needs assessment and little time before a proposal is due. In contrast, a new city councilor may ask a social work staff member to provide a more comprehensive community assessment, and that councilor may be able to provide adequate resources and more time to carry out a longer, more involved assessment. If you are short on funds and time, consider using publically available data, including data available from government sources, the local chapters of the United Way, and nonprofit organizations. You might also consider including a focus group and/or a community forum. If you have more time and/or resources, you may add targeted surveys, key informant interviews, and/or larger surveys. Exhibit 10.4 shows the interrelationships among time frame, budget, expertise, and possible designs in developing a community needs assessment.

In sum, key considerations about needs assessments, the scope of the type of information you need, how you intend to use the data, political considerations, and available funding and time influence the methods you choose. For examples of community needs assessments and to see a sample assessment conclusion, see Exhibit 10.5.

Assessing Specific Population Needs and Social Problems

Social workers often work with community members who are vulnerable, at risk, or otherwise in need of particular services. These may include runaway youth, older adults, people with HIV/AIDS and their families, persons with disabilities, working families who are poor, and former psychiatric inpatients. Likewise, social workers often work to alleviate issues in the community. Creating or continually modifying services to effectively and efficiently meet the needs of specific populations or to target services at a specific issue is critically important. It can help ensure long-term program funding. Needs assessments often focus on a particular population or social problem. General needs assessments and those targeted to a specific population or community challenge use the same process and data collection methods.

The goal of a community needs assessment is to learn about a community from the perspective of a particular challenge or the needs of a particular population. In

TIME FRAME	FINANCES	RESEARCHER EXPERTISE	POSSIBLE DESIGN	
6 months–1 year (or even longer) to complete	Grants or other significant funding in excess of $1500 *	Primarily research and/or evaluation staff with some experience in needs assessment*	• Probability surveys • Personal interviews	**EXHIBIT 10.4** *Considerations for Needs Assessment Designs*
3–6 months to complete	Small grants or funding ($500–$1500)	Primarily staff with some experience in research	• Small targeted surveys	
Less than 3 months	Very small grants or funding ($500 or less)	Primarily agency staff or students who have other commitments and limited research or statistical expertise	• Focus group • Community forum • Unobtrusive measures including secondary data collection from agency files	

Resources (left vertical axis, arrows pointing up and down)

Scientific Rigor (right vertical axis, arrows pointing up and down)

* *Note:* In needs assessment projects that are funded by larger grants, a professional organization may be used.

Source: Royse, Staton-Tindall, Badger, & Webster, 2009

the process of conducting a community needs assessment, social workers strive to understand the history and characteristics of a population or challenge and to profile the specific dimensions associated with the population or challenge. When assessing the needs of a population, it is important to identify the following: (1) the population's perspective on the community and its patterns of resource availability; (2) the community's strengths, issues, and problems from the perspective of a specific population; and (3) the differences between groups in the community, such as the dominant values of each and the methods of oppression and discrimination the dominant group(s) in communities use to subjugate other populations. For needs assessments focused both on populations and community challenges, learning about the power structure of the community while learning about other aspects of the structure of the community is helpful. Questions about resource distribution and decision-making processes can help uncover these dynamics (Netting et al., 2017). For example, if a social worker is investigating the needs of a Filipino population within a city, asking key informants about the Filipino leaders'

EXHIBIT 10.5

Examples of Needs Assessments

- Community Action of the Franklin, Hampshire, and North Quabbin Regions in Massachusetts conducted a comprehensive community needs assessment for 2015–2017 that provides an overview of the community economic and social conditions. They will use this document to identify major issues and needs and design to strategies to address them within their service area.
- The Fairfax County Department of Family Services–Office for Children published a community assessment for Head Start Programming in 2015. The document provides the latest information on trends in the service area, including data about health, dental, nutritional, and special education needs of the children eligible for Head Start in their service area.
- The Princeton Department of Human Services in Princeton, New Jersey, published a community needs assessment in 2014. The assessment identifies community needs in the areas of housing, food, health care, employment, transportation, legal matters, and safety. They found that residents prioritized their need for a living wage, job training, and affordable medical care.
- Spectrum Health Care System in Kent County, Michigan identified community health needs in their needs assessment for 2014. They will use the data for problem and asset identification, and policy and program development.

Summary: The need for affordable housing in the District of Columbia (Washington, DC)

The data gathered through the Needs Assessment demonstrate that:

- the need for affordable housing is significant;
- the majority of households in DC were nonfamily households (either single people or unrelated people);
- housing construction has been booming, but the majority of housing was built over 50 years ago;
- the majority of areas are majority renters;
- the most common problem is housing costs exceed what residents can afford, especially for renters and those with household incomes that are half of the area median income or less; and
- based on current projections, there will be 33,000 more households with extremely low incomes than affordable units available to these households.

Source: Tatian et al., 2015

relationships with leaders of the wider community may help the social worker learn about power, dominance, and oppression. If the needs assessment focuses on a particular community challenge, such as homelessness, researchers may ask key informants about the history of the location of shelters in the community, the history behind the funding patterns for homeless services, and/or the relationship

A needs assessment can be used to determine how a potential change in a community will impact the human social fabric of the community. Researchers may conduct this type of assessment to analyze the potential social impacts of any policy, plan, program, project, or proposed facility—for example, a new development project or a change to an existing facility. This type of assessment discerns the potential ways in which a change—such as a new housing, commercial property, or transportation development—may affect how people live, work, recreate, relate to one another, and organize as a community, or change their norms, values, and beliefs. All types of impacts, including social, cultural, demographic, economic, social–psychological, and political, may be assessed (IOCPG, 2003).

Census data, surveys, key informant interviews, focus groups, public meetings, and historical documents are all useful data sources for conducting social impact assessments. Giving affected populations the opportunity to be heard through the assessment and to therefore have input into the decision-making process about a proposal is key to the social impact assessment process. The assessment can measure population characteristics, community structures, resources, and potential individual and family changes (IOCPG, 2003).

Social Work: Practice in Action–Social Impact Assessment

A semirural community near an urban area in New Mexico was under threat of significant disruption from a proposed 14-acre development. This proposed development could have significantly changed the social fabric and quality of life of neighborhood residents. The Rio Grande Educational Collaborative proposed a 35,000 square foot learning facility on land that had been planned for a storm water drainage pond. Students and faculty affiliated with The Resource Center for Raza Planning engaged in data collection through the use of census data, historical documents, previous studies about the site, survey interview data, key informant interviews, and focus group data. They collected data related to the programmatic and facility characteristics. At the conclusion of their assessment, they produced an 82-page report, and presented their findings to the public and to decision-makers. Their findings included community concerns about traffic and parking, property values, and the potential displacement of residents. They recommended criteria for site selection for the facility and offered alternative activities for the site that reflected community preferences. While the residents were supportive of the learning programming, the ultimate impact of the facility on the community would be a negative one. County officials rejected the proposed development; instead, a water retention pond with walking trails and a working community farm were built on the site.

Source: Cordova, 2011

EXHIBIT 10.6

Social Impact Assessment

of key providers to political decision-makers in the community. Exhibit 10.6 provides an example of a needs assessment that focuses on the human social impact of a proposed change, and Exhibit 10.7 provides an example of a needs assessment that focuses on a particular community challenge.

EXHIBIT 10.7

*Community
Practice and
Child Welfare
Assessment*

A social worker working in child welfare services in a small community can engage in community practice in a variety of ways. One social worker in child welfare was working in a community within a county characterized by higher-than-average rates of poverty, substance abuse, and criminal violations. A substantial number of children in the county endure prolonged childhood sexual abuse. These children are initially placed in foster care, but many are removed shortly thereafter and placed in residential facilities because they express their acute emotional disruptions in dangerous or out-of-control behaviors. Residential care is more costly than foster care, and it has implications for both the current quality of life and for the future community integration of the children.

Due to the behaviors children who have been abused display, the social worker forms a group of caseworkers, supervisors, foster parents, former foster children, and allies in other organizations to complete a needs assessment. After reviewing previous needs assessments of foster children in that community, as well as U.S. Census data, public health data, juvenile court data, educational data, and other administrative data, the group decides to use a survey to complete the needs assessment. All foster parents and those providing any services to foster children, including teachers, complete the survey. The survey is designed to elicit strengths, resources, and stressors.

The plan is, as a group, to analyze the data, integrate the survey data with previous data and studies, and issue a report, which will include recommendations, to the child welfare supervisor for the county. The group will ask the supervisor to share the needs assessment with other local decision-makers, including politicians, in an effort to change policy and possibly raise funds for additional services, if needed.

Asset Mapping

Social workers using a strengths-based approach in community work seek to learn about and identify the people, institutions, and organizations in the community, as well as those who work on behalf of that community. In order to effectively address the challenges that face communities using a strengths-based approach, social workers must possess knowledge of the resources (or assets) available to work on local issues. The key to this approach is the idea that, collectively, the resources available within the community offer the capacity to address local issues. **Asset mapping** is a technique to systematically learn about a variety of different types of assets that could be helpful in an intervention. It prepares the way for an intervention that focuses on effectiveness and interdependencies within a community and that seeks to empower people by identifying ways that people can contribute to a community change effort (Hillier & Culhane, 2013). Like individual, family, and group assessments, asset mapping provides information that can be useful in planning a community intervention.

The community mapping process is the first stage of an asset-based community intervention, generally called the asset-based community development approach.

McKnight and Kretzmann (1996) first developed this approach, and today the Asset-Based Community Development Institute at Northwestern University spearheads its use. Using a strengths-based approach, the first activity of community practice is to inventory—to "map"—the assets of a community. These assets include members of the community, both those that currently participate in community affairs and those who do not, as well as institutions and formal and informal organizations. Conducting an inventory of the assets of individual people requires the identification of the abilities, talents, gifts, and capacities of community members. For example, community members may have underutilized home repair, child/older adult care, craft, music, and other types of skills. Exhibit 10.8 provides an example of the topics included in an individual capacity inventory. Researchers mapping assets would first ask people questions on these topics and then ask them to prioritize their skills and to comment on their involvement in community activities, their interests in starting a small business, and their current business activities. Researchers would also map formal and informal organizations and associations that exist within the community, including economic, education, political, religious, and kinship groups. Associations can include many types of formal and informal organizations and groups, such as self-help groups that assist with addictions, youth groups, environmental groups, and charitable groups. Institutions can include parks, libraries, schools of all types, law enforcement, hospitals, and other health care resources. Exhibits 10.9 and 10.10 provide examples of community asset mapping tools for associations/organizations and institutions. Several helpful asset

CATEGORY	EXAMPLE OF SKILLS	
Health	Caring for an older adult or person with a mental illness	**EXHIBIT 10.8**
Office	Typing, writing letters, telephone skills	
Construction and Repair	Painting, roof repair, tuckpointing, demolition	*Capacity*
Maintenance	Washing windows, mowing lawns, gardening	*Inventory for*
Food	Catering, bartending, baking, washing dishes	*Individuals*
Child Care	Caring for children, assisting with field trips	
Transportation	Driving a taxi, truck, or ambulance; hauling	
Operating Equipment and Repairing Machinery	Repairing electronics, using a forklift	
Supervision	Completing forms, planning work for others	
Sales	Operating a cash register, selling services	
Music	Singing, playing an instrument	
Security	Guarding property, installing security systems	
Other	Sewing, upholstering, managing property	

Source: Adapted from Kretzmann & McKnight, 1993

EXHIBIT 10.9	Types	Examples of Types
Capacity Inventory for Associations/ Organizations, Abbreviated List	Artistic	Artists coalition
	Business	Business association
	Charitable Groups and Drives	American Red Cross, United Way
	Church Groups	Service, prayer, youth, women's and men's, choir
	Civic	Lions and Rotary Clubs
	Collectors Groups	Stamps, antiques
	Community Centers	Senior centers
	Ethnic Associations	League of Americans of Ukrainian Descent
	Health and Fitness	Basketball league
	Interest	Antique car owners, book clubs
	Local Media	Local cable TV, local community radio
	Mutual Support	La Leche League, Alcoholics Anonymous
	Neighborhood	Block Group, Community Development Corporation
	Outdoor	Biking, hiking, rollerblading
	Political	Ward, Democratic Party
	School	Parent-Teacher Association
	Service/Nonprofits	Habitat for Humanity

Source: Adapted from McKnight & Block, 2010

EXHIBIT 10.10	TYPES	EXAMPLES OF CAPACITIES WITHIN TYPES
Sample Capacity Inventory for Local Institutions	Historic/Arts Council Groups	Training, Personnel, Space/Facilities, Materials/Equipment
	Hospitals/Health Care Facilities	Expertise, Financial
	Libraries	Expertise, Materials, Fundraising Resources
	Local Government	Expertise, Space/Facilities, Financial
	Military facilities	Expertise, Speakers
	Older Adult Facilities	Expertise, Speakers, Space/Facilities
	Parks	Personnel, Space/Facilities, Materials/Equipment
	Police	Personnel, Authority, Financial
	Public Transportation	Expertise, Financial, Authority
	Schools	Personnel, Space/Facilities, Students, Financial

Source: McKnight & Block, 2010.

mapping tools are available on the Internet, including the U.S. Department of Housing and Urban Development (HUD) "Connecting to Success: Neighborhood Networks Asset Mapping Guide."

The process of mapping assets will vary depending on your needs, sponsor, and resources. While some circumstances may lend themselves to a thorough mapping process in a relatively short period of time, in other circumstances, the mapping process may take a year or longer. Like a community needs assessment, asset mapping provides a foundation for a community intervention, yet it is also a process that may continue while an intervention is underway. Chapter 11 will discuss the next steps for using community mapping data for an intervention.

PLANNING

A needs assessment process will bring many issues, challenges, and ideas to the fore-front. The planning phase involves sorting through and prioritizing them to be able to move forward with an intervention. To make these choices, a set of criteria must be developed to provide the structure needed to select the most important issues/ideas in a fair manner. The criteria can include any or any combination of the following:

- Seriousness or frequency of an issue

- Cost of the issue, or resources needed to address the issue

- Feasibility of affecting the issue

- Readiness of the community to recognize and address the issue

- The long-term impact or benefit of addressing an issue, or in implementing an idea

Ideally, the criteria is developed in an collaborative, democratic manner with community members as well as with people that may provide technical expertise, such as in public health, health, community development, that can provide important information in the process (such as through a voting process or in a community forum). Setting the criteria to select can occur at any point in the process from the beginning to the end of the needs assessment process. After setting the criteria, a democratic process can also be used to then apply the criteria to the issues/ideas generated in the community needs assessment process to plan for an intervention (University of Kansas Work Group for Community Health and Development, 2016).

SKILLS FOR COMMUNITY-BASED PARTICIPATORY RESEARCH [EPAS 4]

The community analysis and needs assessment process offers valuable opportunities to engage in community-based participatory research. This research methodology involves engaging a wide group of people who are either direct stakeholders or who are interested in the community and/or the research. Involving community members, representatives of organizations, elected officials, and/or other researchers in the process makes the research more informed by and responsive to the community's needs.

The following key principles guide the participatory research method (Sohng, 2013):

- Seek to identify and work with communities as a whole and to strengthen the social bonds of community by engaging community members.

- Use a strengths-based approach. Identify, build on, and promote strengths and assets, as well as social structures and processes that promote community involvement in decision-making.

- Seek to collaborate with partners in all phases of the research. In particular, use community members' knowledge, share information and resources among all involved, and maintain an equitable decision-making process among the partners.

- Structure the process so members of the community and community groups have the power and ability to act on research findings.

- Seek to promote and develop the capacity of local people and organizations to create and sustain any change that may occur as a result of the research process and outcomes.

Participatory research can be used with a variety of research tools and techniques. The research process itself is a mechanism by which to enhance the well-being of communities through the inclusion of community members and organizations in all phases of the research, including the development of the research question. Using the research method to promote the community and collaborative processes increases the likelihood that the data and analysis will accurately reflect needs and that community residents will engage in action to fulfill those needs.

It is important to recognize and respect the centrality of the community experience to community experts. In acknowledging the multiple realities that are brought to bear in any community context, community-based participatory research is consistent with critical social construction. Participatory action-research empowers community members to transform their lives. Exhibit 10.11 provides an example.

The Floating Hospital (TFH), located in New York City, provides primary health care for families and children in homeless shelters. Academic researchers partnered with TFH to engage in a community-based approach to advocate for health care for homeless children. They used the strengths-based approach by identifying TFH's strengths through gathering internal agency data and client case summaries. They also used empowerment by engaging in "photovoice," by using pictures taken by clients to record the barriers to accessing education faced by homeless children. TFH enhanced its capacity by collaborating with other community agencies for data sharing. They also created advocacy briefs to provide the facts and tell client stories to be used in their advocacy. Ultimately, they were able to create the resources needed to advocate with the New York General Assembly for medical resources for homeless children so that they meet the health requirements for public education (such as vaccinations). They found that as they worked closely with the community, their capacity to advocate for the needs of homeless children was enhanced.	**EXHIBIT 10.11** *Community-Based Participatory Research to Advocate for Homeless Children*

Source: Fetherman & Burke, 2014

CONTEMPORARY TRENDS IMPACTING COMMUNITY PRACTICE

Twenty-first century community social work practice comes with many opportunities and challenges. Social workers often intervene in low-income communities that face unique challenges with recent political, economic, and social trends, such as the following (Mondros & Staples, 2013; Ohmer & DeMasi, 2009; Putnam & Feldstein, 2003: Weil, Reisch, & Ohmer, 2013):

- *The devolution, or decentralization, of control of many federally funded programs and policies, including those that support community practice:* Increasingly, states are relying on nonprofit and for-profit organizations to deliver social services. This decentralization and cuts in funding have increased the importance of involving communities and neighborhoods in informing, designing, and delivering services and in raising local funds to pay for them. For example, some federal block grants for child welfare give state and local governments the power to allocate funds, which offers opportunities for community participation. Social workers are frequently in a position to contribute to the local-level discussions about the federal funds through their work with state and local agencies, public hearings on regulations, and legislative testimony. Social workers have also helped raise private and public funds to pay for resources in their communities.

- *The increasingly multicultural composition of society:* Hispanics are the largest minority group in the United States. The U.S. is expected to become a majority-minority in 2044, which means that the minority population (i.e., non-Whites) will be the majority of the population (U.S. Census Bureau, 2015b). The increase in minority populations in communities offers social workers the opportunity to advocate for greater inclusion, reduced conflict between races and ethnicities, participation, decreases in disparities in income and wealth, and social justice through increased attention to community issues that impact these populations such as immigration, bilingual education, and health care.

- *The increasing poverty and inequality in the fabric of our economic, social, racial, and ethnic relations:* Poverty has increased in recent decades, and despite the ending of the Great Recession with decreasing unemployment, the number of people living in poverty has remained the same as before the Great Recession (2008–2009) (Kneebone & Holmes, 2016). Income and wealth inequalities are the most extreme they have been since prior to the Great Depression due to such factors as the decline in unions, outsourcing of employment, stagnation of wages, high unemployment, and changes in tax policy (Saez, 2015). Social workers will continue to play a central role in working with and advocating for a more inclusive and responsive community for all citizens. For example, differential access to technology and the Internet is a significant barrier for many individuals and communities in their employment efforts, particularly those that are low income.

- *The widening venues and locations for community practice:* Social workers have increased opportunities to work with different types of communities, including those that organize around identity (or shared experiences), geography, and faith. For example, social workers may work with an online community of people with a similar medical diagnosis, a planning group for HIV/AIDS prevention funding, people living in a specific neighborhood, or people of various faiths. Social workers may also work in communities that are experiencing poverty for the first time, such as inner-ring and outer suburbs.

- *The increasing integration of community practice ideas and strategies into other models of practice:* For example, policy-makers are increasingly viewing elements of community practice as a part of work with individuals, families, and groups. Newer practices in services for children and families and for older adults increasingly use community-based service practice models. For example, social workers are increasingly using Assertive Community Treatment, a community-based, intensive, wrap-around case management program for intervening with individuals with severe mental illness (Slade, McCarthy, Valenstein, Visnic, & Dixon, 2012).

- *Distrust of political institutions:* Hyper-partisanship among political candidates and in national and state legislatures has created an intense atmosphere of estrangement and distrust among the American public. Social workers can engage with politicians and political groups to encourage respectful dialogue and bipartisan collaboration on social issues.

- *The decline of democratic participation and civic engagement:* The decline of social capital, including the networks, norms, and trust that facilitate collective action, is a growing concern among community practitioners. The degree to which citizens engage in public life affects community practice, including the identity and shared values in a community. Not all participation and engagement has positive effects but much of it does, and social workers can work to energize and mobilize a diverse array of individuals and groups to be engaged in public life within their communities.

Having discussed several important trends impacting community practice in the U.S., the next section will focus on the world as a community. This discussion will broaden the topic of community practice, and set the stage for Chapter 11, in which community intervention, termination, and evaluation will be explored.

THE WORLD AS A COMMUNITY

Ease of travel, communication, and economic interdependence impact social work practice in the U.S. and will certainly grow in influence in coming decades. This section discusses global interdependence (the connectedness of all nations) and its implications for domestic community social work practice.

Global Interdependence: Implications for U.S. Practice

Global interdependence influences social work practice in the U.S. in many ways, especially with regard to political, social, and technological events. Four of the primary influences are discussed as follows (Healy, 2008; Reisch, 2013):

- Due to increased migration in all parts of the world, *culturally competent skills and an understanding of the social problems* associated with refugee status and transborder issues are important for social workers in most U.S. communities. Migration occurs as a result of international events, political forces, and natural forces, such as disasters. For example, increased internal political tensions in Syria resulting from the recent widespread political upheaval in the Middle East caused almost 5 million people to seek safety and aid in neighboring countries by July 2016 (United Nations Office for the Coordination of Humanitarian Affairs, 2016).

- Using critical thinking, social workers *seek information from multiple sources,* rather than just from Western sources, about meeting common social challenges such as homelessness, poverty, violence, street children, HIV/AIDS, unemployment, increasing longevity, runaway contagious disease, and growing divisions between the "haves" and the "have-nots." Mutual inquiries and information sharing are increasingly relevant as these conditions are addressed on a worldwide basis.

- Social workers recognize the need to *build global organizations and coalitions* to work on issues that are interlinked. The actions of and activity in one country influence the social and economic well being of other countries, as well as the world's overall social health. For example, social work is involved in international groups engaged in public health initiatives that respond to: (1) natural disasters that cross country borders, (2) activities of financial institutions that impact the world economy, and 3) nuclear accidents worldwide.

- Social workers *seek new ways of using technology* to advance universal human rights. Social media and other technology have vast potential as tools for sharing agendas and materials and collaborating toward meeting basic human needs.

Approaches for a Global Community [EPAS 1]

A global perspective is gaining importance in community social work practice, as economic, demographic, and social consequences of globalization effect their practice. For example, due to global market forces, practitioners must confront widening income and wealth inequality in their community practice. The following points will be helpful in developing a global perspective and expanding your thinking as a global citizen (adapted from Ramanathan & Link, 2004, pp. 225–230).

1. *Making a personal review of global awareness:* Developing global awareness first requires an awareness of your present orientation. For example, how often do you keep up with news about other countries or about international organizations, such as the World Trade Organization (WTO)? How often do you think about economic and/or social conditions in other countries? Do you know where your clothing and shoes are made, where your food is grown, and under what conditions?

2. *Expanding knowledge of social work practice in a range of countries:* Another factor in expanding your awareness is learning about and gaining an appreciation of social work practices in other countries. What you learn about practices in other countries through cultural exchanges with their social services or by reading about their practices can inform your practice in your location. Do you, either consciously or unconsciously, consider yourself the expert and deem other countries' approaches secondary or inferior? Awareness of this issue is vitally important to your approach.

3. *Understanding "cultural humility" and respect for language:* Understanding the dynamics of culture and its implications for access to power and resources can lead to highly effective professional relationships. For example, think about the

degree to which you understand the ideas of cultures other than your own, the degree to which your language is respectful of other cultures, and whether you avoid assuming your culture is the worldwide norm. Cultural humility can help build engage and trust and fosters understanding between yourself and community members.

4. *Analyzing global policy instruments built upon consensus:* An understanding of global policy statements that apply to issues of concern to social workers around the world provides an understanding of the foundation upon which social work practice is built and build common ground. Relevant documents include the UN Convention on the Rights of Persons with Disabilities, the UN Convention on the Rights of the Child, and the UN Convention Against Torture (Oliver & Sapey, 2006; Reichert, 2007; Richards-Schuster & Pritzker, 2015).

5. *Becoming historically aware:* Understanding the historical context of U.S. policies is essential to the development of a global perspective. For example, an understanding of how U.S. policies affect the economic situations of other countries can assist in a broader understanding of immigration patterns in the U.S. Regularly accessing reputable domestic and international media sources that provide historical context for current news is one way to further your understanding.

6. *Becoming aware of privilege:* An appreciation of the privilege associated with economic power can contribute to the development of a global perspective. For

© THEGIFT777

example, awareness of your technological privilege and of issues of distributive justice, energy resources, and other dimensions related to the distribution of resources and the ethics associated with it can be illuminating. In-person exposure to domestic and international populations without the same level of access to resources you have enjoyed can assist in raising your awareness.

7. *Reviewing values and ethics:* The ability to understand the global application of the NASW *Code of Ethics* (2008) is key to a global perspective. For instance, do you respect the dignity of all the peoples of the earth, or just the dignity of people in the U.S.? Are you preoccupied with material goods? How do you reconcile this focus with the fact that global resources are finite and inequitably distributed?

8. *Evaluating local variations and uniqueness:* As a social worker, you are obliged to balance the tension between upholding universal principles that will strengthen the profession and valuing individual and local expressions of differences. The goal of social work practice is not to make everything the same, but to promote a "unified purpose" (Ramanathan & Link, 2004, p. 230).

STRAIGHT TALK ABOUT COMMUNITY PRACTICE

In addition to these forces and trends, globalization has led to deindustrialization and the outsourcing of traditional "blue-collar" as well as "white-collar" jobs. In particular, the loss of well-paying manufacturing jobs to lower-wage markets in other countries has made it more difficult for low-income populations with little formal education and training to access well-paying jobs. The corresponding economic insecurity has resulted in weaker local institutions such as churches, schools, and businesses. Areas of concentrated poverty have left increasing numbers of poor communities isolated from economic development, making it difficult for families in those communities to take advantage of mainstream social and economic opportunities. For example, it may be more difficult for people in low-income communities to access available living-wage job opportunities if the jobs are located far from the community and if transportation options are limited.

A related trend is the gentrification of metropolitan areas with rapidly growing populations. Gentrification occurs when low-income communities experience a physical renovation that results in increased property values and decreasing affordability. Property owners wishing to take advantage of increasing property values may convert their properties into high-cost housing, which can force low-income families to seek housing elsewhere, changing the social fabric of the community (Ohmer & DeMasi, 2009). These issues reflect many of the major dimensions of contemporary society that challenge all human service professions, and they also present unique and exciting opportunities for the renewal of vibrant community practice.

The American Academy of Social Work and Social Welfare Grand Challenges for Social Work Initiative identify financial capability and asset building for all as an area that the profession should address. Lack of financial capability and assets contribute to poverty and social inequality, two key concerns for the social work profession. Social workers have been involved in this work since the founding of the profession, and are today involved in related practice, policy, and research efforts. For example, social workers help families obtain resources to take care of basic needs, such as public benefits, and low-cost food and housing, as well as economic empowerment work, and financial education and coaching.

GRAND CHALLENGE

Building Financial Capability for All

Sherraden and colleagues (2015) lay out the professional obligation to help clients achieve financial security in a number of ways:

1. *Gain financial capability*: Social workers must help clients gain financial knowledge and skills, as well as access to sound financial products and services. This involves helping people to strengthen their financial behavior, as well as to change institutions that provide financial tools.
2. *Build assets*: Financial stability is also gained with financial wealth (e.g., personal savings, retirement plans, and home and small business ownership). Social workers must be involved in helping families gain a financial foothold through building wealth that can have intergenerational effects.

How might the mandate to practice financial capability and asset building be applied to community engagement and assessment? To familiarize yourself with financial capability and asset building, visit the Grand Challenges website and read Working Paper No. 13, *Financial Capability and Asset Building for All* (Sherraden et al., 2015) at: http:// aaswsw.org/wp-content/uploads/2016/01/WP13-with-cover.pdf. (See Exercise #a1 for additional exploration of engaging and assessing communities for financial capability and asset building within the context of the Brickville community.)

CONCLUSION

This chapter has introduced the concept of community as a place in which individuals and groups find identity and meaning in their various roles. Most important for social workers, community is an arena that impacts all areas of practice, and social workers in many settings engaging in generalist practice will benefit from a working knowledge of community practice. Community is the structure that supports interaction and connectedness among people over time, and it can be understood using various theories and perspectives. The characteristics of the community in which people live and grow have important implications for the resources and opportunities available to community residents. Having considered community engagement, assessment, and the global community, in the next chapter, we will examine community intervention strategies, termination, evaluation, and follow-up processes.

MAIN POINTS

- Communities play a critical role in the lives of workers and clients, even in traditional individual, family, and group practice.

- There are multiple definitions, types, functions of, and approaches to community, including traditional and postmodern approaches.

- Community engagement and assessment involves many skills and practice behaviors, including community analysis, needs assessment, community asset mapping, and community-based participatory research.

- Various factors, including the population and/or problem focus, aid in determining the assessment approach.

- Contemporary trends and globalization are changing community social work practice.

- A global perspective is imperative to contemporary community engagement and assessment.

- Understanding traditional and contemporary perspectives helps social workers view community through many different lenses.

- Skills of engagement, assessment, and intervention in community social work build on those relevant for social work practice with individuals, families, and groups. In addition, you will find the skills of participatory action-research useful as an ethnographic approach to your work.

EXERCISES

a. Case Exercises

1. Go to www.routledgesw.com/cases and click on the Brickville case (click on "Start This Case"). To familiarize yourself with the case, under the "Engage" table, review the Introduction, "You, the Social Worker," and Critical Thinking Question #1. Consider the following: your employer, the Brickville Community Development Corporation (CDC), wants to engage and assess the community about their financial capability and assets. You will start with approaching and engaging with other community institutions about this topic before engaging and assessing individual community residents. What kind of institutions would be involved in the financial capability and assets of community residents?

What kind of information might you want from the other institutions to learn about the residents' financial capability and their assets?

2. Go to www.routledgesw.com/cases and click on the Riverton case (click on "Start This Case"). Familiarize yourself with the Riverton Town Map (under "Explore This Town" case study tool), the Sociogram (case study tool), and the Interaction Matrix (case study tool). Answer the critical thinking questions on the Riverton case. What other players would you add to the interaction matrix?

3. After completing Exercise #2, consider the following case. In your position as social worker at the Alvadora Community Mental Health Center, you have observed that there are some strained connections between the center's staff and the Hispanic community it serves. You would like to learn more about the Hispanic community, both to become more culturally competent and to learn more about the needs of the community. You decide to explore the idea of a community analysis.

   a. Define the type of community you would study.

   b. Discuss the approach you might take to conduct a community analysis. What type of information would you seek? Who would you involve? With whom might you talk?

4. After completing Exercises #2 and #3, you decide to conduct a community needs assessment. Using the material in Chapter 10, create a plan for a community needs assessment of the Hispanic population in Riverton. Include the sources of data and the assessment approach that you plan to use.

5. Go to www.routledgesw.com/cases and become familiar with the Sanchez family. Review the material in the chapter that discusses the world as a global community. Identify and describe the ways in which the Sanchez family context in particular is shaped by each of the four dimensions of global interdependence. Add any other ways you think would make an impact.

6. The Chapter 10 section "Approaches for a Global Community" discusses points that could be helpful in creating a global perspective for social work practice. Apply 4 of the 8 points in the chapter to work with the Sanchez family. In your application, focus your discussion on the ways in which you can accomplish each of the tasks to create a global perspective toward the larger goal of being a culturally competent social worker.

7. Go to www.routledgesw.com/cases and become familiar with the Brickville case. Using the Brickville community redevelopment scenario, create a 10-question survey that could be used for a community needs assessment.

b. Other exercises

8. Select a community of which you are a member. Reflect on an issue that your community faces. What is the issue? How might you conduct a community analysis of your community? How might you conduct a needs assessment of your community? Create a thorough plan for each in a 1–2 page paper.

9. Select a community within which you are a member. Using the "Create Your Own Ecomap" template at www.routledgesw.com/cases, create a sociogram of your community.

10. Using Exhibit 10.6 as an example, create a scenario that begins with an individual case(s), and the need for a community needs assessment becomes apparent. Discuss the methods you would use to conduct the needs assessment in a 1–2 page paper.

11. Using Exhibit 10.5 as an example, search media sources for another real-life situation in which development threatens a community and an impact assessment could be useful in the decision-making process. In a 1–2 page paper, describe the situation and discuss how a social impact assessment could be conducted.

Social Work Practice with Communities: Intervention, Termination, and Evaluation

Passion begins with a burden and a split-second moment when you understand something like never before. That burden is on those who know. Those who don't know are at peace. Those of us who do know get disturbed and are forced to take action.

Wangari Maathai

It isn't enough to talk about peace. One must believe in it. And it isn't enough to believe in it. One must work at it.

Eleanor Roosevelt

Key Questions for Chapter 11

1. How can I use theory and perspectives to guide the development of intervention, terminations, and evaluation with communities? [EPAS 8 and 9]
2. What models can I use to intervene in communities? [EPAS 8]
3. How do I utilize evidence to practice research-informed practice and practice-informed research to guide intervention, termination, and evaluation with communities? [EPAS 4]
4. How can I apply social work values and ethics to community intervention, termination, and evaluation? [EPAS 1]

The Brickville community is in a quandary. Although the community needs redevelopment, the current proposal to completely overhaul the physical structures in the community, including razing some buildings, has stirred major controversy among current community residents, neighborhood social service providers, and sympathetic outsiders. The community has had little input into the plan, and they are fearful that many current residents would no longer be able to afford to live in the neighborhood after the redevelopment. Some do not like the plan itself, fearful that the planned changes in community real estate will change the look and character of the area. Others do not trust the developer who has proposed the redevelopment. Some residents think that, despite any drawbacks, the proposal and developer should be supported. A supporting group (Brickville Community Benefits Alliance) and an opposing group (Vision Brickville) formed and are actively engaged in community organizing to attract people and move their agendas forward.

L IKE SOCIAL WORK PRACTICE WITH INDIVIDUALS, FAMILIES, AND GROUPS, the second phase of practice with communities is engagement and assessment. We have previously covered the initial phases of engagement and assessment with communities. Intervention, termination, evaluation, and follow-up are the middle and ending phases of work with all client system levels. As noted in Chapter 10, community practice is a broad term that includes grassroots community organizing, community development, human service program development, planning and coordination, and advocacy (Weil, Gamble, & Ohmer, 2013). There are many types of community interventions, all of which are based on the data gathered and process used for community assessment. The aim of community practice interventions is to shape and create institutions and communities that respond to community needs. Community-level interventions, terminations, evaluations, and follow-up concentrate on the community level but also impact individual, family, and group change. Focusing on the community and on individuals, families, and groups requires the social worker to use many skills to begin the intervention and to facilitate the termination, evaluation, and follow-up processes.

This chapter explores community practice from the intervention plan through the termination, and evaluation and follow-up phases. In this chapter, we discuss practice models, which are based on theoretical perspectives, for community interventions, and we provide an overview of social work interventions for communities. The chapter continues with a look at the final phase of community practice—the termination process and the evaluation and follow-up processes. You will learn about the most recognized models for community intervention: Planning/Policy, community capacity development, and social advocacy, as well as the ways in which they can be mixed in practice (Rothman, 2008).

SOCIAL WORK THEORY AND MODELS FOR COMMUNITY INTERVENTION [EPAS 8 AND 9]

As we discussed in Chapter 10, theory provides a lens through which to understand and analyze communities. For example, you can apply the strengths approach to communities in general through the identification of assets and possibilities within a community, including the individuals and groups in that community. You can achieve the empowerment approach by helping the community to realize its capacity to build on its strengths (Netting, Kettner, McMurtry, & Thomas, 2017).

Community practice models, which are primarily based in the concepts and language of systems, ecological, power, change, and politics theories, guide community interventions (Netting et al., 2017). As Exhibit 11.1 notes, systems theory helps to demonstrate that planned community change reverberates throughout a community and affects units within and outside of a community. Therefore, when you choose a community intervention, you should consider the possibility that community change may affect more people than you intend. In the Brickville situation, implementing the redevelopment could affect the surrounding

THEORIES	CONTRIBUTIONS TO COMMUNITY PRACTICE	
Social Systems	Reveals that changes in one community unit impact other units	**EXHIBIT 11.1**
	Indicates that changes in subunits also influence the larger community	*Ways in Which*
	Allows comparisons between the functioning of different communities	*Theories Contribute to*
Ecological	Sheds light on relationships among community units	*Community Practice*
	Recognizes that community groups compete for limited resources	
	Recognizes that groups without power must adapt to community norms	
	Acknowledges the interconnections and mutual shaping of physical and social structures	
Power, Change, and Politics	Reveals the influence of external sources of resources on local communities	
	Views the community as divided into "haves" and "have-nots"	
	Focuses heavily on the "isms" such as racism	
	Acknowledges the role of power in all interpersonal transactions	

Source: Netting, et al., 2017

communities through, for example, Brickville residents moving into neighboring communities and increasing the rents in those communities or through increasing the amount of property taxes collected from Brickville residents when the redevelopment is complete.

Ecological theory's focus on competition for limited resources, which can affect the relationship among units within a community or between communities, informs community interventions. Community interventions can account for competition and limited resources. Power, change, and politics theories emphasize the ways in which external forces influence local communities. Community intervention can use the influence of external forces to increase a community's power and control over internal affairs and in relationships with other persons and institutions that possess power.

As highlighted in Chapter 10, the data from the community assessment process are the basis for community change efforts, which often use a blend of approaches. The models most common in the literature are Rothman's (2008) three models of community practice: planning/policy, community capacity development, and social advocacy. These three models, explained in the remainder of this section, have a common goal to improve social, economic, and/or environmental well-being, and they share several common elements including the following (Rothman, 2008; Weil & Gamble, 2009; Weil, Gamble, & Ohmer, 2013):

- the formulation of a change goal,

- roles for staff,

- leaders and members,

- a process of selecting issues to work on,

- a target of the change effort,

- assessment of resources needed to produce change, and

- an understanding of the role of organizations in the change process.

Planning/Policy

The **planning/policy model** of community intervention focuses on data and logic to achieve community change, using experts to assist in the process of studying problems and applying rational planning techniques. Social workers using social planning also factor in political considerations and advocacy in the intervention process, but the primary emphasis is on rational planning.

The planning/policy model can be implemented in a range of practice situations. Social workers engage in social planning efforts when they participate in efforts to envision, develop, coordinate, deliver, and improve human services. Planning is needed for all types of human services (i.e., child welfare, health, aging) and topics (i.e., gang violence, neighborhood development), and by myriad of hosts, such as local, state, or federal governments, faith-based organizations, and community councils (Sager & Weil, 2013). As one example, social workers prioritize data when they are involved in comprehensive planning, such as working with city officials to create a plan for homeless shelters or for prison facilities for the community. In these situations, data, such as U.S. Census data, local government data, or data generated by local nonprofits, are the primary considerations for making decisions. Social workers often use statistics, computer modeling, and forecasting techniques with this model (Rothman, 2008; Weil & Gamble, 2009).

Community Capacity Development

Community capacity development focuses on fostering the local community collective ability to accomplish change by building relationships and skills that help solve local problems in a cooperative manner. Participant consensus is thus the optimal decision-making process for this model. Community capacity development is consistent with the strengths-based approaches of community asset mapping (discussed later in this chapter).

The community capacity development model emphasizes building competency of community members, groups, and the community as a whole through self-help and local problem solving. Common themes within this approach include empowerment, solidarity (e.g., achieving harmonious interrelationships among diverse persons), participation in civic action within a democratic process, and the development of leadership among local leaders. For example, neighborhood associations and clubs may work to educate themselves on ways to address a trash dumping problem, or settlement houses may attempt to prevent violence and crime by assisting local citizens and leaders in organizing summer activities for youth. The work of the U.S. Peace Corps, in which international volunteers work with local communities to create a project or increase capacity in an ongoing community effort, is another example of the community capacity development model. A Peace Corps volunteer may work with local schools to develop their capacity to improve the schools' hygiene facilities and lower the rate of illness and disease. To do this, a volunteer could work with a local committee involved with the school and help them to raise money, prioritize needs, make plans, contact experts within or outside of the community, and carry out other tasks needed for the project (Rothman, 2008; Weil & Gamble, 2009).

Social Advocacy

The **social advocacy model** is based in conflict, power dependency, and resource mobilization theories of power and politics (discussed in Chapter 10). This model is both process- and task-oriented and focuses on shifting power relationships and resources to affect institutional change by applying pressure to a target (e.g., persons and/or institutions) that has created or exacerbated a problem. Through this model, beneficiaries achieve empowerment when they feel a sense of mastery in influencing community decision-making.

A helpful example of the social advocacy model is the work of Greenpeace. To seek solutions to environmental dilemmas, such as climate change, Greenpeace nonviolently confronts decision-makers and those who may influence decision-makers. The goal of their nonviolent actions is to promote public dialogue about environmental issues and to pressure decision-makers (Greenpeace, n.d.). As described in Quick Guides 35 and 36, there is a wide variety of social advocacy activities, including but not limited to testifying, protesting, striking, and walking on picket lines (Rothman, 2008; Weil & Gamble, 2009).

QUICK GUIDE 35   PROVIDING TESTIMONY

Social workers often provide testimony to legislative and planning committees at the local, state, regional, and national levels. The main purpose of testimony is to share information and ascertain public opinion. The following steps are helpful when preparing to provide testimony:

1. Learn about how legislative proposals (bills) work their way through the process in the legislature. Who has sponsored or co-sponsored the bill? To what committee(s) has your bill been assigned? What are the possible outcomes of committee work on the bill? Where would the bill go next if the committee approves the bill? Has a similar bill been introduced in the other chamber?
2. Learn about the history of the topic and bill. Has this bill been proposed before? Who sponsored it? What happened to the bill? Did the general public already vote on the topic through referendum? Has this bill already been amended?
3. Engage in research about the topic. Research existing statutes that the bill seeks to amend, revise, supplement, or delete. If possible, research the cost of the bill, if enacted.
4. Engage in research about the politics of the bill. Which individuals or what groups are working for the bill? Against the bill? What are their perspectives?
5. Research the committee membership. Who is the chair? What is his/her perspective on the topic of your bill? Who else is on the committee? What are their interests and those of their constituents? How have they voted on this topic before?
6. Determine how long your testimony should be, and, depending on time, draft a written statement that: (1) provides factual data, including cost estimates, needed to support or refute the opposition's key points; (2) analyzes the proposed changes/additions to present law; (3) discusses any new problems that attempts to solve existing problems may create; and/or (4) provides any suggestions for needed amendments.

When delivering your testimony, consider the following:

7. Use effective nonverbal communication. Dress professionally, make eye contact, and display a calm and confident demeanor.
8. Start your testimony by introducing yourself and the organization you represent. Use full titles to address committee members. At the beginning and end of your testimony, thank the committee

chair and decision-makers for allowing you to speak. State your name and background information related to the topic at hand (such as where you live, your credentials, or your connection to the topic). Clearly state your request for the outcome of the decision-making process.

9. Describe your involvement with the topic, including any helpful context or background. If the testimony is related to your employment, provide your employer's name and interest in the topic.

10. Describe how the topic affects you or your clients. Provide factual and general information, as well as anecdotes. Describe how the pending decision will positively or negatively affect you or your clients and include a description of who will benefit and who will be hurt by the decision.

11. Connect the topic to evaluation of the policy change outcomes. For example, would the proposal provide benefits for the affected? The community? What is most important in this decision?

12. End by thanking the committee again, and offer to be of further assistance. If possible, leave a copy of your written statement with the committee.

13. Convey passion for the topic you are addressing, balanced with professionalism.

14. If you are asked questions, maintain your professionalism. Do not take questions personally, but rather state facts and your position on the bill. Offer to get facts or call on someone else to help, if needed.

Remember that a vote can be the result of a particular amendment to the bill, budget projections, position of party leadership, or complex interrelationships between procedural and substantive issues—not necessarily the subject of the bill.

Source: Kleinkauf, 1981; Oregon Legislature, n.d.; Work Group for Community Health and Development at the University of Kansas, 2012.

QUICK GUIDE 36   ACTIVITIES TO PROMOTE SOCIAL CHANGE

Conduct petition drives
Conduct public hearings
Develop relationships with decision-makers
File complaints
Lobby decision-makers
Organize boycotts
Organize public demonstrations
Organize strikes
Provide testimony
Recruit and develop leaders
Register voters
Use legal action
Use media
Write letters to legislators and/or the media

Source: Bobo, Kendall, & Max, 2010; Work Group for Community Health and Development at the University of Kansas, 2012

Applying Community Practice Models to Case Examples

Exhibit 11.2 provides a case example and applies each type of model to the example.

| EXHIBIT 11.2 | CASE #1 |

Applying Community Practice Models to Case Examples

CASE #1

In a case similar to Brickville, another city struggles with redevelopment efforts. The south side of a large Midwestern city is a low-income community populated mostly by Latino and African American populations. The other parts of the city are mainly populated with White, non-Latino, middle- and high-income families. The south side of the city has a history of oppression, including poorer quality schools and less public funding for roads and other infrastructure. In addition, it has a past history of discrimination against minority families in mortgage lending, which led to a very high rate of minorities living in rental housing rather than owning homes. Over the past half-century, real estate developers have made several half-hearted efforts to redevelop the residential and commercial parts of the community, with little success. However, several real estate developers are now working to redevelop different areas of the community, and all are requesting public funding (in addition to bank loans) for their development efforts. While some developers are working with current residents, most of them have not asked community groups or local political leaders for their input or feedback on the redevelopment plans.

The Planning/Policy Model: Using the Planning/Policy model, the community group or local political leader would request that city planners generate data or utilize previously existing data to create a redevelopment plan for the community to which all developers would have to adhere.

The Community Capacity Development Model: Using the Community Capacity Development model, one or more community groups from the affected area would begin a process of developing their ability to create a comprehensive community redevelopment plan that they could present to real estate developers and/or city officials.

The Social Advocacy Model: Using the Social Advocacy model, one or more community groups from the affected area would utilize pressure tactics on a targeted decision-maker to affect the outcome of decisions about public funding for the projects, such as specific city elected or appointed officials.

CASE #2

In May 2011, Joplin, Missouri, experienced an EF-5 tornado—the highest-strength rating—that destroyed one-third of the city and killed 161 people, including one teen who had received his high school diploma that day. Homes, businesses, a hospital, and the local high school were destroyed (Shelton, 2012). Organizations and religious groups

EXHIBIT 11.2

Continued

provided tremendous resources, including basic needs (i.e., shelter, food), health services, crisis mental health services, and debris cleanup.

The community faced the challenging task of rebuilding a large part of their area, including public institutions. To carry out this task and gain consensus among citizens regarding planning efforts, city leaders created a Citizen Advisory Recovery Team (CART) to provide a citizen voice for Joplin residents in the decisions involved in rebuilding. CART focuses on economic development, school and community facilities development, housing and neighborhood development, and infrastructure and the environment. CART membership consists of a diverse set of Joplin citizens. To gain community input into planning, a series of community meetings and open houses have been held for comments regarding a master plan for community redevelopment and the selection of a master developer. Citizens have expressed interest in developing a walkable community that includes diverse, affordable, and sustainable housing (Joplin Area CART, n.d.).

The Planning/Policy Model: By employing professional planners and other experts who are contributing their technical knowledge and expertise in the planning effort, the Joplin community is also using the Planning/Policy model.

The Community Capacity Model: The Joplin community is most clearly using the Community Capacity Development model because community members are utilizing their abilities to create a redevelopment plan with extensive community input. Involved community members are exercising and building their leadership skills by facilitating a process whereby other citizens can participate in a democratic process.

The Social Advocacy Model: The Joplin community may use the Social Advocacy model, under certain circumstances. For example, if the authorities would not seriously consider the decisions CART makes, CART may organize activities to apply pressure to targeted decision-makers.

Blending Models

While we present models here in a "pure" form, in practice they are often blended in a variety of ways (Rothman, 2008; Weil & Gamble, 2009). While the same blend occurs more than once, the first model mentioned emphasizes the blended approach:

You Can Incorporate Community Capacity Development into the Planning/Policy Model with the use of citizen input into a data-driven planning process. For example, the St. Louis, Missouri, Mental Health Board (hereafter referred to as "The Board") periodically completes a needs assessment on the mental health services of

St. Louis in order to identify the largest unmet needs. The Board then creates a multiyear plan to allocate funding to best meet those needs. Throughout the process, the Board receives feedback from mental health providers and consumers. In this way, the board mixes the two models through the strong reliance on data (Planning/Policy) and the use of citizen and provider input into the planning process (Community Capacity Development) (Rothman, 2008). In another example, data about the increase of rape on college campuses (Planning/Policy) spurred the creation of an on-campus group whose participants were taught how to identify activity that could result in sexual violence and to intervene as bystanders (Community Capacity Development) (Banyard, Moynihan, & Plante, 2007).

You Can Incorporate Social Advocacy into the Planning/Policy Model by emphasizing the use of data and logic in policy advocacy efforts. For instance, the Board can use the needs assessment and funding allocation plans to advocate for policy changes at the local, state, and/or national levels via intensive education and lobby efforts. These changes work to improve services for those with mental health challenges. In this manner, the Board uses data (Planning/Policy) and advocacy efforts (Social Advocacy) to implement community change (Rothman, 2008).

You Can Incorporate Planning/Policy into the Community Capacity Development Model (with an emphasis on the Capacity Development Model) by utilizing institutions that primarily assist communities to increase their capacity to deliver resources to their residents. For example, based on the results of a needs assessment, the Mental Health Board could work with neighborhood providers to strengthen local communities' response to mental health needs, emphasizing a local problem-solving process for working with individuals with chronic mental illness. In a second example, **Community Development Corporations** (CDCs) are resident-driven organizations that exist to provide assistance to the community. This assistance can include facilitating housing improvements throughout the community, or supporting businesses and commercial real estate efforts, and involvement in child care, community centers, and other components in the community. A board of residents, business owners, and/or local government officials govern the CDCs. The CDCs can use data-informed approaches, such as creating small business assistance programs, creating **cooperatives** (i.e., member-owned/operated businesses), or rehabilitating affordable housing in the community (Garkovich, 2011). Both examples emphasize developing the capacity of local communities (Capacity Development) using data and logic (Planning/Policy) to make decisions about the focus of community change efforts (Rothman, 2008).

You Can Incorporate Social Advocacy into the Community Capacity Development Model to encourage networks of community stakeholders to put pressure on decision-makers to improve the community. All types of communities can use this mixed approach on a wide variety of targets for policy and practice decisions. For example, a neighborhood group may learn about the plans to build a casino in their community and decide to fight it by lobbying key decision-makers, delivering petitions, and/or picketing the local government. A group of parents of children who are LGBTQ may decide to engage in an online effort to advocate for civil rights for lesbian, gay, bisexual, transgender, and questioning (LGBTQ) people in their community. Their efforts may include a sit-in at the office of a local elected official to ask for her or his support. This mixed approach emphasizes using community capacity (Community Capacity Development) with social advocacy techniques in situations where this mix will maximize the possibility for community change (Rothman, 2008).

You Can Incorporate Planning/Policy into the Social Advocacy Model to use data and logic to support advocacy efforts. This blend can best describe the efforts of many prominent social work pioneers in history, such as Jane Addams, John Dewey, Margaret Sanger, and others. These pioneers based their arguments about child labor, housing codes, food and drug safety, and other issues on data and logical arguments. Today, "think-tanks" such as the New America Foundation and others provide well-researched factual reports that social advocacy groups use to press for change. Therefore, mixing tactics that bring pressure to bear on decision-makers (Social Advocacy) with data and logic (Planning/Policy) most closely aligns with the roots of the profession (Rothman, 2008).

You Can Incorporate Community Capacity Development into the Social Advocacy Model to create strong networks of people engaged in advocacy, which can also focus on developing leadership, empowering participants, and building solidarity. This mixture is most apparent in long-term social advocacy efforts, such as the gay rights movement, the environmental movement, and the women's rights movement. This mix of pressure tactics and techniques (Social Advocacy) and developing the skills and knowledge of community members (Community Capacity Development) creates long-term aptitude for community intervention (Rothman, 2008).

These models, both in pure and mixed forms, offer ways to analyze and describe community interventions. The possibilities for interventions when mixing the models are endless. You can alter the degree of the secondary model in the mix. For example, many faith-based organizations focus on Community Capacity Development, emphasizing programming for empowerment, leadership development, and solidarity through self-help group work, and engage in only a small amount of Social Advocacy (Rothman, 2008). While there are several other conceptual frameworks for community interventions that provide helpful practice models (see for example Weil, Gamble, & Ohmer, 2013), the models described here provide a starting point for many types of community intervention. Exhibit 11.3 provides an example of mixing the models. Next we discuss intervention strategies and skills needed for intervention.

EXHIBIT 11.3 *Blending Models*	The majority of the world's leading scientists agree that global warming is a serious challenge to the long-term viability and sustainability of the planet. Therefore, global warming is the focus of community practice efforts worldwide. In 2008, Bill McKibben, a professor at Middlebury College, found 350.org, an organization that works to build political pressure to promote action that lessens global warming and climate change. Specifically, the goal of 350.org is to lower the amount of carbon dioxide in the atmosphere below 350 parts per million, the limit that scientists advocate as the maximum amount the atmosphere can absorb without leading to climate change. 350.org uses the latest scientific data about global warming from the world's leading scientists, which provides a solid evidence base for their work. 350.org encourages localities around the world—nations, cities, towns, and villages—and groups of individuals to build their community capacity by organizing individuals and groups to collaborate with them on campaigns. Local activist groups around the globe coordinate to sponsor events. For example, after the November 2012 election, 350.org began a "Do the Math Tour" in which McKibben and 350.org traveled the county to coordinate with local groups to build a movement through events that featured actors, artists, and musicians. 350.org also engages in social advocacy to both educate policy leaders by testifying to legislative committees, and to pressure them to make policy decisions that would lessen global warming. For example, the Keystone Pipeline is a proposed oil pipeline that would run from the tar fields in Canada to the Gulf of Mexico. Scientists maintain that mining the tar fields would release large amounts of carbon into the air, which would contribute to the problem of global warming. In 2011, 350.org organized protests in front of the White House to raise concern among the public about the pipeline and to put pressure on President Obama to halt plans to build the pipeline. Their work was at least partially successful: On February 24, 2015, President Obama vetoed the Keystone Pipeline. 350.org provides an example of an effort that blends two models, with their emphasis on building community capacity and social advocacy.

Source: Adapted from 350.org (n.d.).

CONTEMPORARY TRENDS AND SKILLS FOR THE MIDDLE PHASE OF COMMUNITY WORK: INTERVENTION [EPAS 8]

Community intervention is action to improve community conditions and quality of life for residents or members. This discussion will focus on the intervention strategies useful for implementing the community practice models mentioned earlier. These strategies can be useful in any of the models discussed, as they are often blended within interventions. We will discuss community social and economic development, community asset mapping, and community organizing. We will also cover the skills of conducting meetings and participating in decision-making, as these are useful skills within many community practice interventions.

© 350.org

© 350.org

Community Social and Economic Development [EPAS 1 and 8]

Community social and economic development (hereafter referred to as "community development"), also called "locality development" and "community building," is an often-ambiguous term with a variety of definitions. In this text, it is a community intervention method that seeks to maximize human potential by focusing on social relationships and the environment in order to improve the physical and social fabric of communities (Rubin & Rubin, 2008). Community development emphasizes social development through relationship-building, education, motivation for self-help, and leadership development. It encourages local participation in community efforts toward the goal of strengthening democracy at the local community level and can include efforts to revitalize institutions. Community development focused on economics includes economic development, affordable housing, employment services, and other activities. Often community social development and community economic development efforts are simultaneous and interdependent, and they can be viewed as a continuum.

Community development may include professions from many fields, including business, sociology, anthropology, psychology, and others (Gamble & Hoff, 2013). Community development work most closely aligns with the Community Capacity Development model discussed earlier, because its goal is to mobilize communities to solve problems and effectively work with institutions, rather than to engage in Social Advocacy or Planning/Policy work. However, community development work also can use a mix of models, depending on the needs at the time.

The following assumptions drive community development (Cnaan & Rothman, 2008, pp. 247–248):

- People may need to become aware of a common problem and create a desire to act in order to solve problems.

- A diverse group of people across various dimensions of diversity (i.e., race, ethnicity, socioeconomic status, etc.) adds value and authenticity to the efforts and ensures that they serve the interests of more than one group of people.

- Democratic decision-making and participatory democracy values and fosters local self-determination.

- Empowerment, or the capacity to solve problems by working with the authorities and institutions that affect the lives of community members, is a central goal of community development.

- The primary constituents of the community development social worker are community members and community organizations, rather than those who hold more power.

• Planned change is preferred to inaction that allows current conditions to continue.

Community Development Skills   The most commonly used practice skills are group work skills. Group work, covered extensively in Chapters 8 and 9, is a major part of community development work, as this type of work is often conducted in meetings. To ensure success, community development social workers must employ task group work skills including leadership; communication; problem solving; and managing group function and processes such as educating, forming groups, seeking consensus, encouraging group discussion, and focusing to solve concerns and problems common to the group. Other skills include analyzing community issues and facilitating the increase of communication among community members (Cnaan & Rothman, 2008).

As discussed in Chapter 9, promoting indigenous leadership in group work directed at community development requires the ability to distribute leadership as widely as possible. The facilitation of effective task meeting is one example of a leadership skill that social workers may use or teach to indigenous leaders. Quick Guide 37 provides an overview of the tasks involved in effective meeting facilitation. These tasks can be distributed among individuals during meetings or handled by a small group as a way to learn and exercise leadership skills.

In task groups, using decision-making processes that promote full participation is an important skill. Decision-making for groups can be handled in many ways, including the **parliamentary procedure**, or **Robert's Rules of Order**, and **consensus decision-making**. Quick Guide 38 provides an overview of Robert's Rules of Order, and Quick Guide 39 provides an overview of consensus decision-making. Both types of decision-making processes are common in task groups, depending on the context of the work. Social workers need to be familiar with decision-making processes to fully participate as individuals and to help others participate.

Recruitment of new participants is an ongoing and important community development skill. Participants involved in community development work are often volunteers, and recruitment, training, monitoring, and rewarding of volunteers is important to the success of the long-term goals. The most effective ways to recruit participants include focusing on people who are most likely to join, using a well-formed recruiting message, using multiple recruitment methods, providing orientation for new participants, and making it easy to join activities. Volunteer activities have to be calibrated to fit the skills, time, and interests of volunteers and be meaningful to them (Cnaan & Rothman, 2008).

Community Development Programs   Community economic development (CED) approaches use economic approaches to develop the capacities of low-income people and neighborhoods (Robinson & Green, 2011). Programs that fall into

QUICK GUIDE 37   ELEMENTS OF EFFECTIVE MEETINGS

STAGE	ELEMENT	NOTES
Preparation	Goals	Develop goal(s) for each meeting.
	Site	Establish a meeting site that is familiar, accessible, perceived as safe, and has parking.
	Date/Timing	Set a date and time that is convenient for the majority of (would-be) participants.
	Facilitator	The facilitator is involved in setting the agenda.
	Agenda	Include the speaker's name in each agenda item, information about the item, and a time limit. Discuss easy items first, followed by hard and then moderate decisions.
	Food	Offer food at various times, unless disruptive.
	Recruitment/Turnout	Provide oral and written meeting announcements and remind people a few days prior to the meeting.
	Meeting Roles	Assign roles ahead of time, including facilitator, note-taker, timekeeper, presenters, and greeter.
	Room Logistics	Set up chairs, AV equipment, flipchart, sign-in table, food/drink, and microphone.
	Background Materials	Prepare background materials about pending decisions and preliminary proposals to discuss.
Meeting	Timeliness	Begin and end the meeting on time.
	Welcome, Introductions	Begin with a warm welcome and introductions to set a positive tone, regardless of the turnout.
	Agenda	Review the agenda with the group and make changes as needed.
	Meeting Rules	Explain any rules, including decision-making rules.
	Discussion	Encourage discussion of various viewpoints; encourage all to speak by drawing out quieter people, limiting those who dominate, and encouraging respect for viewpoints; summarize; and bring closure to discussion.
	Focus	Bring the group back to the agenda if discussion wanders.
	Ending	Summarize meeting results, decisions, and needed follow-up. Thank people for attending.
Follow-up	Notes	Prepare and disseminate meeting notes quickly.
	Thank People	Contact people, especially new people, to thank them for their contribution to the meeting, to encourage follow-up on commitments for action, and to encourage them to attend the next meeting.

Source: Adapted from Bobo, Kendall, & Max, 2010; Minieri & Getsos, 2007

QUICK GUIDE 38   UTILIZING ROBERT'S RULES OF ORDER

Many formal groups, such as Boards of Directors, committees, and policy-making groups, use some form of a formal decision-making process. *Parliamentary procedure,* or *Robert's Rules of Order,* are often used because they are well known, help to maintain order, and allow actions to be taken in an expedient and consistent manner. Although the process can be quite complex, some groups utilize the general rules without learning the minutia. Understanding the major concepts of parliamentary procedure is a critical skill for facilitating and participating in a meeting.

Robert's Rules of Order provide a structured, democratic (majority rules) mechanism whereby formal groups can engage in efficient and fair decision-making. The following are major elements of the process:

- The use of a *motion* to introduce a proposal. Any idea for the group's consideration must be introduced as a motion (i.e., "I move that . . ."). Only one motion can be considered at a time.
- The *seconding* of a motion to move a proposal forward for discussion. A motion cannot move forward in the process unless someone other than the person who made the motion "seconds" the motion (i.e., "I second the motion"). Without a second, a motion dies and is not discussed.
- The use of *debate/discussion* to enable participants to present perspectives and ask questions about a motion. After a motion is made and seconded, the facilitator can open discussion about the motion, and group members can ask questions of the author of the motion.
- *Amendments* to reflect revisions to an original motion based on the debate/discussion. During the discussion, one or more participants may offer an amendment to clarify or narrow the motion. This amendment must be voted on before the original motion is voted on. A majority vote is required to pass an amendment.
- *Majority rules* (i.e., a minimum of 51% of members agreeing) to establish a motion as a decision.

Source: Adapted from Robert III, Honermann, & Balch, 2011

QUICK GUIDE 39   UTILIZING CONSENSUS FOR DECISION-MAKING

Real change, at the individual, family, group, community, or organizational level, comes from persons who are personally committed to a decision or direction in which they fully participated. **Consensus decision-making**, or a cooperative process in which all members develop and agree to support a decision that is in the best interests of the whole group, can be effective in situations in which the following conditions are present:

- Participants feel a genuine stake in the decision.
- Participants share a common purpose and values.
- Participants trust each other.
- Participants are willing to put the best interests of the group over personal preferences.
- Participants can share their ideas and opinions freely, without fear of ridicule.
- Enough time is available for the process.
- Participants can engage in active listening and consider different points of view.

After meeting preparation work, the process:

- Explores the issue toward the goal of developing an informed, shared understanding of the facts and the issue.

- Establishes decision criteria, including such factors as interests/needs that must be met, resource constraints, and possible ramifications of decisions.
- Develops and discusses a written preliminary proposal.
- Tests for consensus, asking participants whether they can live with the proposal (original or amended), whether it meets the decision criteria, and whether it is the best decision possible.
- Reaches agreement by restating the proposed decision and ensuring that participants can support the implementation of the proposal.

Source: Adapted from Dressler, 2006

this approach include the following (Robinson & Green, 2011; Rubin & Rubin, 2008):

- *Individual Development Accounts (IDAs)*: IDAs are matched saving accounts for low-income employed persons who meet income guidelines. IDA programs involve financial education and case management. IDA funds can be spent on approved assets, such as a home, home repair, starting or expanding a small business, or secondary education.

- *Employment training and placement:* Job training programs prepare people for employment opportunities and assist participants in securing and maintaining their employment.

- *Support of small and home-based businesses:* Programs are available to assist people to start and expand small business, including training, technical assistance, support, and linkages to small business loans.

- *Financial education and credit building:* Nonprofit and for-profit organizations provide financial education to build client financial knowledge and also help people build their credit score.

- *Services to help low-income families purchase a home:* Homeownership services are available to assist families to build their credit, locate and secure a home, obtain affordable financing, avoid foreclosure, and maintain their homeownership.

- *Assistance for families:* to file their federal and state taxes and receive the Earned Income Tax Credit (EITC), which is a refundable tax credit for working, low-income families.

- *Human-rights work* (i.e., fair housing, civil rights, environmental justice, disability, and sexual orientation discrimination).

There are many examples of community social and economic development work. Youth development work often involves leadership development and relationship skills as well as job training and employment placement services (Chaskin,

EXHIBIT 11.4

Detroit, Michigan Promotes Community Social and Economic Development

The economic changes of the past few decades have brought empty boulevards, an abandoned train station, empty high-rises, shuttered storefronts, and semideserted neighborhoods to Detroit, Michigan. In striving to revitalize the local economy, the community is paying particular attention to self-reliance. One example is the reimagining of the growing amount of vacant land in the downtown area toward a new, sustainable, local food system. Community and commercial gardens are springing up on land leased from the city, providing employment and volunteer opportunities. In addition to selling produce at local farmers markets during the summer, some gardens are also installing hoop houses, in which food can be grown year-round. There are also plans for indoor tilapia and shrimp farms, tree farms, and other uses of the land that will facilitate employment and sustainability (Sands, 2015). The emergence of a local food system has been spurred by the Detroit Food Policy Council, which works to create the local policy conditions to facilitate the expansion of a "sustainable local food system that promotes food security, food justice, and food sovereignty in the city of Detroit" (Detroit Food Policy Council, 2016).

Source: Detroit Food Policy Council, 2016; Sands, 2015

2010; Wheeler & Thomas, 2011). Domestic violence services can include education, financial education, credit building, IDA services, and economic advocacy (Family Resource Center, 2016). Building community partnerships for school-based services, such as physical and mental health services, counseling, mentoring, and other programs, is an example of community development work focused primarily on social development (Poole, 2009). Work with immigrants and refugees can include community development work, including financial literacy; assistance for small business owners to start, expand, and strengthen their business; and lending for small businesses and micro business loans through a peer lending program as well as case management, translation, education, and other services (International Institute St. Louis, 2016). Some community development focuses solely on improving the physical environments of communities through efforts such as the production of affordable housing, the development of commercial space in low income communities, and/or the redevelopment of entire streets. Exhibit 11.4 provides an example of community development.

Asset-Based Community Development

We discussed community asset mapping as an assessment strategy in Chapter 10. You can use the community data you gather as part of the assessment process in the community intervention. After collecting the data, the next step is to group all of the data into categories, such as capabilities of individuals, including those marginalized within the community, associations, local institutions, physical assets, and (potential) leaders. Exhibit 11.5 provides examples of the types of information you can

EXHIBIT 11.5

Community Assets

Associations
Animal Care Groups
Anti-Crime Groups
Block Clubs
Business Organizations
Charitable Groups
Civic Events Groups
Cultural Groups
Disability/Special Needs Groups
Education Groups
Elderly Groups
Environmental Groups
Family Support Groups
Health Advocacy and Fitness
Heritage Groups
Hobby and Collectors Groups
Men's Groups
Mentoring Groups
Mutual Support Groups
Neighborhood Groups
Political Organizations
Recreation Groups
Religious Groups
Service Clubs
Social Groups
Union Groups
Veteran's Groups
Women's Groups
Youth Groups

Local Economy
Banks
Barter & Exchange
Business Associations
CDCs
Chamber of Commerce
Consumer Expenditures
Corporations & Branches
Credit Unions
For-Profit Businesses
Foundations
Institutional-Purchasing Power
and Personnel
Merchants

Physical Space
Bike Paths
Bird Watching Sites
Campsites
Duck Ponds
Fishing Spots
Forests/Forest Preserves
Gardens
Housing
Natural Habitats – Coastal,
Marine, Amphibian
Parking Lots
Parks
Picnic Areas
Playgrounds
Star Gazing Sites
Streets
Transit Stops and Facilities
Vacant Land & Buildings
Walking Paths
Wildlife Center
Zoos

Individuals
Gifts, Skills, Capacities,
Knowledge and Traits of:
Activists
Artists
Entrepreneurs
Ex-Offenders
Older Adults
Parents
People with Disabilities
Students
Veterans
Welfare Recipients
Youth

Institutions
Community Colleges
Fire Departments
Foundations
Hospitals
Libraries
Media
Museums
Nonprofit Organizations
Police Departments
Schools
Social Service Agencies
Universities

Source: Kretzmann & McKnight, 2005

group in each category. As a social worker, building your relationship with all of these types of assets, as well as relationships between these types of assets, is a key ingredient in a community change effort. Building strong networks among these assets will strengthen the social fabric of the community and build capacity as a whole community. For example, a social worker may be involved in establishing a network of social service providers, representatives of educational institutions, and business leaders in communities to work on local community challenges. Social workers may need to identify the self-interest of the various groups when recruiting them to become involved, such as mentioning to local businesses that strengthening their ties to organizations serving local youth also involves the possibility of expanding their pool of future labor. These efforts can result in a more self-reliant community.

As relationships are built, the ability of the community to solve problems locally increases. Social workers prompt associations and institutions to increase their contributions to community efforts. For example, social workers can facilitate and support organizations in their work to develop websites, and they can contact local newspapers and radio stations to aid the flow of useful information. The process of community asset development may involve community meetings to develop a local vision and the strategies to implement this vision. Faith communities (such as churches or synagogues), faith networks (such as ministerial alliance), associations (such as clubs or groups), or institutions (such as a local school district or large employer) can sponsor community planning processes. After the planning process, the planning group can seek outside resources, if needed, to carry out a community plan. Bringing in outside resources, such as foundations, government actors, and others, *after* creating a plan ensures that community plans are truly resident-driven. If the group brings in outside resources during the planning process, careful participatory planning must occur to ensure that citizens' knowledge and views about what is good for the community are heard and considered. The outcomes of a participatory, community-driven planning process reflect the desires of the residents (Weil, 2013).

In addition to community development work, community social work practice interventions also include community organizing. Having considered community development, our discussion now turns to community organizing as a standalone community intervention that can be integrated into community development.

Community Organizing

Community organizing is a practice skill that entails using a process to mobilize people and their resources to identify problems and advocate for change to improve the quality of life in marginalized communities (Ohmer & Brooks, 2013). Community organizing skills can be used within any of the three models of community practice mentioned earlier (planning/policy, community capacity development, and social advocacy). The target of community organizing efforts can aim at a wide variety of targets, including local, state, and federal government officials; legislators; private landlords; corporate CEOs; and officials of the global organizations. For example, in the Brickville case, the supporting and opposing groups both target public officials, who have control over the public resources needed for the budget of the redevelopment effort.

While community organizing work typically focuses on a particular change effort, such as passing a local ballot issue about sales tax, the form that community organizing takes can vary widely. Community organization can include accepting and working with the existing power relationships, or **consensus organizing**, and challenging the existing power relationship, or **direct action organizing**.

Exhibit 11.6 describes the continuum of services as framed by the degree to which people accept the existing power relationships within a community. The left side of the exhibit depicts consensus organizing. Consensus organizing involves developing strong relationships and partnerships among and between community members and stakeholders and with people and institutions that are external to the community and hold power that can facilitate community change.

External powers can include government officials, landlords who own rental property in the community, and/or private business owners. Engaging in consensus community organizing brings together community participants and uses the power structure as a partner in the change effort. Exhibit 11.7 shows the assumptions of the consensus organizing approach.

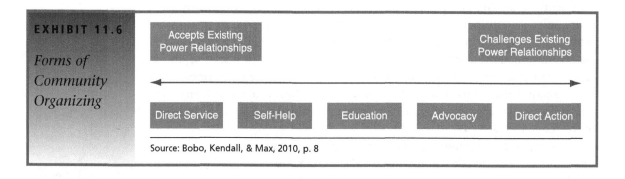

EXHIBIT 11.6

Forms of Community Organizing

Accepts Existing Power Relationships

Challenges Existing Power Relationships

Direct Service   Self-Help   Education   Advocacy   Direct Action

Source: Bobo, Kendall, & Max, 2010, p. 8

EXHIBIT 11.7

Assumptions of the Consensus Organizing Approach

- Ordinary people can and should be involved in creating sustainable community change.
- It is important to identify and build on community strengths and assets, rather than deficits.
- Potential leaders are everywhere and often need recognition and support to thrive.
- The organizer must be a selfless promoter of others.
- The organizer must seek to achieve self-interest for residents and external partners.
- Powerful people and institutions want to assist with community change.

Source: Adapted from Ohmer & DeMasi, 2009

The right side of Exhibit 11.6 represents direct action community organizing, or **conflict organizing**. This form of community organizing assumes that a disadvantaged population must be organized to make demands on a target for equal treatment/resources, with the larger goal of gaining power and changing the structure of power. With conflict organizing, the power structure is not seen as a partner but more as a target of action (Ohmer & DeMasi, 2009). The targets of conflict organizing are those with power in the community to make change, such as landlords and government officials—the same people and institutions with which consensus organizers seek to create partnerships.

In the Brickville example, both sides could use consensus or conflict organizing. Using conflict organizing, both groups could organize their supporters to press public officials and the developer to demand more power in the decision-making process about the redevelopment plan. In contrast, both sides could use consensus organizing by attempting to partner with the developer and/or the public officials, and gain input through a collaborative process.

Community Organizing Skills   The three essential elements for community organizing along the continuum are empowering individuals, building and strengthening community bonds, and building progressive organizations (Rubin & Rubin, 2008). Organizers can empower individuals by (1) encouraging participation, (2) arranging tasks so individuals experience success and build their confidence to engage in public affairs, (3) organizing tasks so individuals' involvement is meaningful and builds leadership skills, and (4) recognizing and supporting their efforts (Minieri & Getsos, 2007). Building progressive organizations involves a mission to promote social equity and participatory democracy processes (Rubin & Rubin, 2008), such as Robert's Rules of Order or consensus.

People build bonds by developing a shared sense of community. When individuals work together to determine common community issues, analyze the issues, select issues on which to work, develop and implement strategies, and engage in evaluation toward a common goal, they create bonds and social networks (Rubin & Rubin, 2008). In the process of community organizing, once organizers have built relationships, they identify common challenges with a core group. As new members are continually recruited, the core group works to enact change, even of a small magnitude (Ohmer & DeMasi, 2009).

The ultimate desired outcomes of community organizing efforts frame many aspects of community practice. For example, at the conflict end of the organizing continuum, the final desired outcome is to alter the balance of power so that resources are more equitably distributed, while at the other end of the continuum, in Exhibit 11.6, strong partnerships between community residents and external power sources that result in tangible resources is the desired outcome (Ohmer & DeMasi, 2009). For example, in the Brickville case, using conflict organizing, both supporting and opposing groups could ultimately seek to change the balance of power between themselves and the developer and public officials. Using consensus

<table>
<tr>
<td>

EXHIBIT 11.8

Community Organizing to Encourage People of Faith to Vote and Facilitate the Process

</td>
<td>

In several communities, houses of worship are the springboard for community organizing efforts to encourage people to vote and facilitate the electoral process. For example, community organizers are engaged in a "Rock the Muslim Vote" campaign to register Muslims to vote. They work in mosques and Islamic centers in the Los Angeles area. These efforts are encouraging Muslims to vote so their voices are amplified in political campaigns, and ultimately in community affairs (Pogash, 2016). In another example, community organizers are working in Ohio to ensure that the state law that purges infrequent voters from voting rolls does not disenfranchise African American voters. Community organizers are working in predominantly black churches to help congregants check the Secretary of State's public records to see if they are still registered to vote. If they are not still registered, they help them become registered (Yi, Rothman, & Burty, 2016, July 31)

Source: Pogash, 2016; Yi, Rothman, & Burty, 2016, July 31

</td>
</tr>
</table>

organizing, the groups would seek to build strong and enduring partnerships among all of the players, and seek to gain build relationships with the powerful decision makers that will endure past the current issue of the redevelopment. This difference affects the importance of specific skills, such as analyzing the power of a target, prioritizing issues on which to work (conflict organizing), building relationships with external resources, and brokering relationships between community groups and institutions (consensus organizing) (Bobo, Kendall, & Max, 2010; Ohmer & DeMasis, 2009).

A Generalist Approach to Community Intervention [EPAS 4]

Depending on the context of the community intervention, generalist social work practitioners often integrate aspects of community organizing and community development activities into their practice. For example, in many communities, a shared identity, bonds between residents, the skills for public discourse, the ability to determine priorities, the skills to work together on common challenges, and leadership skills all must be developed for community change efforts to be possible. Social workers can play an important role in helping develop these prerequisites. Social workers who work primarily with individuals, families, and groups have opportunities to support the development of these skills and to encourage people to participate in community efforts.

There are many ways that social workers can help build the capacity of individuals to engage in community interventions. At the interpersonal level, social workers emphasize collaboration with their clients to optimize individuals' rights, strengths, and capabilities. Social workers discuss power and control with their clients to increase clients' awareness of these dynamics in their everyday lives and in community activities. Social workers can regard clients as citizens, consumers, and partners in change efforts and can use dialogue to raise client awareness about sociopolitical realities. As first suggested by educator Paulo Freire (1973), social workers educate clients about the social conditions, patterns of resource distribution, oppression, and other social and environmental factors that contribute to their situation using respectful discussion and questioning. Social workers help prepare and support people to engage in collective action.

Social workers strive to provide evidence-based interventions in community practice. Creating a body of research to inform evidence-based practice (first introduced in Chapter 4) has proven challenging due to the complexity of community interventions, the difficulties of community research, and many organizations' lack of capacity to engage in research. Yet, social workers must conduct or locate research before intervening. Quick Guide 40 lists sample resources for locating evidence on community practice interventions. Exhibit 11.9 provides research findings about the most effective community intervention activities that social workers undertake (Ohmer & Korr, 2006).

Social workers also engage in social planning efforts when they participate in proposing that elected officials or human service planning councils take action They engage by writing letters, testifying to committees, becoming a member of planning committees, and/or organizing others to lobby planning councils. As part of that process, social workers can carefully create opportunities for community members to

QUICK GUIDE 40   EXAMPLES OF PUBLIC AND PRIVATE EFFORTS TO PROMOTE EVIDENCE-BASED COMMUNITY PRACTICE

Children, Families, and Communities

1. Harvard Family Research Project, Harvard Graduate School of Education
   The Evaluation Exchange is a periodical that contains new lessons and emerging strategies for evaluating programs and policies, particularly those focused on children, families, and communities.

Community Change

2. The Aspen Institute report, *Building Knowledge about Community Change,* summarizes key learning over the past fifteen years about how to evaluate community change initiatives and how to identify strategies for enhancing the evidence base for improving conditions in poor communities. The conclusions in the report are based primarily on the experiences of a group of comprehensive community initiatives (CCIs) in the United States and the United Kingdom.

Health

3. King's Fund
   The policy paper, *Finding Out What Works,* provides information about the effectiveness of health initiatives in Britain.

QUICK GUIDE 40 CONTINUED

Early Childhood, Health Care, and Housing

4. Centers for Disease Controls and Prevention: Community Preventative Services Task Force
   The Community Guide includes systemic reviews of interventions in early childhood development programs, culturally competent health care, and housing.

Housing

5. U.S. Department of Housing and Urban Development (HUD)
   The Program Evaluation Division of HUD has done much research on housing issues, including projects such as costs of homelessness, fair housing accessibility, and comprehensive initiatives such as "Moving to Opportunity."

Mental Health in Communities

6. National Registry of Evidence-based Programs and Practices (NREPP)
   Sponsored by the Substance Abuse and Mental Health Services Administration, NREPP is an online, searchable registry of mental health and substance abuse interventions.

Neighborhood Research, Policy, and Practices

7. Economic and Social Research Council
   The Centre for Neighbourhood Research (CNR) identifies, evaluates, and synthesizes existing social science research on social, economic, and political processes relevant to neighborhood policies and practices in the UK.

Violence Prevention

8. The Center for the Study and Prevention of Violence (CSPV), University of Colorado, Boulder
   Blueprints for Violence Prevention is a project of CSPV that identifies outstanding violence and drug prevention programs that meet a high scientific standard of effectiveness.

Miscellaneous

9. The Campbell Collaboration
   This international research network prepares, maintains, and disseminates systematic reviews on a wide variety of topics related to social welfare and community practice.
10. Laura and John Arnold Foundation Evidence-Based Policy and Innovation
    This nonprofit organization provides evidence about social interventions.
11. Social Care Institute for Excellence
    This charity organization provides evidence-based practice tools and evidence about programs.
12. Society for Community Research and Action, Division 27 of the American Psychological Association (APA)
    The Society provides access to research on community interventions.
13. Society for Child and Family Policy and Practice, Division 37 of the American Psychological Association (APA)
    The Society provides information about services and service structures for children and youth.
14. Community Toolbox
    Their databases of best practices promote community health and development.

Sources: Ohmer, 2008; Thyer, 2008

EXHIBIT 11.9

Effectiveness of Community Practice

Community practice interventions are often complex, with multiple community locations, goals, and activities that make them difficult to evaluate for compliance and fidelity. Community practice interventions can have:

1. a positive impact on facilitating citizen participation, including increasing collective action and community involvement;
2. facilitate personal and collective competencies among participants, including increasing self-esteem, personal and community empowerment, leadership and political skills, and community pride and belonging;
3. a positive impact on improving the physical, social, and economic conditions of communities (i.e., creating and improving affordable housing, increasing homeownership, improving infrastructure and physical appearance, increasing income, investment, and employment, improving high school education, and reducing the sale of alcohol to and its use among young people);
4. the potential for no effect (many studies indicate that interventions do not affect the physical and economic attributes of the communities); and
5. greater likelihood of involving the community organizing efforts of older female residents, African Americans, and Hispanics (other factors that help to explain and predict citizen participation include interest in the problems the program was attempting to solve, neighborhood perceptions and relationships, and length of residency).

Community practice interventions more easily improve citizen participation and associated benefits (i.e., improving collective action and personal and political skills of participants) than they improve complex physical, social, and economic problems in poor communities. Therefore, social work strategies should simultaneously focus on developing ways to strengthen citizen participation and building the capacity of individuals.

Source: Ohmer & Korr, 2006.

participate so that their participation is meaningful and effective, rather than a token effort to "involve" residents. For example, social workers invite community residents to testify at public hearings about proposals to close schools in their neighborhood and help prepare them to testify. Social workers also seek resident involvement in neighborhood committees and work to ensure that residents can voice their opinions, participate fully in decision-making, and assist to implement decisions. Social workers also make connections between disparate situations, so that the needs of individuals are connected to broader efforts and wider structures. For example, if a social worker encounters a resident whose child has lead poisoning, the social worker may be able to link this "case" to a broader "cause" of a community problem with lead poisoning due to the old housing stock in the neighborhood and the reluctance of landlords to remediate the lead in their units. Social workers also invite residents to participate in community-wide efforts to alleviate and prevent the problem, such as lead paint screenings in schools and programs to help tenants test for lead paint in their apartments.

GLOBAL APPROACHES FOR COMMUNITY SOCIAL WORK PRACTICE

While all types of social work practice methods, including casework, group work, and family work, are used around the world, community social work practice is an intervention method that offers unique contributions. Social workers are concerned about poverty and social issues that they encounter in every country, yet large differences in the scope and severity of social issues exist. While a social worker can address poverty and social issues that she or he encounters on a small scale through individual, family, and group social work interventions and can apply a social welfare approach through offering governmental income and/or health assistance, widespread poverty and disasters in countries without social safety nets often require a community practice approach (Healy, 2008). Exhibit 11.10 provides an overview of strategies to link local social work practice with global social work practice, particularly focused on community practice. While any of the models described in this chapter may be appropriate, given a specific community context, we next turn our attention to community development and community organizing using global approaches at home and in other countries.

International Social Work Community Development

As with domestic social work community development practice, the international spectrum of social and economic development activities is broad and has many actors. Some large international organizations (e.g., the United Nations Development Programme, World Health Organization, World Bank, International Monetary Fund) and national players, such as U.S. Agency for International Development (USAID) and the U.S. Peace Corps, play important roles in community development work in developed and developing countries through funding, facilitation, oversight, and management of community development projects and programs. There are also organizations that operate from within the U.S. that support and facilitate international community development; for example, they engage in strategic planning, fundraising, and other activities that support practice outside of the U.S.

Organizations engaged in international community development work, physically located both locally and abroad, facilitate and plan small business loans, credit guarantees, the provision of primary health care, and the creation of large-scale physical projects (such as the building of dams), among other activities. Nongovernmental organizations, such as the International Red Cross, CARE, Catholic Relief Services, and Save the Children, also focus on self-sustaining development projects that have long-reaching positive effects on communities. Examples

- Concentrating on community development as a focus for practice and the incorporation of community development approaches in all social work practice.
- Extending the practice of policy advocacy to international forums.
- Developing techniques to enable the disadvantaged and oppressed to find a voice not merely in national forums, but also globally, in international solidarity.
- Making effective use of new technologies to link workers and community groups globally.
- Including global forces as a critical component of problem analysis and consciousness raising.

The global local web

- Establishing social work roles and positions in international nongovernmental organizations (NGOs) and United Nations (UN) agencies.
- Incorporating a strong human rights analysis alongside more traditional social work needs-based practice.
- Seeking opportunities for social workers to develop internationalist understandings through exchange programs and international courses in schools of social work.
- Developing further analysis and research about the link between the global and the local across social work knowledge, values, and skills.

Source: Ife, 2000, pp. 62–63; Reisch, 2013

include forming local cooperatives, introducing farming techniques, and facilitating preventive health care projects and local sanitation projects (e.g., digging wells and building latrines) (Healy, 2008).

The goal of international community development projects is to reach the point at which the community can sustain them. Organizers most often employ local-level development, in which the community takes responsibility for the work. Local-level development requires and allows the persons experiencing the problem or need to plan and implement the strategies for improvement. The local-level approach requires social workers to focus on the development of relationships with community members, groups, and institutions so that development projects are truly locally determined and directed (Healy, 2008). Exhibit 11.11 provides an

EXHIBIT 11.11

Key Strategies and Programs for International Local-Level Development

- *Basic literacy courses:* Social workers can recruit and train teachers from local communities to provide basic literacy instruction that conforms to local culture, and socioeconomic realities and that responds to the desires of the local population.
- *Primary school education:* Primary school education is a key element to development. Social workers can support children seeking an education and can work with the local community to provide needed resources.
- *Basic health care:* Social workers can recruit and train staff from local communities to provide basic health care. Social workers can also be involved in education about basic hygiene, immunizations, and disease prevention efforts.
- *Adult education, basic training, and capacity building:* If a community wishes, social workers can facilitate adult basic education or training in such fields as agriculture, forestry, or marketing for small businesses.
- *Awareness-raising and empowerment:* Through informal or formal dialogue, social workers can assist individuals, families, groups, and communities to understand their life situation, whether it be oppression, exclusion, poverty, drug addiction, or something else. This understanding includes recognition of the forces that have led to and reinforce the present situation. This realization can lead to change efforts.
- *Local income-generation programs:* Social workers can be involved in education or the facilitation of programs that lead to higher income generation at the individual, family, or community level. Such programs can lead to better farming methods, increased number of or profitability of small businesses, or large community-wide industries, such as food processing plants.
- *Credit schemes and people's banks:* To overcome community members' inability to access financial credit through formal institutions, social workers can be involved in local level, small lending programs (for example, see Exhibit 11.12).
- *Community-based self-help programs:* Social workers can help facilitate a planned community response to a community need, such as developing a local program to assist the disabled, mentally ill, or AIDS orphans.
- *Leadership development:* Social workers can support existing leaders and train new ones.
- *Local organization and institution promotion and capacity building:* Social workers may be involved in helping create or promote local institutions, such as those that oversee education or community recreation.
- *Linking local organizations to government agencies and international structures:* Social workers can provide information, support, and connections between local organizations and external resources.
- *Comprehensive community development programs:* Social workers can help facilitate the integration of development efforts to create a holistic effort.

Source: Cox & Pawar, 2013, pp. 199–220

An effort to loan one Bangladeshi woman $27 dollars has evolved into a worldwide movement to help the poor escape dire poverty by providing micro-credit. Many poor small business owners lack the money to purchase needed raw goods or supplies for their business, and they depend on high-cost credit from moneylenders. The Grameen (which means "village") Bank was founded on the idea that small loans with reasonable terms would make a large difference in the lives of the poor. The bank began as a very small effort in 1983, and now has over 2,500 branches in 81,000 villages in Bangladesh, with a loan repayment rate of 96%.

The bank offers loans without collateral requirements, a credit history, or any legal instruments. The bank makes loans to a self-made group of five friends, rather than an individual. When one wants to take out a loan, the other group members must approve. Members of the group provide encouragement, support, and practical assistance to one another. The groups from each village attend weekly meetings in their village, in which they collect loan repayments, accept loan applications, and undertake activities to foster community bonds and provide education about important topics. The positive social pressure the group has exerted has facilitated a high repayment rate of the small loans. The Grameen Bank borrowers also commit to "The Sixteen Decisions," a list of values and activities that foster healthy living, communal action, and education for children.

EXHIBIT 11.12

International Community Development Case Example: Grameen Bank

overview of key strategies and programs for local-level community development. Exhibits 11.12 and 11.13 provide case examples of international community development work that implements several of the strategies and programs.

Globalization and Community Organizing in Social Work Practice [EPAS 8]

Similarities exist between community organizing efforts at the international level and efforts in the U.S. For example, regardless of the setting or context, empowering individuals, building and strengthening community bonds, and building progressive organizations are appropriate community organizing goals. Community organizing skills are similar, as they focus on a particular change effort.

Community organizing efforts, both in the U.S and abroad, are closely related to global issues; therefore, local issues must be viewed within globally interconnected systems (Reisch, 2013). For example, international migration of workers from the poorer to wealthier countries, and from countries engaged in civil conflict to those at peace has left large numbers of workers, some of whom are not documented, vulnerable to employer abuse and exploitation due to their tenuous legal status, and desperate to generate income to support themselves and their families in their home countries. A worldwide effort has ensued to build the power of immigrant workers to raise their wages and improve their working conditions by bringing together labor organizing and community organizing. These efforts mostly use direct action, or

EXHIBIT 11.13

International Community Development Case Example: Micro-Financing Partners in Africa

Micro-Financing Partners in Africa (MFPA) is a U.S.-based organization that provides grants to strengthen and expand micro-financing, employment, and health programs in Africa. MFPA raises money in the U.S. through donor appeals and fundraising events. They provide funds to partner organizations working in Tanzania, Kenya, Uganda, Rwanda, and the Democratic Republic of Congo on a wide variety of projects designed to help people provide for their own needs within their families and within their communities, and promote health within their communities. They carry out their mission through four primary projects: providing funds for small business loans, providing funds for gifts of animals (such as cows) that generate income from products (such as milk), vocational skills training, and supporting cooperative ventures, such as a cooperatively owned soy farm and bakery. They have recently added a health program that promotes healthy pregnancies and births.

One example of their work is the financial support they provide for small businesses in Tanzania. A local organization organizes women into small groups of neighbors, and teaches them business skills. When they finish with their training, one woman starts a small business with loan funds, typically about $50. Business can be a wide variety of things that will sell in their local community, such as selling fried fish, tailoring, or raising rabbits. When she finishes repaying her loan from her business profits, the next woman in the group can apply for a loan. Each of the women support one another in their business, because their success means that they can apply for a loan (MicroFinancing Partners in Africa, n.d.).

conflict, organizing strategies, and activities to gain changes in public policy (Hanley & Shragge, 2009). Other global community organizing efforts focus on the domestic violence immigrants experience (Kasvin & Tashayeva, 2004), workers' rights (International Labor Rights Forum, n.d.), child welfare issues related to deportation of immigrants, global warming (350.org, n.d.), and a host of other interrelated issues in the global interconnections of systems. Due to the transnational nature of local issues, such as unemployment, environmental problems, and public health challenges, local development work must be accomplished within the framework of globalization of human challenges. For example, community development work that intends to impact the local economy must consider the global economic climate, rather than just the local market.

Community social work practice, just like social work practice with other systems levels, ends with the termination and evaluation phase. The next section will consider trends that impact this phase, as well as the skills needed to professionally master the ending phase of social work community practice.

CONTEMPORARY TRENDS AND SKILLS FOR THE ENDING PHASE OF COMMUNITY SOCIAL WORK: TERMINATION, EVALUATION, AND FOLLOW-UP

Community social work practitioners join the community in change efforts and facilitate the community leadership of the tasks required. Often, community practice accomplishments are the result of months and even years (or decades) of work and consist of many smaller change efforts. For example, social workers may engage in community development struggles to rid the community of child lead poisoning. This overarching change effort can involve tasks to change local policy regarding rental housing, work with landlords to remediate lead paint, promote local school screening for child lead poisoning, and work with the local public health clinic to create an outreach program to prevent lead poisoning and reach persons potentially affected. Each of these may have involved lengthy efforts.

Achieving the goals of community change efforts, whether smaller goals achieved in the process of working toward a larger goal or the larger goal itself, leads us to the next phase of the change effort, termination and evaluation.

Community Social Work Practice Endings

Termination in community social work practice can be more complex than termination with other clients. Community practice can involve long-term change efforts (such as Brickville's redevelopment efforts that would take many years) that are complex, with the potential involvement of many players and institutions in the process. The termination phase in community practice is often termination of the social worker from the community (if moving on to other responsibilities), of the social worker's sponsoring organization from a community change effort (if the organization can no longer participate for some reason), or termination of people or institutions from community change efforts, which may continue without them. Termination of one change effort can also occur when the community has prioritized other needs, such as a situation where the community is grappling with a natural disaster. For example, a social worker may terminate with a community lead prevention and remediation effort if lead poisoning levels drop dramatically and/or if local leadership is effectively working on the issue and no longer need the social worker's assistance.

As in terminations with other clients, endings can be emotional, particularly if the intervention has been longstanding. Building relationships is a key element to all types of community practice; therefore, the social worker's role in termination is to "help [participants] examine their accomplishments, review their experience together, and prepare for the future" (Garvin & Galinsky, 2013). Social workers may also facilitate the expression and integration of positive and negative emotions, which can include such feelings as elation and joy about successes achieved and/or such negative emotions as disappointment, rejection, abandonment, or anger, depending on the circumstances of the termination. The social worker and community participants can celebrate milestones and successes along the way toward larger goals, even if those currently involved do not see an intervention through to the final, hoped-for result.

Endings and Follow-Up in Community Practice Utilizing Strengths and Empowerment A social worker employing strengths and empowerment approaches facilitates the community process of reviewing progress toward identified goals and developing strategies for sustaining changes. In social work community practice, the social worker can invite each participant to review and reflect on her or his individual experience in the change effort, including strengths brought to the process, any change they personally experienced, and plans for contributing to the maintenance of the change(s). Engaging individual members in this process can provide closure for all involved. Like group work practice, participants can also use other participants' reflections to examine their own growth processes.

As community social work practice often involves the use of task groups, many elements of and skills needed in group work terminations may apply. For example, using a strengths-based perspective, the social worker can help the members of the group to reflect on the strengths they developed as they engaged in community change efforts. The social worker can use the group ending as an opportunity to provide feedback on the individual, group, and community changes she or he observes.

The termination process can employ a strengths perspective even when community goals are not realized. Participants can review the community and group strengths that existed at the outset of their efforts, those strengths they gained or mobilized during the process, and those strengths participants can carry with them after the formal change effort has ended. While the members (and the social worker) may be dismayed at not achieving desired goals, strategizing about ways in which participants can continue to work toward achieving the goals can, in fact, be empowering.

As in terminations with individuals, families, and groups, a key element of the termination process with communities is a focus on sustaining the gains achieved, such as community bonding, leadership skills, civic engagement, and/or the continuation and growth of community networks and community programs. Regardless of the circumstances of the termination, a focus on community strengths and the positive outcomes of the intervention can energize community members and institutions to continue their efforts. If the termination occurs because the community intervention achieves its goal, the community can build on their successes and begin the assessment, intervention, and evaluation process anew.

Following-up involves helping to sustain any gains from the intervention. Follow-up may involve many people and institutions, particularly if the social worker (and his/her sponsoring organization) supplied many resources for the intervention. Follow-up also involves honoring any commitments made during the intervention and termination process, and welcoming any new actors into the change process. New actors, such as new community participants or institutions, may need to become involved to continue the community change efforts if professional social work resources will not be available. For example, let's consider the social worker involved in the change efforts related to lead paint discussed earlier. If the social worker was transferred to a different school and needed to terminate from the efforts, the social worker would transfer responsibilities to another leader in the effort, such as a co-worker, parent, local development organization staff member, other community resident, or a group of professionals involved in the effort, so that the change effort could continue. Following up involves ensuring that the new leaders have the resources they need to continue the efforts. However, if the local leadership was not sufficiently developed to maintain the community change effort, despite follow-up, the effort would discontinue. Exhibit 11.14 provides an example of a termination of a community organizing effort.

Evaluation of Social Work Practice with Communities [EPAS 9]

Similar to evaluation with individuals, families, and groups, evaluation of social work community practice interventions can assess the process along the way (i.e., **process evaluation**); the extent to which goals were achieved (i.e., **outcome evaluation**); and the social worker's skills in the intervention phase. Just as the community change effort was a collaborative process, so too is the evaluation. Community participation is important throughout the change effort in order to empower participants, and during the evaluation process, collaboration as an equal partner in this process leads to a feeling of ownership of the information. The evaluation process seeks to determine the value of something and differs from monitoring the intervention (Netting et al., 2017).

The evaluation process begins as an element of the intervention design, and may be predetermined by an organization, a funder, or other decision-maker. It requires social workers and community members first to determine: (1) if both the process and outcomes will be evaluated, (2) the ways in which the process and outcomes will be evaluated, and (3) the means by which data will be collected as the basis for the evaluation. Evaluation of community change efforts may include examinations of the personal, interpersonal, and community levels. Evaluation of the community effort may include an evaluation of the group work involved, which is covered extensively in Chapter 9.

Preferably, the evaluation process will include both qualitative and quantitative data to provide information about the process of community change and progress on the desired outcomes at the personal, interpersonal, and community levels. Methods may include pre- and post-measures of community functioning. These measures include, but are not limited to, the use of validated and standardized

EXHIBIT
11.14

*Termination,
Evaluation,
and Follow-Up*

Communities Facilitating Opportunity (CFO) is an organization that conducts community organizing through a federation of twenty-five local faith-based institutions. One area of their work focuses on the lack of affordable housing production in their community for over a decade. The work of the CFO leaders and members, with the support of staff members, included years of conducting research with both affected individuals, public officials, and others involved in the affordable housing production and maintenance system, holding numerous meetings with relevant public officials to demand answers to questions about the lack of quality affordable housing in their community and drawing media attention to the problem. The housing department failed time and time again to deliver on promises, despite the availability of federal funding dedicated to the production of affordable housing for the city. CFO also called attention to official city and federal audits that demonstrated a significant level of dysfunction and corruption within the city housing department. One project that they focused on was the renovation of two small houses in a working class neighborhood at a cost that exceeded twenty times the assessed value of those properties. The housing agency used many tactics to disempower citizen input, such as verbally promising to take action and not following through, and yelling and saying demeaning things to CFO leaders and members. CFO finally decided to hold a public meeting to directly address public officials in front of a large number of their constituents. They specifically invited the mayor and other local public officials to attend the meeting to directly engage the public and the leadership of their local government.

The overall goals of members for this CFO campaign were to establish: (1) an accountable city government, (2) a working program for the repair of homes, (3) a way to hold absentee landlords accountable, (4) protection from predatory mortgage lenders, and (5) a focus on building communities—not just homes. In the meeting, the group pointed out that $18 million in funds flowed annually through the city housing agency in a haphazard, nontransparent way. They offered specific policy proposals, such as establishing a $5 million fund for minor home repair to add to existing monies, targeting neighborhoods where the existing housing stock was strained. Two weeks after the public meeting, the City Manager moved all personnel out of the city housing agency to other city agencies, saying that he had concluded that the city housing agency was often controlled by outside special interests, that housing services were fragmented, and that there was no comprehensive approach for building and selling houses. A completely new staff was needed to correct these deep problems. CFO members would be involved in elements of restructuring and re-staffing the organization.

Termination: When the CFO leadership and membership recognized that at least one of the intervention goals was met, they terminated the campaign; the city was now more accountable for decisions about affordable housing production. The restructuring of the housing agency fundamentally shifted who had the power to make decisions about affordable housing in the city. As follow-up, CFO, along with its partners, monitored the rebuilding of a branch of local government that implements housing and community development. CFO action helped provide the necessary pressure to create change in the

**EXHIBIT
11.14**

Continued

structure of the local government. CFO decided to end its tactics designed to put pressure on the city and to instead work with the City Manager to create a new agency that
would be transparent and accountable, with the hopes that new personnel could meet
their other goals.

   Using the strengths perspective, CFO engaged in reflection to discern group and
community strengths present from the beginning and those gained through the intervention. CFO leadership and membership also engaged in a group process to review
their accomplishments and to discern future movements. The CFO focused on building
their strength as an organization, bonding, leadership skills, knowledge of and engagement with civic affairs and city personnel, and the continuation and growth of their
network of organizations in the community.

Evaluation: Evaluation of this community practice intervention occurred both in the
short-term and the long-term. Throughout the long campaign, the social worker assisted
leaders to facilitate their own reflection, member reflection about the degree to which
they met short-term goals, and documentation of the process. Short-term goals in this
case include obtaining: meetings with involved parties and public officials; information;
commitments of action; actions taken; and media coverage. Long-term efforts were
evaluated over many years, and required documentation of media coverage, turnout at
public meetings, and the amount and type of responsiveness of public officials and
decision-makers. CFO also collected data on the housing problems over the years from
the housing agency, federal agencies, and others. Evaluation also included the extent to
which members realized increasing confidence, leadership skills, personal speaking
skills, organizing skills, and feelings of efficacy. Methods included review of meeting
minutes and other organization (i.e., internal reports); interviews with staff, CFO leadership, and members; and public documents.

Source: Speer & Christens, 2011

measures; direct observation by the social worker to document change; use of publically available data (i.e., U.S. Census data and others); administrative data from
public departments such as policy, public health, child welfare, police, and others;
GIS mapping (discussed in Chapter 10); and feedback from other professionals
(Ohmer, 2008).

   One good example of a community evaluation process comes from a
community development effort in Perth, Western Australia. The aim of the evaluation was to compare the quality of life in a community that had experienced
community development initiatives with the quality of life in a nearby community
that had not experienced the initiatives. The residents used the Australian Unity
Wellbeing Index to rate individual and neighborhood well-being. Additionally,
the evaluation compared residents' well-being to national averages (Blunsdon &
Davern, 2007).

STRAIGHT TALK ABOUT COMMUNITY INTERVENTION, TERMINATION, EVALUATION, AND FOLLOW-UP

Community social work practice, including the intervention, termination, and evaluation and follow-up phases, offers many rewards and challenges. One challenging aspect of some types of community social work practice is long hours at salaries less than those in individual, family, and group practice. Further, community social work practice can involve working during the day with professionals in organizations and institutions and in the evenings and on weekends with community participants. Efforts to change institutions, policies, and practices can take a long time, and there may be many setbacks along the way. Tangible rewards and successes for the work may be few and far between, which can lead to burnout (Rubin & Rubin, 2008).

The rewards include the personal satisfaction of working to change environments to better meet the needs of and to provide empowerment opportunities for individuals and communities. Many community practitioners appreciate the ability to partner with individuals, families, and groups to better their lives, while avoiding the view of persons as clients, which can involve diagnostic labels, treatment plans, and a primarily individualistic perspective. In community practice, community members are involved in making decisions that affect their lives, sometimes for the first time. Helping people gain their voices and work toward large-scale social change is work toward social justice. The variety of tasks completed, the joy of successes, and the wide autonomy and flexibility are other factors that draw and keep social workers in community practice (Rubin & Rubin, 2008).

Community practitioners must have the energy for long-term work and must be able to see value in the process and effort involved, rather than just in the outcomes. The occasional victories, even short-term or small, must be enough to sustain community practitioners. The community practitioner must celebrate small gains. She must often work diligently on short-term or immediate goals, while keeping the larger, systemic, institutional change in focus.

CONCLUSION

This chapter has presented the range of social work community practice as an important client system level for generalist practitioners. Engaging in community practice offers social workers the opportunity to influence their environments to create communities that are truly responsive to the needs of all members. Community interventions, terminations, and evaluations are complex, with a primary focus on the community, and a secondary focus on individual change. Community practice involves developing leaders, facilitating bonding among residents, and other personal and interpersonal work that provides a foundation for

A Grand Challenge for social work identified by The American Academy of Social Work and Social Welfare is reducing extreme economic inequality in the United States. Although the economy is producing more wealth than ever before, business owners are getting most of the revenue, while labor has a shrinking share. In fact, those workers at the bottom of the income distribution have seen their wages decline since 1979, and half of all workers have experienced no or little growth in their hourly wages since 2000. Heads of companies often earn hundreds of times as much income as the ordinary worker. This trend has led to increasing hardship and concentrated income poverty among lower paid workers. The median net wealth of White households is 10 to 20 times greater than the median net worth of African American and Hispanic households.

Lein, Romich, and Sherraden (2015) call for social work involvement in public policy changes to reduce extreme inequality. Community organizing has been occurring across the country to increase earnings from low-skills job through the "fight for $15," or raising the minimum wage to a new standard of $15/hour. Making part-time, shift, and variable work more humane, so that instability in hours and income and unpredictability is minimized. Expansion of the Earned Income Tax Credit (EITC), a refundable tax credit for working, low-income taxpayers, would result in some reduction of poverty and inequality. Expanding child and dependent care to enable stable employment would help working families trying to achieve a stable income and invest in assets. To familiarize yourself with the topic of reducing extreme economic inequality, visit the Grand Challenges website and read Working Paper No. 16, *Reversing Extreme Inequality* (Lein, et al., 2015) at: http://aaswsw.org/grand-challenges-initiative/12-challenges/reduce-extreme-economic-inequality/. (See Exercise #a1 to learn more about how you could become involved in community practice in your community to reduce extreme inequality.)

GRAND CHALLENGE

Reduce Extreme Economic Inequality

community change. Such complexity requires the social worker to possess skills with various clients in order to implement the community intervention and facilitate the termination and evaluation processes.

MAIN POINTS

- Community intervention uses guided community practice models, which are primarily based in the concepts and language of systems, ecological, and power, change, and politics theories.

- The three most common models of community intervention are Rothman's (2008) three models of community practice: planning/policy, community capacity development, and social advocacy. These models can be blended to best match the context of the community change effort.

- The intervention strategies of community social and economic development, community organizing, and community asset mapping aim to improve community conditions and the quality of life for community residents or members.

- Community social work practice, including community development and community organizing, makes unique contributions as an intervention method both domestically and around the globe.

- Termination in community practice can be more complex than termination with other client systems because of the potential involvement of many players and institutions in the process.

- Social work community practice evaluations and follow-up assess the process along the way, the extent to which goals are achieved, and the social worker's skills in the intervention phase.

EXERCISES

a. Case Exercises

1. To apply your learning of the Grand Challenge to reduce extreme inequality that was highlighted in this chapter, visit the Grand Challenges website and read Working Paper No. 16, *Reduce Extreme Inequality* (Lein et al., 2016) at: http://aaswsw.org/wp-content/uploads/2016/01/WP16-with-cover-2.pdf.

   Research whether there are any community interventions in your community that might reduce extreme income inequality. For example, is there an organization or coalition working to do any of the following:
   a. Raise the minimum wage in your community?
   b. Create or expand a state-EITC?
   c. Pressure employers or local or state change policy to require more predictability of income for low-wage workers?

2. Go to www.routledgesw.com/cases and review the video of the Alvadora neighborhood association meeting within the Riverton case. In groups, begin a role-play where the video ends and continue the discussion. Did the Chair of the committee vote? If not, what may have occurred? If the committee delays their vote, what additional information might be helpful to the decision-making process? Summarize the points of view. Which arguments are most persuasive? How might you vote if you were on the committee? What result would you prefer? Compare your preferences with classmates.

3. After completing Exercise #1, discuss the following questions with your classmates. What other information would you need to make a decision? If you were the Chair, what might you have done differently? What elements of Robert's

Rules of Order were used in the Alvadora video? What elements were not used? How might other elements have been used? How might that have changed the course of actions in the video?

4. Go to www.routledgesw.com/cases and become familiar with the Riverton case file, especially the "Your History" section. Choose either the planning/policy, community capacity development, or social advocacy models of community intervention described in Chapter 11 and describe a possible community intervention for Riverton to address the concerns about the coal-fired power plant. Describe a community intervention using a second model and compare and contrast the intervention with the first intervention. What are some key differences?

5. Go to www.routledgesw.com/cases and become familiar with the Riverton case file. You would like to begin to address community concerns and issues using a community social and economic development approach. What issues could you address? How would you address the issues using a community social and economic development approach?

6. Go to www.routledgesw.com/cases and become familiar with the Riverton case file. With many types of community interventions, recruiting allies from diverse groups adds to the strength of the intervention. Describe how you would recruit from various populations within Riverton to participate in a community intervention.

7. Go to www.routledgesw.com/cases and become familiar with the Brickville case. An evaluation of the youth group community empowerment effort could entail many different types of activities. Create a 5–7 question key informant interview guide that the youth group could use for evaluation purposes to gather feedback about the level of involvement and empowerment of neighborhood residents. The interviews would include faith leaders, neighborhood leaders, politicians, and professionals who serve the community through area nonprofits.

b. Other exercises

8. Choose a social issue that is important to you. Assume the role of a community developer. How would you address the issue using community development skills and techniques?

9. Choose a social issue that is important to you. Assume the role of a community organizer. How would you address the issue using community organizing skills and techniques?

10. Review the categories and examples of assets in Exhibit 11.5. List all of the types of assets present in your community (i.e., campus or neighborhood) within each of the categories.

CHAPTER 12

Social Work Practice with Organizations: Engagement, Assessment, and Planning

"Why study organizations?" There are two answers to this question. The first answer is that we have become a society of organization. Our lives are shaped by organizations, from birth to death. . . . The second is that if we want to change key aspects of our lives and/or society, we almost inevitably must change organizations.

Tolbert & Hall, 2016, pp. 1–2

Key Questions for Chapter 12

1. What competencies do I need to engage and assess organizations? [EPAS 6 and 7]
2. What are the social work behaviors that enable me to effectively engage and assess organizations? [EPAS 6 and 7]
3. How can I use evidence to engage in research-informed practice and practice-informed research to guide my engagement with and assessment of organizations? [EPAS 4]
4. How can I apply social work values and ethics to engagement with and assessment of organizations? [EPAS 1]
5. How can I determine whether an organization is culturally competent? [EPAS 2]

Organizations are the structure through which social services are delivered. For example, the RAINN organization (www.routledgesw.com//rainn/engage/components) provides vital social services to people who have experienced sexual trauma. RAINN staff and volunteers provide safe, secure, confidential services, emotional support, information, and referrals 24/7 through their website. To carry out their work, they have a wide array of collaborative partners, including local rape crisis centers, university-based evaluators, donors, and legal consultants. Learning more about this nontraditional social service agency can aid in understanding more about traditional agencies, and provides ideas of how social services agencies may be structured in the future to include more online service delivery.

INFLUENCING ORGANIZATIONS CAN RESULT IN IMPROVED services for clients. You may think of organizations as small, supportive structures that help to organize an interconnected jumble of work that needs accomplishing, or as large bureaucracies that are unresponsive to client needs or individual efforts to improve them. Organizations are "formally structured arrangements of people, tools, and resources brought together to achieve predetermined objectives through institutionalized strategies" (Barker, 2014, p. 304). Social workers work in many types and sizes of organizations and use their knowledge of organizations to promote the best interest of their clients. Although there has been considerable growth in the number of social workers choosing independent practice settings, the majority today works in agency-based organizational settings (Bureau of Labor Statistics, 2016).

This chapter focuses on the nature of organizations and social work agencies, particularly as experienced by social work practitioners. Theoretical perspectives on and dimensions of organizations will be explored. We will also discuss the engagement, assessment, and planning processes with organizations. The discussion emphasizes the social worker's interface with organizations and the ways in which organizational functions shape professional practice. The chapter will also examine the skills needed for organizational engagement, assessment, and planning and will close with a discussion about types of organizations most often used for social service delivery.

UNDERSTANDING ORGANIZATIONS

Organizations address individual, family, group, and community needs. Organizations, like other clients, can be understood through theories, models, and perspectives. Prior to moving into the change process, a theoretical understanding of organizations can assist social workers in the process of engagement, assessment, planning, intervention, termination, evaluation, and follow-up. In this next section, organizations will be described as social systems, as well as from the integration of contemporary theories of organizations.

Organization as a Social System

As discussed in earlier chapters, general systems theory posits that a system, such as an organization, is composed of intersecting components that are part of larger systems, such as the community at large and society. Organizations, therefore, acquire resources from their environments and return products or services to their environment. Understanding organizations requires understanding that organizations exchange resources with their environments (Brueggemann, 2013b). In the assessment and planning processes, which are described later in this chapter, social workers can examine the extent to which subsystems, such as funders, other organizations, or networks of organizations, meet the needs of the organization. The organization can use this information to advocate for a higher level of functioning of a subsystem, which will ultimately benefit the organization and those being served.

Contemporary Theories and Organizations

Organizational and management theory that relates to organizations of all types has a history that dates back to the late 1800s. In helping to understand organizations, today's theories emphasize (1) the role of culture in helping to understand how organizations define and pursue collective goals; (2) the idea of quality as the benchmark in organizational structures, processes, and evaluation; (3) respect for how tasks are accomplished as a factor as important as the outcomes of programs and services; and (4) recognition that there is no one correct approach to structuring organizations. Many aspects of an organization, including size, mission, clients, and staff qualifications, are important to consider when structuring an organization and developing a management style (Netting, Kettner, McMurtry, & Thomas, 2017).

Dimensions of Organizations

The characteristics and qualities that exist within social services organizations affect both service delivery to clients and the employee experience. The three most important dimensions of these differences are: (1) purpose of the organization, (2) structure of governance, and (3) the internal power relations. Let us turn to an exploration of each of these areas.

Organization Purpose

The stated purpose of an organization is the rationale for the organization's existence. While organizational objectives state the ways in which organizations work toward their goals, the purpose describes the concerns of the organization in broad terms. The three types of purposes are: (1) filling a public mandate, (2) providing a particular service, and (3) fostering social change related to an ideological concern to which the organization is committed.

Organizations Sanctioned by Law   The law sanctions organizations in several ways. First, organizations sanctioned by federal and state law ("public organizations") provide mandated social services that are widely recognized by the public. For example, adult protection services, available in all fifty states, are usually housed

© Digital Vision

within a large and visible state organization. Social workers representing these organizations are expected to act in the best interests of adults who cannot protect themselves against abuse, neglect, or exploitation; carry out the activities of daily living; or manage their own affairs. Public organizations are directly accountable to the community, as they derive the vast majority of their funding through tax revenue (i.e., federal, state, county, or local government funds).

Second, most social services are offered through nonprofit organizations designated as **501(c)3** organizations by the U.S. Internal Revenue Service (IRS). As a 501(c)3 organizations, nonprofit organizations are sanctioned by the law to meet specified public needs. Designated nonprofit organizations are exempt from paying taxes on organizational income, and donors are allowed to deduct contributions from their taxes (Holland, 2013).

Organizations with Service Goals   Organizations with service goals develop as a result of an agreed-upon need or concern and are often started by and operated by professionals. For example, youth at risk of dropping out of school are often seen gathering together in groups in blighted areas. Adolescent high school drop-outs are a high-risk population for poverty, health concerns, and criminal activity. Organizations providing youth services offer prevention services to help youth avoid dropping out, assist adolescent drop-outs in acquiring tangible resources, and provide legal assistance and referrals to addictions treatment. Service goals define the work of the organization and the social need addressed by the organization.

Organizations Arising from Social Movements Some **grassroots organizations**, which are organizations started by citizens rather than professionals, arise in response to ideological positions on particular social problems. The early development of shelters for women experiencing intimate partner violence is an example of a

EXHIBIT 12.1

Example of Public and Non Profit Organizations

The *Area Agencies on Aging* (AAA) is a network of *public* agencies across the country that provides a comprehensible and coordinated system of community-based services for older adults in localities across the U.S. Services can include nutrition programs, case management, abuse prevention programs, legal assistance, personal assistance, and other programs. The AAAs are public organizations because they are directly funded through tax dollars, and overseen by the U.S. Department of Health and Human Services.

NATIONAL AGING SERVICES NETWORK

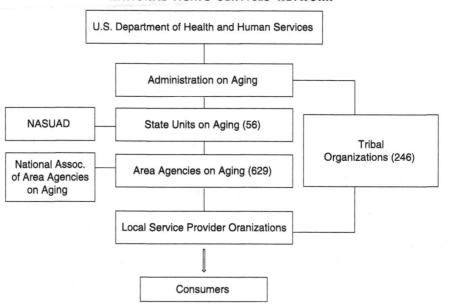

Source: National Association of Area Agencies on Aging, 2016

The *Alzheimer's Association* (AA) is the leading, global voluntary health organization in Alzheimer's care and support, and the largest private, nonprofit funder of Alzheimer's research. Through over 70 agencies across the country, AAs provide services such as referrals for resources, family education, support, respite care, and other services to families impacted by Alzheimer's disease. The AAs are *private* organizations because they are not directly supported through tax dollars, but rather through private funds, and are overseen by a Board of Directors.

Casa de Esperanza was started to meet the need for a culturally competent domestic violence shelter in St. Paul, Minnesota. While there were well-established domestic violence shelters in Minnesota, there was a lack of culturally appropriate services for Latina women. However, not long after it started, the vast majority of those assisted were Anglo and African American, despite the pervasive problem of family violence for Latina women. However, the board and staff knew that within the Latino community, there was a real need for education, prevention, and safe haven. In response, new programs were developed to serve the community and attract Latinas, including a Women's Empowerment program, support groups, advocacy, supportive listening, a 24-hour crisis line, a children's therapeutic program, children's advocacy, and structured daily activities, such as therapeutic dance and Spanish lessons.

Strong resistance within the Latino community to speaking openly about the problem of domestic violence existed, and the message of Casa's leaders was met with hostility and animosity. Exposing women's experience of family violence challenged the image of a happy family, and brought a private matter out into the open, potentially embarrassing family members.

The organization struggled to sort through these cultural forces, and answer important questions. While the mission statement stated that the agency existed to "eliminate oppression and its violence against women and children," many board and staff members felt a unique responsibility to work within the Latino community. This responsibility had further implications regarding expectations for bilingual and bicultural staff and publications, definitions of eligibility for services. Most significantly, should women in crisis be turned away from the shelter because they were not Latina? Receipt of public funding for the shelter required that clients be served on a "first-come, first-served basis," so no shelter or service slots could be reserved for Latinas.

In response, the organization created new programs and services to educate the community about Latino family violence, and conduct outreach to Latinas. Staff and volunteers also began to network with other Hispanic organizations to increase awareness about the problem of family violence. As the organization grew, questions about identity persisted. Were they an organization serving primarily Latinos, or a multicultural organization? The contradictions woven into the fabric of the operations needed to be addressed.

In early 1997, the Board went through a strategic planning process to grapple with their identity. Ultimately, the organization moved from being primarily a shelter to today becoming an organization that served a wide variety of needs of the Latino/a population regarding domestic violence. This affirmation created a need for a new approach to program development and operations, community relations, and an overhaul of the agency systems. Shelter services changed in duration, and were delinked from community-wide referral system, resulting in more Latina women being served. The emphasis of the organization moved away from shelter to prevention, community education and support, and policy advocacy for Latinos. For example, staff (1) offered expanded case management and referral networks to support women who live with their abusers or other family members; (2) worked to build the cultural competence of

EXHIBIT 12.2

Change the Mission?

EXHIBIT 12.2

Continued

other nonprofits; (3) engaged in advocating for public policies that better protected women; and (4) formed strategic alliances with other organizations to influence policy makers, judges, and law enforcement officials. To correspond with the new emphasis on the community as an agent of change, the mission was changed to "Mobilize Latinas and Latino communities to end domestic violence."

Source: Casa De Esperanza, n.d.; Sandfort, 2005.

© Chris Fertnig

social movement, a political effort designed to change some aspect of society. A social movement is led by citizens whose commitments and energies are channeled into a political movement, and organizations are created to implement the long-term work of the social movement. A more recent example is the Black Lives Matter movement, which developed into a chapter-based national organization. As organizations are created and mature, professionals, such as social workers, are often employed. Frequently, the founders, professionals, and volunteers of such organizations are indigenous to the movement, which means they have personally experienced the oppression that is the focus of the organization. Professionals and volunteers often have extraordinary commitment to the mission of the organization (Hardina, 2013).

Structures of Governance

Organizational structure, much like family structure, refers to the ways in which members, tasks, and units relate to one another. The structure shapes the rules, or norms, of the organization. Some of the rules are explicit, such as personnel policies, and others are implicit, such as the best ways to influence the decision of an administrator. These rules, governed by organizational culture (discussed later) may be communicated openly to employees and volunteers, while others may be communicated nonverbally or through interpretation of decisions. In the next section, three kinds of organizational structures will be explored as representative of those found in many contemporary agencies: bureaucracies, project teams, and functional structures.

Bureaucracies   Many human service organizations, including state and local government organizations and nonprofits, are structured as a bureaucracy; therefore, social workers benefit from knowledge about the structure of their employing organization.

German sociologist Max Weber invented the term **bureaucracy** as a conceptual type, rather than a reality, of structure. The following ten points describe the characteristics of a bureaucracy (Netting et al., 2017):

- Each position in the organization has a limited area of authority and responsibility.

- Control and responsibility are concentrated at the top of a clear hierarchy.

- The activities of the organization are documented in a central system of records.

- The organization employs highly specialized workers based on expert training.

- Staff demands require full-time commitment, and each position represents a career.

- Activities are coordinated through clearly outlined rules and procedures.

- The relationships among workers are characterized by impersonality.

- Recruitment is based on ability and relevant technical knowledge.

- The private and public lives of the organization's members are distinct.

- Promotions in the organization are made by seniority and/or achievement.

Several aspects of bureaucracy have been incorporated into the organizational experiences of many professionals, even those in smaller organizations. For example, the notion that recruitment is based on ability, rather than a relationship with other staff members, is a widely accepted idea of fairness in employment practices. On the other hand, the top-down, hierarchical authority or the impersonality of relationships among members is often an aspect of bureaucracies that challenges employees. The organizations that most often display the characteristics of bureaucracies are those embedded in large systems, such as local, state, or federal government; therefore, older adult/child protection, public health and mental health, and corrections, are fields in which bureaucratic approaches are most common.

Project Teams   In a sharp contrast with bureaucracy, **project teams** consist of a group of people who collectively work on organizational challenges or opportunities through committee or task force structures (Brueggemann, 2013b). Project teams are a flexible way to accomplish work tasks, because the committees may exercise their best collective judgment in decision-making, and the group has minimal hierarchy. Often, such groups find maintaining this structure challenging for many reasons, such as the growth of the group and limitations imposed by a higher authority. Sometimes organizations structured as bureaucracies create project teams within them to accomplish certain tasks.

For example, a group of women and men concerned about intimate partner violence may use a project team approach to develop and operate an organization that provides services to survivors of intimate partner violence. The intended services include a domestic violence shelter, therapy, and violence prevention programming. Team members may structure the organization of the shelter staff so that everyone shares the tasks of managing the agency's physical space, and identical salaries are paid to everyone. The project team structure has many positive aspects; however, the structure may be challenged by those with concerns relating to the appropriateness of some duties for those staff with higher educational degrees (e.g., the appropriateness of a person with a master's degree answering phones or vacuuming the shelter office). The project team approach can be challenged as organizations hire new workers who demand a competitive salary, or as their budget grows from funding or accountability sources (such as a Board of Directors) that require a hierarchal structure.

Functional Structures   When an agency becomes too large for a single person to administer, a layer of personnel will be added. These administrative additions are usually divided by function or area of responsibility—thus the name **functional structures**. Exhibit 12.3 shows an organizational chart that visually lays out a functional structure of the RAINN organization.

In a community agency, for example, the executive director may appoint an experienced social worker as the program director of the youth services department and appoint another as the program director of the affordable housing development unit. In this situation, the two mid-level administrative leaders would be equals and may form a management team that works directly with the executive director in larger administrative functions and decisions. Frequently, these administrative roles are added to already existing direct service roles, particularly in smaller

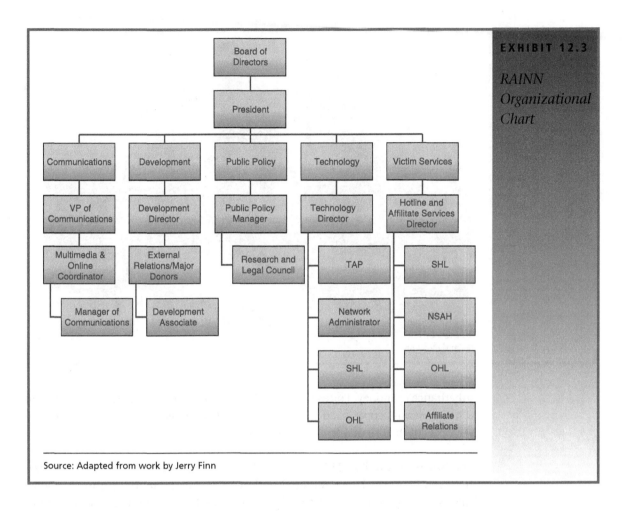

EXHIBIT 12.3

RAINN Organizational Chart

Source: Adapted from work by Jerry Finn

organizations. For example, the program director of the youth services programs would retain responsibility for actually implementing one of the programs. As the agency grows larger, the program directors may not provide the direct services due to the heavy demands of the supervisory and administrative activities.

Internal Power Relations

While organizations have overt arrangements of power, such as hierarchical arrangements of personnel, they also have unofficial power arrangements that are subtle and are unique to the organization. Chapter 3 discusses several sources of power for social workers, including agency, expert knowledge, interpersonal, and legitimate power.

Traditional Authority   Authority attributed by title or ancestry, such as someone with powerful family ties, is **traditional authority.** This type of authority is most often seen in the U.S. as based on profession, family relationships, and history or

© CandyBox Images

inheritance of money. For example, CEOs of large corporations are often related to other powerful people, such as former presidents or other CEOs, and are frequently members of the original family who started the business.

Charismatic Authority   This type of authority is an unstable dynamic in organizations. As contrasted to traditional authority, the **charismatic authority** model suggests that a captivating personality (rather than heritage, ideas, skills, or commitments) is the variable required to gain power by consensus. This form of authority is often displayed in state and national elections when, for example, entertainers and celebrities run for and win public office without previous political experience. Such authority is often present with founders of human service agencies who are successful at the necessary start-up tasks of garnering supporters, raising funds, recruiting an initial board of directors, and other tasks that involve persuasion.

Rational/Legal Authority   This authority is based on ability to achieve outcomes and, like charismatic authority, is persuasive rather than coercive. An example of a person with **rational/legal authority** is an agency staff member who is an expert in program development and program evaluation. A staff member with a particular expertise and a track record of accomplishments in the area of expertise is likely to be persuasive in an appeal to initiate new programs. Large human service agencies, particularly bureaucracies, often contain staff members with rational/legal authority because the staff is able to specialize and develop expertise. Staff in smaller organizations can also develop rational/legal authority, depending on their backgrounds, interests, opportunities, and agency needs.

In social work practice, these forms of authority can exist on a continuum (i.e., from noninfluential to very influential) and/or commingle. For example, human service organizations may have an executive director who was the founder and began the position with a great deal of charismatic authority and who developed rational/legal authority while in the position by developing expertise as an administrator. Another executive director may have initially had mainly traditional authority due to a connection with a powerful family member in human services and/or also has or developed charismatic authority due to strong persuasion skills.

Intersections among Dimensions of Organizations

Thus far, the discussion has focused on dimensions of organizations that influence practice and the social worker's experience. These dimensions, purpose, structures of governance, and internal power relations, often intersect in practice, and some dimensions are likely to be intertwined. For example, a domestic violence shelter, whose purpose reflects a social movement and ideological position, is more likely to adopt a project team rather than a bureaucratic structure. With feminist organizational roots, a domestic violence shelter is also more likely to be subject to charismatic or rational/legal authority, as social workers with strong interpersonal skills may tend to take on leadership roles even without a formal position of authority.

Understanding interconnections among these dimensions aids to understand the nature of organizations and develop a framework for examining their distinctions and impact on social workers. Ultimately, understanding possible interconnections can assist in discerning the combination of dimensions that best fit the talents and work styles of workers. For example, some social workers learn that an organization structure characterized by project team approach and rational/legal authority is the best fit for them because they would prefer to work within a more flexible organizational structure. Gaining knowledge about agency dimensions also helps to recognize the ways in which agencies in various environments can most effectively and efficiently help clients reach their goals.

Social Work Practice in Host Settings

Many social workers practice in **host settings**, such as hospitals, residential care facilities, public and private schools, and correctional facilities. Host settings are organizations in which social workers provide social services as a secondary activity. The following are examples: (1) the primary service in a school is education, yet social workers provide services to augment and support the educational goals; (2) various programs maintained by the court system, aimed at diversion or advocacy, often include social workers; and (3) housing programs and disability projects employ social workers to support the main goal of the organization. Next, we will discuss two situations with both opportunities and challenges: being a guest in a host setting, and being a member of an interprofessional team.

Guest Status Expectations and privilege accompany a **guest status** for a social worker practicing within a host setting. Professionals of other disciplines in the setting may not understand the scope of the social work role, and have inaccurate expectations—too high or too low—of the social worker. For example, a social worker in a hospital setting may find that other professionals assume that a social worker is only qualified to give referrals to clients, rather than engage in the myriad of activities for which they are qualified. At the same time, social workers may experience the privilege of working with other professionals on a team that is able to accomplish more than a social worker could independently. The experience of social worker Diane can illustrate the point.

> Diane is a recent Bachelor's in Social Work (BSW) graduate hired to facilitate discharges in a residential psychiatric treatment center that has a positive reputation in the community. A staff psychiatrist serves as medical director, and the executive director has a graduate degree in public health. Diane is the first social worker ever employed by the center. The nursing staff had responsibility for discharge work until the number and pace of discharges outgrew their capacity to conduct discharge planning along with their other nursing duties.
>
> Diane is warmly welcomed by staff, who hopes that she will fill an acute organizational need. Diane is hopeful that she will gain new competencies and behaviors because she will be exposed to different perspectives and practices for treatment strategies, medication, and ethics. She knows that she will have the opportunity to observe first-hand the work of the psychiatrist, the public health administrator, nurses, and others and learn about the ways in which different professional perspectives can assist clients.
>
> While many of these hopes were realized, Diane also discovers that she does not have a role in decision-making about discharges; rather, the other staff expect her to simply carry out the instructions she is given. The exclusion from the decision-making process occurs because she is viewed as extraneous to the discharge (medical) decisions, rather than for any personal reason. Further, Diane has noticed a lack of professional, dignified treatment of some staff toward patients but is ambivalent about notifying officials about it. Because she is excluded from decision-making, Diane feels undervalued, and more as a guest than a valued team member.
>
> While she understands that the center is primarily a medical facility and medical issues take priority over other concerns, she also understands the potential value of her involvement in decision-making about discharge planning activities. She knows she has much more to contribute than she is currently allowed, and wishes to create the possibility of articulating her possible contributions in a way that will facilitate the staff's appreciation and growth, rather than engendering their resistance and resentment. Specifically, she knows that she needs to educate the staff about the complexities of discharge planning (for example, the need for day programming, employment,

training, housing, emotional support, family support, and income support) and about the possible contributions that she could make to addressing these complexities within the decision-making process about the timing of discharge and the appropriate placement for patients. In the future, she may also want to address several practices that are inconsistent with socially just and respectful treatment.

Clearly, a guest status within an organization brings unique challenges for social workers. Some professionals with a guest status function as part of interprofessional teams (discussed in the next section), while others work side-by-side with other professionals (in multiprofessional settings). Social workers who have a guest status must exhibit effective professional behaviors concerning the education of other professions about the roles and responsibilities of social workers. Building credibility and networks of support within host organizations, a keen sense of timing, and displaying diplomacy are key skills in this process. On the other hand, social workers in host settings must also advocate for themselves and their professional obligations for client services.

Interprofessional Teams   Projects and programs that include members of several professions (e.g., health professions, public health, public administration, and social work) create **interprofessional teams.** These teams can provide an enriching and exciting atmosphere in which to practice social work. Although the social work profession emphasizes a holistic view of clients, social workers join many helping professionals in delivering services in a fragmented fashion. Many families seeking the assistance of social workers are also involved with other helping professionals, such as vocational counselors, non-social work therapists, psychologists, income maintenance specialists, physicians—including psychiatrists—and community support workers.

In an interprofessional setting, all professions carry equal power and share decision-making responsibilities—the value is in the total contribution of an integrated approach. In order to be effective, each profession must value the contribution of others. Social workers need competent collaborative skills when working with other professionals, including conflict mediation skills. A truly interprofessional setting is challenging to implement in practice. For example, in many medically oriented interprofessional teams, physicians are dominant and appear to have a privileged standpoint, while in others, you may find a social worker as the leader/facilitator of the team. The socialization of many professions can encourage narrow views to bias the perspective of the chosen profession over other perspectives. Nevertheless, even with such challenges, interprofessional settings offer vast opportunities to wrestle with the challenges of providing an integrated, highly skilled approach in the best interests of clients, as well as to explore the internal dynamics of teaming through the lens of multiple realities.

ORGANIZATIONAL ENGAGEMENT, ASSESSMENT, AND PLANNING [EPAS 4, 6, AND 7]

This section spotlights the process of organizational engagement, assessment, and planning, including the sources of data and information for the assessment. These phases are important to undertake to ensure that organizations implement their mission and serve community needs most effectively and efficiently. For example, the RAINN organization (http://routledgesw.com//rainn) engages, assesses, and plans prior to implementing an intervention (and evaluating the intervention as well). These phases set the stage for the organizational change process of intervention, termination, evaluation, and follow-up. The section closes with a discussion about integrating the information gleaned in the assessment.

Engaging the Organizations

Engagement of an organization first involves the perception of the organization as a client. An organization is comprised of many individuals and systems, yet the social worker must view the entire organization as a client in order to participate in the change process with an organization. This first step in the change process uses many of the skills needed for engagement with individuals, families, groups, and communities, namely, the active listening skills and research, evaluation, and analyzing skills discussed in previous chapters. Engagement with organizations involves working directly with all clients and staff, within the perspective of the organization.

Social workers can engage organizations for the change process as an employee, volunteer, interested citizen, or as a consultant, although most often the change process occurs with employing organizations. Social workers often see the need for organizational change, so the organization can operate more efficiently and effectively, provide a higher quality of services, and better address human needs. For example, social workers who work for a school system may identify the need to make a change in the schools and begin to engage other social workers, teachers, principals, administrators, committees, and task groups across the school district and even across districts to address a specific organizational need. Social workers may also engage organizations as part of advocacy efforts. For instance, a social worker might engage with a public agency that serves older adults to advocate for better handling of cases involving abuse, neglect, or exploitation of older adults. Social workers may also engage with a community of organizations, such as a network of homeless shelters, to work for changes across many organizations, such as to coordinate data management systems to better meet the needs of clients who are homeless, are struggling with substance abuse, and have a chronic mental illness. In all these cases, engagement skills used with other clients are necessary.

Assessment of Organizations

The overall assessment of organizations involves both research into the internal environment of the organization, or the internal mechanisms within organizations, and the external environment with which the organization receives and provides resources, such as funders, accreditation organizations, suppliers of goods and services, clients, other organizations, and others. The following assessment framework, an integration of previous frameworks, may be helpful in the assessment task (Gitterman & Germain, 2008; Netting et. al., 2017) and are more fully described in the following:

Internal Assessment

- Legal basis, mission, by-laws, and history

- Administrative structure and management style

- Program structure, programs, and services

- Organizational culture (i.e., physical surroundings, public relations, language, procedures, social justice/diversity)

- Personnel policies and procedures

- Resources (i.e., financial, technological, personnel)

External Assessment

- Relationship with funders and potential funders

- Relationship with clients

- Relationship with organizations in network (i.e., referrals and coalitions)

- Relationships with political figures

- Relationships with others (regulatory bodies, professional associations, etc.)

Assessment of an organization, similar to assessment with all clients, involves gathering data. Like community assessment, data can be gathered through observation, written documents, key informant interviews, publically available data, service statistics, previous organizational assessment (partial or full), administrative data, other data, and focus groups. Depending on the size of the organization to be assessed, a public forum and survey data may also be appropriate ways to gather data (Gitterman & Germain, 2008; Netting et al., 2017; O'Conner & Netting, 2009).

Organizations often create documents that may be helpful in the assessment process. These include organizational charts, policy and personnel manuals, procedure manuals, job descriptions, meeting minutes, and annual reports. Information from media sources and reports from other organizations can also be useful.

Elements of an Internal Assessment

The internal structures and dynamics of an organization affect many aspects of service delivery of the organization, as well as the employee experience (Grace, McClellan, & Yankey, 2009). The following section discusses the elements of an organization that can be part of an organizational assessment.

Legal Basis   Organizations must be recognized by the law to legitimately operate. The **legal basis** for public organizations is a statute or executive order, while a private organization has a legal basis in the articles of incorporation. These documents authorize an organization to officially exist, and define the parameters for their operations.

Mission Statement   Most organizations create a **mission statement**, which is a concise, broad statement of the purpose of the organization that describes a shared vision. While the statement is too broad for details, the statement identifies the client needs the organization meets, the population served, and the intended client outcomes. The details about programs, services, organizational structure, and other specifics are outlined in other documents, such as annual reports, an organizational chart (discussed later in this section), and program descriptions. The mission statement states why the organization exists and is less changeable than programs and services. Revising a mission statement is needed if an organization perceives a mismatch between the mission statement and current client needs and organization activities. For example, many child welfare agencies were founded in the early 20th century as orphanages and needed to revisit their mission statements in light of the focus in child welfare on home-based placements. Exhibit 12.4 provides an example of a mission statement.

By-laws   The way in which a nonprofit organization governs itself is described in the **by-laws.** By-laws are legal documents that describe the structure and abilities of the board of directors, such as the composition of the board, terms of the members, permanent committees, voting rights, and other matters that concern governance. The by-laws are typically brief, and the rules about them vary from state to state.

EXHIBIT 12.4 *Mission Statement, Longview Community Center*	Our mission is to enhance the quality of life of older adults, children, and families in the regional area by serving their basic needs by providing: (1) Access to education, counseling and health services; (2) Recreation and social program; (3) Daily nutritional meals.

History   Like other clients, organizations create history that defines and impacts the future of the organization. Important aspects of history include the founding of the organization, major funders, influential staff members and administrators, accomplishments, and challenging periods.

Administrative Structure and Management Style   Organizations often depict their administrative structure on an organizational chart that shows the units of the organization, and their relationship to one another. The management style of the organization can be seen in the way work is allocated, decisions are made, the nature of the supervision of employees, and how conflict is handled. Some elements of the management style will be included in written documents, while others can be learned from staff members.

Structure of Programs, Services, and Activities   Human service organizations provide programs and services and/or carry out activities to meet overall organizational goals and objectives. An assessment process would include a review of official documents where these are described, and review the extent to which the programs, services, and activities are consistent with the overall mission, goals, and objectives of the organization, as well as are based on evidence-based practice.

Organizational Culture   Organizational culture consists of many factors, including history, philosophy, styles of communication, patterns of decision-making, expectations, collective preferred personal styles of social workers, myths, behaviors, and formal and informal rules. Culture is also shaped by the purpose, structure of governance, and internal power relations. While not reflected in the mission statement or any one official document, the organizational culture is, nevertheless, an important element that shapes aspects of the agency's work and employees' experiences. For example, the extent to which social workers are expected to work overtime without financial compensation or earned time off, or if practicum students take shifts of being "on call," both represent the types of issues that are shaped by organizational culture. Exhibit 12.5 discusses the dimensions of organizational culture. Exhibit 12.6 helps you review your own organizational style.

While the concept of organizational culture is intangible and imprecise, culture is an important dynamic of any organization. In the next section, additional dimensions that shape services will be discussed, including the legal basis, mission statement, by-laws, physical surroundings, public relations, procedures, and social justice/diversity factors.

Physical Surroundings   If organizations have a physical presence that clients see, the interior and location of an organization can provide some information about its culture to clients. An organization with dark, messy physical surroundings and/or little privacy for client interactions could be an organization with a culture that places a lower priority on the potential impact of physical surroundings on client

EXHIBIT 12.5 *Dimensions of Organizational Culture*	*Observed behavioral regularities* when people interact, including their language, customs, traditions, and rituals *Group norms* that evolve as standards and values for working together *Espoused values* that the organization is trying to achieve *Formal philosophy*, which are the board policies and ideologies that direct the work *Rules of the game*, often known as "the ropes" *Climate*, which is the physical layout and how it feels *Embedded skills*, the ability to pass along competencies to the next generation *Habits of thinking, mental models, and/or linguistic paradigms* are things taught to new members as they are socialized to the organization *Shared meanings*, which are group understandings that develop as they work together *Root metaphors or integrating symbols*, the ideas, feelings, images, and even physical layout that represent the group's artifacts *Formal rituals and celebrations*, which are ways that a group celebrates key events that reflect important values or events

Source: Schein, 2010 pp. 15–16; O'Connor & Netting, 2009

outcomes than a clean organization with bright lighting and plenty of space for private interviews. To best serve their clients, many human service agencies are located near their clients' homes, often in low- and middle-income communities. While many social workers are not employed by organizations that are housed in luxurious surroundings and/or in upscale locations, the physical atmosphere and location of an organization reflects and impacts aspects of organizational culture, and impacts employee well-being (Shier, 2012). The organizational environment is an important area to learn about the organization's culture.

Public Relations   Organizations reflect their culture in their **public relations** activities and products (Brueggemann, 2013b). Public relations is the practice of managing communication between an organization and the public. Organizations seek to gain support from a positive communication both from the public at large and from specific groups, such as funders, politicians, client populations, and even employees. Organizations can use a variety of mediums to manage their public information and image, such as websites, social media, blogs, printed materials, print newspaper articles and commentaries, radio and televisions public service announcements and appearances, and face-to-face encounters. An organization's public image gives clues about the organization's culture.

Language   The **language** used in agency settings includes the tone, range of sentiment, and degree of empathy and respect expressed. In previous chapters, we discussed postmodern ideas about the role of language and the way people create and sustain meanings based on language. Using postmodernism concepts, language

Using the key below, rate yourself on the items listed here to review your organizational style. Add other items you think are important. Be prepared to discuss this survey in class and to apply it to your field placement. What obstacles do you encounter in fulfilling these points?

EXHIBIT 12.6

Rate Your Organizational Style

☐ I offer positive feedback to my colleagues for behaviors that contribute to effective services.

☐ I involve my colleagues in seeking changes in policies and programs to improve the quality of services.

☐ I value learning about my colleagues' points of view. For example, I seek feedback that will help me to enhance my competencies and behaviors. When I have a complaint, I discuss it with the person directly involved.

☐ I involve others in arranging opportunities to discuss practice/policy issues/topics.

☐ I communicate congratulations to others regarding professional or personal vents/accomplishments.

☐ I come prepared for all types of meetings.

☐ I make positive contributions at meetings.

☐ I refrain from idle gossip at work.

☐ I make more positive than negative comments at work.

☐ _____

☐ _____

Key:0 (not at all) **1** (a little) **2** (a fair amount) **3** (a great deal) **4** (best that could be)

Source: Adapted from Gambrill, 2013

both reflects and shapes the thoughts and feelings expressed. Therefore, the language used in organizations reflects and shapes the self-perceptions of the social workers, their work, and their clients. For example, social workers' use of disrespectful language toward and about clients violates the *Code of Ethics* (NASW, 2008), displays a violation of the core commitment to respect people and treat them with dignity, and can affect other social workers through a culture of disrespect. While some organizations may attempt to justify pejorative language patterns by stating that staff members need to "blow off steam," the lack of respectful, strengths-based language can have a powerful, detrimental impact on organizational culture. In another example, the language used to describe the members of the Board of Directors or administrators can affect the perception staff has of the competence of their leaders and the value they place on their work. Describing board members as "thoughtful, informed decision-makers," even when staff do not agree with a decision, implies to clients that the organization has a culture of respect.

Procedures   A simple **procedure**, such as greeting a new client, asking them to sit down, inviting them to an office from the waiting room, or giving them paperwork, strongly impacts the quality of the experience of becoming a client and maintaining that status. Social workers must be respectful and sensitive about the explanation of the procedures concerning such matters as confidentiality, fees, appointment times, and negotiations in scheduling appointments. These aspects are relevant as a social worker's expression of respect for clients but also as clearly understood agency policy. Quick Guide 41 provides an opportunity to assess client and employee treatment regarding procedures at an organization familiar to you.

Social Justice/Diversity Factors   Aspects of social work practice that affirm social justice and support diversity can be nurtured and sustained across all client types, including organizations. Unless organizations promote social justice through policies and practices, clients may find their social workers to be "nice people" but feel victimized by unjust organizational practices. To fully promote social justice, organizations may arrange the internal administrative practices of the agency to reflect diversity, cultural competence/humility, and social justice concerns. For example, posters, magazines, and signs in the waiting area can reflect multiple languages and cultures to convey a welcoming atmosphere for clients from diverse backgrounds. Activities and services that clearly take into account cultural values, such as food at events that reflect ethnic food traditions and restrictions, and materials available in multiple languages, send a message. Activities and services can also honor history of groups and/or reflect histories of oppression for specific populations. Just as ethnically dominant white middle-class social workers struggle to become competent in working with other cultures, so must organizations assess their culture competency and the extent to which the organization works toward social justice goals. Exhibit 12.7 addresses some of the assumptions that underlie

QUICK GUIDE 41 DIGNITY ASSESSMENT AND HUMAN SERVICES GUIDE

Complete the following assessment using an organization with which you are familiar.

1. Persons seeking services from my agency are more likely to experience:

____ a poorly maintained waiting room   ____ a warm and well-furnished waiting room

____ a place to sign in and be told to take a seat   ____ a courteous and personal greeting

____ having their name called out and being told to "follow me" to the office   ____ being personally met and invited to "follow me" to the office

____ nonverbal cues from the staff that they are a bother   ____ nonverbal cues that suggest we are glad they are here

____ treatment that says "you are another case"   ____ treatment that says "you are a person"

2. Persons seeking services in my agency are more likely to be:

____ treated as problems that need to be solved   ____ treated as partners in a mutual process of deciding how to proceed

____ given treatment based on the medical model   ____ provided treatment based on a competency model

____ seen as problems   ____ seen as people with issues and needs

____ seen as needing an expert   ____ seen as the expert

3. Employees within my setting are more likely to experience:

____ getting written memos about new changes   ____being asked for input about new changes

____ an expectation of independent work without much support   ____being supported in their roles

____ wishing for another job   ____ joy in coming to work

____ feeling like their consumers are not important to the agency   ____ feeling their consumers are important to the agency

____ feeling like they are a drain to the community   ____ feeling like they are a resource to the community

____feeling unimportant to the agency   ____feeling important to the agency

____lack of respect for other employees   ____respect for other employees

4. My experience with the organizational culture is that:

____ respect for human diversity is ignored   ____respect for human diversity is valued

____ membership in the community is blocked to those who are different   ____membership in the community is open to all

____ social services are at best tolerated   ____social services are willingly supported

Source: Adapted from Locke, Garrison, & Winship, 1998, pp. 278–279

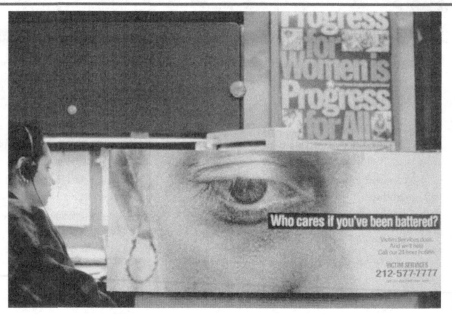

Validating client experience

Organizations that are culturally competent display the following characteristics:

- Respect the unique, culturally defined needs of various client populations.
- Acknowledge culture as a predominant force in shaping behaviors, values, and institutions
- View natural systems (i.e., family, community, faith communities, healers) as the primary mechanism of support for minority populations
- Start with the "family" as defined by each culture, as the primary and preferred point of intervention
- Acknowledge that minority people are served in varying degrees by the natural system
- Recognize that the concepts of "family," "community," etc., are different from various cultures and even for subgroups within cultures
- Believe that diversity within cultures is as important as diversity between cultures
- Function with the awareness that the dignity of the person is not guaranteed unless the dignity of his/her people is preserved
- Display understanding that minority clients are usually best served by persons who are part of or have knowledge about their culture
- Acknowledge and accept that cultural differences exist and have an impact on service delivery
- Treat clients in the context of their minority status, which creates unique mental health issues for minority individuals, including issues related to self-esteem, identity formation, isolation, and role assumptions

EXHIBIT 12.7

Continued

- Advocate for effective services on the basis that the absence of cultural competence in any part of the organization compromises the cultural competency of the entire organization
- Respect the family as indispensable to understanding the individual, because the family provides the context within which the person functions and is the primary support network of its members
- Recognize that the thought patterns of non-Western peoples, though different, are equally valid and influence the ways in which clients view problems and solutions
- Respect cultural preferences that value process rather than product, and harmony or balance within one's life rather than achievement
- Acknowledge that when working with minority clients, process is as important as product
- Recognize that taking the best of the Western and non-Western worlds enhances the capacity of all
- Recognize that minority people have to at least be bicultural, which in turn creates its own set of mental health issues such as identity conflicts resulting from assimilation
- Function with the knowledge that some behaviors are the expression of adjustments to being different
- Understand when values of minority groups are in conflict with dominant society values

Source: Adapted from Sue, Rasheed, & Rasheed, 2015

organizational practices and approaches that are critical to address in the process toward culture competency.

Personnel Policies and Procedures   The size and legal basis of an organization are important factors in the creation of staff policies and procedures; small, newly created nonprofit organizations have relatively simple and concise policies and procedures. Having fewer policies and procedures lends itself to flexibility and creativity but also more uncertainty about responsibilities, processes, and scope of work. Larger, public organizations often have highly formal, complex policies and procedures, which creates a more constricted work environment, yet also provides a structure to better navigate a more multifaceted set of activities and responsibilities. Nevertheless, the development of written policies and procedures, including a plan for recruitment, selection, development, evaluation, and termination, is important. Some organizations also develop plans to address personnel changes and issues, such as to enhance staff diversity or develop career pathways for employees within the organization.

Resources (i.e., Financial, Technical, and Personnel)   Other types of resources are also important to organizations. For example, the adequacy of the financial resources of organizations can be assessed through annual and monthly budgets, where income and liabilities are documented. **Technical resources** include the facilities and equipment of the organization, such as the office space, computers, software, and cell phones. **Personnel resources** include the number and capacity of current staff, including their knowledge, skills, and expertise.

Elements of an External Assessment

The external environment of organizations consists of many players. The assessment process focused on the external environment reviews the individuals, groups, organizations, and policies that impact operations. The external environment can offer opportunities and challenges for organizations, and maintaining a focus on relationships with external players is important. The following section discusses those elements external to an organization that can be considered as part of an organizational assessment.

Relationship with Funders and Potential Funders An assessment process should uncover the sources of agency funding, as well as the nature of the relationship between the organization and each funding source. For example, the assessment process would uncover the amount and percentage of the overall budget received from each funding source. The funding sources could include government appropriations and contracts, donations, investment income, fees, fundraising events and activities, and profit-making activities. A source of funding that constitutes nearly half or more of the organization's overall budget indicates a strong relationship. Organizations that rely on a diverse source of funds have increased program and staff flexibility compared to those that rely on fewer sources.

Relationship with Clients Human service organizations rarely have the resources to serve all people who live in their service area; therefore, organizations create client eligibility requirements for programs and services. An assessment in this area may include examining how clients are recruited and deemed eligible, the manner in which clients are treated who are not eligible for services, the degree to which clients are mandated to receive services, and which organizations are sources of referrals.

Relationship with Organizations in Service Network (i.e., Referrals and Coalitions) Constructive, professional relationships with other organizations are imperative to a positive community perception and to the ability of the organization to function effectively. Organizations that deliver similar services often have motivation to work together to meet community needs, yet often compete for funding from similar sources. Therefore, strong relationships between similar organizations benefit the community through stronger service delivery and collective advocacy efforts. However, forming these relationships can be challenging due to competition for resources. An assessment of this aspect would uncover the nature of the relationship with similar and referring organizations, and those with whom the organization networks. Quick Guide 42 provides guidance on the types of organizational partnerships.

Relationships with Political Figures   Elected and appointed officials often carry considerable influence over public opinion about and resources for both public and private organizations. An assessment would investigate the key political figures for an organization and describe the organization's relationship with them.

QUICK GUIDE 42   GUIDE TO NONPROFIT ORGANIZATIONAL PARTNERSHIPS

A local nonprofit organization, Citizens Against Climate Change (CACC), would like to expand their influence without necessarily expanding their organization. They are exploring the idea of partnering with other organizations either locally, statewide, regionally, nationally or internationally. The forms of partnership from which they could choose are:

Task force: Task forces are temporary, flexible structures to address a community challenge to be resolved in a relatively short period of time. Membership includes representatives of all types of organizations focused on similar challenges. While the advantages include pooling of resources, ease of short-term commitment, and flexibility in structure, disadvantages include lack of organizational engagement and commitment, resources, and general trust due to the short-term nature of the arrangement.

For example, CACC could decide to create a task force with organizations to promote the creation of bike lanes on local roads.

Collaborative: Collaborative partnerships can be relatively long-term and involve sharing of resources, such as staff and funds, to engage in sustained service delivery among member organizations. Each member organization provides a unique contribution to combined work. Collaborative organizations can work closely over time and are often motivated to reduce costs, receive funding that otherwise would not be available, or fulfill unmet, complex needs. Advantages include resource sharing, expansion and improvement of services, while challenges include potential competition for similar funding opportunities and creating consensus among diverse partners.

For example, CACC could decide to create a collaborative partnership to deliver ongoing cycle safety courses and bike clubs for community members.

Coalition: Coalitions are groups formed of organizations to take joint action, such as lobbying elected officials, through collective action. While most coalitions have informal structures and fluid membership, some are formal organizations. Member organizations pool resources and devote staff and members to take action. The loose structure and fluid membership is both a strength (i.e., fairly easy to recruit like-minded organizations) and a challenge (i.e., challenge to create consensus with organizations that are diverse and do not work together regularly).

For example, CACC could decide to form or join a coalition to advocate for additional state transportation dollars to be devoted to walkable-bikeable community projects, such as sideways, bike lanes, bike corridors, and traffic-calming infrastructure improvements on side roads.

Interfaith Alliance: While faith communities are the lead organizations in Interfaith Alliances (IA), these organizational partnerships also involve other nonprofits, local groups and institutions (e.g.,

QUICK GUIDE 42   CONTINUED

public health departments, or child welfare departments). Advantages of IA include (1) faith communities offer a place of recruitment of active individuals who are motivated by their faith to take action on issues, (2) faith communities can add credibility to efforts to address societal needs, and (3) faith communities can also offer many types of resources. As with other partnerships, challenges include developing consensus among diverse groups and individuals.

For example, CACC could join an Interfaith Alliance at the local or national level to engage in advocacy about emissions standards for autos or to fund complete composting systems for food waste at schools.

Affiliation with national/international organizations: National and international organizations sponsor local chapters to work at a smaller level (e.g., state) to carry out their agenda. Local chapters benefit from affiliation by increased political influence, access to funding, and networks with similar-sized organizations across the country or world. Challenges include reaching agreement among diverse groups with varying agendas, and/or forfeiting some decision-making powers at the local level to the national/international organization.

For example, CACC could join with other, similar groups to create a chapter of Greenpeace, an international organization focused on climate change.

Social movement: Organizations can participate in social movements by joining with broad-based coalitions and national organizations dedicated to the same cause. Social movements are often the mechanism for marginalized and oppressed groups to obtain access to resources and political rights, as well as for allies to support them in their advocacy through organizational resources. Rather than a single organization, the work of a movement is carried out through partnerships of multiple organizations and coalitions to generate public support and links to decision-makers and funders.

For example, CACC could join with organizations such as the Global Campaign for Climate Action, 350. org, and other networks that are working with organizations and groups around the world to create political pressure worldwide for action on climate change.

Source: Adapted from Hardina, 2013; Netting et al., 2017

QUICK GUIDE 43   NONPROFIT ORGANIZATIONAL ASSESSMENT

Using an organization with which you are familiar, complete the following assessment:

Internal assessment:

• *Legal basis, mission, by-laws, and history*

___ The legal basis is clearly stated in appropriate documents.

___ The mission statement is current, accurate, specifies reason for existence and expected outcomes.

___ The by-laws are relevant, current, and accurately portray the needs of the organization.

• *Administrative structure and management style*

___ Fit the mission and services of the organization.

___ Transparent and structured lines/systems for decision-making exist.

___ Clear communication lines exist for dissemination of decisions.

___ Roles are clearly defined.

___ Decision-making involves broad participation as practical and appropriate.

• *Program structure, programs, and services*

___ Continual monitoring and assessment of the structure, processes, and programs occurs

___ Program evaluation data is collected, used, and linked to systematic improvements

___ Programs and services reflect evidence-based practice.

___ The need for programs and services is well-documented.

• *Organizational culture i.e., physical surroundings, public relations, language, procedures, social justice/diversity)*

___ Physical infrastructure is well-suited to current and anticipated needs.

___Physical infrastructure enhances effectiveness.

___ Informal expectations are clearly articulated and supported by staff.

___ Communications plan and strategy is in place and updated on a frequent basis.

• *Personnel policies and procedures*

___ Recruitment, selection, orientation, supervision, training and development, performance appraisal, termination, and grievance processes identified.

___ Relationships between and among positions, and position qualifications identified.

• *Resources (i.e., financial, technological, personnel)*

___ Funding is sufficient, comes from diverse sources, fits mission, and provides insulation from market instabilities.

___ Board members embrace fundraising as a core role.

___Board fundraising plans in place.

___ Electronic data systems sufficiently gather and report appropriate data regarding clients, staff, volunteers, program outcomes, and financial information.

___ Comprehensive, integrated system used for measuring organization's performance and progress on continual basis.

___ Programs and services are efficient, effective, and high quality.

___ Programs and services are well-defined and fully aligned with mission.

___ A system is in place to collect data about gaps in ability of existing programs to meet recipient and community-wide needs.

___ New ideas are continually offered to meet service gaps.

___ Communications carry a consistent and powerful message.

___ Marketing materials are professional, used consistently, and are current.

___ Materials are provided in multiple languages as needed, and reflect diversity.

___ Policies and procedures reflect systems that are culturally competent.

___ Diversity is characterized as an asset.

___ Organizational resources devoted to staff continuing education are sufficient.

___ Technology needs (e.g., computers, phones, etc.) are adequately met.

___ Website is sophisticated, comprehensive, interactive, and regularly maintained.

___ Positions adequately and appropriately staffed, vacancies quickly filled.

___ Staff are capable, committed, and bring complementary skills and momentum for improvement.

QUICK GUIDE 43   CONTINUED

External Assessment

• *Relationship with funders and potential funders*

___ Fundraising skills and expertise is adequate for funding needs.

___ Sustainable revenue-generating activities used.

___ System for regular communication and reporting with current funders used.

___ Feedback from current funders sought and considered.

___ System to cultivate potential funders used and continually updated.

___ Ideas for revenue diversification continually considered.

• *Relationship with clients*

___ System to actively recruit and involve clients in offering feedback is used.

___ System to actively involve clients in making decisions is used.

___ When possible, clients work collaboratively with staff in important roles, such as volunteer positions of leadership.

• *Relationship with organizations in network (i.e., referrals and partnerships)*

___ Strong, positive relationships with similar and related organizations exist.

___ Presence on relevant partnerships evident, and leadership roles appropriately taken.

___Reciprocity sought with relevant organizations.

• *Relationships with political figures*

___ Strong, high-impact, relationships using regular communication with a variety of political entities (i.e., local, state, and federal government) and community leaders exists.

___ Proactively and effectively influences policymaking at the local, state, and/or national level.

___ Participate in substantive policy discussions with opinion and political leaders.

Source: Adapted from: Netting et al., 2017; Marguerite Casey Foundation, 2012

ORGANIZATIONAL ENGAGEMENT, ASSESSMENT, AND PLANNING IN GENERALIST PRACTICE [EPAS 1, 6, AND 7]

While administrators have official roles and responsibilities, and therefore are naturally involved in the organizational change process, social workers in direct practice with individuals, families, groups, and communities, including generalist practitioners, must also be involved with the organizational change process. Both generalist practitioners and administrators are bound by the NASW *Code of Ethics* (NASW, 2008) Section 3.09 to work to improve services, to carry out their ethical obligations even if employer structures are challenging, and to act to eliminate discrimination in organizations.

What does the ethical obligation to participate in organizational change mean for social workers who are not administrators? Social workers must always learn about as many aspects of their affiliated organization as possible. Many organizational problems emerge through the experiences of clients or members of the community, and defining and documenting client or community member problems is a powerful way to make a strong case for organizational change. Social workers can engage others in identifying and documenting client problems to which the organization contributes (Gitterman & Germain, 2008). As discussed in Chapter 13, successful organizational change efforts often involve many individuals and groups.

Organizational engagement and assessment involve many of the same competencies and behaviors used with other clients. Discussed in the next section are those skills needed to effectively begin the organizational change process.

SKILLS FOR ENGAGEMENT, ASSESSMENT, AND PLANNING WITH ORGANIZATIONS

In addition to the skills previously mentioned in this chapter, (i.e., active listening, research and analysis, group facilitation, and documentation skills), integration of the data gathered in the assessment process must occur to provide direction to the next phases of the change process. One method is the **SWOT** (i.e., strengths, weaknesses, opportunities, and threats) **analysis**. In a SWOT analysis, organizational staff identify and assess both internal and external forces that impact the organization (Hardina, 2013) that can be the basis for developing the plan for intervention and change.

Another method of organizational assessment is a **force-field analysis** (FFA) (Hardina, 2013; Pippard & Bjorklunc, 2004). The FFA is a mechanism to gather and sort all of the information and data gathered in the assessment process and to provide the basis for a plan for an intervention, as will be discussed in Chapter 13.

An FFA is a method of identifying and assessing the forces that impact a decision about an issue by organizing the assessment data. To begin, a social worker would identify the forces that could impact the outcomes of change efforts, meaning constraints that work to prevent a change and advantages that will help overcome resistance to change. The forces could include influential individuals who could shape the opinion of others or who are decision-makers; organizations, committees and task forces; groups; and political parties. The technique enables a social worker to make a decision about whether to move forward with a change process, and if so, to create a plan based on an evaluation of the forces working for and against a proposed change (Hardina, 2013).

For example, the school social worker mentioned earlier has documented that LGBTQ students experience a higher number of social and academic problems in

EXHIBIT 12.8

SWOT Analysis

The Hispanic Community Development Center (HCDC), a Hispanic-serving, three-year-old nonprofit organization, wanted to increase their capacity to provide additional services to a growing Hispanic population in the community. While HCDC has been providing food, rent, and utility assistance and ESL classes for three years with one paid staff member, the Board wants to increase their capacity to provide health services to the population in response to high rates of teen pregnancy, HIV/AIDS, and poor oral health.

In their planning process, they used a Strengths, Weaknesses, Opportunities, and Threats (SWOT) analysis to analyze the factors affecting change in the organizations and the strengths and weaknesses both inside and outside of the organization. The SWOT analysis was conducted to help decide between two options: either attempting to raise funds to deliver health services themselves or partnering with an organization(s), such as the public health department, for service delivery at HCDC.

	Strengths	Weaknesses
Internal	• Reputation among Hispanics • History in community • Reputation among non-Hispanics • Only Hispanic-serving nonprofit • Evidence of need of health services • Diverse board with community connections	• Lack capacity to deliver health services • Lack of paid enough staff • Little experience in raising money • Little experience in partnering
	Opportunities	**Threats**
External	• Potential partnership with local institutions (i.e., public health department, university) • Potential coalition building with other human service organizations • Create HCDC capacity to meet growing needs	• Other institutions may deliver services without HCDC • If deliver services, increase financial and liability risk • Partner institutions may require proof of documentation status of clients • If fail, damage reputation

Ultimately, the organization decided to attempt to raise money and deliver the health services themselves rather than partner with another organization. The primary reasons for this decision was to avoid the requirement that HCDC clients show proof of documentation status and to preserve their reputation among Hispanics in the community. The Board decided to attempt to raise funds and to request training from other health organizations.

Source: Adapted from Larson & McGuiston, 2012

middle and high school than other students. The social worker has completed an organizational assessment and would like to synthesize the information to determine whether and how to move forward. Working with a group of students who self-identify as LGBTQ, the social worker would like to engage in a change process to provide more comprehensive services to this population across the school district. After engaging and assessing the organization, the LGBTQ work group conducted an FFA to determine whether to proceed in the change process and to assist in developing an intervention plan.

As seen in Exhibit 12.9, there are many forces that support an initiative to provide more comprehensive support services to LGBTQ teens, including student leaders, student government, and high school principals. Neutral forces, including the association of principals and school counselors, could support or oppose a change process and do not yet have an opinion about the possibility. Through lobbying and education, these neutral forces could become supporters and, therefore, may become the focus of such efforts in the intervention phase. The forces that are opposed to providing support services, including several influential teachers, the parent association and others, would work against a change process. As other forces are discovered, they could be added to the analysis. The FFA is one tool to assist the LGBTQ work group in making a decision whether to proceed with their efforts, and in making an intervention plan.

The advantage of an FFA are numerous—the individuals, groups, and coalitions relevant to the issue are identified, as well as the driving and restraining forces most likely to effect the change effort. The strength of each force is assessed and ranked, and the amenability to change of each force is ranked as high, low, or uncertain. A plan for change is then created based on the information contained in the FFA. The FFA is a simple technique that can be used with groups of all sizes as a group decision-making tool that fosters creativity and critical thinking. The social worker must demonstrate keen group facilitation skills to achieve a balance of forces for and against change, to avoid the domination of a minority of the group, and to encourage the group to be specific (Pippard & Bjorklund, 2004).

SUPPORTING FORCES	NEUTRAL FORCES	OPPOSING FORCES
Student leaders	Principal Association	Four influential teachers
Student government	School counselors	Parent Association
All high school principals	Local TV and radio station	Two student groups/clubs
American Civil Liberties Union	Chair of the School	Three School Board members
Three School Board members	Board	All middle school principals
Local activists		

EXHIBIT 12.9

Force Field Analysis, Assessment of Forces Impacting LGBTQ Initiative

Planning with Organizations

Sometimes an organizational assessment process is focused on one aspect of an organization, and a decision-making person or group (such as a program director, administrator, or Board of Directors) can review the data and make a decision. At other times, an assessment process will surface many organizational issues, challenges, and ideas to the forefront. In that case, like in community assessment, the planning phase for organizations involves sorting through and prioritizing the issues to be able to move forward with an intervention. A set of criteria is needed to provide structure and fairness to the decision-making process. The criteria can include any or any combination of the following:

- Seriousness or frequency of an issue

- Cost of the issue, or resources needed to address the issue

- Feasibility of affecting the issue

- Readiness of the community to recognize and address the issue

- The long-term impact or benefit of addressing an issue, or in implementing an idea

Criteria may be set at any point in the process. Organizations may select to have some combination of administrators, staff and/or the Board of Directors set the criteria and make a decision about whether and how to move forward with an intervention by applying the criteria. After setting the criteria, a democratic process can also be used to then apply the criteria to the issues/ideas generated in the community needs assessment process to plan for an intervention (University of Kansas Work Group for Community Health and Development, 2016).

STRAIGHT TALK ABOUT PRACTICE WITHIN ORGANIZATIONS

Different types of organizations offer distinct professional rewards, opportunities, and challenges. Expectations and experiences differ from organizational setting to setting, and work style preferences that fit one type of organization may not be a match at another organization or type of organization. The following discussion will highlight several of the different types of social service organizations.

Although working for public organizations brings challenges, there are advantages unique to employment with public agencies. Compared to working within the private (i.e., nonprofit and for-profit) sector, needed services can be offered to clients with less consideration given to cost effectiveness because services may be required by law, and therefore, there are fewer demands for demonstrated outcomes than in nonprofit and for-profit organizations. In stable economic times, social workers within public agencies enjoy relative predictability and job security, with highly structured job levels and raise structures, especially in the military and federal government. Social workers in public organizations typically earn higher salaries than in some nonprofit settings (excluding hospitals) (Bureau of Labor Statistics, 2016). Many clients who served in public organizations are those without many alternatives; therefore, social workers within these agencies are implementing the historical preference of social work for working on behalf of the poor. Lastly, social workers in public organizations gain invaluable experience with a wide range of client issues and with clients with complex problems.

The number of social workers at for-profit social service agencies, such as private practices and for-profit health care systems, is projected to grow in coming years (Bureau of Labor Statistics, 2016). In contrast to public and nonprofit organizations, for-profit (or proprietary) agencies seek to produce a financial profit for their owners or shareholders. Social workers in residential care facilities, medical and psychiatric hospitals, long-term care for persons with disabilities, home health services, health maintenance organizations, substance abuse treatment centers, correctional settings, and child welfare services may be in for-profit settings.

Depending on the type of services provided, social workers in for-profit organizations may enjoy a more comfortable physical setting, more resources, use of cutting-edge interventions and treatment modalities, and higher expectations of efficiency and effectiveness than in other settings. Salaries, however, are generally similar at for-profits and nonprofits (Whitaker & Wilson, 2010). In some for-profit settings, a wide socioeconomic diversity of clients may seek services. Social workers may also enjoy the opportunities to advocate for the primary goal of client-centered human services to meet community needs, rather than a profit.

Most social service organizations are nonprofit (Holland, 2013). Advantages to working for a nonprofit organization include the following: (1) for some nonprofits, social workers generally have less need to advocate internally to maintain the historical commitment to serving the poor; (2) the funding base is often a diverse mixture of sources, including grants, contracts, memberships, fee for service, investment, donations, and events (Netting et al., 2017); (3) social work employees may enjoy more autonomy, flexibility, and creativity in service delivery due to the multitude of funding sources; and (4) social workers in faith-based nonprofit organization can implement their religious traditions and beliefs in their employment setting.

While there are other types of organizations beyond public, for-profit, and 501(c)3 nonprofit organizations (i.e., hybrid nonprofit and social enterprises, whereby nonprofit organizations engage in commercial activity (Brunell, Moray, Stevens, & Fassin, 2016), other classifications of 501(c)), these three are the central types of organizations that employ social workers. While generalities may be helpful, each setting offers a unique working environment. Social workers who explore types of organizations may gain more insight about the best fit for their preferred work style and career aspirations. Both for-profit and nonprofit organizations can engage in advocacy. Quick Guide 44 provides more details on the types of advocacy activities in which organizations engage.

QUICK GUIDE 44 ORGANIZATIONAL POLICY ADVOCACY ACTIVITIES

Complete the following tool about organizational policy advocacy activities using an organization with which you are familiar. Completing this assessment can shed light on the degree to which organizations use opportunities to engage in policy activities for the benefit of their clients and organization. Organizations that engage in few of these could consider expanding their policy advocacy activities to more opportunities, such as those listed here.

In the past, our agency has:

(Organizational Activities)

___Testified at public hearings held by the city council, state legislature, or other decision-making body.

___Participated in legislative or policy working groups with government officials.

___Engaged in nonviolent civil disobedience (i.e., deliberately broke a law to draw attention to unjust government policies, programs, or actions).

___Sent unique letters, e-mails, faxes, or texts to the city council, the mayor, local government agency directors, or senior staff members regarding legislation, government policies, government programs, or other issues that affect our clients.

___Participated in rallies, protests, vigils, and/or demonstrations to draw attention to an issue that affects our clients.

___Attempted to engage television, radio, print, or web-based media reporters to give attention to legislation, government policies, government programs, or other issues that affect our clients.

___Submitted letters to the editor or op-ed pieces to the local media regarding legislation, government policies, government programs, or other issues related to our client population.

___Helped draft legislation.

___Sponsored or cosponsored forums or other community events to educate the general public about legislation, government policies, government programs, or a social issue.

___Submitted formal comments on rules, regulations, strategic plans, or other administrative governmental documents.

___Met with the city council members, the mayor, and/or local government agency directors or senior staff to discuss legislation, government policies, government programs, or other issues that affect our clients.

___Contacted city council members, the mayor, and/or local government agency directors or senior staff to discuss legislation, government policies, government programs, or other issues that affect our client populations.

___Participated in letter-writing campaigns, "sign-on" letters, "call-in days," postcard drives, petition drives, or email drives to contact public officials about legislation, government policies, government programs, or other issues that affect our clients.

___Submitted articles In our newsletter about legislation, government policies, government programs, or other issues that affect our clients.

___Posted fact sheets, issue briefs, articles, and/or testimony about legislation, government policies, government programs, or other issues that affect our client population on our website.

___Invited council members and/or the mayor to visit our program(s) to educate them about the issues that affect our clients.

___Actively participated in coalitions related to our area of service or issue of concern. (*Actively participated means attended and gave input at coalition meetings, joined and actively participated in coalition committees, attended coalition events, etc.*)

(Direct Client Activities)

___Met with and/or distributed written information to clients to educate/inform them about legislation, government policies, government programs, or upcoming public policy activities, (e.g., meetings, public hearings).

___Solicited input from clients to inform our agency's advocacy priorities.

___Included clients when making visits to the city council, state representatives, or other decision-makers.

___Provided skill-building workshops to clients to encourage their public policy participation. *Skill building may include writing and giving testimony, writing letters, making phone calls, meeting with decision-makers, and other tactics.*

___Met with clients to help them formulate direct action strategies around issues of their choice.

___Conducted voter registration drives.

___Facilitated transportation for clients to encourage their participation in public policy activities and/or to vote at the polls.

Source: Adapted from Plitt & Shields, 2009

A focus on mass incarceration for the past several decades in the United States has resulted in the world's largest proportion of people in prison. The expansion of the criminal justice system, or mass incarceration, is a social justice issue. This challenge has been identified by the American Academy of Social Work and Social Welfare as one of the twelve Grand Challenges for Social Work.

In addition to the overwhelming financial cost, Pettus-Davis and Epperson (2016) provide an overview of this problem from a social justice perspective:

> The exponential growth of incarceration in the United States is a compelling problem not only because of sheer numbers, but also because of who is most affected. The majority of the imprisoned population is made up of people of color and people suffering from poverty or behavioral health disorders. For these reasons, social workers and the American public increasingly understand mass incarceration as unaffordable (p.4).

GRAND CHALLENGE

Promote Smart Decarceration

GRAND
CHALLENGE

Continued

Smart decarceration interventions build on structural and behavioral interventions that have been shown to reduce incarcerated populations. They include (1) diverting criminal offenders from prison by first implementing alternatives to incarceration, (2) reducing recidivism and thereby reduce prison populations, and (3) reinvesting criminal justice resources into treatment and prevention.

With its long history of reform efforts and focus on social justice, the social work profession is well suited to provide leadership toward promoting decarceration. Society needs to explore and evaluate a range of alternatives to transform the criminal justice system incarceration, including multidisciplinary approaches to policy and practice intervention. Social work can promote cross-sector and transdisciplinary collaboration to encourage evidence-based practice toward smart decarceration. Consider the dimensions of organizations discussed in this chapter. How can organizations be structured to promote cross-sector and transdisciplinary collaborative work? To familiarize yourself with smart decarceration, visit the Grand Challenges website and read Working Paper No. 4 (Pettus-Davis & Epperson, 2015) at http://aaswsw.org/wp-content/uploads/2015/12/WP4-with-cover.pdf. (See Exercise #a1 for additional exploration of engaging and assessing communities for financial capability and asset building within the context of the Brickville community.)

CONCLUSION

This chapter has introduced organizations as an important arena for the social work change process. Social workers in direct practice and their supervisors are uniquely informed about the impact of organizational operations on clients. Social workers may best be able to identify unmet client needs, and initiate a change process designed to meet the best interests of the client—whether that be an individual, family, group, or community. Social workers, therefore, have a mandate to engage people in the organization and external to the organization, and learn about both the internal and external environments of organizations to competently lead and participate in organizational change processes. In addition to engagement, this chapter focused on the assessment process to provide the foundation needed to initiate the change process, as well as the planning process. Organizations are an important context of generalist social work practice with all types of clients. Chapter 13 will focus on organization intervention strategies, termination, evaluation, and follow-up processes.

MAIN POINTS

- Social workers work in many types of and sizes of organizations and use their knowledge to promote the best interests of their clients.

- Organizations, like other clients, can be understood using various theories, models, and perspectives, including systems theories and contemporary organizational and management theories.

- Three main dimensions of difference between organizations are: (1) purpose of the organization, (2) structure of governance, and (3) internal power relations.

- Social workers also practice in host settings, which are organizations in which social workers provide social services as a secondary activity.

- Social workers in a variety of roles can change organizations to provide a higher quality of services.

- The overall assessment of organizations involves both a review of the internal environment of the organization, and the external environment.

- The NASW *Code of Ethics* (2008) provides direction to both generalist and advanced specialist social workers to work to improve services, carry out their ethical obligations in the work place, and to act to eliminate discrimination in organizations.

- A helpful skill in the assessment process is a force-field analysis (FFA), a tool to sort information and data gathered in the assessment process and aid in the planning process to make decisions about the change process.

- The type of organization in which a social worker is employed offers different professional rewards, opportunities, and challenges.

EXERCISES

a. Case Exercises

1. Log onto http://routledgesw.com//rainn/engage/components and read about RAINN's service components. Draft a short mission statement for RAINN.
2. Log onto www.routledgesw.com/cases and review the Sanchez family case. Imagine you were hired as a social worker approximately three months ago at a community center that serves the Sanchez family. As you have settled into your job responsibilities, you notice some tensions within the agency. Several social workers are grumbling at "the way things are around here." As you consider the reasons for your feelings of being unsettled, you decide to gather information about the organization to gain a better understanding of the dynamics. Referring back to the chapter, discuss ways in which you might obtain knowledge about each factor, and how each factor could influence the experience of staff members (one paragraph for each): purpose, structure of governance, and internal power relations.

3. After you have completed Exercise #1, you still are not sure about the dynamics that have led you to feel unsettled, and co-workers to grumble. You decide to learn more about the agency, but are not quite ready to undertake a full organizational assessment. You decide to start your mini-assessment by focusing on culture. Using the concepts described in the chapter, describe the elements of culture that exist in the center, and how you would go about learning them, to include the types of individuals you might interview, the documents you would seek, the groups you would access, and any other source of information you might use. Justify your choices.

4. Log onto www.routledgesw.com/cases. Review the Riverton case file (i.e., Your History and Your Concerns). View the community sociogram, and note all of the organizations and their relationships to one another. Develop a sociogram for an organization with which you are familiar.

5. Using the Riverton case (at www.routledgesw.com/cases), answer the Critical Thinking Question #2.

6. Using the Riverton case (at www.routledgesw.com/cases), answer the Critical Thinking Question #3 by assuming that the organization is the client. What would be your next steps after deciding that an organization in the community is the client? Which organization is the client (use the sociogram and/or town map to review the possibilities)?

7. Go to www.routledgesw.com/cases and become familiar with the Brickville case. Several events have occurred that prompt the Brickville CDC to conduct an organizational assessment. First, the Brickville CDC has been asked to join the coalition that is working for the redevelopment plan. Second, as part of the needs assessment outcomes, the youth development organization encouraged the Brickville CDC to become more politically engaged for the benefit of the neighborhood. The CDC director has stated that the organization has never taken a stance on an issue before. Olivia and her colleagues have decided to work toward organizational change and create a process whereby the Brickville CDC can take a stance on neighborhood issues. In a brief, 1-page paper, discuss the elements of an internal assessment that would need to be included to assess for political engagement. Explain the rationale for your choices.

b. Other exercises

For the following exercises, write a 1–2 page paper with your findings.

8. Choose an organization with which you are familiar. Familiarize yourself with the elements of an organizational assessment, as discussed in Chapter 12. Interview a person familiar with the organization to gather as much information as possible related to the internal and external elements of an organizational assessment. As part of the interview, ask whether the organization has completed an organizational assessment in the past and whether there are any written documents that describe the assessment that you could review.

9. Using the SWOT diagram in Exhibit 12.8 as an example, complete a SWOT diagram for an organization with which you are familiar. Briefly explain and justify the contents of your SWOT analysis.

10. Using the examples of forms of partnership in Quick Guide 42, describe the forms of partnerships that a nonprofit, "Men Against Sexual Assault," could take if they wanted to expand their influence without expanding their organization.

11. Using Exhibit 12.2 as the case (Casa De Esperanza), describe how 3 of the 10 "Dimensions of Organizational Culture," as described in Exhibit 12.5, could be implemented. That is, if Casa De Esperanza wanted to implement a culture that was friendly and welcoming to the Latino community, what would three of the ten "look like"?

Social Work Practice with Organizations: Intervention, Termination, and Evaluation

The time when you need to do something is when no one else is willing to do it, when people are saying it can't be done.

Mary Frances Berry

Key Questions for Chapter 13

1. How can I use theory and perspectives to guide the development of intervention, terminations, and evaluation with organizations? [EPAS 8 and 9]
2. What models can I use to intervene in organizations? [EPAS 8]
3. How do I utilize evidence to practice research-informed practice and practice-informed research to guide intervention, termination, and evaluation with organizations? [EPAS 4]
4. How can I apply social work values and ethics to organizations intervention, termination, and evaluation? [EPAS 1]

CONSIDER THE FOLLOWING SITUATIONS:

Toby, a tenth-grader, left Dan (the social worker)'s office having made the comment that he wished that other kids would just "leave him alone" and that he wished he "knew other kids like him." Toby, who shared with Dan that he thinks he is gay, was the third student that week to say similar things to Dan, who is struggling with a response to the needs of lesbian, gay, bisexual, transgendered, and questioning (LGBTQ) students. Dan has seen these students struggle with bullying, less social integration, and poor school performance, which they often say is due to a lack of acceptance by teachers, administrators, and peers.

Carrie, a social work case manager at a mental health service organization, is at the end at her rope. Four of the clients on her caseload, who are dual diagnosed with a chronic mental illness and a substance abuse issue, have become homeless this month due to the lack of affordable rental housing in the community. The few units that are available in the community are owned by landlords who will not rent to clients of the organization.

These are situations that may prompt organizational change that result from client needs not adequately being met by the agency, the institution, or community. Dan, for example, is realizing that his agency (i.e., the school) may not be responding adequately to the needs of one population. Carrie sees an inadequate response by the community to the housing needs of her clients, which may be worsening their mental health conditions.

Organizational change can range in size from large (e.g., changing the decision-making process within the organization) to small (e.g., changing eligibility for one program, or the working hours for staff members), and from short-term (e.g., creating a short-term project) to long-term (e.g., creating new programs). Large-scale change, such as a legal merger with another organization, can change the nature and mission of organizations. However, small-scale change can also make an important difference to the clients and community, such as offering a new program that allows people who are homeless and have chronic mental illness and substance abuse problems to live in supportive housing while clients work to reduce and eliminate substances from their lives. Both types of changes involve utilizing the change process of engagement, assessment, intervention, termination, and evaluation.

As discussed in Chapter 12, the impetus for organizational change can emerge from many sources, including administrators, direct practice staff, stakeholders, and people outside an organization. Social workers' concerns for an aspect of service, whether ineffective, wasteful, or in some other way troubling, may be the most accessible route to effect change. As frontline staff, social workers are often the first to notice that clients experience difficulty with organizational practices, and they can voice their concerns as part of the engagement, assessment, and planning processes and participate in the next parts of the change process. This chapter will focus on the change process from the perspective of direct service social workers.

After completing the engagement, assessment, and planning processes outlined in Chapter 12, the social worker, with allies who have formed a "change work group" (i.e., a committee of people who are willing to work toward organizational change), must consider possible solutions, develop a change proposal (i.e., intervention) to pursue, select an intervention strategy, and if successful, possibly be involved in the implementation of the intervention, as well as its termination and evaluation. Organizations change in much the same way as individuals. Organizations structured as bureaucracies tend to change slowly because of their complex systems. Organizations of any size with a long history can resist change because staff feel that "we have always done things this way," and change may require a great deal of effort. Organizations with a more open, flexible structure, like people who are flexible, tend to make purposeful changes easily. Based on assessments, social workers collaborating with a change work group must choose the intervention strategy to best match the organization and the context of the change.

This chapter will examine ideas social workers in change work groups can use to change policies, programs, projects, and practices within organizations. Based on the engagement, assessment, and planning phases of the change process, the next three steps—intervention, termination, and evaluation and follow-up—can help organizations to become more responsive to the individuals, families, groups, and communities they serve. First discussed are approaches, perspectives, and models for interventions with organizations. In the next section, a framework for organizational change is provided. The challenges and methods for implementing the organizational change are explored, followed by a discussion of termination and evaluation of change in organizations. The chapter ends with an overview of the challenge of maintaining a hopeful stance with clients regarding organizational change.

© gosphotodesign

APPROACHES, PERSPECTIVES, AND MODELS FOR INTERVENTIONS WITH ORGANIZATIONS [EPAS 8 AND 9]

Approaches, perspectives, and models that are grounded in theory can be used to describe organizations and inform the change process for organizations. In the following section, the organization is described using self-learning, systems, social ecology, power and politics, postmodernist, and social constructionist approaches. We will discuss each approach as well as the implications for the social worker working within an organization.

Self-Learning Model

Gambrill (2013) describes the **self-learning model** as a contemporary organizational climate that emphasizes the ability of organizations to self-correct when needed. The increasing emphasis on accountability and accessibility to clients, increasing use of information technology, and a limited resource pool lead to the ability of the organization to improve the quality of its decisions and develop new knowledge. This model maintains that organizations seek and use corrective feedback from internal and external sources by ongoing monitoring and continuously soliciting feedback from clients about their experiences with services and from other stakeholders who provide information about the external environment of the organization. This model also assumes a rational process in which all members of an organization agree on the mission, goals, and objectives of the organization and work collaboratively to achieve them. Although no organization perfectly implements its mission, goals, and objectives, the self-learning model has widespread applicability in well-focused organizations with clear goals and values committed to quality improvement. An organization that seeks feedback from many stakeholders—clients, funders, referral sources, political leaders and others—and considers this feedback when deciding whether to make change is using a self-learning model.

This model is closely related to the **ecosystems perspective**, described fully in Chapter 1 as a perspective focused on the fit between the environment and a human system. As mentioned in Chapter 1, the ecosystems perspective can relate to all clients, including work within organizations to create more responsive policies and programs (Gitterman & Germain, 2013). The model is also related to the **social ecology approach**, which assumes that the organization is continually interacting with and adapting to its environment. An organization must continue to adjust and adapt to environmental changes in order to survive and prosper. According to the social ecology approach, change efforts may emanate from changes that occur externally, which has created a need for change in some part of the organization. For example, when economic conditions force many families to seek services, different policies and procedures may be needed to adequately serve the larger number of clients with a higher level of needs. Social workers need to pay attention to changes in the organization's environment (e.g., new funding sources, a change in an area of social policy, new political support for an idea about human services) and help the organization strategize to make needed changes (Cummings & Worley, 2014).

Social workers within organizations that are using the self-learning model contribute to an organizational culture focused on receiving feedback from the internal and external environment, learning, and seeking knowledge about ways to improve their functioning and programs/services. This model is well-recognized in organizations that are involved in networks of organizations, have close relationships with their funders, and/or have a highly developed internal evaluation and feedback systems.

Systems Model

The **systems model**, also related to the ecosystems approach, recognizes an organization as a system composed of individuals, subsystems, rules, roles, and processes operating within the wider environment. Using a systems approach, change in one part of the organization can create changes in other parts of the organization. This model asserts that efforts involved in organizational maintenance and survival need to be balanced with achieving organizational goals. Thus, an administrator using this model needs to balance the resources spent fundraising with resources on strategic planning and program implementation.

An example of systems model is the idea that changing a program's eligibility requirements may result in other programs having fewer, more, or different types of prospective clients. It could also result in changes to other organizations, such as referral sources, having fewer, more, or different prospective clients. It could affect the number of staff employed, the budget of programs throughout the organization, and the outcomes of the program.

In another example, change within an organization may be pursued due to job stress, staff disagreements, and unmet social and emotional needs of employees that, unaddressed, have potential to divert workers from their commitments. Change efforts in this model are more likely to include such maintenance functions as clarification of goals, improving morale, and emphasizing better communication among employees. The systems model can clearly be seen in such activities as agency retreats, training sessions, and requests for staff feedback on redefining agency direction (Campbell, 2000). In an important respect, this approach recognizes the impact of human service work by acknowledging the stresses that accompany working within organizations, and recognizing the necessity to attend to the human side of the professionals who constitute the organization and engage in the work.

Power and Politics Model

Assuming that the organization is essentially an entity where decisions are made in a political context, the **power and politics model** emphasizes competition for resources, personal advancement, and inter- and intrapower struggles. The model asserts that the primary path to change requires strategic access to decision-makers and/or the people who have the greatest power and primary influence over decision-makers. This model is related to the **critical social construction** approach, first introduced in Chapter 1, as a postmodern approach. The approach is based in an analysis of power, which recognizes that any social group can shape its beliefs to its own benefit at the expense of other groups (Hartman, 1994). The analysis of power includes questioning the power relationships between decision makers and others, which can lead to using the power and politics model of organizational change.

The power and politics model can be used within or outside of an organization and with any size organization. For example, using it within an organization, a common tactic is to work to convince influential people that the proposed change, such as starting a new program, is both in the organization's and the individual's personal best interest. Using it outside of an organization, a common tactic is to apply pressure from outside sources, such as the media, to gain the support of influential people for a change (Pfeffer, 1992). The model reflects the reality of conflict over resources and power that can emerge in change efforts, and the necessity of consideration of the role that politics and power play in change efforts.

Postmodern Approaches

As discussed in Chapter 1, in a postmodern view of change, actions, interactions, and patterns of relationships play an important role in the change process. Interaction patterns between people and between units become stable, dominate, and occur repeatedly in a dynamic process. The language used in organizations can serve to reinforce the patterns and processes (Hasenfeld, 2000).

Recognizing the power of language, the process of making meaning through social interactions, and the potential for taking part in reshaping their world, social workers can engage with people, groups, and committees within bureaucratic organizations to influence the development of individual and organizational approaches by paying particular attention to the language used and how people make sense of the language used. There is nothing inevitable about the structures and processes that shape and guide institutions or practice—people have created them and have the ability to change them. Changes to improve the organization's functioning can occur through understanding the language, symbols, relationships, and dialogues that structure the organization, and using dialogue to explore the perceptions, values, ideologies, ideas of reality, and assumptions held by staff members, stakeholders, and decision-makers for the organization (Hasenfeld, 2000). While not an easy or quick process for change, the importance of dialogue and language cannot be overstated.

Social Constructionist Approach

A social constructionist approach to organizational change emphasizes the impact that social processes, such as dialogue, have on the perception of social reality, which impacts the prospects for change. Therefore, dialogue about an organization's problem has an impact on the perception of problems, and can be one of the most effective tools in building support for a change proposal. Using this approach during an organizational change process means paying particular attention to the way in which dialogue is approached, and how the dialogue shapes people's perceptions. Dialogue that is continuous, patient, and respectful can positively impact the view of staff about the change proposal, which can serve to break down structural barriers to organizational change.

Organizations rarely use only one approach or model in change efforts; they usually use a mixture. These approaches and models offer perspectives on change efforts, offer a lens through which change efforts can be viewed, and offer ideas to social workers involved in organizational change efforts. In the next section, we will explore a framework for intervention with organizations. We will discuss recruiting allies into a "change work group," choosing feasible solution(s), selecting a change strategy, implementing the change strategy (i.e., intervention), terminating the change effort, and evaluating the change effort and resulting program or project.

FRAMEWORK FOR ORGANIZATIONAL CHANGE

Promoting change within organizations can be challenging. Sometimes change is needed because there is an issue, but other times, it is due to an opportunity, such as new funding opportunities. Exhibit 13.1 gives examples of the origins of organizational change efforts.

EXHIBIT 13.1 *Origins of Organizational Change*	The origins for organizational change can occur internally from staff members, administration, or members of the Board of Directors, or externally from other organizations, funders, or others. Consider the following examples: *Annie works for the Santa Clara County Social Service Agency (SSA). Years ago, she noticed that the client population was increasingly diverse, with growing numbers of Asian, Hispanics, Hawaiian/Pacific Islander, Black, and multiracial clients. At a staff meeting, she initiated a discussion about culturally competent practice, and most of the staff agreed that they did not know enough about it and needed to know more. Her supervisor agreed that this issue needed to be studied, with the possibility of educating staff, and making changes to the organization. He authorized a committee, chaired by Annie, and asked her to recruit other staff for the committee. Over many years, major organizational changes occurred as a result of committee efforts. Three separate committees composed of staff at various levels now meet on a regular basis to discuss cultural issues and promote agency-wide change. One committee consisted of representatives from separate employee committees that are organized primarily by race or ethnicity. They collaboratively discuss and make policy recommendations to the SSA*

EXHIBIT 13.1

Continued

director. The second committee includes the agency director and various managers, and makes decisions about policies. The third committee consists of representatives of department cultural committees (i.e., one each in adult and aging, families and children, etc.). This committee monitors the progress being made regarding culturally responsive policies, procedures, and training programs related to improving client services in each department, and solicits staff feedback. All three committees contribute to increased intergroup collaboration, the direct involvement of the agency director, increased capacity for employees on all levels to be heard, and increased focus on shaping policy for cultural competency.

Source: Adapted from Chun-Chow & Austin, 2008

Ethan works for The Island, an agency that does exemplary work with disadvantaged adolescents and their families. Even though Ethan loved the direct services and clinical work, he felt that he was working solely toward the goal of teens and their families adjusting to challenging community situations, rather than also encouraging them to try to improve community conditions. The surrounding community struggled with high unemployment, poor housing, underperforming public schools, and needed more responsive local politicians. In talking with his co-workers, he realized that many felt that way. He invited his co-workers to join him informally at lunch to discuss possibilities, including evidence-based programs that sought to involve clients directly with community systems. Eventually, committee members engaged in work—one team located a recent community assessment about youth and family involvement in their community, another team engaged in an organizational assessment, including speaking informally to other staff, administrators, and community leaders about the issue, while a third team researched evidence-based community programming for youth. The Island administrators eventually agreed to appoint a formal committee to work on the idea. Out of these efforts came new programming. Youth civic action teams now work out of local community centers, in partnership with The Island staff, to address community issues of concern to teen members and their peers. The goal is to assist youth to be key agents of change in activities with the potential to transform the community conditions that create problems in their lives.

Source: Adapted from Evans, Hanlin, & Prillehensky, 2007

It can be helpful to have a framework—a rough guide map—to guide such efforts. This section will discuss the need to create a change work group, develop feasible solutions, a proposal, and the selection of strategy and tactics for the intervention.

Gathering Allies and Creating a Change Work Group

Organizational change often requires the resources of more than one person. A group, informal or formal, adds credibility and power to a change effort and also allows members to share work. Even if the engagement and assessment process began with one person, social workers will want to identify supporters and allies while assisting with the change process. Volunteers will vary from passively supportive to highly active. Those who are supportive may change their involvement level throughout the process, with some people beginning as mildly supportive and, at some periods, actively joining the work, while others that may begin as active members of a change work group may lessen their work responsibilities at certain times. The key is to continually recruit allies through formal and/or informal (word of mouth) methods and change work group members throughout the change process, so that even if membership of the group changes, a change work group is always in place to support the effort. While some change processes are short-term, many are long-term and require a great deal of energy and allies (Packard, 2009).

In the ally recruitment process, social workers must raise the concerns discovered in the assessment process in staff and committee meetings and in discussions with their colleagues. When trying to garner support for a change proposal from other colleagues, social workers will want to be as explicit as possible and use real-world client examples when applicable. Statements about problems that are in clear, behavioral, and values-oriented terms are the most effective. In these discussions, the client problems must be translated into potential solutions in which the organization can participate. For example, if you think the problem is that LGBTQ adolescents in a school district need additional social and administrative support, the social worker must first consider solutions in which the organization can participate. Can each school in the district partner with the local mental health center to provide education about sexuality and gender to all students? Should the partnership provide in-school or in-home family therapy related to sexuality and adolescents in order to promote family acceptance and support? Should the partnership provide individual therapy? Should the school district provide services without organizational partners, either in-school or in-home? Should the school district engage the parent–teacher association in their efforts? Rather than provide therapy, should the school refer LGBTQ students to private therapists? Or should the school provide services more quietly, so as not to arouse opposition, by providing, but not widely marketing, support services through the counseling department? Translating the problem into potential solutions will help others understand, propose other solutions, and have input into decisions. After recruiting allies into a change work group and establishing the group dynamics—leadership, decision-making, and other aspects (see Chapter 9)—the group must generate possible solutions and select one solution to address the problem.

Considerations for the Development of Feasible Solutions for Organizational Change [EPAS 4]

The change work group, including the social worker, must ultimately develop a potential solution to the identified problem(s) that is acceptable to the decision-maker(s) and that addresses the identified client problem to the best of the organization's ability, based on the information gathered and analyzed in the engagement and assessment process. The proposed solution is a change proposal, which varies in shape, such as a formal, written document for more in-depth change proposals or an oral presentation for smaller change proposals. Decision-makers for change proposals within organizations can be colleagues (who may be able to make decisions about small changes related to organizational practices, such as changing the way the telephone is answered or email is sent), administrators, including the executive director or director, members of the board of directors, legislative bodies, or funders of the organization. Additionally, the change work group must also select a feasible solution that is based in evidence-based practice (as first defined and discussed in Chapter 4). There are several important *considerations* for selecting feasible solutions, including the following:

1. Depending on the scope of the problem, potential solutions, and size of the organization, the change work group must account for *resistance to change,* as discussed in Chapter 12 (Tolbert & Hall, 2016). According to systems theory, all organizations seek to maintain the status quo, or stability. **Inertia** can impede change by preserving a stable state that actively works against change. Change work groups must expect some opposition to change, regardless of the specifics, because change takes energy away from other pursuits (Gambrill, 2013) and individuals have preferences for stability (Tolbert & Hall, 2016).
2. Employee attitudes and behaviors impact the success of change efforts (Packard, 2013). Therefore, the amount of organizational *effort* and *risk* involved is an important consideration (Packard, 2013). Those change processes that will require considerable time, energy, and/or risk to the organization involve in-depth change and will greatly challenge the change work group. If, for example, an organization has spent significant resources on a program, the process for ending that program may take a long time. In another example, a change proposal that involves implementing activities that are new to the organization, such as a new type of therapy, may be perceived as highly risky to the financial stability and reputation of the organization. A high level of effort and risk inherent in a change proposal typically translates to a high level of challenge for the change proposal.
3. The change process may encounter *competition* for resources (e.g., financial, relationship, attention, etc.) from other change processes. The assessment process should have uncovered any other change process occurring within the organization, as well as any plans that will structure future change efforts. For example, organizations often create **strategic plans**, which are long-term formal plans for the organization's future. These plans often involve incremental, highly focused modifications to current operations that are projected to contribute to a preferred result for the organization (Austin & Solomon, 2009). A change process occurring in another part of the organization can

impact a change proposal if the organization does not have enough resources to consider or implement more than one change proposal at a time.

4. The organization must possess the *ability* to implement the change, experience a *need* for change, and the change proposal must *match with the mission and values* of the organization (Packard, 2013). The engagement, assessment, and planning processes, depending on the methods used, may have made administrators and staff aware of a possible problem or opportunity, potential solutions or options, and the possibility of an organizational change effort. If not, staff members and administrators must become aware of the problem, become dissatisfied with the current situation, and perceive that a proposed solution will alleviate the problem. In sum, the organizational system that supports the current structure that creates or exacerbates the problem must become weakened.

5. You must consider *perceived advantages and disadvantages* to the organization and staff (Packard, 2013). For example, if potential solutions will result in more work for a particular staff member or group of staff, the person(s) or unit(s) involved should be consulted before choosing a solution. Others' input may shape the change proposal itself or strengthen the support for the proposed solution; their suggestions and concerns can be considered and possibly addressed in the solution and change strategy (discussed later in this chapter). Consulting with person(s) or unit(s) may garner their support. If possible, implementing a solution should be shared widely.

6. Gathering *history* on the organization's policy-making efforts or program changes will provide helpful context to future change efforts. For example, did prior change efforts induce staff disgruntlement or staff support? Were changes perceived as coming from the top down (i.e., imposed from administrators) or from the bottom up (i.e., suggested by staff)? Long-term staff members may be helpful sources of historical information.

7. In discussions with other staff members about potential solutions, the change work group should also gather an initial impression about change ideas and the degree to which they are *understandable,* and likely be met with apathy, resistance, or support. The change work group must learn about formal and informal groupings of staff members and charismatic leaders within the organization and account for the sentiment of such "subgroups" and leaders in the change proposal.

8. Prior to developing a change proposal, the change work group must engage in *evidence-based practice* by researching the identified problem and potential solutions using evidence-based literature (Packard, 2013). This information must be integrated with the expertise of the change work group as well as the values, experiences, and expressed wishes of the client.

9. The *timing* of a proposed solution can significantly impact the proposal's reception. For example, the time in which one administrator is leaving an organization and a new administrator is arriving is a window of opportunity for some change proposals. The change work group may take advantage of

this vacuum of administrative power by proposing changes to organizational practices (possibly including a change that was not acceptable to the outgoing administrator), such as a policy that allows staff and/or clients to be part of the committee that screens and interviews candidates for administrative positions.

These considerations speak to the need for a comprehensive process to determine a solution or option. Some considerations may be more important than others, and there may be special considerations for certain organizations. Developing a change proposal involves thinking through such considerations. Your proposal may also be impacted by your chosen change strategy (discussed later in this chapter). Additionally, the proposal may evolve as you garner more information.

Change Proposal Structure   The change proposal may be in the structure of a policy, program, project, personnel, or practice, or some combination (Kettner, 2002; Netting et al., 2017). The **policy** approach involves a formal statement regarding the direction for a course of action. A policy change often involves the decision of people with high decision-making authority, such as administrators, elected officials, or a board of directors, that involves large-scale change to create new or amend existing policy. For example, a change work group in a school system that is striving to create improved services to LGBTQ students in the school district may determine that the most effective change strategy is to work toward a harassment policy that would include harassment based on sexual orientation.

A **program** approach involves the creation of or change to "structured activities, [which are] designed to achieve a set of goals and objectives" (Netting et al., 2017, p. 306). Programs are designed to provide services to clients and are long-term activities. These are often high-profile aspects of an organization because clients interact with, and know organizations for, their programs. For example, a program approach to the perceived unmet needs of LGBTQ adolescents in the school system would be to create an education program about sexual orientation for all students. **Projects** are similar to programs but are typically smaller and more flexible, can be adapted to changing needs relatively easily, and are not permanent. A demonstration project, a short-term test of an idea, can be a less controversial way of implementing change. For example, the education program described earlier could be implemented for a specific time period, such as a semester, with the possibility of extension of the program in the spring semester and the possibility of changing the program in the first semester, as needed. A change in **personnel** can address different types of problems in programs and projects. Staff members within organizations may lack the specific competencies or practice behaviors to effectively work within programs or projects, and a personnel approach is needed. A personnel approach can include additional education, internships, change in responsibilities for staff, or complete change of staff. Changes that involve personnel must be undertaken carefully, with a thorough examination to determine if such a change will better serve the client (rather than simply change office dynamics). Using the example of the unmet needs of the LGBTQ adolescents, the proposed solution may be to educate teachers to become more supportive of LGBTQ adolescents in the school. Lastly, a change for an organization can involve a **practice** approach, or the way in which organizations implement basic functions, which may or may not be formally described in written documents. For example, a subset of counselors or teachers may become the unofficial resource and support persons for LGBTQ adolescents in each school, so LGBTQ adolescents have supportive adults in each school (Netting et al., 2017). Exhibit 13.2 provides a summary of these approaches. Exhibit 13.3 provides a case example of an organization that implemented these approaches to change.

Selecting an Organizational Change Strategy [EPAS 4]

Thus far, the social worker has completed the engagement, assessment, and planning process; gathered allies; and created a change work group. Together with the change work group, the social worker has taken many factors into consideration when developing a proposed solution, including evidence-based practice, and made a decision about a specific change proposal or intervention to pursue that entails a change in the organization. The next step in the process is to determine the strategy for making a change. A **strategy** is an overall approach to a change effort. In contrast, a **tactic** refers to specific actions, or skills, taken to implement a strategy (Hardina, 2013). This section will include discussion of strategies, while the next section focuses on tactics, or specific skills, needed to implement strategies.

Change Strategies   There are three basic strategies for organizational change: collaborative, campaign, or conflict (Brager, Specht, & Torczyner, 1987). A **collaborative** change is one in which the change work group and the decision-maker(s) *agree that some type of change in the organization is required,* and cooperation is needed to create a joint effort to create change in the organization. The change work group and the decision-maker(s) need to create a partnership to communicate, plan, and coordinate and share tasks to implement a change. All parties involved agree that a change is needed; therefore, the group's decisions will determine the approach (i.e., whether a policy, program, project, personnel, or practice); the ways in which the resources needed can be obtained; and other details of implementation. Choosing this strategy means that there is little opposition to a change, and the change can best be carried out collaboratively. For example, if the change work group and the school principal and administrators agree that LGBTQ adolescents need additional support and that the school should and can assume a supportive role, the change work group and administrators could partner in a change effort to determine the form that the support would take (e.g., further education of teachers, support groups, and/or education of the students) and to implement the change.

APPROACH	DEFINITION
Policy	A formally adopted statement that reflects goals and strategies or agreements on a settled course of action.
Program	Prearranged sets of activities designed to achieve a set of goals and objectives.
Project	Similar to programs, but have a time-limited existence and are more flexible so that they can be adapted to the needs of a changing environment.
Personnel	Persons who are in interaction within the change arena.
Practice	The way in which organizations or individuals go about doing business. Practices are less formalized than policies and may be specific to persons or groups.

Source: Netting, Kettner, McMurtry, & Thomas, 2017, p. 308

EXHIBIT 13.2

Approaches to Organizational Change

The local mental health organization has a long-standing program for persons with chronic mental illness who also have a substance abuse problem (i.e., clients with co-occurring disorders). In recent years, the social work case managers have noticed increasing difficulty locating affordable, decent rental housing for clients in the co-occuring disorders program. The social work case managers have convened a change work group, and they are considering a variety of change approaches, including the following:

A policy approach: The change work group may approach the administration and the board of directors to change organizational policy, so the organization can move from only providing social services to an organization that also owns and manages afford-able, supportive housing for clients.

A program approach: The change work group may propose to the administration that the organization seek to partner with local private landlords to provide the intensive, on-site case management and supportive services needed to maintain a stable living environment through a live-in care provider. The organization will guarantee that the rent and utilities will be paid on time and that the apartment will be kept clean. The live-in care provider will be the first-responder for any problems in the building that involve the client.

A project approach: This change would be the same as the program change (described earlier), but would involve a six-month trial period. During the trial period, the social worker who is overseeing the project reports weekly to the administrator, who then reports on the project monthly to the board of directors. Ongoing adjustments will be made to the project as needed. If the project is deemed successful, the board of directors may consider creating a long-term program.

A personnel approach: Using this approach, social workers will be trained to become trainers to the family members of clients about being live-in case providers to their

EXHIBIT 13.3

A Dearth of Affordable Rental Housing: A Case Example of Approaches to Change

family member with chronic mental health challenges. The trained live-in family members will allow clients to live with their families, and alleviate the need for rental housing.

A practice approach: Using a practice approach, social workers will learn different approaches for assisting clients to live together in their current rental housing, so that at least two clients can live in each apartment. This will have the effect of housing more clients with the same number of rental units.

A **campaign** strategy is used when *communication can occur* between the decision-makers and the change work group, but there is *no agreement that a change is needed.* The key to this strategy is the willingness of the decision-makers to listen to arguments on behalf of a change proposal. The decision-makers may need additional information or persuasion. For example, if the change work group and the school principal and administrators do not agree that LGBTQ adolescents need additional support from the school, the change work group could choose a campaign strategy of providing additional information, developing persuasive arguments, and arranging regular communication about this topic with the principal and administrators.

The third strategy, **conflict**, can be used when *the decision-makers are opposed to a change and are unwilling to communicate with the change work group.* Due to the lack of communication, the change work group is unable to educate or persuade the decision-makers through organizational processes, and is only able to influence the decision-makers through a public conversation. This change strategy involves efforts to draw support from a wider group of supporters and often involves public conflict. The conflict strategy often involves heated and/or passionate discussion that includes negative reactions and is therefore not typically used as a first change option. For example, if the school principal and administrators do not agree that the school can take a role in providing additional support for the LGBTQ adolescents, and are unwilling to communicate with the change work group about the topic, the change work group could choose to take a conflict strategy. The group may decide to organize a march or rally to apply additional pressure to the decision-makers to begin communicating with the group. Exhibit 13.4 provides an overview of change strategies and tactics.

Contemporary Tactics and Skills for Interventions with Organizations

The skills needed for interventions with organizations are built on the skills for intervention covered in previous chapters (i.e., relationship skills in Chapter 3; intervention skills with individuals, families, groups, and communities in Chapters 3–12). In addition to basic intervention skills, social workers need specific skills for working with change processes in organizations. The following tactics, or

RELATIONSHIP OF DECISION-MAKERS AND CHANGE WORK GROUP	TACTICS	EXHIBIT 13.4
Collaboration Decision-makers and change work group agree (or are easily convinced to agree) that change is needed, and resources must be allocated for a change.	1. Implementation 2. Capacity Building 　a. Participation 　b. Empowerment	*Strategies and Tactical Behaviors*
Campaign Decision-makers are willing to communicate with the change work group, but do not agree that a change is needed or that resources are needed for a change.	1. Education 2. Persuasion 　a. Co-optation 　b. Lobbying 3. Mass Media Appeal	
Contest Decision-makers oppose change and/or allocation of resources and are unwilling to communicate with the change work group.	1. Bargaining and Negotiation 2. Group Actions	

Adapted from Netting, Kettner, McMurtry, & Thomas, 2017, p. 312

skills, are organized by the strategy with which they are most commonly associated. The terms tactics and skills are used interchangeably in the following section.

For collaborative change strategies:

Implementation Skills Implementation skills are those that involve solving problems and making decisions about logistics. Examples include engaging in research about an issue, developing written materials relating to the change proposal (e.g., written proposals, fact sheets), creating and facilitating task groups and workshops, and communicating with interested parties and decision-makers (Schneider & Lester, 2001).

Capacity Building Building the capacity of client systems has two components: (1) participation, or involving members of the client system in the change process and (2) empowerment of clients through participation in the effort. These efforts, both a process and an outcome, can improve the ability of client systems to remove real or perceived barriers to participation in change processes, and increase the likelihood of clients participating in future change processes.

　To elaborate on the earlier example of the principal and administrators agreeing that LGBTQ adolescents in the school needed additional support and that the school could take a role in providing additional support, these collaborative change skills could be used to create a new program. The change work group can use supporters and friends of LGBTQ students and LGBTQ students themselves to provide assistance with every aspect of the program, including researching, analyzing, and creating program ideas; facilitating groups; educating other students and education personnel about their unmet needs; and other tasks. Involving the LGBTQ students and student supporters in this effort can increase their competence in these skills, and potentially enable them to teach them to others in a manner appropriate to their stage of life development.

For campaign change strategy:

Education   Education involves communication skills, which may include in-person meetings with individuals and groups, formal and informal presentations, written materials, and education materials designed for persons and groups influential with decision-makers. The goal of such efforts is to present different types of information to impact the perception, knowledge, attitude, and opinions of decision-makers through information.

Persuasion   Convincing others to accept and support a particular view of an issue is the goal of persuasion. Skillful communication that appeals to the reasoning of the decision-makers is an essential part of persuasion. The change work group must discern the information or incentives that would be important to the decision-maker and make every effort to appeal to these. Additionally, choosing people with credibility with the decision-makers to communicate with the decision-makers also helps make persuasive argument. One form of persuasion is **co-optation**, defined as minimizing anticipated opposition by including those who would be opposed to a change effort in the change effort (Netting et al., 2017). Including the opposition in the change effort can neutralize the opposition because the opposition was part of designing the change effort and may be able to advance an interest through it. Lobbying is the use of persuasion with targeted decision-makers who are neutral or opposed to the change effort (Schneider Î Lester, 2001). Quick Guide 45 outlines specific skills needed for persuasion.

Mass Media Appeals   This skill refers to the use of all types of media to influence public opinion, as well as the opinion of decision-makers, either directly or indirectly. Involved in this skill is the development and shaping of newsworthy stories that will affect viewer opinion in the hoped-for direction.

In the example of the unmet needs of LGBTQ adolescents in the school setting, these campaign skills can be applied if the change work group and school principals are able to communicate about the need for additional support, but the principals did not agree that additional support was needed and/or that the school could take a role in providing additional support. The change work group can be involved in education efforts with the principal through such efforts as holding meetings or using school media options, such as a school newspaper, to present factual information about LGBTQ adolescents and the challenges they face. The group could also

QUICK GUIDE 45   PERSUASION SKILLS

Persuasion means to convince someone to do something that they might not otherwise do through use of reason. Eight skills of persuasion are:

1. *Target your case on the other person:* Find out as much as you can about the person you wish to persuade, including their roles in organizations as well as individual characteristics. Learning about their values, priorities, goals, motivations, personality, and habits will assist to shape a reasoned argument that appeals to them.

2. *Be clear about "who," "what," and "why":* Create a reasoned argument that includes the essentials and that appeals *to the other person* (not necessarily yourself). The reasoned argument should not be constructed as a debate—there are no winners/losers.

3. *Highlight common ground:* Build your reasoned argument on interests that both sides can agree on, even if lofty (such as "freedom" or "justice").

4. *Keep it simple:* People tend to make decisions by generalizing from a limited amount of evidence. Using a few powerful arguments that provide evidence of a unifying theme, presented in simple and relevant terms, is the most effective.

5. *Appeal to "head" and "heart":* Persuasive arguments include both rational and emotional elements. Pairing case stories or anecdotes told with vivid language with compelling "hard" evidence is particularly effective.

6. *Delivery matters:* Effective verbal delivery includes the use of "I" statements, taking responsibility for your statements, projecting a positive image and adopting an active tone, showing respect to others and giving them credit, telling the truth and showing a willingness to learn from experience. Effective nonverbal behaviors include using a clear and concise tone of voice, being calm, relaxed and confident, using statements that are carefully articulated, and being attentive to the nonverbal behaviors of the other person.

7. *Use dialogue, rather than monologue:* Use active listening by asking for information, summarizing, and testing for understanding. Respond in a constructive way to comments made by the other party. Dissent and disagreement are natural and functional, in that they acknowledge differences of roles, goals, values and personal qualities out of the open.

8. *Work with challenges:* When differences arise in the conversation, one response is to ask more questions. After learning where the other party stands on the matter, ask questions to learn the basis for their position, whether they are interested in reassessing their position, and if they have any ideas for resolving the differences. If confronting the other party, it is helpful to first summarize the other party's concerns and priorities, and discuss any areas of your proposal that would address any of their concerns (i.e., common ground). It can also be helpful to offer your ideas as suggestions, rather than proposals. Above all, avoid hostile or aggressive responses.

Source: Adapted from Manning, 2012

submit op-ed articles and letters to the editor to the local community newspaper. The change work group can also engage in persuasive efforts; the group can appeal to the interests of decision-makers by describing potentially increased academic performance and decreased fighting by LGBTQ adolescents, and increased tolerance for diversity throughout the school that would result from the new program. The change work group can also use co-optation by inviting the principal or another administrator to be part of the change work group (or an advisory committee to the change work group) or by lobbying the principal and other administrators who are neutral or opposed. As part of the lobbying effort, the change work group can also use websites, blogs, and social media, as well as print media, to influence the opinion of other students, staff, parents, and district administrators about the unmet needs of LGBTQ adolescents in the hope that these populations will be persuaded to attempt to influence the principal's opinion.

For contest change strategy:

Bargaining and Negotiation   Discussing a change proposal, with the possibility of both the decision-maker and the change work group making compromises to their preferred change proposal, involves bargaining and negotiation skills. Bargaining and negotiation skills are used when both the decision-maker and the change work group understand the position of one another and understand the change proposal and when there is a sense of urgency on both sides about settling the matter. Rather than confrontation, at the core of this skill is the assumption that both sides use persuasive arguments about their position on a change proposal and that both give and receive accommodation to their preferences in the final decision. This process may involve a third party acting in the role of a mediator (Schneider & Lester, 2001).

Group Actions   Group actions include many activities designed to increase political pressure on decision-makers. These confrontational tactics cover a wide range of legal and illegal activities, including rallies, demonstrations, marches, picketing, sit-ins, vigils, blockages, strikes, slow-downs, boycotts, class action lawsuits, and civil disobedience. Several of these actions require the involvement of attorneys and other professionals, while others are possible with a skilled social worker, change work group, and/or a large group of supporters (Schneider & Lester, 2001).

Ethic and Change Tactics [EPAS 1]   The choice of tactics utilized for a change effort is influenced by a number of factors, to include the type of relationship between the decision-maker(s) and the change work group, the degree to which the sides agree on the goal, the extent of the communication, as well as social work ethics. Actions taken, particularly group actions that can involve confrontation, should be undertaken after careful thought and consideration, as well as after preparing clients involved for any possible negative consequences, such as negative publicity, fines, arrest, lost wages, or physical injury. As mentioned, when there is a moderate amount of agreement and communication between the parties, more cooperative tactics should first be attempted prior to campaign tactics, and conflict-oriented tactics are often the last set of tactics used (Netting et al., 2017). The *Code of Ethics* (NASW, 2008) should always be used as a guide for ethical decision-making.

Returning to the example of the unmet needs of LGBTQ adolescents in a school setting, if the change work group attempts tactics associated with collaborative and campaign strategies without any success, the next set of tactics utilized may be those of the contest strategy. Ultimately, the change work group wants the principal to implement a new program, and the principal has rejected the idea and is unwilling to formally communicate further about the change proposal.

In response, the change work group may consider several different actions in terms of perceived effectiveness, best estimate of any negative consequences of each, and their comfort level with each. The change work group may decide to organize a march to raise awareness of this unmet need. The march can be on public property in front of the school and can occur before or after school hours, so no school or district rules will be violated. This choice of a tactic involves several skills needed by the social worker, including using the research-based evidence about social action in general, and marches in particular, and empowerment work with LGBTQ adolescents in academic settings and integrating the research findings with the professional and client experience and preferences. The social worker may also seek to involve external organizations that specialize in advocacy and diversity issues. If this, or any subsequent actions, successfully persuades the principal and administrators to begin formally communicating again with the change work group, bargaining and negotiation between the principal and the change work group may produce a satisfactory outcome, such as a modified version of a program to be used for one year, as a project, with evaluation occurring throughout and at the end of the year. Exhibit 13.5 provides a case example of the use of strategies and tactics.

The social work case managers of a local mental health organization who work with clients who have co-occurring disorders and are experiencing challenges in locating affordable rental housing have convened a change work group. The goal of the change work group is to pursue a policy change, so the organization can develop and manage affordable rental housing. The decision-makers in this situation are the board of directors, which includes the Executive Director. The work change group is considering a variety of change approaches, including the following:

The change work group may first attempt **collaborative change strategies** with the decision-makers. If all agree that a policy change is needed so the organization can develop and manage affordable rental housing for clients, the work will involve implementation skills. The social worker and change work group may be involved in such activities as locating and presenting data regarding affordable housing development and management, creating written materials relating the policy change, creating and facilitating a task group (which includes clients), and communicating with other housing developers and managers, interested parties and decision-makers. Another tactic used is capacity building. The social worker, with the change work group, would ensure that clients would be involved in the change process, to possibly include

EXHIBIT 13.5

A Dearth of Affordable Housing: Strategies and Tactics

EXHIBIT 13.5

Continued

participating in the change work group itself or selected activities. This involvement can be considered empowerment work with the clients, in that the social workers involved with each participating client can work to build client skills related to organizational change tasks (e.g., participating in task groups and public speaking), and client self-image.

The change work group may decide to begin with **campaign change strategies,** if collaborative change strategies are unsuccessful, or if decision-makers will communicate with the change work group, but do not agree that a policy change is needed. The work change group can utilize education skills, to include conducting in-person meetings with individuals on the board of directors and others who can influence board members, such as long-term employees. The group can also provide formal presentations at the board meetings, as well as create educational materials for these meetings. In addition to education efforts using facts, the work change group must also utilize persuasion to convince the board of directors to accept and support a policy change. The work group attempts to appeal to the interests of board members, to include better meeting the needs of clients, as well as potentially raising new revenue for the organization, and increasing the status of the organization among peer organizations. The change work group carefully chooses persons with credibility to communicate with the board members, to include clients, former clients, and long-time employees. The change work group may also utilize co-optation if they invited a member of the board of directors to join the change work group in determining the exact direction and wording of the policy change proposal. Change work group members may also lobby board members about the policy change.

The change work group may decide, after unsuccessfully attempting a campaign change strategy, to utilize a **contest change strategy.** After careful thought and deliberation, the change work group may utilize a group action to raise the pressure on the members of the board of directors. For example, the change work group may decide to organize a rally, march, or a vigil, along with other similar service providers who are experiencing the same challenges with affordable rental housing. The publicity materials specifically request that organizations respond to the need for affordable rental housing for the chronically mentally ill. If board members feel there is some urgency in settling the situation, the change work group may engage in **bargaining and negotiation** with the board of directors. In this process, the two sides may agree on a policy change for the organization that looks similar to, but is the same as, the original policy change sought by the change work group.

Similar to change efforts with other client systems and levels of practice, not all change efforts are successful. Change work groups may need to change strategies or tactics, and the end result of the change process may differ from the original proposals. A proposed program may be a short-term, small project, a policy change may differ from the original intention, and an attempt to create a project may require a policy change. Some change efforts are not successful at all, and the status quo is maintained. At this point, the social worker, along with the change work group, must reassess the situation to determine next steps. The change effort may benefit from starting over at the engagement and assessment phase to determine if the identified unmet need may still be as urgent, or other data needs to be collected. Alternatively, the change effort may need to begin anew at the intervention stage, where the decision to pursue an intervention, the type of intervention, and/or the change strategy may need revisiting. An evaluation of the process so far will help determine if different directions may yield more successful results, toward the goal of better meeting the needs of the client. Overall, advocates for change at all client system levels benefit from persistence because many factors may be impacting the possibility of change, including external factors, such as a poor economy. Many change efforts take a long time, even years (Schenider & Lester, 2001). If the change process has been successful thus far, the next step is to implement the change process within the organization, as discussed in the next section.

IMPLEMENTING ORGANIZATIONAL CHANGE

If the change work group has been successful in its work to create an organizational change, the next step is to implement the organizational change. At this point, the change effort converts to administrative functions, such as a new or modified policy, program, project, personnel, or practice change. A change in one element of the organization, such as a new policy, can often impact change in another area, such as a new program, project, or even another policy change. For example, a policy change that affects the members of a committee that screens and interviews candidates for administrative positions will result in practice changes: clients will now be recruited for the committee and educated about organizational personnel procedures, interviewing techniques, and written evaluation process for interviews. Those changes that involve policy, program, or project most significantly impact organizations, and those that impact personnel and practices, while important, may not represent an in-depth change to the organization. The following discussion applies to implementing a new or modified program or project, including developing goals, objectives, and evaluation criteria and possibly using a Gantt chart to guide the time frame of activities. Implementing a new or modified program or project involves similar components.

Implementation Structure

Successful programs and projects need structure to guide implementation and for evaluation purposes, although the elements for a project may be less elaborate than those for a program due to the short-term nature of a project. The elements of a program include goals and objectives, timelines, eligibility criteria, rules and procedures, an evaluation plan, and a management information system (Hardina, Middleton,

Montana, & Simpson, 2007). **Goals** are broad statements related to an ideal state for a target, such as population or community, while **objectives** are steps toward reaching the goals. Objectives can relate to an outcome, a specific task, a process, or the means to completing a task. A **timeline** spells out in detail the activities that will carry out the goal and objectives, with specific deadlines in place. The **eligibility criteria** define the group of clients who can participate in the program, while the rules and procedures provide the structure for the day-to-day functioning of the program, such as the roles that individuals will play, the decision-making process, the responsibilities for each person involved, and the process for delivering the program. The **evaluation plan** provides the details about the instruments and/or data to be collected on a timetable and the identity of those that will collect, analyze, and report on the program data. The **management information system** is the process for collecting program data and is often a type of software or Internet-based application.

For example, if the change work group focused on the unmet needs of LGBTQ adolescents is successful in promoting a new program within the school to better educate, support, and nurture LGBTQ students, the next step is to create the elements of a program. The change work group, the school social worker, and/or administrators can create program goals and objectives, and corresponding evaluation criteria, such as the following (Hardina et al., 2007):

- *Program goal:* To enhance the academic and social functioning of LGBTQ students and their supporters in Jefferson High School.

- *Outcome objective:* By December 2018, at least one support group and three sexual orientation educational sessions will be offered to students.

- *Evaluation criteria:* Number of support groups and educational sessions offered.

- *Process objective:* By November 30, 2019, recruit at least ten students for an LGBTQ support group through one-to-one contact and advertising in the school.

- *Evaluation criteria:* Number of students recruited, number of in-person recruiting contacts made, amount of school newspaper coverage.

- *Process objective:* By October 2018, create outlines of two different curricula related to sexual orientation education for consideration by the administration.

- *Evaluation criteria:* Number of existing curricula reviewed, number of curricular outlines created.

Gantt Chart

An important component of planning program implementation is specifying activities that will implement objectives and a time frame for each of them so that

ACTIVITY	SEPT	OCT	NOV	DEC
Produce recruitment materials and begin recruiting for support group	X			
Locate and review at least three sexual orientation education curricular materials	X			
Create at least two outlines of a sexual orientation education curricular		X		
Recruit five students		X		
Recruit five additional students			X	
Facilitate one weekly support group			X	X
Conduct one education session			X	
Conduct two education sessions				X

Source: Adapted from O'Connor & Netting, 2009

EXHIBIT 13.6

Gantt Chart, LGBTQ Support Group and Sexual Orientation Education

actions can be undertaken in a logical, sequential order. The specification of activities and a corresponding time frame can be viewed in a **Gantt chart**, as displayed in Exhibit 13.6 (O'Connor & Netting, 2009). A Gantt chart provides a visual display of the activities that must be undertaken and the time frame for the completion of each activity, which can be helpful in both implementing a program and evaluating the success of the implementation (discussed later in this chapter). The Gantt chart depicts a sample of the activities to be completed for implementation of an LGBTQ support group and sexual orientation education sessions.

In addition to the activities in the Gantt chart, client eligibility criteria, program rules and procedures, and a management information system will be created to track the program participants, as well as overall evaluation criteria for the program.

Challenges to Implementation

Due to the complexity of organizations, implementation of a change effort can be fraught with difficulty. The organization may be facing challenges imposed by external constraints, such as a scarcity of available funding for the change proposal. The challenges faced by social workers who are attempting to implement a change can include the following (Winship & Lee, 2012):

Change Participant Affects   Although the change process has been successfully approved and authorized, the staff members involved in actually implementing the change may have a significant impact. Change proposals often encounter resistance from staff members with a different perspective or philosophy or who simply have a personal conflict with a member of the change work group. Staff members may oppose the change for many reasons, including a different worldview about the potential for change in people and organization, a distrust of nonexperts (or experts), or a fear of conflict, among other reasons. If the staff member was opposed to the change initially, the staff member may covertly express her or his opposition through inaction or subversion, may simply incorrectly implement the change due to a lack of understanding or skill or may decide to implement the change with her or his unique style such that the original intent is not realized.

Generality of the Change   Changes that are major in scope, such as policy changes, tend to be worded too generally; therefore, the implementation of the change may suffer from distortion because the staff member making the change may not understand or be suited to make the intended change.

Organizational Supports   Change proposals may be adopted with low levels of commitment by the decision-makers, and the implementation consequently may suffer from inadequate financial, planning, implementation, and other types of resources. A partial implementation of a change proposal may mean that the change is unsuccessful, when a complete implementation may have resulted in a highly successful implementation. A decision-maker's perspective on change may be affected by relationships with other organizations because a change could potentially create or exacerbate competition with other organizations or unnecessarily duplicate another organization's program. This could happen while the administrator is trying to create a stronger relationship with another organization. In short, support for the implementation by the organization's decision-makers can be affected by many factors other than the merits of the change proposal. Exhibit 13.7 provides an example of the ways in which staff resources impact change efforts.

EXHIBIT 13.7 *Organizational Challenges of Implementing Change*	The death of an infant under the supervision of the San Mateo County Human Services Agency (HAS) ultimately led to a decision to seek accreditation in all eligible agency services by the Council on Accreditation (COA). Accreditation by an outside body, such as the COA, provides an external, unbiased "stamp of approval" on an organization and is a confirmation of the highest level of professionalism of an organization. The process of seeking accreditation is a challenging, arduous, resource-laden process of organizational self-assessment toward meeting specific standards supported by documented evidence. Ultimately, the goal is to build capacity of the organization toward better organization and client outcomes. A "change work group," the Quality Assurance and Accreditation Committee, consisted mostly of administrators, while smaller subcommittees were established of staff members. As the two-year process got underway, it was clear that some staff on the subcommittees were passive and/or resistant to the work. In general, staff were not

EXHIBIT 13.7

Continued

highly motivated to respond to communication or meet deadlines for deliverables. Staff lacked clarity about the importance of the work, and questioned how the work involved in seeking accreditation would help clients. They were also frustrated that they were asked to work overtime to meet their regular job requirements as well as accomplish tasks needed for accreditation efforts. Some staff felt that the process devalued their many years of practice experience and reflected judgment on the quality of service they had been providing.

In response to early problems, the value of the accreditation process to client services and service outcomes was clarified. Additionally, communication systems were clarified, administrators provided more encouragement to accomplish tasks and assistance in balancing work priorities, and "tip sheets" on relevant topics were delivered to each subcommittee. Yet, even after staff better understood the importance of the work to their clients, staff were resistant to solve the problems unearthed in the process, such as a lack of formal written procedures, documentation, and evaluation in all areas required by COA. Administrators repeatedly reminded staff of the importance of the work to client outcomes, and encouraged them to take some ownership of the process as a legacy of their work at the agency. Finally, a mock site visit by COA volunteers (prior to the "real" site visit by COA evaluators) led to clarification for the staff of the inadequacies of the products produced thus far and an increased focus to complete the work as required by the COA. While challenged to finish the work within deadlines, staff then felt a higher level of camaraderie with one another and administrators, who also worked overtime during this period. Ultimately, HSA received accreditation by COA.

Source: Winship & Lee, 2012

TERMINATION, EVALUATION, AND FOLLOW-UP OF CHANGE IN ORGANIZATIONS

The next phase in the change process, termination, can apply to the change process and/or termination from the clients of the organization. Most social workers engaged in a change effort from within an organization will continue to participate in the work of the organization as an employee or a volunteer and will be engaged in follow-up activities following an intervention. In a sense, many organizations experience continual change processes, as the organization seeks to maintain programs and services that are relevant to clients' needs.

If the change process has been unsuccessful, the change work group may decide to begin anew at the assessment phase to gather more information and consider different possible unmet needs as the basis for a new intervention effort. The group may also decide to pursue a change effort based on the same unmet need, but with a different change proposal and/or a different strategy for change. Alternatively, the change work group may decide to abandon intervention efforts for now and disband. In this case, termination by the change work group from the change process may occur until the next unmet need is identified, when the change process can begin anew (possibly with a different change work group).

If the change process has been successful, the end of the change effort may occur when the change proposal has been approved by the decision-makers, or after the policy, program or project change has occurred, and an evaluation has determined that the change has positively impacted the organization. The change work group may be disbanded either after the approval or implementation and evaluation (or may stay together and begin the next organizational change effort). Follow-up effects may involve continuing to monitor the effects of a change within an organization, such as through program evaluation efforts.

When the change work group is disbanded, as with other client systems, the termination may evoke an emotional response from participants, and group termination processes may be helpful (see Chapter 9). Change work groups are one type of task group, and members may have built relationships with one another. Just as in other groups, the role of the social worker in termination is to help the group members examine and celebrate their experiences and accomplishments and discuss the ways in which their shared experiences and skills may be useful to the participants in the future (Garvin & Galinsky, 2013). Social workers may also facilitate the expression and integration of positive and negative emotion, depending on the circumstances of the termination. While change work group members are likely to experience fewer emotional responses than those of other client systems, social workers must always be attuned to the possibility of emotional reactions.

Evaluation of Social Work Practice with Organizations

Similar to evaluation with social work practice with individuals, families, groups, and communities, evaluation of social work practice with organizations is an important part of the change process. The evaluation process can focus on the change process itself, as well as the result of the change process (i.e., the new or changed policy, program, or project that resulted from the change process). The evaluation of both the change efforts and evaluation of policies, programs, and projects have similar components.

Evaluation of an advocacy effort or of a program or project begins with a decision about the measurable objectives, usually made at the beginning of a change effort. The evaluation process begins as an element of the change effort and requires a decision: (1) if both the process and outcomes will be evaluated, (2) the ways in which the process and outcomes will be evaluated, and (3) the means by which data will be collected as the basis for the evaluation. The goal of the evaluation process is to determine the *value* of something, which differs from simply monitoring an intervention (Netting et al., 2017).

Types of Evaluation For both the change process and the implementation of programs and projects, there are three types of evaluation that can be used to assess the objectives: (1) process, (2) outcome, or (3) impact evaluation. A **process evaluation** focuses on the *degree to which the effort operated well.* For example, did the change work group have a sufficient number of persons for the work involved? What methods were used to recruit persons to the change work group? If evaluating a program, a process evaluation could focus on whether sufficient resources were available for the program, the ways in which decisions were made as a group, or whether there was sufficient and timely communication between staff members implementing a program. An **outcome evaluation** focuses on *information about specific results* that the effort achieved. Questions to be answered may ask: did the work group successfully arrange meetings with decision-makers? Create educational materials? Were there any policy changes? Were new programs or projects created as a result of policy changes?

An outcome evaluation for a program focuses on the results of program efforts. For example, did support groups meet? Were educational trainings held? The objectives for the program should be reviewed, and success in their achievement should be noted. An **impact evaluation** reviews the *impact of the efforts,* such as individual or community-level behavioral changes (Edwards & Yankey, 2006). For example, in relation to advocacy efforts, is there a new decision-making process in the organization that is more participatory? In relation to a new program, are LGBTQ adolescents achieving at higher academic levels as a result? Have clients experienced behavioral changes as a result of a new policy, program, or project? Have specific changes occurred in the community, such as decreased suicides or increased involvement in community programs?

Structure of Evaluation   The structure of evaluation involves four specific concepts: inputs, activities, outputs, and outcomes. **Inputs** are those resources necessary to implement a change effort or a program. Inputs can include funding, equipment, staff, time, expertise, and other resources needed for the effort or program. **Activities** are those actions that organizations take to produce change. Activities can include attending meetings, creating flyers, interviewing clients, and conducting assessments. **Outputs** are products that emerge from the activities. Outputs are often measured by a number (e.g., number of clients served by a program, flyers produced, or hours worked). **Outcomes** are the benefits gained or changes that have occurred as a result of the activities. Outcomes may relate to behavior, skill, knowledge, attitudes, values, condition, or other attribute. In essence, the outcomes are the impact made by the change effort or program (Dudley, 2014).

Logic Model   A **logic model** is a graphic depiction of the relationship of inputs, activities, outputs, and outcomes. Logic models provide a way to demonstrate the links between resources, efforts, accomplishments, and the impacts of change efforts and programs (Hardina, 2013). They are created at the beginning of a change effort, such as creating a program or project, to understand how all of the different parts interact with one another, and are very useful for evaluation. Exhibit 13.8

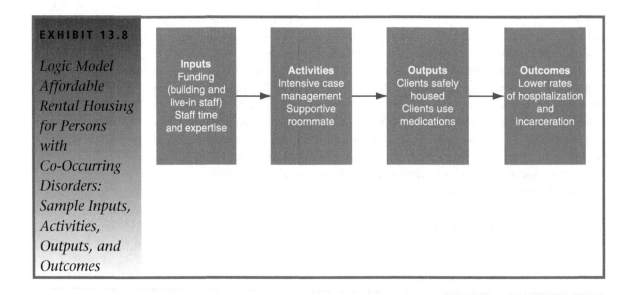

EXHIBIT 13.8

Logic Model Affordable Rental Housing for Persons with Co-Occurring Disorders: Sample Inputs, Activities, Outputs, and Outcomes

Inputs
Funding (building and live-in staff)
Staff time and expertise

Activities
Intensive case management
Supportive roommate

Outputs
Clients safely housed
Clients use medications

Outcomes
Lower rates of hospitalization and incarceration

provides an example of a logic model used for a program of rental housing for dual-diagnosed clients.

In this example, funding is needed to purchase and/or renovate an apartment building (*input*), so that clients can be housed with a trained, supportive roommate and provided with intensive case management (*activities*). These activities may result in clients being housed in a decent, affordable unit, leading a more stable life, and being compliant with their medication (*output*), so that fewer clients would be homeless and/or incarcerated (*outcome*). This logic model can be useful in making a persuasive argument to a decision-maker who is interested in decreasing the number of dual diagnosed clients who are hospitalized or incarcerated. Other decision-makers may be interested in other outcomes, such as lowering levels of homelessness among persons who are dual diagnosed in the community to improve the relationship between the police force and the organization. Logic models provide a rational connection between inputs, activities, outputs, and outcomes and are often used in evaluating change efforts, programs, and projects (Hardina, 2013).

Information and Data Sources Developing and maintaining an adequate system for tracking information and data about change efforts, as well as programs and projects, is the backbone of the evaluation process. Information (hard copy and/or electronic) that may be helpful includes the following (Schneider & Lester, 2001):

- Minutes of meetings, logs of activities, sign-in sheets

- Information noting time spent on activities, appointments, assessments, client progress, activities in need of completing, and accomplishments

- Client evaluation materials, including standardized measures

- Organization strategic plans, mission, value statements, goals, objectives, and timelines

- Media coverage

- Funding sources, amounts, responsibilities, and required communications

- Information about key individuals to change efforts or programs/projects

- Government organizations related to the change effort and/or programs/projects

- Previous internal and external evaluations of advocacy efforts and programs/projects

- Records about previous internal and external advocacy efforts.

As with evaluations of community change efforts, the evaluation process ideally includes qualitative and quantitative data to provide information about the process and outcomes of organizational change. Methods may include pre- and post-measures of organizational and/or community functioning, such as validated and standardized measures, direct observation, use of publically available data (i.e., U.S. Census data and others), and feedback from other professionals.

Roles in Evaluation   Generalist social work practitioners commonly contribute in several ways to the evaluation efforts. Social workers can lead and/or assist with evaluation efforts by helping maintain organizational records, submitting data for an analysis, participating in interviews and/or focus groups, or creating questions to be used in the evaluation process. Participation on evaluation teams and committees provides a way for social workers to learn about and direct the evaluation efforts, and some social workers function in the role of researchers to collect, analyze, and report on quantitative and qualitative data. Organizations benefit from well-designed and executed evaluation efforts.

STRAIGHT TALK ABOUT ORGANIZATIONAL LIFE

This chapter has highlighted both the challenging and the exhilarating aspects of social work practice with change in an organizational setting. Social workers can be tempted to view the organization as a source of challenges in practice. Sometimes organizations can be perceived as posing confounding or complex barriers to the helping process due to policies, procedures, and practice requirements.

In much the same way that some people blame their families for their challenges, some social workers point to the organization as the source of the problem when work becomes challenging or proves more difficult than expected. Shifting responsibility for challenges to organizations relieves the burden of responsibility from the social worker for a role in those organizational challenges. Social workers may not always fully understand the practice constraints inherent in organizations (such as constraints on practice by funders or regulators) and may find it easier to adopt a cynicism that eases their sense of responsibility. A related problem can occur if the social worker joins with the clients to collude about the problems of the organization as the source of the clients' challenges. In doing so, the social worker may feel temporarily relieved by engaging the client in her or his desperation with the organizational system. However, such collusion can convey a sense of hopelessness to the client, when the social worker's goal may be to convey a sense of hopefulness about the client's situation. In its most extreme implication, a hopeless stance may promote a generalized, scornful distrust of all helping efforts. The client may generalize that all helping efforts are ineptly carried out by social workers who are helpless and caught in troubled organizational structures that fail to implement their mission statements. Social workers, at times, must identify problematic agency policies or obstacles to clients. An element of empowerment practice is creating an alliance with clients, or a joint effort designed to promote more effective responses to clients. However, social workers must be able to convey an overall hopeful message to clients about their interaction with an organization.

At the same time, social workers must invest in a thorough engagement, assessment, and planning process prior to initiating in change efforts within and for an organization. For example, social workers need to understand the dynamics of bureaucracies and the slow nature of change within bureaucracies before engaging in a change effort. Social workers can be discouraged to enact change by their senior colleagues who believe that change efforts will create no effect or who are afraid of being sanctioned or fired if they attempt to create change without first building credibility.

Social workers who facilitate organizational change efforts must be well-informed, and have completed the earlier phases of the change process, knowing that every change effort will encounter resistance. In addition to understanding the organization, social workers must also understand their own strengths and weaknesses, and enlist allies to assist with the effort. However, a social worker who does not address any problematic organizational policy or practice due to fear of criticism or loss of employment is likely to have a difficult time in a social work career. Social work practice requires principled, thoughtful, and respectful risks across all settings to fully implement the work of the profession.

CONCLUSION

Organizations are structures that shape and facilitate social work practice. The change process in organizations provides an opportunity to offer improved services

In the history of the United States, some groups of people have long endured prejudice, discrimination, and exclusion from success in education and employment. A challenge for social work, identified by the American Academy of Social Work and Social Welfare, is to end racial and social injustice, dismantle inequality, and end unfair practices.

"The Grand Challenge of Promoting Equality by Addressing Social Stigma," by Goldbach, Amaro, Vega, and Walter (2015), describes the problems associated with social stigma and opportunities for social workers to end these problems. They describe stigma as "negative labeling" based on characteristics that others perceive as undesirable and distinguishing them from the rest of society. Stigma results in social disadvantage and loss of opportunities throughout life because of inequality, and leads to less favorable outcomes regarding health, academic achievement, income, wealth, and others. Stigma can be based on race and ethnicity, gender, sexual orientation, immigration status, age, ability status, health-related domains, housing status, and others.

The authors suggest a number of steps that social workers can take to reduce stigma, including examining social work's role as an agent of social control in society that has supported inequality (compared to the principles of the professions), and working to unearth unconscious biases of social workers. They also suggest engaging in employment-based training to reduce bias in service delivery, as well as active participation in public policy efforts to reduce inequality.

One effort that can be taken is at the organizational level. Organizations can make efforts to overcome stigma that is built into institutional arrangements. Stigma can result in biases built into organizations, even when they are unrecognized. Organizations can examine the assumptions built into their policies, practices, programs, personnel to determine where biases may be present that are reinforcing social stigmas. For example, unexamined biases could exist in such policies as the length of time a participant is allowed to participate in a program, the process of taking clients off waiting lists for services, or recruitment sources of programs. To consider these questions further, please familiarize yourself with Working Paper No. 18, *Promoting Equality by Addressing Social Stigma* (Goldbach et al., 2015) at http://aaswsw.org/wp-content/uploads/2016/01/W16-The-Grand-Challenge-of-Promoting-Equality-by-Addressing-Social-Stigma1-1-2.pdf. (To consider these questions further, see Exercise #a1 at the end of this chapter.)

GRAND CHALLENGE

Achieve Equal Opportunity and Justice

to clients. While the change process can be lengthy and complex, the process is an opportunity to make changes that positively impact a large number of people, including entire communities. Most organizations undergo at least modest change on a regular basis due to changes in many factors, such as funding, relationships, personnel, accreditation requirements, or accountability requirements, and staff members are in a unique position to implement the change process based on feedback and critical thinking about clients' needs as experienced by staff working directly with clients. While organizations can seem vague and too complex to change, understanding and impacting organizations is important to social work practitioners on all levels because of the significant impact on clients and practitioners. Taking an active role in shaping the organization is a significant aspect to generalist social work practice.

MAIN POINTS

- The approach of an organizational change effort will be impacted by the results of the engagement and assessment process, as well as the approach, perspective, or model utilized.

- The organizational change effort is facilitated by using a framework.

- Gathering supporters and allies into a change work group, considering important factors when choosing a change proposal, and selecting an organizational change strategy are vital steps in the intervention.

- Social workers consider social work ethics when choosing specific tactics to utilize for the change process.

- The implementation of an organizational change is facilitated by a structure, as well as consideration of challenges to implementation that can impede the implementation.

- Termination of a change effort can occur after a change proposal has been successful or after the implementation of the change.

- The evaluation phase can include evaluation of the change effort as well as evaluation of the change, such as a program or a project.

- Social workers should exercise caution about identifying organizational challenges with clients and only do so while maintaining a hopeful stance about the ability of the organization to assist the client.

EXERCISES

a. Case Exercises

1. To apply your learning of the Grand Challenge to promote equality by addressing social stigma that was highlighted in this chapter, visit the Grand Challenges website and read Working Paper No. 18 (Goldbach, Amaro, Vega, & Walter, 2015). Then, go to www.routledgesw.com/cases and become familiar with the RAINN case. Under the "Evaluate Your Results" tab, review both "The Purpose of RAINN evaluation data" and "What Data Can't Tell Us" sections. Consider whether there are any data collected that could provide hints about potential organizational bias in RAINN service delivery? Are there

any evaluation questions that cannot be answered with the data collected, yet, if it could, may shed light on some implicit bias in the organization?

2. Go to www.routledgesw.com/cases and become familiar with the Carla Washburn case, including reviewing her client history, concerns, and goals. Explore the town map and determine those organizations that may be able to assist Carla with her concerns and goals. Choose one of the organizations and consider the way(s) in which the organization may be able to assist Carla with one or more of her concerns and/or goals. Imagine that you are employed by the organization, and the assistance needed for Carla is currently not offered by the organization. Using the material from Chapter 13, describe the following:
   - The type of approach, perspective, or model with which you most closely identify
   - The way in which you would go about creating a change work group
   - Two to three possible solutions to Carla's concern or goal with which the organization could assist
   - Two to three considerations that are important to consider in deciding on the change proposal

3. Go to www.routledgesw.com/cases and become familiar with the Riverton case, including the history, concerns, and goals, as well as the town map and the interaction matrix. Imagine that you decide to work to find a solution to the problem of public intoxication by working with the organizations in the community as a "nonemployee."

   Which organizations would you approach to develop a community-wide response to this problem? What kind of changes might be needed in those organizations to better meet the unmet needs of the clients in the community? What steps might you take to facilitate the development of a change work group in these organizations? What might be some feasible solutions that organizations could implement through a partnership?

4. Go to www.routledgesw.com/cases and become familiar with the Brickville case. After an organizational assessment related to organizational engagement in political affairs, the Brickville CDC decided to move forward with a change proposal to engage more fully in local politics. The social worker, Olivia, and her colleagues formed a committee to work on the organizational change effort. For this change effort, create a goal, outcome objective, and evaluation criteria. In addition, create 2–3 process objectives and corresponding evaluation criteria for the change effort.

5. Using the Brickville case scenario described in Exercise #3, describe a policy, program, project, personnel, and practice approach to more fully engaging in local politics as an organization.

6. Go to www.routledgesw.com/cases and become familiar with the RAINN case by reviewing the RAINN Components and Ecomap. Discuss the approaches, perspectives, and models discussed in this chapter (i.e., self-learning model, social ecology approach, systems model, power and politics model, postmodern

approaches, and social constructionist approach) related to RAINN. If you were to describe RAINN using each one of these, what would you notice in particular? How would you be able to tell whether the approach, perspective, or model was relevant to RAINN?

b. Other Exercises

7. Review Exhibit 13.3. Create a different policy, program, project, personnel, or practice approach to the case than those provided.
8. Review Exhibit 13.3. Create an approach to change that mixes these approaches.
9. You are a social worker at an organization that provides treatment for adolescents who have alcohol and drug addiction issues. Yesterday, you suggested that the organization extend the service hours of the organization into the evenings and weekends so that the families of the clients would have greater access to meet with the staff, participate in treatment planning, and provide additional face-to-face support for their children. The staff was enthusiastic about the idea, and you agreed to the director's request that you compose a written proposal to be discussed at the next staff meeting.

   In your weekly meeting with your supervisor, you learn that she is upset with you. In your discussion, she is curt and states that you may not have taken into account the increased amount of work that extended service hours would entail. She states that increased service hours will have a negative impact on her life in terms of her social life and time with family members, and cost the agency additional funds. Considering the material discussed in Chapter 13, discuss the factors that may have led to this encounter in terms of creating a change proposal. Discuss possible next steps for this change process.
10. Using the two scenarios in Exhibit 13.1, create a problem statement that could be used in a change effort. The problem statement should be explicit, clear, and behavioral and should include values-oriented terms and client examples.
11. Using the case scenario in Exhibit 13.7, apply the key points in Quick Guide 45. What steps could have been taken to be more persuasive to those opposed?

REFERENCES

350.org. (n.d.). No KXL. Retrieved from http://350.org/kxl-victory/

Abramson, J. (2009). Interdisciplinary team practice. In A.R. Roberts (Ed.), *Social workers' desk reference* (2nd ed.) (pp. 44–50). New York: Oxford University Press.

Alissi, A.S. (2009). United States. In A. Gitterman & R. Salmon (Eds.), *Encyclopedia of social work with groups* (pp. 6–12). New York: Routledge.

American Academy of Social Work & Social Welfare. (2016). Grand challenges: About. Retrieved from http://aaswsw.org/grand-challenges-initiative/about/

Anderson, K.M. (2013). Assessing strengths. Identifying acts of resistance to violence and oppression. In D. Saleebey (Ed.), *The strengths perspective in social work practice* (6th ed.) (pp. 182–202). Boston: Pearson.

Anderson, K., Cowger, C., & Snively, C. (2009). Assessing strengths: Identifying acts of resistance to violence and oppression. In D. Saleebey (Ed.), *The strengths perspective in social work practice* (5th ed.) (pp. 181–200). Boston: Pearson Education, Inc.

Aotearoa New Zealand Association of Social Workers (ANZAWS). (2007). Code of ethics. Retrieved from http://anzasw.nz/summary-of-the-code-of-ethics/#1455661759310-739c7231-9145

Association for the Advancement of Social Work with Groups, Inc. (2013). Standards for social work practice with groups, second edition. Retrieved from www.aaswg.org/files/AASWG_Standards_for_Social_Work_Practice_with_Groups.pdf.

Atwood, J.D., & Genovese, F. (2006). *Therapy with single parents. A social constructionist approach*. New York: The Haworth Press.

Austin, M.J., & Solomon, J.R. (2009). Managing the planning process. In R.J. Patti (Ed.), *The handbook of human services management* (pp. 321–337). Thousand Oaks, CA: Sage Publications.

Bailey, S.J., Haynes, D.C., & Letiecq, B.L. (2013). "How can you retire when you still got a kid in school?": Economics of raising grandchildren in rural areas. *Marriage & Family Review, 49*, 671–693.

Banyard, V.L., Moynihan, M.M., & Plante, E.G. (2007). Sexual violence prevention through bystander education: An experimental evaluation. *Journal of Community Psychology, 35*(4), 463–481.

Barker, R.L. (2014). *The social work dictionary* (6th ed.). Washington, DC: NASW Press.

Barsky, A.E. (2010). *Ethics and values in social work*. New York: Oxford University Press.

Barth, R.P. (2013). Adoption: Overview. In C. Franklin (Ed.), *Encyclopedia of social work [E-reader version]*. Washington, DC, and New York: National Association of Social Workers and Oxford University Press. DOI: 10.1093/acrefore/9780199975839.013.5

Bathgate, L. (2016). 5 practical points for social workers on interdisciplinary teams. *The New Social Worker, 23*(1), 14–15.

Bavelas, J., De Jong, P., Franklin, C., Froerer, A., Gingerich, W., Kim, J., Korman, H., Langer, S., Lee, M.Y., McCollum, E.E., Jordan, S.S., & Trepper, T.S. (2013). *Solution focused therapy treatment manual for working with individuals* (2nd ed.). Retrieved from www.sfbta.org/researchdownloads.html

Beaulaurier, R.L., & Taylor, S.H. (2007). Social work practice with people with disabilities in the era of disability rights. In A.E. Dell Orto & P.W. Power

(Eds.), *The psychological and social impact of illness and disability* (5th ed.) (pp. 53–74). New York: Springer Publishing.

Beck, J.S. (2011). *Cognitive therapy for challenging problems: What to do when the basics don't work.* New York: Guilford Press.

Benard, B., & Truebridge, S. (2013). A shift in thinking. Influencing social workers' beliefs about individual and family resilience in an effort to enhance well-being and success for all. In D. Saleebey (Ed.), *The strengths perspective in social work practice* (6th ed.) (pp. 203–220). Boston: Allyn & Bacon.

Berg, R.D., Landreth, G.L., & Fall, K.A. (2013). *Group counseling concepts and procedures* (5th ed.). New York: Routledge.

Berg-Weger, M. (2016). *Social work and social welfare. An invitation* (4th ed.). New York: Routledge.

Berg-Weger, M., Rubio, D.M., & Tebb, S. (2000). The caregiver well-being scale revisited. *Health and Social Work, 25*(4), 255–263.

Berman-Rossi, T., & Kelly, T.B. (2003). *Group composition, diversity, the skills of the social worker, and group development.* Presented at the Council for Social Work Education, Annual Meeting, Atlanta, GA, February.

Berzin, S.C., Singer, J., & Chan, C. (2015). *Practice innovation through technology in the digital age: A grand challenge for social work.* Working Paper No. 12, American Academy of Social Work and Social Welfare Grand Challenges for Social Work Initiative. Retrieved from http://aaswsw.org/grand-challenges-initiative/12-challenges/harness-technology-for-social-good/

Bliss, D.L. (2015). Using the social work advocacy practice model to find our voices in service of advocacy. *Human Service Organizations: Management, Leadership & Governance, 39,* 57–68.

Bloom, M., Fischer, J., & Orme, J.G. (2009). *Evaluating practice: Guidelines for the accountable professional* (6th ed.). Boston: Allyn & Bacon.

Blunsdon, B., & Davern, M. (2007). Measuring wellness through interdisciplinary community development: Linking the physical, economic and social environment. *Journal of Community Practice, 15*(1/2), 217–238.

Bobo, K., Kendall, J., & Max, S. (2010). *Organizing for social change.* Santa Ana, CA: The Forum Press.

Boland-Prom, K.W. (2009). Results of a national study of social workers sanctioned by state licensing boards. *Social Work, 54*(4), 351–360.

Bond, C., Woods, K., Humphrey, N., Symes, W., & Green, L. (2013). Practitioner review: The effectiveness of solution focused brief therapy with children and families: A systematic and critical evaluation of the literature from 1990–2010. *Journal of Child Psychology and Psychiatry, 54*(7), 707–723.

Bos, H.M.W., Knox, J.R., van Rijn-van Gelderen, L., & Gartrell, N.K. (2016). Same-sex and different-sex parent households and child health outcomes: Findings from the National Survey of Children's Health. *Journal of Developmental & Behavioral Pediatrics, 37*(3), 179–187.

Bowlby, J. (1982). *Attachment and loss: Vol. 1, Attachment* (2nd ed.). New York: Basic Books.

Brager, G., Specht, H., & Torczyner, J. (1987). *Community organizing.* New York: Columbia University Press.

Breton, M. (2006). An empowerment perspective. In C.D. Garvin, L.M. Gutiérrez, & M.J. Galinsky (Eds.), *Handbook of social work with groups* (pp. 58–75). New York: Guilford Press.

Briar-Lawson, K., & Naccarato, T. (2013). Family services. In C. Franklin (Ed.), *Encyclopedia of social work [E-reader version].* Washington, DC, and New York: National Association of Social Workers and Oxford University Press. DOI: 10.1093/acrefore/9780199975839.013.145

Brill, C. (1998). The new NASW code of ethics can be your ally: Part I. Focus Newsletter. Retrieved from www.naswma.org/displaycommon.cfm?an=1&subarticlenbr=96

Briskman, L., & Noble, C. (1999). Social work ethics: Embracing diversity? In J. Fook & B. Pease (Eds.), *Transforming social work practice: Postmodern critical perspectives* (pp. 57–69). London: Routledge.

Brown, N.W. (2013). *Creative activities for group therapy.* New York: Routledge.

Brueggemann, W.G. (2013a). History and context for community practice in North America. In

M. Weil's (Ed.), *The handbook of community practice* (pp. 27–46). Thousand Oaks, CA: Sage Publications.

Brueggemann, W.G. (2013b). *The practice of macro social work* (4th ed.). Belmont, CA: Thomson Higher Education.

Brunell, J., Moray, N., Stevens, R., & Fassin, Y. (2016). Balancing competing logic in for-profit enterprises: A need for hybrid governance. *Journal of Social Entrepreneurship*, 1–26. DOI: 10.1080/19420676.2016.1166147

Bureau of Labor Statistics. (2016). Occupational outlook handbook, social workers. Retrieved from www.bls.gov/ooh/community-and-social-service/social-workers.htm#tab-1

Butler, C. (2009). Sexual and gender minority therapy and systemic practice. *Journal of Family Therapy*, *31*(4), 338–358.

Campbell, D. (2000). *The socially constructed organization*. London: Karnac Books.

Carter, L., & Matthieu, M. (2010). *Developing skills in the evidence based practice process*. St. Louis, MO: Washington University in St. Louis. Presented March 12, 2010.

Casa de Esperanza. (n.d.). History. Retrieved from https://www.casadeesperanza.org

Cattaneo, L.B., & Goodman, L.A. (2015). What is empowerment anyway? A model for domestic violence practice, research, and evaluation. *Psychology of Violence 5*(1), 84–94.

Chandler, S.M. (2013). The application of collaboration models to family group conferencing. *Journal of Policy Practice*, *12*(1), 3–22.

Chaskin, R.J. (2010). The Chicago School: A context for youth intervention, research and development. In R.J. Chaskin (Ed.), *Youth gangs and community intervention: Research, practice, and evidence* (pp. 3–23). New York: Columbia University Press.

Chaskin, R.J. (2013). Theories of community. In M. Weil's (Ed.), *The handbook of community practice* (pp. 105–121). Thousand Oaks, CA: Sage Publications.

Chee, L.P., Goh, E.C.L., & Kuczynski, L. (2014). Oversized loads: Child parentification in low-income families and underlying parent–child dynamics. *Families in Society: The Journal of Contemporary Social Services*, *95*(3), 204–212.

Chen, E.C., Budianto, L., & Wong, K. (2011). Professional school counselors as social justice advocates for undocumented immigrant students in group work. In A.A. Singh & C.F. Salazar (Eds.), *Social justice in group work. Practical interventions for change* (pp. 88–94). New York: Routledge.

Child, Youth, and Family (n.d.). *The Family Group Conference*. Retrieved from www.cyf.govt.nz/keeping-kids-safe/ways-we-work-with-families/family-group-conference-or-fgc.html

Chun-Chow, J., & Austin, M.J. (2008). The culturally responsive social service agency: The application of an evolving definition to a case study. *Administration in Social Work*, *32*(4), 39–64.

Cnaan, R.A., & Rothman, J. (2008). Capacity development and the building of community. In J. Rothman, J. Erlich, & J. Tropman (Eds.), *Strategies of community intervention* (7th ed.) (pp. 243–262). Peosta, Iowa: Eddie Bowers Publishing Co., Inc.

Coles, R.L. (2015). Single-father families: A review of the literature. *Journal of Family Theory & Review*, *7*(2), 144–166.

Collins, D., Jordan, C., & Coleman, H. (2013). *An introduction to family social work* (4th ed.). Belmont, CA: Brooks/Cole.

Collins, K.S., & Lazzari, M.M. (2009). Co-leadership. In A. Gitterman & R. Salmon (Eds.), *Encyclopedia of social work with groups* (pp. 299–302). New York: Routledge.

Comer, E., & Meier, A. (2011). Using evidence-based practice and intervention research with treatment groups for populations at risk. In G.L. Greif & P.H. Ephross (Eds.), *Group work with populations* (3rd ed.) (pp. 459–488). New York: Oxford University Press.

Congress, E.P. (2004). Cultural and ethical issues in working with culturally diverse patients and their families: The use of the culturagram to promote cultural competent practice in health care settings. In A. Metteri, T. Krôger, A. Pohjola, & P. Rauhala (Eds.), *Social work visions from around the globe* (pp. 249–262). Binghamton, NY: Haworth.

Congress, E.P. (2015). The culturagram. In K. Corcoran & A.R. Roberts (Eds.), *Social workers' desk reference*

(3rd ed.) (pp. 1011–1018). New York: Oxford University Press.

Corcoran, K. (2009). Using standardized tests and instruments in family assessments. In K. Corcoran & A.R. Roberts (Eds.), *Social workers' desk reference* (3rd ed.) (pp. 388–392). New York: Oxford University Press.

Corcoran, K. (2015). How clinical social workers can easily use rapid assessment tools (RATs) for mental health assessment and treatment evaluation. In K. Corcoran & A.R. Roberts (Eds.), *Social workers' desk reference* (3rd ed.) (pp. 358–364). New York: Oxford University Press.

Corcoran, K., & Fischer, J. (2013). *Measures for clinical practice and research: A sourcebook, Volume 1: Couples, families, and children* (5th ed.). New York: Oxford University Press.

Cordova, T.L. (2011). Community-based research and participatory change: A strategic, multi-method community impact assessment. *Journal of Community Practice, 19*(1), 29–47.

Council on Social Work Education (CSWE). (2012). Educational Policy and Accreditation Standards. Washington, DC: Author.

Council on Social Work Education (CSWE). (2015). Educational Policy and Accreditation Standards. Washington, DC: Author. Retrieved from www.cswe.org/File.aspx?id=81660

Cox, D. & Pawar, M. (2013). *International social work: Issues, strategies, and programs*. Thousand Oaks, CA: Sage Publications.

Cross, T.L. (2013). Cultural competence. In C. Franklin (Ed.), *Encyclopedia of social work*. Washington, DC, and New York: National Association of Social Workers and Oxford University Press.

Cross, T.L., Bazron, B.J., Dennis, K.W., & Isaacs, M.R. (1989). *Toward a culturally competent system of care*. Washington, DC: Georgetown University Development Center.

Cummings, T.G., & Worley, C.G. (2014). *Organizational development and change* (10th ed.). Mason, OH: South-Western Cengage Learning.

De Jong, P. (2009). Solution-focused therapy. In K. Corcoran & A.R. Roberts (Eds.), *Social workers' desk*

reference (3rd ed.) (pp. 268–275). New York: Oxford University Press.

De Jong, P. (2013). Interviewing. In C. Franklin (Ed.), *Encyclopedia of social work [E-reader version]*. Washington, DC, and New York: National Association of Social Workers and Oxford University. DOI: 10.1093/acrefore/978019975839.013.209

De Jong, P. (2015). Solution-focused therapy. In K. Corcoran & A.R. Roberts (Eds.), *Social workers' desk reference* (3rd ed.) (pp. 268–274). New York: Oxford University Press.

De Jong, P., & Berg, I.K. (2013). *Interviewing for solutions* (4th ed.). Belmont, CA: Brooks/Cole.

De Jong, P., & Cronkright, A. (2011). Learning solution-focused interviewing skills: BSW student voices. *Journal of Teaching in Social Work, 31*, 21–37.

DeFrain, J., & Asay, S.M. (2007). Epilogue: A strengths-based conceptual framework for understanding families worldwide. In J. DeFrain & S.M. Asay (Eds.), *Strong families around the world: Strengths-based research and perspectives* (pp. 447–466). New York: Haworth Press, Inc.

DeNavas-Walt, C., & Proctor, B.D. (2015). U.S. Census Bureau, Current Population Reports, P60-252, *Income and Poverty in the United States: 2014*, U.S. Government Printing Office, Washington, DC.

deShazer, S. (1984). The death of resistance. *Family Process, 23*, 11–21.

Detroit Food Policy Council. (2016). The DFPC is. . . Retrieved from http://detroitfoodpolicycouncil.net/

Diller, J.V. (2015). *Cultural diversity: A primer for the human services* (5th ed.). Stamford, CT: Cengage Learning.

Doel, M., & Kelly, T.B. (2014). *A-Z of groups & group-work*. New York: Palgrave Macmillan.

Dolgoff, R., Harrington, D., & Loewenberg, F.M. (2012). *Ethical decisions for social work practice*. Itasca, IL: F.E. Peacock.

Dombo, E.A. (2011). Rape: When professional values place vulnerable clients at risk. In J.C. Rothman (Ed.), *From the front lines: Student cases in social work ethics* (3rd ed.) (pp. 185–188). Boston: Allyn & Bacon.

Dominelli, L. (2014). Promoting environmental justice through green social work practice: A key challenge for practitioners and educators. *International Social Work*, *57*(4), 338–345. DOI: 10.1177/0020872814524968

Donaldson, L.P. (2004). Toward validating the therapeutic benefits of empowerment-oriented social action groups. *Social Work with Groups, 27*(2), 159–175.

Dressler, L. (2006). *Consensus through conversation.* San Francisco, CA: Berrett-Koehler Publishers, Inc.

Dudley, J.R. (2014). *Social work evaluation: Enhancing what we do* (2nd ed.). Chicago: Lyceum Books, Inc.

Dudziak, S., & Profitt, N.J. (2012). Group work and social justice: Designing pedagogy for social change. *Social Work with Groups, 35*, 235–252.

Dunst, C.J., & Trivette, C.M. (2009). Capacity-building family-systems intervention practices. *Journal of Family Social Work, 12*, 119–143.

Dunst, C.J., Trivette, C.M., & Deal, A.G. (2003). *Enabling and empowering families: Principles and guidelines for practice.* Newton, MA: Brookline Books.

Dybicz, P. (2015). From person-in-environment to strengths: The promise of postmodern practice. *Journal of Social Work Education, 51*(2), 237–249.

Early, T.J., & Newsome, W.S. (2005). Measures for assessment and accountability in practice with families from a strengths perspective. In. J. Corcoran (Ed.), *Building strength and skills. A collaborative approach to working with clients* (pp. 359–393). New York: Oxford University Press.

East, J.F., & Roll, S.J. (2015). Women, poverty and trauma: An empowerment practice approach. *Social Work, 60*(4): 279–286.

Eaton, Y.M., & Roberts, A.R. (2009). Frontline crisis intervention. Step-by-step practice guidelines with case applications. In A.R. Roberts (Ed.), *Social workers' desk reference* (2nd ed.) (pp. 207–215). New York: Oxford University Press.

Eaton-Shull, Y.M. (2015). Crisis intervention with individuals and groups: Frameworks to guide social workers. In K. Corcoran & A.R. Roberts (Eds.), *Social workers' desk reference* (3rd ed.) (pp. 217–222). New York: Oxford University Press.

Edleson, J.L., Lindhorst, T., & Kanuha, V.K. (2015). *Ending gender-based violence: A grand challenge for social work.* Working Paper No. 10, American Academy of Social Work and Social Welfare Grand Challenges for Social Work Initiative. Retrieved from http://aaswsw.org/grand-challenges-initiative/12-challenges/stop-family-violence/

Edwards, R.L., & Yankey, J.A. (2006). *Effectively managing nonprofit organizations.* Washington, DC: NASW Press.

Ellis, R.R., & Simmons, T. (2014). Coresident grandparents and their grandchildren: 2012. Washington, DC: Current Population Reports, P20-576, U.S. Census Bureau,

Ephross, P.H. (2011). Social work with groups: Practice principles. In G.L. Grief & P.H. Ephross (Eds.), *Group work with populations at risk* (3rd ed.) (pp. 3–14). New York: Oxford University Press.

Epstein, M.H. (2004). *Behavioral and emotional rating scale: A strengths-based approach to assessment* (2nd ed.). Austin, TX: PRO-ED.

Epstein, M.H., Mooney, P., Ryser, G., & Pierce, C.D. (2004). Validity and reliability of the Behavioral and Emotional Rating Scale (2nd edition): Youth Rating Scale. *Research on Social Work Practice, 14*(50), 358–367.

Evans, S.D., Hanlin, C.E., & Prillehensky, I. (2007). Blending ameliorative and (transformative approaches in human service organizations: A case study. *Journal of Community Psychology, 35*(3), 329–346.

Falicov, C.J. (2013). *Latino families in therapy.* New York: Guilford Publications.

Family Resource Center. (2016). Redevelopment Opportunities for Women. Retrieved from https://www.frcmo.org/services/row/

Fetherman, D.L., & Burke, S.C. (2014). Using community-based participatory research to advocate for homeless children. *Social Work in Public Health, 31*(1), 30–37.

Finlayson, M.L., & Cho, C.C. (2011). A profile of support group use and need among middle-aged and older adults with multiple sclerosis. *Journal of Gerontological Social Work, 54*, 475–493.

Fischer, J., & Orme, J.G. (2013). Single-system designs. In C. Franklin (Ed.), *Encyclopedia of social work [E-reader version]*. Washington, DC, and New York: National Association of Social Workers and Oxford University Press. DOI: 10.1093/acrefore/9780199975839.013.360

Fleming, J. (2009). Social action. In A. Gitterman & R. Salmon (Eds.), *Encyclopedia of social work with groups* (pp. 275–277). New York: Routledge.

Floersch, J. (2013). Social work practice: Theoretical base. In C. Franklin (Ed.), *Encyclopedia of social work [E-reader version]*. Washington, DC, and New York: National Association of Social Workers and Oxford University Press. DOI:10.1093/acrefore/9780199975839.013.621

Fook, J., & Pease, B. (Eds.). (2016). *Transforming social work practice: Postmodern critical perspectives.* New York: Routledge.

Fortune, A.E. (2015). Terminating with clients. In K. Corcoran & A.R. Roberts (Eds.), *Social workers' desk reference* (3rd ed.) (pp. 697–704). New York: Oxford University Press.

Franklin, C., Jordan, C., & Hopson, L.M. (2015). Effective couple and family treatment. In K. Corcoran & A.R. Roberts (Eds.), *Social workers' desk reference* (3rd ed.) (pp. 438–447). New York: Oxford University Press.

Freedenthal, S. (2013). Suicide. In C. Franklin (Ed.), *Encyclopedia of social work [E-reader version]*. Washington, DC, and New York: National Association of Social Workers and Oxford University Press. DOI: 10.1093/acrefore/9780199975839.013.137

Freire, P. (1973). *Education for critical consciousness.* New York: Seabury Press.

Fruhauf, C.A., & Hayslip, B. (2013). Understanding collaborative efforts to assist grandparent caregivers: A multileveled perspective. *Journal of Family Social Work, 16*(5), 382–391.

Furman, R., Bender, K., & Rowan, D. (2014). *An experiential approach to group work* (2nd ed.). Chicago: Lyceum Books, Inc.

Gamble, D.N., & Hoff, M.D. (2013). Sustainable community development. In M. Weil (Ed.), *The handbook of community practice* (pp. 215–232). Thousand Oaks, CA: Sage Publications.

Gambrill, E. (2013). *Social work practice: A critical thinker's guide.* New York: Oxford University Press.

Garkovich, L.E. (2011). A historical view of community development. In J.W. Robinson, Jr., & G.P. Green (Eds.), *Introduction to community development* (pp. 11–34). Los Angeles, CA: Sage Publications.

Garland, J., Jones, H., & Kolodny, R. (1965). A model for stages of development in social work groups. In S. Bernstein (Ed.), *Explorations in group work: Essays in theory and practice* (pp. 12–53). Boston: Boston University School of Social Work.

Garvin, C.D. (2015). Developing goals. In K. Corcoran & A.R. Roberts (Eds.), *Social workers' desk reference* (3rd ed.) (pp. 560–565). New York: Oxford University Press.

Garvin, C.D., & Galinsky, M.J. (2013). Groups. In C. Franklin (Ed.), *Encyclopedia of social work [E-reader version]*. Washington, DC, and New York: National Association of Social Workers and Oxford University Press. DOI: 10.1093/acrefore/9780199975839.013.167

Gibson, D.M. (2013). Ambiguous roles in a stepfamily: Using maps of narrative practices to develop a new family story with adolescents and parents. *Contemporary Family Therapy, 35*, 793–805.

Gilligan, C. (1993). *In a different voice.* Cambridge, MA: Harvard University Press.

Gitterman, A., & Germain, C.B. (2008). *The life model of social work practice: Advances in theory and practice* (3rd ed). New York: Columbia Press.

Gitterman, A., & Germain, C.B. (2013). Ecological framework. In C. Franklin (Ed.), *Encyclopedia of social work [E-reader version]*. Washington, DC, and New York: National Association of Social Workers and Oxford University Press. DOI: 10.1093/acrefore/9780199975839.013.118

GLAAD. (2014). Accelerating acceptance. Retrieved from www.glaad.org/publications/glaad-accelerating-acceptance

Goldbach, J., Amaro, H., Vega, W., & Walter, M.D. (2015). *The Grand Challenge of promoting equality by addressing social stigma. Grand Challenges for Social Work Initiative.* Working Paper No. 18. Washington, DC: American Academy of Social Work and Social Welfare. Retrieved from http://aaswsw.org/

wp-content/uploads/2016/01/W16-The-Grand-Challenge-of-Promoting-Equality-by-Addressing-Social-Stigma1-1-2.pdf

Goldberg, A.E., & Allen, K.R. (2013). *LGBT-parent families. Innovations in research and implications for practice.* New York: Springer.

Gonzáles-Prendes, A.A., & Brisebois, K. (2012). Cognitive-behavioral therapy and social work values: A critical analysis. *Journal of Social Work Values & Ethics, 9*(2), 2–21.

Goodman, H. (2004). Elderly parents of adults with severe mental illness: Group work interventions. *Journal of Gerontological Social Work, 44*(1/2), 173–188.

Grace, K.S., McClellan, A., & Yankey, J.A. (2009). The nonprofit board's role in mission, planning and evaluation. Washington, DC: BoardSource.

Grady, M., & Drisko, J.W. (2014). Thorough clinical assessment: The hidden foundation of evidence-based practice. *Families in Society: The Journal of Contemporary Social Service, 95*(1), 1–10. DOI: 10.1606/1044-3894.2014.95.2

Grant, D. (2013). Clinical social work. In C. Franklin (Ed.), *Encyclopedia of social work [E-reader version].* Washington, DC, and New York: National Association of Social Workers and Oxford University Press. DOI: 10.1093/acrefore/9780199975839.013.63

Gray, M. (2011). Back to basics: A critique of the strengths perspective in social work. *Families in Society: The Journal of Contemporary Social Services, 92*(1), 5–11.

Greene, G.J., & Lee, M.Y. (2011). *Solution-oriented social work practice.* New York: Oxford University Press.

Greenpeace. (n.d.). About us. Retrieved from www.greenpeace.org/usa/what-we-do/

Gregg, B. (2012). *Human rights as a social construction.* New York: Oxford University Press.

Greif, G., & Ephross, P.H. (Eds.). (2011). *Group work with populations at risk* (3rd ed.). New York: Oxford University Press.

Grief, G.L., & Morris-Compton, D. (2011). Group work with urban African American parents in their neighborhood schools. In G.L. Grief & P.H. Ephross (Eds.), *Group work with populations at risk* (3rd ed.) (pp. 385–398). New York: Oxford University Press.

Gumz, E., & Grant, C. (2009). Restorative justice: A systematic review of the social work literature. *Families in Society: The Journal of Contemporary Social Services, 90*(1), 119–126.

Hahn, S.A., & Scanlon, E. (2016). The integration of micro and macro practice: A qualitative study of clinical social workers' practice with domestic violence survivors. *Affilia: Journal of Women and Social Work, 31*(3), 331–343.

Hall, J.C. (2011). A narrative approach to group work with men who batter. *Social Work with Groups, 34,* 175–189.

Hamilton, B.E., Martin, J.A., Osterman, M.J.K., Curtin, S.C., & Mathews, T.J. (2015). *Births: Final data for 2014.* Hyattsville, MD: National Vital Statistics Reports, 64(12). Retrieved from www.cdc.gov/nchs/data/nvsr/nvsr64/nvsr64_12.pdf

Hanley, J., & Shragge, E. (2009). Organizing for immigrant rights. *Journal of Community Practice, 17*(1), 184–206.

Hardina, D. (2002). *Analytical skills for community organization practice.* New York: Columbia University Press.

Hardina, D. (2013). *Interpersonal social work skills for community practice.* New York: Springer.

Hardina, D., Middleton, J., Montana, S., & Simpson, R.A. (2007). *An empowering approach to managing social service organizations.* New York: Springer Publishing Company.

Hardy, K.V., & Laszloffy, T.A. (1995). The cultural genogram: Key to training culturally competent family therapists. *Journal of Marital and Family Therapy, 21,* 227–237.

Harr, C.R., Brice, T.S., Riley, K., & Moore, M. (2014). The impact of compassion fatigue and compassion satisfaction on social work students. *Journal of the Society for Social Work and Research, 5*(2), 233–251.

Harrington, D., & Dolgoff, R. (2008). Hierarchies of ethical principles for ethical decision making in social work. *Ethics and Social Welfare, 2*(2), 183–196.

Hartman, A. (1994). *Reflection & controversy: Essays on social work.* Washington, DC: NASW Press.

Hartman, A., & Laird, J. (1983). Family-centered social work practice. New York: Free Press.

Harvey, A.R. (2011). Group work with African American youth in the criminal justice system: A culturally competent model. In G.L. Grief & P.H. Ephross (Eds.), *Group work with populations at risk* (3rd ed.) (pp. 264–282). New York: Oxford University Press.

Hasenfeld, Y. (2000). Social welfare administration and organizational theory. In R.J. Patti (Ed.), *The handbook of social welfare management* (pp. 89–112). Thousand Oaks, CA: Sage Publications.

Hawkins, J.D., Jenson, J.M., Catalano, R.F., Fraser, M.W., Botvin, G.J., Shapiro, V., Bender, K.A., Brown, C.H., Beardslee, W., Brent, D., Leslie, L.K., Rotheram-Borus, M.J., Shea, P., Shih, A., Anthony, E.K., Haggerty, K.P., Gorman-Smith, D., Casey, E., Stone, S., & the Coalition for Behavioral Health. (2015). *Unleashing the power of prevention.* Working Paper No. 10, American Academy of Social Work and Social Welfare Grand Challenges for Social Work Initiative. Retrieved from http://aaswsw.org/grand-challenges-initiative/12-challenges/ensure-healthy-development-for-all-youth/

Haynes, K.S., & Mickelson, J.S. (2010). *Affecting change* (7th ed.). Boston: Pearson.

Head, J.W. (2008). *Losing the global development war.* Leiden, The Netherlands: Martinus Nijhoff Publishers.

Healy, L.M. (2008). *International social work: Professional practice in an interdependent world.* New York: Oxford University Press.

Healy, L.M. (2013). International social work: An overview. In C. Franklin (Ed.), *Encyclopedia of social work [E-reader version].* Washington, DC, and New York: National Association of Social Workers and Oxford University Press. DOI: 10.1093/acrefore/9780199975839.013.137

Healy, L.M., & Link, R.J. (2012). *Handbook of international social work: Human rights, development, and the global profession.* New York: Oxford.

Henriksen, R.C., & Maxwell, M.J. (2016). Counseling the fastest growing population in America: Those with multiple heritage backgrounds. *Journal of Mental Health Counseling, 38*(1), 1–11.

Henwood, B.F., Wenzel, S.L., Mangano, P.F., Hombs, M., Padgett, D.K., Byrne, T., Rice, E., Butts, S.C., &

Uretsky, M.C. (2015). *The grand challenge of ending homelessness.* Working Paper No. 9, American Academy of Social Work and Social Welfare Grand Challenges for Social Work Initiative. Retrieved from http://aaswsw.org/grand-challenges-initiative/12-challenges/end-homelessness/

Herbert, R.J., Gagnon, A.J., Rennick, J.E., & O'Loughlin, J.L. (2009). A systematic review of questionnaires measuring health-related empowerment. *Research and Theory for Nursing Practice: An International Journal, 23*(2), 107–132.

Hillier, A., & Culhane, D. (2013). GIS applications and administrative data to support community change. In M. Weil's (Ed.), *The handbook of community practice* (pp. 827–844). Thousand Oaks, CA: Sage Publications.

Hodge, D.R. (2005a). Social work and the House of Islam: Orienting practitioners to the beliefs and values of Muslims in the United States. *Social Work, 50*(20) 162–173.

Hodge, D.R. (2005b). Spiritual life maps: A client centered pictorial instrument for spiritual assessment, planning, and intervention. *Social Work, 50*(1), 77–87.

Hodge, D.R. (2013). Implicit spiritual assessment: An alternative approach for assessing client spirituality. *Social Work, 58*(3), 223–230.

Hodgson, J.L., Lamson, A.L., & Kolobova, I. (2016). A biopsychosocial-spiritual assessment in brief or extended couple therapy formats. In G.R. Weeks, S.T. Fife, & C.M. Person (Eds.), *Techniques for the couple therapist: Essential interventions from the experts* (pp. 213–217). New York: Routledge.

Hohman, M. (2012). *Motivational interviewing in social work practice.* New York: The Guilford Press.

Hohman, M., Pierce, P., & Barnett, E. (2015). Motivational interviewing: An evidence-based practice for improving student practice skills. *Journal of Social Work Education, 51*(2), 287–297.

Holland, T. (2013). Organizations and governance. In C. Franklin (Ed.), *Encyclopedia of social work [E-reader version].* Washington, DC, and New York: National Association of Social Workers and Oxford University Press. DOI: 10.1093/acrefore/9780199975839.013.275

Holland, T.P., & Kilpatrick, A.C. (2009). An ecological system—social constructionism approach to family practice. In A.C. Kilpatrick & T.P. Holland (Eds.), *Working with families. An integrative model by level of need* (5th ed.) (pp. 15–31). Boston: Pearson.

Hong, P.Y., & Song, I.H. (2010). Globalization of social work practice: Global and local responses to globalization. *International Social Work, 53,* 656–670.

Hudson, R.E. (2009). Empowerment model. In A. Gitterman & R. Salmon (Eds.), *Encyclopedia of social work with groups* (pp. 47–50). New York: Routledge.

Hull, G.H., & Mather, J. (2006). *Understanding generalist practice with families.* Belmont, CA: Thomson Brooks/Cole.

Human Rights Education Association (n.d.). Simplified version of the University Declaration of Human Rights. Retrieved from www.hrea.org/index.php?base_id=104&language_id=1&erc_doc_id=5211&category_id=24&category_type=3&group=

Ife, J. (2012). *Human rights and social work: Towards rights-based practice.* New York: Cambridge University Press.

Institute for Healthcare Improvement (IHI). (2016). Person-and family-centered care. Retrieved from www.ihi.org/Topics/PFCC/Pages/Overview.aspx

International Association for Social Work with Groups, Inc. (IASWG) (2015). *Standards for social work practice with groups* (2nd ed.). New York: IASWG, Inc. Retrieved from www.iaswg.org/standards

International Federation of Social Workers and the International Association of Schools of Social Work (IFSW & IASW). (2012). Statement of ethical principles. Retrieved from http://ifsw.org/policies/statement-of-ethical-principles/

International Institute St. Louis. (2016). Economic development. Retrieved from www.iistl.org/edintro.html

International Labor Rights Forum. (n.d.). Workers around the world face serious threats for democratically organizing – an internationally recognized freedom. Retrieved from www.laborrights.org/issues/right-organize-bargain

Interorganizational Committee on Guidelines and Principles for Social Impact Assessment (IOCPG). (2003). Principles and guidelines for social impact assessment in the United States. *Impact Assessment and Project Appraisal, 21*(3), 231–250.

Iowa State University Extension and Outreach. (2016). Needs assessment strategies for community groups and organizations. Retrieved from www.extension.iastate.edu/communities/assess

Jackson, K.F., & Samuels, G.M. (2011). Multiracial competence in social work: Recommendation for culturally attuned work with multiracial people. *Social Work, 56*(3), 235–245.

Jankowski, P.J., Hooper, L.M., Sandage, S.J., & Hannah, N.J. (2013). Parentification and mental health symptoms: Mediator effects of perceived unfairness and differentiation of self. *Journal of Family Therapy, 35,* 43–65.

Janzen, C., Harris, O., Jordan, C., & Franklin, C. (2006). Family treatment: Evidence-based practice with populations at risk. Belmont, CA: Thomson Brooks/ Cole.

Jenson, J.M., & Howard, M.O. (2013). Evidence-based practice. In C. Franklin (Ed.), *Encyclopedia of social work [E-reader version].* Washington, DC, and New York: National Association of Social Workers and Oxford University Press. DOI: 10.1093/acrefore/9780199975839.013.137

Johnson, S.K., von Sternberg, K., & Velasquez, M.M. (2015). Motivational interviewing. In K. Corcoran & A.R. Roberts (Eds.), *Social workers' desk reference* (3rd ed.) (pp. 684–691). New York: Oxford University Press.

Joplin Area CART. (n.d.). Joplin Area CART. Retrieved from https://www.facebook.com/JoplinAreaCART

Jordan, C., & Franklin, C. (2013). Assessment. In C. Franklin (Ed.), *Encyclopedia of social work [E-reader version].* Washington, DC, and New York: National Association of Social Workers and Oxford University Press. DOI: 10.1093/acrefore/978019997583 9.013.137

Jordan, C., Franklin, C., & Johnson, S.K. (2015). Treatment planning with families: An evidence-based approach. In K. Corcoran & A.R. Roberts (Eds.), *Social workers' desk reference* (3rd ed.) (pp. 433–438). New York: Oxford University Press.

Jung, M. (1996). Family-centered practice with single parent families. *Families in Society, 77*(9), 583–590.

Kagle, J.D. (2013). Recording. In C. Franklin (Ed.), *Encyclopedia of social work [E-reader version]*. Washington, DC, and New York: National Association of Social Workers and Oxford University Press. DOI: 10.1093/acrefore/9780199975839.013.33.

Kagle, J.D., & Kopels, S. (2008). *Social work records* (3rd ed.). Long Grove, IL: Waveland Press, Inc.

Kalyanpur, M., & Harry, B. (2012). Cultural reciprocity in special education. Building family-professional relationships. Baltimore, MD: Brookes Publishing Company.

Kasvin, N., & Tashayeva, A. (2004). Community organizing to address domestic violence in immigrant populations in the U.S.A. *Journal of Religion and Abuse, 6*(3/4), 109–112.

Kaye, M. (1980). *We speak in code: Poems & other writings*. Pittsburgh, PA: Motheroot Publications.

Kelley, P. (2013). Narratives. In C. Franklin (Ed.), *Encyclopedia of social work [E-reader version]*. Washington, DC, and New York: National Association of Social Workers and Oxford University Press. DOI: 10.1093/acrefore/9780199975839.013.259

Kelley, P., & Smith, M. (2015). Narrative therapy. In K. Corcoran & A.R. Roberts (Eds.), *Social workers' desk reference* (3rd ed.) (pp. 287–292). New York: Oxford University Press.

Kelly, M.S., Kim, J.S., & Franklin, C. (2008). Solution-focused brief therapy in schools. A 360-degree view of research and practice. New York: Oxford University Press.

Kelly, T.B., Lowndes, A., & Tolson, D. (2005). Advancing stages of group development: The case of virtual nursing community of practice groups. *Groupwork, 15*(2), 17–38.

Kemp, S.P., & Palinkas, L.A. (2016). *Strengthening the social response to the human impacts of environmental change*. Working Paper No. 5, American Academy of Social Work and Social Welfare. Retrieved from http://aaswsw.org/wp-content/uploads/2015/12/WP5-with-cover.pdf

Kettner, P.M. (2002). *Achieving excellence in the management of human service organizations*. Boston: Allyn & Bacon.

Kilpatrick, A.C. (2009). Levels of family need. In A.C. Kilpatrick & T.P. Holland (Eds.), *Working with families. An integrative model by level of need* (5th ed.) (pp. 2–14). Boston: Pearson.

Kilpatrick, A.C., & Cleveland, P. (1993). Unpublished course materials. University of Georgia School of Social Work.

Kim, A., & Barak, M.E.M. (2015). The mediating roles of leader–member exchange and perceived organizational support in the role stress–turnover intention relationship among child welfare workers: A longitudinal analysis. *Children & Youth Services Review 52*, 135–143.

Kim, H., & Hopkins, K.M. (2015). Child welfare workers' personal safety concerns and organizational commitment: The moderating role of social support. *Human Service Organizations: Management, Leadership & Governance, 39*, 101–115.

Kim, H., Ji, J, & Kao, D. (2011). Burnout and physical health among social workers: A three-year longitudinal study. *Social Work, 56*(3), 258–268.

Kim, J.S. (2013). Strengths perspective. In C. Franklin (Ed.), *Encyclopedia of social work [E-reader version]*. Washington, DC, and New York: National Association of Social Workers and Oxford University Press. DOI: 10.1093/acrefore/9780199975839.013.382

Kingsley, G.T., Coulton, C.J., & Pettit, K.L. (2014). *Strengthening communities with neighborhood data*. Washington, DC: Urban Institute.

Kisthardt, W.E. (2013). Integrating the core competencies in strengths-based, person-centered practice. In D. Saleebey (Ed.), *The strengths perspective in social work practice* (6th ed.), pp. 53–78. Boston: Allyn & Bacon.

Kleinkauf, C. (1981). A guide to giving legislative testimony. *Social Work* (July), 297–303.

Kneebone, E., & Holmes, N. (2016). U.S. concentrated poverty in the wake of the Great Recession. Washington, DC: Brookings Institution. Retrieved from www.brookings.edu/research/reports2/2016/03/31-concentrated-poverty-recession-kneebone-holmes

Knight, C. (2012). Social workers' attitudes towards engagement in self-disclosure. *Clinical Social Work Journal, 40*, 297–306.

Kohli, H.K., Huber, R., & Faul, A.C. (2010). Historical and theoretical development of culturally competent social work practice. *Journal of Teaching in Social Work, 30*, 252–271.

Koop, J.J. (2009). Solution-focused family interventions. In A.C. Kilpatrick & T.P. Holland (Eds.), *Working with families. An integrative model by level of need* (5th ed.) (pp. 147–169). Boston: Pearson.

Koren, P.E., DeChillo, N., & Friesen, B.J. (1992). Measuring empowerment in families whose children have emotional disabilities: A brief questionnaire. *Rehabilitation Psychology, 37*, 305–310.

Kresak, K.E., Gallagher, P.A., & Kelley, S.J. (2014). Grandmothers raising grandchildren with disabilities: Sources of support and family quality of life. *Journal of Early Intervention, 36*(1), 3–17.

Kretzmann, J. P. & McKnight, J. L. (1993). *Building communities from the inside out: A path toward finding and mobilizing a community's assets.* Evanston, IL: Center for Urban Affairs and Policy Research.

Kretzmann, J. P., McKnight, J., & Puntenney, D. (2005). *Discovering community power: A guide to mobilizing local assets and your organization's capacity.* Chicago, IL: Asset-Based Community Development Institute, School of Education and Social Policy, Northwestern University.

Kurland, R. (2007). Debunking the "blood theory" of social work with groups: Group workers are made and not born. *Social Work with Groups, 31*(1), 11–24.

Kurland, R., & Salmon, R. (1998). *Teaching a methods course in social work with groups.* Alexandria, VA: Council on Social Work Education.

Kurland, R., Salmon, R., Bitel, M., Goodman, H., Ludwig, K., Newmann, E.W., & Sullivan, N. (2004). The survival of social group work: *A call to action. Social Work with Groups, 27*(1), 3–16.

Larson, K., & McGuiston, C. (2012). Building capacity to improve Latino health in rural North Carolina: A case study in community-university engagement. *Journal of Community Engagement and Scholarship, 5*(1), 14–23.

Laurio, A. (2016). A grand challenge for social work: Isolation seen as a critical social problem. *NASW News, 61*(6), 7, 9.

Leahy, M.M., O'Dwyer, M., & Ryan, F. (2012). Witnessing stories: Definitional ceremonies in narrative therapy with adults who stutter. *Journal of Fluency Disorders, 37*, 234–241.

Lee, M.Y. (2015). The miracle question and scaling questions for solution-building and empowerment. In K. Corcoran & A.R. Roberts (Eds.), *Social workers' desk reference* (3rd ed.) (pp. 308–316). New York: Oxford University Press.

Lee, M.Y., & Greene, G.J. (2009). Using social constructivism in social work practice. In A.R. Roberts (Ed.), *Social workers' desk reference* (2nd ed.) (pp. 294–299). New York: Oxford University Press.

Lein, L., Romich, J.L., & Sherraden, M. (2015). *Reversing extreme inequality. Grand Challenges for Social Work Initiative.* Working Paper No. 16. Washington, DC: American Academy of Social Work and Social Welfare. Retrieved from http://aaswsw.org/wp-content/uploads/2016/01/WP16-with-cover-2.pdf

Lesser, J.G., O'Neill, M.R., Burke, K.W., Scanlon, P., Hollis, K., & Miller, R. (2004). Women supporting women: A mutual aid group fosters new connections among women in midlife. *Social Work with Groups, 27*(1), 75–88.

Levy, R. (2011). Core themes in a support group for spouses of breast cancer patients. *Social Work with Groups, 34*, 141–157.

Libal, K.R., & Harding, S. (2015). *Human rights-based community practice in the United States.* SpringerBriefs in Rights-Based Approaches to Social Work. New York: Springer.

Life Crisis Services. (n.d.) Suicide Assessment. St. Louis, MO: Author.

Locke, B., Garrison, R., & Winship, J. (1998). *Generalist social work practice: Context, story, and partnerships.* Pacific Grove, CA: Brooks/Cole.

Logan, S.L.M. (2013). Family: Overview. In C. Franklin (Ed.), *Encyclopedia of social work [E-reader version].* Washington, DC, and New York: National Association of Social Workers and Oxford

University Press. DOI: 10.1093/acrefore/9780199975839.013.545

López, L.M., & Vargas, E.M. (2011). En dos culturas: Group work with Latino immigrants and refugees. In G.L. Greif & P.H. Ephross (Eds.), *Group work with populations at risk* (3rd ed.) (pp. 144–145). New York: Oxford University Press.

Lotze, G.M., Bellin, M.H., & Oswald, D.P. (2010). Family-centered care for children with special healthcare needs: Are we moving forward? *Journal of Family Social Work, 13,* 100–113.

Lubben, J., Gironda, M., Sabbath, E., Kong, J., & Johnson, C. (2015). *Social isolation presents a grand challenge for social work.* Working Paper No. 7, American Academy of Social Work and Social Welfare Grand Challenges for Social Work Initiative. Retrieved from http://aaswsw.org/grand-challenges-initiative/12-challenges/eradicate-social-isolation/

Lum, D. (2004). *Social work practice and people of color: A process stage approach* (5th ed.). Belmont, CA: Thomson Brooks/Cole.

Lum, D. (2011). *Culturally competent practice: A framework for understanding diverse groups and justice issues.* Belmont, CA: Brooks/Cole Cengage Learning.

Lum, D. (2013). Culturally competent practice. In C. Franklin (Ed.), *Encyclopedia of social work [E-reader version].* Washington, DC, and New York: National Association of Social Workers and Oxford University Press. DOI: 10.1093/acrefore/9780199975839.013.137

Lundahl, B.W., Kunz, C., Brownell, C., Tollefson, D., & Burke, B.L. (2010). A meta-analysis of motivational interviewing: Twenty-five years of empirical studies. *Research on Social Work Practice, 20*(2), 137–160.

Lundy, C. (2011). *Social work, social justice, and human rights: A structural approach to practice.* North York, ON: University of Toronto Press.

MacDonald, S-A. (2016). Attempting to engage in "ethical" research with homeless youth. *Intersectionalities: A Global Journal of Social Work Analysis, Research, Polity and Practice, 5*(1), 126–150.

Macgowan, M.J. (1997). A measure of engagement for social group work: The Groupwork Engagement Measure (GEM). *Journal of Social Service Research, 23,* 17–37.

Macgowan, M.J. (2000). Evaluation of a measure of engagement for group work. *Research on Social Work Practice, 10,* 348–361.

Macgowan, M.J. (2006). The group engagement measure. A review of its conceptual and empirical properties. *Journal of Groups in Addiction & Recovery, 1*(2), 33–52.

Macgowan, M.J. (2009a). Evidence-based group work. In A. Gitterman & R. Salmon (Eds.), *Encyclopedia of social work with groups* (pp. 131–136). New York: Routledge.

Macgowan, M.J. (2009b). Measurement. In A. Gitterman & R. Salmon (Eds.), *Encyclopedia of social work with groups* (pp. 142–147). New York: Routledge.

Macgowan, M.J. (2013). Group dynamics. In C. Franklin (Ed.), *Encyclopedia of social work [E-reader version].* Washington, DC, and New York: National Association of Social Workers and Oxford University Press. DOI: 10.1093/acrefore/9780199975839.013.166

Macgowan, M.J., & Hanbidge, A.S. (2015). Best practices in social work with groups. In K. Corcoran & A.R. Roberts (Eds.), *Social workers' desk reference* (3rd ed.) (pp. 734–745). New York: Oxford University Press.

Macgowan, M.J., & Levenson, J.S. (2003). Psychometrics of the Group Engagement Measure with male sex offenders. *Small Group Research, 34*(2), 155–169.

Macgowan, M.J., & Newman, F.L. (2005). Factor structure of the Group Engagement Measure. *Social Work Research, 29*(2), 107–118.

Mackelprang, R.W., & Salsgiver, R.O. (2015). *Disability: A diversity model approach in human service practice* (3rd ed). Chicago: Lyceum Books, Inc.

Madigan, S. (2011). *Narrative therapy.* Washington, DC: The American Psychological Association.

Mallon, G.P. (2014). Lesbian, gay, bisexual, and transgender (LGBT) families and parenting. In C. Franklin (Ed.), *Encyclopedia of social work [E-reader version].* Washington, DC, and New York: National Association of Social Workers and Oxford

University Press. DOI: 10.1093/acrefore/9780199975839.013.158

Malmstrom, T.K., & Morley, J.E. (2013). Frailty and cognition: Linking two common syndromes in older persons. *Journal of Nutrition, Health, & Aging, 17*, 723–725.

Manning, T. (2012). The art of successful persuasion: Seven skills you need to get your point across effectively. *Industrial and Commercial Training, 44*(3), 150–158.

Manning, W.D., Brown, S.L., & Stykes, J.B. (2014). Family complexity among children in the United States. *Annals of American Academic Political Social Science, 654*(1), 48–65.

Manor, O. (2009). Systemic approach. In A. Gitterman & R. Salmon (Eds.), *Encyclopedia of social work with groups* (pp. 99–101). New York: Routledge.

Maramaldi, P., Berkman, B., & Barusch, A. (2005). Assessment and the ubiquity of culture: Threats to validity in measures of health-related quality of life. *Health & Social Work, 30*(1), 27–36.

Marguerite Casey Foundation. (2012). Organizational capacity assessment tool. Retrieved from http://caseygrants.org/resources/org-capacity-assessment/

Mason, J.L. (1995). Cultural competence self-assessment questionnaire: A manual for users. Portland, OR: Portland State University, Research and Training Center on Family Support and Children's Mental Health. Retrieved from www.racialequitytools.org/ resourcefiles/mason.pdf

McCullough-Chavis, A., & Waites, C. (2008). Genograms with African American families: Considering cultural context. In C.Waites (Ed.), *Social work practice with African-American families: An intergenerational perspective* (pp. 35–54). New York: Routledge.

McGeorge, C.R., & Carlson, T.S. (2011). Deconstructing heterosexism: Becoming an LGB affirmative heterosexual couple and family therapist. *Journal of Marital and Family Therapy, 37*, 14–26. DOI: 10.1111/j.1752-0606.2009.00149.x

McGoldrick, M. (2015). Using genograms to map family patterns. In K. Corcoran & A.R. Roberts (Eds.), *Social workers' desk reference* (3rd ed.) (pp. 413–426). New York: Oxford University Press.

McGoldrick, M., Gerson, R., & Petry, S. (2008). *Genograms assessment and intervention* (3rd ed.). New York: W.W. Norton & Company.

McGowan, B.G., & Walsh, E.M. (2012). Writing in family and child welfare. In W. Green and B.L. Simon (Eds.), *The Columbia guide to social work writing* (pp. 215–231). New York: Columbia University Press.

McKnight, J.L., & Block, P. (2010). *The abundant community: Awakening the power of families and neighborhoods*. San Francisco, CA: Berrett-Koehler Publishers.

McKnight, J.L., & Kretzman, J.P. (1996). *Mapping community capacity*. Evanston, IL: Institute for Policy Research. Retrieved from www.racialequitytools.org/resourcefiles/mcknight.pdf

McLaughlin, B., Ryder, D., & Taylor, M.F. (2016). The effectiveness of interventions for grandparent caregivers: A systematic review. *Marriage & Family Review*, 1–23. DOI: 10.1080/01494929.2016.1177631

McWhirter, P.T., Robbins, R., Vaughn, K., Youngbull, N., Burks, D., Willmon-Haque, S., Schuetz, S., Brandes, J.A., & Nael, A.Z.O. (2011). Honoring the ways of American Indian women: A group therapy intervention. In A.A. Singh & C.F. Salazar (Eds.), *Social justice in group work. Practical interventions for change* (pp. 73–81). New York: Routledge.

Meyer, C. (1993). *Assessment in social work practice*. New York: Columbia University Press.

MicroFinancing Partners in Africa. (n.d.). About us. Retrieved from http://microfinancingafrica.org/about-us/#Our-History

Middleman, R.R., & Wood, G.G. (1990). *Skills for direct practice in social work*. New York: Columbia University Press.

Miley, K.K., O'Melia, M.W., & DuBois, B.L. (2016). *Generalist social work practice: An empowering approach* (8th ed.). Boston: Pearson Allyn & Bacon.

Miller, C.C. (2014). The divorce surge is over, but the myth lives on. *New York Times*. Retrieved from www.nytimes.com/2014/12/02/upshot/the-divorce-surge-is-over-but-the-myth-lives-on.

html?smid=fb-nytimes&smtyp=cur&bicmp=AD&
bicmlukp=WT.mc_id&bicmst=1409232722000&b
icmet=1419773522000&_r=4&abt=0002&abg=0

Miller, L. (2012). *Counselling skills for social work.* London, Thousand Oaks, CA: Sage Publications.

Miller, W.R., & Rollnick, S. (2013). *Motivational interviewing: Helping people change* (3rd ed.). New York: The Guilford Press.

Minieri, J., & Getsos, P. (2007). *Tools for radical democracy.* San Francisco, CA: Jossey Bass.

Minuchin, P., Colapinto, J., & Minuchin, S. (2007). *Working with families of the poor* (2nd ed.). New York: The Guilford Press.

Minuchin, S. (1974). *Families & family therapy.* Cambridge, MA: Harvard University Press.

Missouri Department of Social Services. (n.d.) Family Intervention Plan. Jefferson City, MO: Author.

Mondros, J., & Staples, L. (2013). Community organization. In C. Franklin (Ed.), *Encyclopedia of social work [E-reader version].* Washington, DC, and New York: National Association of Social Workers and Oxford University Press. DOI: 10.1093/acrefore/9780199975839.013.74

Morgan, A. (2000). *What is narrative therapy?* Adelaide, South Australia: Dulwich Centre Publications.

Morrow-Howell, N., Gonzales, E., Matz-Costa, C., & Greenfield, E.A. (2015). *Increasing productive engagement in later life.* Working Paper No. 8, American Academy of Social Work and Social Welfare Grand Challenges for Social Work Initiative. Retrieved from http://aaswsw.org/grand-challenges-initiative/12-challenges/advance-long-and-productive-lives/

Moxley, D. (2013). Interdisciplinarity. In C. Franklin (Ed.), *Encyclopedia of social work [E-reader version].* Washington, DC, and New York: National Association of Social Workers and Oxford University Press. DOI: 10.1093/acrefore/9780199975839.013.200

Mulroy, E. (2013). Community needs assessment. In C. Franklin (Ed.), *Encyclopedia of social work [E-reader version].* Washington, DC, and New York: National Association of Social Workers and Oxford University Press. DOI: 10.1093/acrefore/9780199975839.013.73

Musick, K., & Meier, Ann. (2009). Are both parents always better than one? Parental conflict and young adult well-being. *Rural New York Minute, 28,* 1.

Myerhoff, B. (1982). Life history among the elderly: Performance, visibility and remembering. In J. Ruby (Ed.), *A crack in the mirror: Reflexive perspectives in anthropology* (pp. 99–117). Philadelphia: University of Pennsylvania Press.

Nakhaima, J.M., & Dicks, B.H. (2012). A role for the religious community in family counseling. *Alliance for Strong Families and Communities.* Retrieved from: www.alliance1.org/sites/default/files/fis/PPF/PDFs/nakhaima_76_6.pdf

National Alliance on Mental Illness. (NAMI). (2013). Cognitive behavior therapy (CBT). Retrieved from www.nami.org

National Association of Area Agencies on Aging. (2016). About n4a. Retrieved from www.n4a.org/about

National Association of Cognitive-Behavioral Therapists (NACBT). (n.d.). Cognitive behavioral therapy. Retrieved from www.nacbt.org/whatiscbt.aspx

National Association of Social Workers (NASW). (2007). *Indicators for the achievement of the NASW Standards for cultural competence in social work.* Washington, DC: NASW. Retrieved from www.socialworkers.org/practice/standards/NASWCulturalStandardsIndicators2006.pdf

National Association of Social Workers (NASW). (2008). Code of ethics. Washington, DC: NASW. Retrieved from https://www.socialworkers.org/pubs/code/code.asp

National Association of Social Workers (NASW). (2013a) *NASW guidelines for social worker safety in the workplace.* Washington, DC: NASW.

National Association of Social Workers (NASW). (2013b). *Standards for social work case management.* Washington, DC: NASW.

National Association of Social Workers (NASW). (2015a). *Indicators for the achievement of the NASW Standards for Cultural Competence in Social Work Practice.* Washington, DC: NASW. Retrieved from www.socialworkers.org/practice/standards/index.asp

National Association of Social Workers (NASW). (2015b). *Cultural and linguistic competence in the social work profession. Social work speaks: National Association of Social Workers policy statements.* Washington, DC: NASW Press.

National Association of Social Workers (NASW). (2015c). *Professional self-care and social work. Social work speaks: National Association of Social Workers policy statements.* Washington, DC: NASW Press.

National Association of Social Workers (NASW). (2015d). *Standards and indicators for cultural competence in social work practice.* Washington, DC: Author. Retrieved from www.socialworkers.org/practice/standards/PRA-BRO-253150-CC-Standards.pdf

National Center for Cultural Competence. (n.d.). Definitions of cultural competence. Retrieved from www.ncccurricula.info/culturalcompetence.html

Netting, F.E., Kettner, P.M., & McMurtry, S.L., & Thomas, L. (2017). *Social work macro practice.* Boston: Pearson Allyn & Bacon.

New York Times. (2015, Nov. 17). Block by block: Jackson Heights. *New York Times.* Retrieved from www.nytimes.com/2015/11/17/realestate/block-by-block-jackson-heights.html

Newhill, C.E. (1995). Client violence toward social workers: A practice and policy concern. *Social Work, 40,* 631–636.

Nichols, M.P. (2014). *The essentials of family therapy* (6th ed.). Boston: Pearson.

Nilsson, P. (2014). Are compassion and empathy bad for professional social workers? *Advances in Social Work, 15*(2), 294–305.

O'Connor, M.K., & Netting, F.E. (2009). *Organization practice: A guide to understanding human service organizations.* Hoboken, NJ: Wiley.

Obama, Barack. (2008, Feb. 5). Speech of February 5, 2008 [transcript]. *New York Times.* Retrieved from www.nytimes.com/2008/02/05/us/politics/05text-obama.html?_r=1

Ohmer, M.L. (2008). Assessing and developing the evidence base of macro practice: Interventions with a community and neighborhood focus. *Journal of Evidence-Based Social Work, 5*(3/4), 519–547.

Ohmer, M.L., & Brooks, F. (2013). The practice of community organizing. In M. Weil (Ed.), *The handbook of community practice* (pp. 233–248). Thousand Oaks, CA: Sage Publications.

Ohmer, M.L., & DeMasi, K. (2009). *Consensus organizing: A community development workbook.* Thousand Oaks, CA: Sage Publications.

Ohmer, M.L., & Korr, W.S. (2006). The effectiveness of community practice interventions: A review of the literature. *Research on Social Work Practice, 16*(2), 132–145.

Ohmer, M.L., Sobek, J.L., Teixeira, S.N., Wallace, J.M., & Shapiro, V.B. (2013). Community-based research: Rationale, methods, roles, and considerations for community practice. In M. Weil's (Ed.), *The handbook of community practice* (pp. 791–807). Thousand Oaks, CA: Sage Publications.

Oliver, M., & Sapey, B. (2006). *Social work with disabled people.* New York: Palgrave Macmillan.

Oregon Legislature. (n.d.). How to testify before a legislative committee. Retrieved from www.leg.state.or.us/comm/testify.html/

Packard, T. (2009). Leadership and performance in human services organizations. In R.J. Patti (Ed.), *The handbook of social welfare management* (pp. 143–164). Thousand Oaks, CA: Sage Publications.

Packard, T. (2013). Organizational change in human service organizations. In C. Franklin (Ed.), *Encyclopedia of social work [E-reader version].* Washington, DC, and New York: National Association of Social Workers and Oxford University Press. DOI: 0.1093/acrefore/9780199975839.013.272

Paniagua, F.A. (2014). *Assessing and treating culturally diverse clients* (4th ed.). Los Angeles, CA: Sage Publications.

Papell, C.P., & Rothman, B. (1962). Social group work models: Possession and heritage. *Journal of Education for Social Work, 2*(2), 66–77.

Papero, D.V. (2015). Bowen family systems theory. In K. Corcoran & A.R. Roberts (Eds.), *Social workers' desk reference* (3rd ed.) (pp. 456–462). New York: Oxford University Press.

Paris, R., & DeVoe, E.R. (2013). Human needs: Family. In C. Franklin (Ed.), *Encyclopedia of social work*

[E-reader version]. Washington, DC, and New York: National Association of Social Workers and Oxford University Press. DOI: 10.1093/acrefore/9780199975839.013.555

Parsons, R.J., & East, J. (2013). Empowerment practice. In C. Franklin (Ed.), *Encyclopedia of social work [E-reader version]*. Washington, DC, and New York: National Association of Social Workers and Oxford University Press. DOI: 10.1093/acrefore/9780199975839.013.128

Payne, M., & Askeland, G.A. (2008). *Globalization and international social work: Postmodern change and challenge*. Burlington, VT: Ashgate Publishing Company.

Peterson, Z. (2002). More than a mirror: The ethics of therapist self-disclosure. *Psychotherapy: Theory, Research, Practice, and Training, 39*, 21–31.

Pettus-Davis, C. & Epperson, M. W. (2015). *Smart decarceration: A grand challenge for social work*. Working Paper No. 16, American Academy of Social Work and Social Welfare Grand Challenges for Social Work Initiative. Retrieved from http://aaswsw.org/wp-content/uploads/2015/12/WP4-with-cover.pdf

Pew Research Center. (2015). U.S. foreign-born population trends. In *Modern wave brings 59 million to U.S., driving population growth and change through 2065: Views of immigration's impact on U.S. society mixed*. Retrieved from www.pewhispanic.org/2015/09/28/chapter-5-u-s-foreign-born-population-trends/#fn-23157-24

Pfeffer, J. (1992). *Managing with power and politics: Influence in organizations*. Boston: Harvard Business School Press.

Pippard, J.L., & Bjorklund, R.W. (2004). Identifying essential techniques for social work community practice. *Journal of Community Practice, 11*(4), 101–116.

Plitt, D.L., & Shields, J. (2009). Development of the Policy Advocacy Behavior Scale: Initial reliability and validity. *Research on Social Work Practice, 19*(1), 83–92.

Pogash, C. (2016, June 1). Unsettling U.S. political climate galvanizes Muslims to vote. *New York Times*. Retrieved from www.nytimes.com/2016/06/02/us/unsettling-political-climate-galvanizes-muslims-to-vote.html

Poole, D.L. (2009). Community partnerships for school-based services. In A. Roberts (Ed.), *Social workers desk reference* (pp. 907–912). New York: Oxford University Press.

Pope, N.D., Rollins, L., Chaumba, J., & Risler, E. (2011). Evidence-based practice knowledge and utilization among social workers. *Journal of Evidence-Based Social Work, 8*, 349–368.

Potocky, M. (2013). Asylum-seekers, refugees, and immigrants in the United States. In C. Franklin (Ed.), *Encyclopedia of social work [E-reader version]*. Washington, DC, and New York: National Association of Social Workers and Oxford University Press. DOI: 10.1093/acrefore/9780199975839.013.193

Putnam, R.D., & Feldstein, L.M. (2003). *Better together: Restoring the American community*. New York: Simon & Schuster.

Ramanathan, C.S., & Link, R.J. (2004). *All our futures: Principles and resources for social work practice in a global era*. Belmont, CA: Brooks/Cole.

Randall, A.C., & DeAngelis, D. (2013). Licensing. In C. Franklin (Ed.), *Encyclopedia of social work [E-reader version]*. Washington, DC, and New York: National Association of Social Workers and Oxford University Press. DOI: 10.1093/acrefore/9780199975839.013.225

Rapp, C.A., & Goscha, R.J. (2012). *The strengths model: A recovery-oriented approach to mental health services*. New York: Oxford University Press.

Rasheed, M.N., & Rasheed, J.M. (2013). Family: Practice interventions. In C. Franklin (Ed.), *Encyclopedia of social work [E-reader version]*. Washington, DC, and New York: National Association of Social Workers and Oxford University Press. DOI: 10.1093/acrefore/9780199975839.013.546

Reamer, F.G. (2013a). Ethics and values. In C. Franklin (Ed.), *Encyclopedia of social work [E-reader version]*. Washington, DC, and New York: National Association of Social Workers and Oxford University. DOI: 10.1093/acrefore/9780199975839.013.134

Reamer, F.G. (2013b). *Social work values and ethics* (4th ed.). New York: Columbia University Press.

Reamer, F.G. (2013c). Social work malpractice, liability, and risk management. In C. Franklin (Ed.),

Encyclopedia of social work [E-reader version]. Washington, DC, and New York: National Association of Social Workers and Oxford University. DOI: 10.1093/acrefore/ 9780199975839.013.977

Reichert, E. (2007). *Challenges in human rights: A social work perspective.* New York: Columbia University Press.

Reichert, E. (2011). *Social work and human rights: A foundation for policy and practice.* New York: Columbia Press.

Reid, K.E. (1997). *Social work practice with groups: A clinical perspective* (2nd ed.). Pacific Grove, CA: Brooks/ Cole.

Reid, K.E. (2002). Clinical social work with groups. In A.R. Roberts & G.J. Greene (Eds.), *Social Workers' Desk Reference* (2nd ed.) (pp. 432–436). New York: Oxford University Press.

Reisch, M. (2013). Community practice challenges in the global economy. In M. Weil (Ed.), *The handbook of community practice* (pp. 47–71). Thousand Oaks, CA: Sage Publications.

Richards-Schuster, K., & Pritzker, S. (2015). Strengthening youth participation in civic engagement: Applying the Convention on the Rights of the Child to social work practice. *Children and Youth Services Review 57,* 90–97.

Ringel, S. (2005). Group work with Asian-American immigrants: A cross-cultural perspective. In G.L. Greif & P.H. Ephross (Eds.), *Group work with populations at risk* (2nd ed.) (pp. 181–194). New York: Oxford University Press.

Robert III, H., Honemann, D.H., & Balch, T.J. (2011). *Robert's rules of order newly revised.* Philadelphia, PA: Da Capo Press.

Roberts, A.R. (2013). Crisis interventions. In C. Franklin (Ed.), *Encyclopedia of social work [E-reader version].* Washington, DC, and New York: National Association of Social Workers and Oxford University Press. DOI: 10.1093/acrefore/ 9780199975839.013.137

Roberts-DeGennaro, M. (2013). Case management. In C. Franklin (Ed.), *Encyclopedia of social work [E-reader version].* Washington, DC, and New York: National Association of Social Workers and Oxford University Press. DOI: 10.1093/acrefore/ 9780199975839.013.42

Robinson, J.W., & Green, G.P. (2011) *Introduction to community development: Theory, practice, and service-learning.* Thousand Oaks, CA: Sage Publications.

Roche, S.E., & Wood, G.G. (2005). A narrative principle for feminist social work with survivors of male violence. *Affilia, 20*(4), 465–475.

Rogers, C. (1957). The necessary and sufficient conditions of therapeutic personality change. *Journal of Consulting Psychology, 22,* 95–103.

Romano, M., & Peters, L. (2015). Evaluating the mechanisms of change in motivational interviewing in the treatment of mental health problems: A review and meta-analysis. *Clinical Psychology Review, 38,* 1–12.

Roscoe, K.D., & Madoc-Jones, L. (2009). Critical social work practice: A narrative approach. *International Journal of Narrative Practice, 1,* 9–18.

Roscoe, K.D., Carson, A.M., & Madoc-Jones, L. (2011). Narrative social work: Conversations between theory and practice. *Journal of Social Work Practice, 25*(1), 47–61.

Rostoky, S.S., & Riggle, E.D.B. (2011). Marriage equality for same-sex couples: Counseling psychologists as social change agents. *The Counseling Psychologist, 39*(7), 956–972.

Rothman, J.C. (2008). Multi modes of community intervention. In J. Rothman, J. Erlich, & J. Tropman (Eds.), *Strategies of community intervention* (7th ed.) (pp.141–170). Peosta, Iowa: Eddie Bowers Publishing Co., Inc.

Rothman, J.C. (2009). An overview of case management. In A.R. Roberts (Ed.), *Social workers' desk reference* (2nd ed.) (pp. 751–755). New York: Oxford University Press.

Rothman, J.C. (2015). Developing therapeutic contracts with clients. In K. Corcoran & A.R. Roberts (Eds.), *Social workers' desk reference* (3rd ed.) (pp. 553–559). New York: Oxford University Press.

Royse, D., Staton-Tindall, M., Badger, K., & Webster, J.M. (2009). *Needs assessment.* New York: Oxford University Press.

Rubin, H.J., & Rubin, I.S. (2008). *Community organizing and development.* Boston: Pearson Allyn & Bacon.

Saez, E. (2015). *The evolution of top incomes in the United States (updated with 2014 preliminary estimates).* University of California, Berkeley, Working Paper. Retrieved from http://eml.berkeley.edu/~saez/saez-UStopincomes-2012.pdf

Safe Connections. (n.d.) Group Assessment Screening. St. Louis, MO: Author.

Sager, J.S., & Weil, M. (2013). Larger-scale social planning: Planning for services and communities. In M. Weil (Ed.), *The handbook of community practice* (pp. 299–325). Thousand Oaks, CA: Sage Publications.

Saint Louis University Pius XII Library (n.d.). Research guides. Retrieved from http://libguides.slu.edu/index.php

Saleebey, D. (2009). *The strengths perspective in social work practice* (6th ed.) Boston: Pearson.

Saleebey, D. (2013). *The strengths perspective in social work practice* (6th ed.). Boston: Allyn & Bacon.

Samudio, M. (2015). Doing family therapy as a new social worker: The dos and don'ts. *The New Social Worker, 22*(1), 6–7.

Samuels, C.A. (2016). Number of U.S. students in special education tickets upwards. *Education Week.* Retrieved from www.edweek.org/ew/articles/2016/04/20/number-of-us-students-in-special-education.html

Sandfort, J. (2005). Casa de Esperanza. *Nonprofit Management & Leadership, 15*(3), 371–382.

Sands, D. (2015). Looking back on a decade of growth in Detroit's urban ag movement. *Model D.* Retrieved from www.modeldmedia.com/features/10-years-urban-ag-091415.aspx

Schein, E.H. (2010). *Organizational culture and leadership.* San Francisco, CA: Jossey-Bass.

Scheuler, L., Diuof, K., Nevels, E., & Hughes, N. (2014). Empowering families in difficult times: The women's economic stability initiative. *Affilia, 29*(3), 353–367.

Schiller, L.Y. (1995). Stages of development in women's groups: A relational model. In R. Kurland & R. Salmon (Eds.), *Group work practice in a troubled society: Problems and opportunities* (pp. 117–138). New York: The Haworth Press.

Schiller, L.Y. (1997). Rethinking stages of group development in women's groups: Implications for practice. *Social Work with Groups, 20*(3), 3–19.

Schiller, L.Y. (2003). Women's group development from a relational model and a new look at facilitator influence on group development. In M.B. Cohen & A. Mullender (Eds.), *Gender and group work* (pp. 16–31). New York: Routledge.

Schiller, L.Y. (2007). Not for women only: Applying the relational model of group development with vulnerable populations. *Social Work with Groups, 30*(2), 11–26.

Schneider, R.L., & Lester, L. (2001). *Social work advocacy.* Belmont, CA: Brooks/Cole.

Schwartz, W. (1961). The social worker in the group. *The Social Welfare Forum,* 146–177.

Sebold, J. (2011). Families and couples: A practical guide for facilitating change. In G.J. Greene and M.Y. Lee (Eds.), *Solution-oriented social work practice* (pp. 209–236). New York: Oxford University Press.

Seligman, M., & Darling, R.B. (2007). *Ordinary families, special children: A systems approach to childhood disability* (3rd ed.). New York: The Guilford Press.

Shakya, H.B., Usita, P.M., Eisenberg, C., Weston, J., & Liles, S. (2012). Family well-being concerns of grandparents in skipped generation families. *Journal of Gerontological Social Work, 55,* 39–54.

Shebib, B. (2015). *Choices: Interviewing and counseling skills for Canadians.* New York: Pearson Canada.

Shelton, M. (2012, May 7). Tornado recovery offers Joplin students new lessons. NPR. Retrieved from www.npr.org/2012/05/07/151950143/tornado-recovery-offers-joplin-students-new-lessons

Sherraden, M.S., Huang, J., Jacobson Frey, J., Birkenmaier, J.M., Callahan, C., Clancy, M., & Sherrden, M. (2015). *Financial capability and asset building for all. American Academy of Social Work and Social Welfare.* Retrieved from http://aaswsw.org/wp-content/uploads/2016/01/WP13-with-cover.pdf

Shier, M.L. (2012). Work-related factors that impact social work practitioners' subjective well-being: Well-being in the workplace. *Journal of Social Work, 12*(6), 402–421.

Shulman, L. (2009). Group work phases of helping: Preliminary phase. In A. Gitterman & R. Salmon (Eds.), *Encyclopedia of social work with groups* (pp. 109–111). New York: Routledge.

Shulman, L. (2011). *Dynamics and skills of group counseling*. Boston: Cengage Learning.

Shulman, L. (2015). Developing successful relationships: The therapeutic and group alliances. In K. Corcoran & A.R. Roberts (Eds.), *Social workers' desk reference* (3rd ed.) (pp. 623–629). New York: Oxford University Press.

Siebold, C. (2007). Everytime we say goodbye: Forced termination revisited, a commentary. *Clinical Social Work Journal, 35*(2), 91–95.

Simon, B. (1990). Re-thinking empowerment. *Journal of Progressive Human Services. 1*(1), 29.

Sims, P.A. (2003). Working with metaphor. *American Journal of Psychotherapy, 57*(4), 528–536

Singh, A.A., & Salazar, C.F. (2011). Conclusion: Six Considerations for Social Justice Group Work. In A.A. Singh & C.F. Salazar (Eds.), *Social justice in group work* (pp. 213–222). Practical interventions for change. New York: Routledge.

Slade, E.P., McCarthy, J.F., Valenstein, M., Visnic, S., & Dixon, L.B. (2013). Cost savings from assertive community treatment services in an era of declining psychiatric inpatient use. *Health Services Research, 48*(1), 195–217.

Sohng, W.S.L. (2013). Community-based participatory research. In C. Franklin (Ed.), *Encyclopedia of social work [E-reader version]*. Washington, DC, and New York: National Association of Social Workers and Oxford University Press. DOI: 10.1093/acrefore/9780199975839.013.69

Sormanti, M. (2012). Writing for and about clinical practice. In W. Green and B.L. Simon (Eds.), *The Columbia guide to social work writing* (pp. 114–132). New York: Columbia University Press.

Sowers, K.M., & Rowe, W.S. (2009). International perspectives on social work practice. In A.R. Roberts (Ed.), *Social workers' desk reference* (2nd ed.) (pp. 863–868). New York: Oxford University Press.

Specht, H. (1990). Social work and the popular psychotherapies. *Social Service Review, 64*, 345–357.

Specht, H., & Courtney, M.E. (1994). *Unfaithful angels: How social work has abandoned its mission*. New York: The Free Press.

Speer, P.W., & Christens, B.D. (2011). Local community organizing and change: Altering policy in the housing and community development system in Kansas City. *Journal of Community & Applied Social Psychology, 22*(5), 414–427.

St. Anthony's Medical Center. (2010). Family Intervention and Planning. St. Louis, MO: Author.

Stamm, B.H. (2010). *The concise ProQOL manual* (2nd ed.). Pocatello, ID: ProQOL.org.

Steger, M.B. (2009). *Globalization*. New York: Sterling Publishing.

Steinberg, D.M. (2014). *A mutual-aid model for social work with groups* (3rd ed). New York: Routledge.

Strand, V., Carten, A., Connolly, D., Gelman, S.R., & Vaughn, P.B. (2009). A cross system initiative supporting child welfare workforce professionalization and stabilization. A task group in action. In C.S. Cohen, M.H. Phillips, & M. Hanson (Eds.), *Strength and diversity in social work with groups* (pp. 41–53). New York: Routledge.

Streeter, C.L. (2013). Community: Overview. In C. Franklin (Ed.), *Encyclopedia of social work [E-reader version]*. Washington, DC, and New York: National Association of Social Workers and Oxford University Press. DOI: 10.1093/acrefore/9780199975839.013.531

Strom-Gottfried, K.J. (2000). Ensuring ethical practice: An examination of NASW Code violations, 1986–97. *Social Work, 45*(3), 251–261.

Strom-Gottfried, K.J. (2003). Managing risk through ethical practice: Ethical dilemmas in rural social work. Presentation at the National Association of Social Workers Vermont chapter, Essex, VT.

Strom-Gottfried, K.J. (2008). *The ethics of practice with minors*. Chicago: Lyceum Books, Inc.

Substance Abuse and Mental Health Services Administration's National Registry of Evidence-based Programs and Practices. (2012). Solution-focused group therapy. Retrieved from http://legacy.nreppadmin.net/ViewIntervention.aspx?id=281

Sue, D.W., Rasheed, M.N., & Rasheed, J.M. (2015). *Multicultural social work practice: A competency-based approach to diversity and social justice.* Hoboken, NJ: John Wiley & Sons.

Supreme Court of the United States. (2015). *Obergefel et al. v. Hodges, Director, Ohio Department of Health, et al.* Retrieved from http://webcache.googleusercontent.com/search?q=cache:W5B8IhdnXt8J:www.supremecourt.gov/opinions/14pdf/14-556_3204.pdf+&cd=2&hl=en&ct=clnk&gl=us

Tariq, S.H., Tumosa, N., Chibnall, J.T., Perry, M.H., & Morley, J.E. (2006). Comparison of the Saint Louis University mental status examination and the mini-mental state examination for detecting dementia and mild neurocognitive disorder—a pilot study. *American Journal of Geriatric Psychiatry, 14,* 900–910.

Tatian, P., Leopold, J., Oo, E., Joseph, G., MacDonald, G., Nichols, A., Woluchem, M., Zhang, S., & Abazajian, K. (2016). *Affordable housing needs assessment for the District of Columbia Phase II.* Washington, DC: Urban Institute.

Tay, D., & Jordan, J. (2015). Metaphor and the notion of control in trauma talk. *Text & Talk, 35(4),* 553–573. DOI: 10.1515/text-2015-0009

Tebb, S.C. (1995). An aid to empowerment: A caregiver well-being scale. *Health and Social Work, 20(2),* 87–92.

Tebb, S.C., Berg-Weger, M., & Rubio, D.M. (2013). The Caregiver Well-Being Scale: Developing a short-form rapid assessment instrument. *Health and Social Work 38(4),* 222–230. DOI: 10.1093/hsw/hlt019

Tervalon, M., & Murray-Garcia, J. (1998). Cultural humility versus cultural competence: A critical distinction in defining physician training outcomes in multicultural education. *Journal of Health Care for the Poor and Underserved, 9(2),* 117–125.

Thompson, L.J., & West, D. (2013). Professional development in the contemporary educational context: Encouraging practice wisdom. *Social Work Education, 21(1),* 118–133.

Thyer, B.A. (2008). Evidence-based macro practice: Addressing the challenges and opportunities. *Journal of Evidence-based Social Work,* (3/4), 453–472.

Thyer, B.A. (2015). Evidence-based practice, science, and social work. An overview. In K. Corcoran & A.R. Roberts (Eds.), *Social workers' desk reference* (3rd ed.) (pp. 1193–1197). New York: Oxford University Press.

Tobert, P.S., & Hall, R.J. (2016). *Organizations: Structures, processes, and outcomes.* New York: Routledge.

Tomasello, N.M., Manning, A.R., & Dulmus, C.N. (2010). Family-centered early intervention for infants and toddlers with disabilities. *Journal of Family Social Work, 13,* 163–172.

Toseland, R.W., & Horton, H. (2013). Group work. In C. Franklin (Ed.), *Encyclopedia of social work [E-reader version].* Washington, DC, and New York: National Association of Social Workers and Oxford University Press. DOI: 10.1093/acrefore/9780199975839.013.168

Turner, H. (2011). Concepts for effective facilitation of open groups. *Social Work with Groups, 34,* 146–156.

U.S. Census Bureau. (2014a). Characteristics of same-sex couple households. 2014 American Community Survey 1-year data file. Retrieved from www.census.gov/hhes/samesex/files/ssex-tables-2014.xlsx

U.S. Census Bureau. (2014b). Poverty status in the past 12 months of families. 2010–2014 American Community Survey 5-year estimates. Retrieved from http://factfinder.census.gov/faces/tableservices/jsf/pages/productview.xhtml?src=bkmk

U.S. Census Bureau. (2015a). Current Population Survey, 2015 Annual Social and Economic Supplement. Retrieved from https://www.census.gov/hhes/families/data/cps2015FG.html

U.S. Census Bureau. (2015b). New Census Bureau report analyses U. S. population projections. CB15-TPS.16. Retrieved from www.census.gov/newsroom/press-releases/2015/cb15-tps16.html

Uken, A., Lee, M.Y., & Sebold, J. (2013). The Plumas Project: Solution-focused treatment of domestic violence offenders. In P. De Jong & I.K. Berg (Eds.), *Interviewing for solutions* (4th ed.) (pp. 333–345). Belmont, CA: Brooks/Cole.

United Nations Office for the Coordination of Humanitarian Affairs. (2016). Syrian Arab Republic. Retrieved from www.unocha.org/syria

United Nations Office of the High Commissioner for Human Rights. (2016). What are human rights? Retrieved from www.ohchr.org/EN/Issues/Pages/WhatareHumanRights.aspx

University of Kansas Work Group for Community Health and Development. (2016). Community Toolbox. Retrieved from http://ctb.ku.edu/en/table-of-contents

Van Hook, M.P. (2014). *Social work practice with families: A resiliency-based approach.* Chicago: Lyceum Books.

Van Soest, D. (2013). Oppression. In C. Franklin (Ed.), *Encyclopedia of social work [E-reader version].* Washington, DC, and New York: National Association of Social Workers and Oxford University Press. DOI: 10.1093/acrefore/9780199975839.013.271

Van Treuren, R.R. (1993). Self-perception in family systems: A diagrammatic technique. In C. Meyer (Ed.), *Assessment in social work practice* (p. 119). New York: Columbia University Press.

Van Wormer, K. (2009). Restorative justice as social justice for victims of gendered violence: A standpoint feminist perspective. *Social Work, 54*(2), 107–116.

Vinter, R.D. (1974). Program activities: An analysis of their effects on participant behavior. In P. Glassner, R. Sarri, & R. Vinter (Eds.), *Individual change through small groups* (pp. 233–243). New York: The Free Press.

Vodde, R., & Giddings, M.M. (1997). The propriety of affiliation with clients beyond the professional role: Nonsexual dual relationships. *Arete, 22*(1), 58–79.

Wagaman, M.A., Geiger, J.M., Shockley, C., & Segal, E.A. (2015). The role of empathy in burnout, compassion satisfaction, and secondary traumatic stress among social workers. *Social Work, 60*(3), 201–209.

Wagner, E.F. (2013). Motivational interviewing. In C. Franklin (Ed.), *Encyclopedia of social work [E-reader version].* Washington, DC, and New York: National Association of Social Workers and Oxford University Press. DOI: 10.1093/acrefore/9780199975839.013.252

Wahab, S. (2005). Motivational interviewing and social work practice. *Journal of Social Work, 5*(1), 45–60.

Walker, L. (2013). Solution-focused reentry and transition planning for imprisoned people. In P. De Jong & I.K. Berg (Eds.), *Interviewing for solutions* (4th ed.) (pp. 318–328). Belmont, CA: Brooks/Cole.

Walsh, J., & Manuel, J. (2015). Clinical case management. In K. Corcoran & A.R. Roberts (Eds.), *Social workers' desk reference* (3rd ed.) (pp. 820–824). New York: Oxford University Press.

Walters, K.L., Spencer, M.S, Smukler, M., Allen, H.L., Andrews, C., Browne, T., Maramaldi, P., Wheeler, D. P., Zebrack, B., & Uehara, E. (2016). *Health equity: Eradicating health inequalities for future generations.* Working Paper No. 19, American Academy of Social Work. Retrieved from http://aaswsw.org/wp-content/uploads/2016/01/WP19-with-cover2.pdf

Walz, T., & Ritchie, H. (2000). Gandhian principles in social work practice: Ethics revisited. *Social Work, 45*(3), 213–222.

Warde, B. (2012). The Cultural Genogram: Enhancing the cultural competency of social work students. *Social Work Education, 31*(5), 570–586.

Weick, A. (1999). Guilty knowledge. *Families in Society, 80*(4), 327–332.

Weick, A., Kreider, J., & Chamberlain, R. (2009). Key dimensions of the strengths perspective in case management, clinical practice, and community practice. In D. Saleebey (Ed.), *The strengths perspective in social work practice* (5th ed.) (pp. 108–121). Boston: Pearson.

Weil, M. (2013). Community-based social planning. In M. Weil (Ed.), *The handbook of community practice* (pp. 265–298). Thousand Oaks, CA: Sage Publications.

Weil, M., & Gamble, D.N. (2009). Community practice model for the twenty-first century. In Roberts (Ed.), *Social workers' desk reference* (pp. 882–892). New York: Oxford University Press, Inc.

Weil, M., & Ohmer, M.L. (2013). Applying practice theories in community work. In M. Weil's (Ed.), *The handbook of community practice* (pp. 123–161). Thousand Oaks, CA: Sage Publications.

Weil, M., Gamble, D.N., & Ohmer, M L. (2013). Evolution, models, and the changing context of community practice. In M. Weil (Ed.), *The handbook of community practice* (pp. 167–193). Thousand Oaks, CA: Sage Publications.

Weil, M., Reisch, M., & Ohmer, M.L. (2013). Introduction: Contexts and challenges for 21st century communities. In M. Weil's (Ed.), *The handbook of community practice* (pp. 3–26). Thousand Oaks, CA: Sage Publications.

Weisman, D., & Zornado, J.L. (2013). *Professional writing for social work practice*. New York: Springer Publishing Company.

West Virginia Board of Social Work Examiners. (n.d.). Level D: LICSW: (Licensed Independent Social Worker) license. Retrieved from www.wvsocial-workboard.org/licensinginfo/regular/licswlicense.htm

Wharton, T.C., & Bolland, K.A. (2012). Practitioner perspectives of evidence-based practice. *Families in Society: The Journal of Contemporary Social Services, 93*(3), 157–164.

Wheeler, W., & Thomas, A.M. (2011). Engaging youth in community development. In J.W. Robinson Jr., & G.P. Green (Eds.), *Introduction to community development: Theory, practice and service-learning* (pp. 209–227). Los Angeles, CA: Sage Publications.

Whitaker, T., & Wilson, M. (2010). *National Association of Social Workers 2009 compensation and benefit study: Summary of key compensation findings*. Washington, DC: NASW.

White, M. (2007). MAPS of narrative practice. NY: WW Norton and Co.

Williams, N.R. (2009). Narrative family interventions. In A.C. Kilpatrick & T.P. Holland (Eds.), *Working with families. An integrative model by level of need* (5th ed.) (pp. 199–223). Boston: Pearson.

Winship, K., & Lee, S.T. (2012). Using evidence-based accreditation standards to promote continuous quality improvement: The experience of San Mateo County Human Services Agency. *Journal of Evidence-based Social Work, 9*(1–2), 68–86.

Wise, J.B. (2005). *Empowerment practice with families in distress*. New York: Columbia University Press.

Wood, G.G., & Roche, S.E. (2001). Representing selves, reconstructing lives: Feminist group work with women survivors of male violence. *Social Work with Groups, 23*(4), 5–23.

Wood, G.G., & Tully, C.T. (2006). *The structural approach to direct practice in social work: A social constructionist Perspective* (3rd ed.). New York: Columbia University Press.

Work Group for Community Health and Development at the University of Kansas. (2012). The Community Tool Box. Retrieved from http://ctb.ku.edu/en/tablecontents/chapter_1033.aspx

World Health Organization. (2012). Global democracy deficit. Retrieved from http://www.who.int/trade/glossary/story037/en/index/html

Yalom, I.D., & Leszcz, M. (2005). *The theory and practice of group psychotherapy* (5th ed.). New York: Basic Books.

Yeager, K.R., & Roberts, A.R. (2015). *Crisis intervention handbook: Assessment, treatment, and research* (4th ed.) (pp. 183–213). New York: Oxford University Press.

Yee Lee, M. (2013). Solution-focused brief therapy. In C. Franklin (Ed.), *Encyclopedia of social work [E-reader version]*. Washington, DC, and New York: National Association of Social Workers and Oxford University Press. DOI: 10.1093/acrefore/9780199975839.013.1039

Yi, H., Rothman, M., & Burty, C. (2016, July 31). Inside Ohio's fight over voting rules. PBS News Hour. Retrieved from www.pbs.org/newshour/bb/inside-ohios-fight-voting-rules/

Young, S. (2013). Solutions for bullying in primary schools. In P. De Jong & I.K. Berg (Eds.), *Interviewing for solutions* (4th ed.) (pp. 308–318). Belmont, CA: Brooks/Cole.

Zandee-Amas, R.R. (2013). A good groups runs itself—and other myths. *The New Social Worker, 20*(1), 10–11.

Zeleznikow, L., & Zeleznikow, J. (2015). Supporting blended families to remain intact: A case study. *Journal of Divorce & Remarriage, 56(4)*, 317–335.

Zelnick, J.R., Slayter, E., Flanzbaum, B., Butler, N.G., Domingo, B., Perlstein, J., & Trust, C. (2013). Part of the job? Workplace violence in Massachusetts social service agencies. *Health & Social Work, 38(2)*, 75–85.

Zur, O., & Lazarus, A.A. (2002). Six arguments against dual relationships and their rebuttals. In A.A. Lararus & O. Zur (Eds.), *Dual relationships and psychotherapy* (p. 3–24). New York: Springer.

CREDITS

Photo 1-A: © Lisa F. Young

Ex 1.1: Copyrighted material reprinted with permission from the National Association of Social Workers, Inc.

Ex 1.2: Healy, L. M. & Link, R. J. (2012). Handbook of international social work: Human rights, development, and the global profession. Used by permission of Oxford University Press.

Photo 1-B: © Lisa F. Young

Ex 1.4: University Declaration of Human Rights used by permission of Human Rights Education Association.

Photo 2-A: © marekuliasz

Ex 2.1: Copyrighted material reprinted with permission from the National Association of Social Workers, Inc.

Ex 2.3: Copyrighted material reprinted with permission from the National Association of Social Workers, Inc.

Ex 2.4: International Federation of Social Workers (IFSW). (2012). Ethics in social work: Statement of principles. Retrieved October 14, 2012 from http://ifsw.org/policies/statement-of-ethical-principles/. Used by permission.

Ex 2.5: New Zealand Association of Social Workers (NZASW). (1993). Code of ethics. Used by permission.

Photo 2-C: © Mark Bowden

QG 3: From Dolgoff/Loewenberg/Harrington. Ethical Decisions for Social Work Practice, 8E. © 2009 Wadsworth, a part of Cengage Learning, Inc. Reproduced by permission. www.cengage.com/permissions

Ex 2.7: From The Propriety of Affiliation with Clients beyond the Professional Role: Nonsexual dual relationships. Arete 22(1) by R. Vodde and M.M. Giddings. © 1997. Reprinted with permission.

Photo 3-A: © Yuri Arcurs

Ex 3.3: From Skills for Direct Practice in Social Work by R. R. Middleman and G.G. Wood. Copyright © 1990. Columbia University Press.

Photo 4-A: © Ron Chapple studios/Thinkstock

Ex 4.1: From Assessing strengths, Identifying acts of resistance to violence and oppression, by K.M. Anderson, C.D. Cowger and C.A. Snively. In The Strengths perspective in social work practice (the d.), by D. Saleebey (Ed.). Copyright Allyn & Bacon, 2009.

Ex 4.2: From Assessing strengths, Identifying acts of resistance to violence and oppression, by K.M. Anderson, C.D. Cowger and C.A. Snively. In The Strengths perspective in social work practice (the d.), by D. Saleebey (Ed.). Copyright Allyn & Bacon, 2009.

Photo 4-B: © fatihhoca

QG 8: Adapted from The Strengths perspective in social work (5th ed.), by D. Saleebey. Copyright © 2009, Allyn & Bacon.

Photo 4-C: © Lisa F. Young

QG 10: Kagle, J. D. & Kopels, S. (2008). Social work records (3rd ed.). Long Grove, IL: Waveland Press, Inc. Used by permission.

Ex 4.8: Adapted from St. Anthony's Medical Center, St. Louis, Missouri. Reprinted with permission.

Ex 4.9: Adapted from St. Anthony's Medical Center, St. Louis, Missouri. Reprinted with permission.

Ex 4.10: Adapted from St. Anthony's Medical Center, St. Louis, Missouri. Reprinted with permission.

QG 11: From Dejong/Berg. Interviewing for Solutions, 4E. © 2013 Wadsworth, a part of Cengage Learning, Inc. Reproduced by permission. Www.cengage.com/permissions

Photo 5-A: © Alexander Raths

Ex 5.1: Adapted from The structural approach to direct practice in social work: A social constructionist perspective (3rd ed.), by G.G. Wood and C.T. Tully. Copyright 2006, Columbia University Press. Reprinted with permission.

Photo 5-B: © Adam Gregor

Photo 5-C: © monkeybusinessimages/Thinkstock

Photo 6-A: © Harry Hu, courtesy of Shutterstock® images

QG 16: Sormanti, M. (2012). Writing for and about clinical practice. In W. Green and B. L. Simon, The Columbia guide to social work writing (pp. 114–132). NY: Columbia University Press.

Photo 6-B: Comstock Images/Thinkstock

Photo 6-D: © Rob Hainer

Ex 6.3: From Culture in special education, by M. Kalyanpur and B. Harry. Copyright 1999, Paul H. Brookes. Reprinted with permission.

Ex 6.4: Van Hook, M.P. (2008). Social work practice with families: A resiliency-based approach. Chicago: Lyceum Books.

Ex 6.5: Van Hook, M.P. (2008). Social work practice with families: A resiliency-based approach. Chicago: Lyceum Books.

Ex 6.6: From Self-perception in family systems: A diagrammatic technique, by R.R. Van Treuren. In assessment in social work practice, by C. Meyer. Copyright 1993, Columbia University Press. Reprinted with permission.

QG 18: Warde, B. (2012). The Cultural Genogram: Enhancing the cultural competency of social work students. Social Work Education, 31(5), 570–586. Used by permission.

Ex 6.7: From The Culturagram, by E. P. Congress. In Social Workers' desk reference (2nd ed.), by A.R. Roberts. Copyright 2009, Oxford Press. Reprinted with permission.

QG 19: Adapted from St. Anthony's Medical Center, St. Louis, Missouri. Reprinted with permission.

Ex 7.1: From Hull/Mather. Understanding Generalist Practice with Families, 1E. © 2006 Wadsworth, a part of Cengage Learning, Inc. Reproduced by permission. www.cengage.com/permissions

Ex 7.2: Sebold, J. (2011). Families and couples: A practical guide for facilitating change. In G. J. Greene and M. Y. Lee, Solution-oriented social work practice (pp. 209–236). NY: Oxford University Press.

Photo 7-A: © Lisa F. Young

Ex 7.3: Adapted from St. Anthony's Medical Center, St. Louis, Missouri. Reprinted with permission.

Ex 7.4: Adapted from St. Anthony's Medical Center, St. Louis, Missouri; Missouri Department of Social Services.

QG 22: From Enabling and empowering families: principles and guidelines for practice, by C.J. Dunst, C.M. Trivette and A.G. Deal. Copyright 2003, Brookline Books. Reprinted with permission.

QG 23: From Enabling and empowering families: principles and guidelines for practice, by C.J. Dunst, C.M. Trivette and A.G. Deal. Copyright 2003, Brookline Books. Reprinted with permission.

Photo 7-B: © Lisa F. Young

Photo 7-C: © monkeybusinessimages/Thinkstock

Photo 8-A: © SerrNovik/Thinkstock

Photo 8-B: © Blaj Gabriel

Ex 8.6: From Teaching a methods course in social work with groups, by R. Kurland and R. Salmon. Copyright 1998, Council on Social Work Education.

Ex 8.7: Kurland, R. & Salmon, R. (1998). Teaching a methods course in social work with groups. Alexandria, VA: Council on Social Work Education.

Photo 8-C: © Yuri Arcurs

Ex 8.8: Adapted from St. Anthony's Medical Center, St. Louis, Missouri. Reprinted with permission.

Ex 8.9: Adapted from Women's Support and Community Services, St. Louis, Missouri.

Photo 9-A: © Design Pics/Don Hammond/Thinkstock

Photo 9-B: © Glynnis Jones

QG 27: From Group Composition, diversity, the skills of the social worker, and group development, by T. Berman-Rossi and T.B. Kelly. Presented at the Council for Social Work Education Annual Meeting, Atlanta, February. Copyright 2003. Reprinted with permission.

Photo 9-C: © Blaj Gabriel

Ex 9.1: Comer, E. & Meier, A. (2011). Using evidence-based practice and intervention research with treatment groups for populations at risk. In G.L. Greif & P.H. Ephross (Eds.) Group work with populations at risk (3rd ed.) (pp. 459–488). New York: Oxford University Press

Ex 9.2: Greif, G. & Ephross, P.H. (Eds.). (2011). Group work with populations at risk (3rd ed.). New York: Oxford University Press.

QG 28: Berg, R.D., Landreth, G.L., & Fall, K.A. (2013). Group counseling concepts and procedures (5th ed.). New York: Routledge.

Photo 9-D: © vm

Photo 9-E: © Yuri Arcurs

QG 30: Berg, R.D., Landreth, G.L., & Fall, K.A. (2013). Group counseling concepts and procedures (5th ed.). New York: Routledge.

Ex 9.7: Berg, R.D., Landreth, G.L., & Fall, K.A. (2013). Group counseling concepts and procedures (5th ed.). New York: Routledge.

Photo 10-A: © vm

Ex 10.2: Adapted from Center of Organizational and Social Research, Saint Louis University.

Ex 10.3: Royse, D., Staton-Tindall, M., Badger, K., & Webster, J.M. (2009). Needs assessment. New York: Oxford University Press.

Photo 10-B: © CREATISTA

Ex 10.4: City of Seattle, Washington. (2012). A Community Assessment of Need for Housing and Services for Homeless Individuals and Families in the Lake City Neighborhood. Retrieved from http://seattle.gov/realestate/pdfs/Needs_Assessment_data_report.pdf

Ex 10.8: Kretzmann, J. P. & McKnight, J. L. (1993). Building communities from the inside out: A part toward finding and mobilizing a community's assets. Evanston, IL: Center for Urban Affairs and Policy Research. Used by permission.

Ex 10.9: McKnight, J. L., & Block, P. (2010). The abundant community: Awakening the power of families and neighborhoods. San Francisco, CA: Berrett-Koehler Publishers.

Ex 10.10: McKnight, J. L., & Block, P. (2010). The abundant community: Awakening the power of families and neighborhoods. San Francisco, CA: Berrett-Koehler Publishers.

Photo 10-C: © THEGIFT777

Ex 11.1: Netting, F. E., Kettner, P. M., McMurtry, S. L., & Thomas, L. (2011). Social work macro practice. Boston: Pearson Allyn & Bacon.

Ex 11.3: Source: 350.org

Photo 11-A: © 350.org

Photo 11-B: © 350.org

QG 36 & 37: Adapted from Organizing for social change, by K. Bobo, J. Kendall, and S. Max. Copyright 2010, The Forum Press. Reprinted with permission.

QG 38: Adapted from New Robert's Rules of Order by L. Rozakis. Copyright 1996, Smithmark Reference.

QG 39: Adapted from Consensus through conversation, by L. Dressler. Copyright 2006, Berrett-Koehler Publishers, Inc. All rights reserved. www.bkconnection.com

Ex 11.5: Kretzmann, J. P. & McKnight, J. L. (2005). Discovering community power: A guide to mobilizing local assets and your organization's capacity. Evanston, IL: Asset-Based Community Development (ABCD) Institute. Used by permission.

Ex 11.7: Ohmer, M.L. & DeMasi, K. (2009). Consensus organizing: A community development workbook. Thousand Oaks, CA: Sage Publications, Inc.

Ex 11.9: Ohmer, M.L. & Korr, W.S. (2006). The effectiveness of community practice interventions: A review of the literature. Research on Social Work Practice, 16(2),132–145. Used by permission.

Ex 11.10: From Localized needs and a globalized economy, by J. Ife in Social work and globalization (Special Issue), Canadian Social Work, 2(1). Copyright 2000.

Ex 11.11: From International social work: Issues, strategies and programs by D. Cox and M. Pawar. Copyright 2006, Sage Publications, Inc. Reprinted with permission.

Ex 11.14: Speer, P. W. & Christens, B. D. (2011). Local community organizing and change: Altering policy in the housing and community development system in Kansas City. Journal of Community & Applied Social Psychology, 22(5), 414–427. Used by permission.

Photo 12-A: © Digital Vision

Ex 12.1: National Association of Area Agencies on Aging. (2012). National aging services network. Retrieved from http://www.n4a.org/about-n4a/join/

Photo 12-B: © Chris Fertnig

Photo 12-C: © CandyBox Images

Ex 12.6: Gambrill, E. (2012). Social work practice: A critical thinkers guide. New York: Oxford University Press.

QG 41: From Locke/Garrison/Winship. Generalist Social Work Practice, 1E. © 1998 Wadsworth, a part of Cengage Learning, Inc. Reproduced by permission. www.Cengage.com/permissions

Ex 12.8: Larson, K., & McGuiston, C. (2012). Building capacity to improve Latino health in rural North Carolina: A case study in community-university engagement. Journal of Community Engagement and Scholarship, 5(1), 14–23.

QG 44: Plitt, D. L. & Shields, J. (2009). Development of the Policy Advocacy Behavior Scale: Initial reliability and validity. Research on Social Work Practice, 19(1), 83–92. Reprinted by permission.

Photo 13-A: © gosphotodesign

Ex 13.1: Evans, S. D., Hanlin, C. E., & Prillehensky, I. (2007). Blending Ameliorative and transformative approaches in human service organizations: A case study. Journal of Community Psychology, 35(3), 329–346. Used by permission.

Ex 13.2: Netting, F. E., Kettner, P. M., McMurtry, S. L., & Thomas, M. L. (2012). Social work macro practice. Boston: Pearson Allyn & Bacon.

Ex 13.4: Netting, F. E., Kettner, P. M., McMurtry, S. L., & Thomas, M. L. (2012). Social work macro practice. Boston: Pearson Allyn & Bacon.

QG 45: Manning, T. (2012). The art of successful persuasion: Seven skills you need to get your point across effectively.

Ex 13.6: O'Connor, M. K., & Netting, F. E. (2009). Organization practice: A guide to understanding human service organizations. Hoboken, NJ: John Wiley and Sons.

Ex 13.7: Winship, K. & Lee, S. T. (2012). Using evidence-based accreditation standards to promote Continuous Quality Improvement: The experience of San Mateo County Human Services Agency. Journal of Evidence-based Social Work, 9(1–2), 68–86.

GLOSSARY / INDEX

Alphabetization is word-by-word.
Locators in *italics* refer to figures, tables, and exhibits.